The Haunted Self

The Norton Series on Interpersonal Neurobiology
Daniel J. Siegel, M.D., Series Editor

The field of mental health is in a tremendously exciting period of growth
and conceptual reorganization. Independent findings from a variety of scientific endeavors are converging in an interdisciplinary view of the mind
and mental well-being. An "interpersonal neurobiology" of human development enables us to understand that the structure and function of the
mind and brain are shaped by experiences, especially those involving emotional relationships.

The Norton Series on Interpersonal Neurobiology will provide cutting-
edge, multidisciplinary views that further our understanding of the complex neurobiology of the human mind. By drawing on a wide range of traditionally independent fields of research—such as neurobiology, genetics,
memory, attachment, complex systems, anthropology, and evolutionary
psychology—these texts will offer mental health professionals a review and
synthesis of scientific findings often inaccessible to clinicians. These books
aim to advance our understanding of human experience by finding the
unity of knowledge, or "consilience," that emerges with the translation of
findings from numerous domains of study into a common language and
conceptual framework. The series will integrate the best of modern science
with the healing art of psychotherapy.

A Norton Professional Book

THE HAUNTED SELF

Structural Dissociation and the Treatment of Chronic Traumatization

Onno van der Hart
Ellert Nijenhuis
Kathy Steele

W. W. NORTON & COMPANY

New York • London

For information about permission to reproduce
selections from this book, write to
Permissions, W. W. Norton & Company, Inc.,
500 Fifth Avenue, New York, NY 10110

Production Manager: Leeann Graham
Manufacturing by Haddon Craftsmen

Library of Congress Cataloging-in-Publication Data

Hart, Onno van der, 1941–
   The haunted self: structural dissociation and the
treatment of chronic traumatization/Onno van der Hart,
Ellert R. S. Nijenhuis, Kathy Steele.
       p. cm.
   "A Norton professional book"
   Includes bibliographical references and index.
ISBN-13: 978-0-393-70401-3
ISBN-10: 0-393-70401-7
1. Psychic trauma—Treatment. 2. Dissociation (Psychology)
3. Dissociative disorders—Treatment I. Nijenhuis, E. R. S.
(Ellert R. S.) . II. Steele, Kathy. III. Title.

RC552.T7H375 2006
616.85'21—dc22   2006046727

W. W. Norton & Company, Inc.,
500 Fifth Avenue, New York, N.Y. 10110
www.wwnorton.com

W. W. Norton & Company Ltd.,
Castle House, 75/76 Wells St., London W1T 3QT

7 9 0 8 6

Contents

Preface

L IFE CAN BE AN ABIDING STRUGGLE FOR PATIENTS who have been chronically traumatized. They typically have a wide array of symptoms, often classified under different combinations of comorbidity, which can make assessment and treatment complicated and confusing for the therapist. Many patients have substantial problems with daily living and relationships, including serious intrapsychic conflicts and maladaptive coping strategies. Their suffering essentially relates to a terrifying and painful past that haunts them. Even when survivors attempt to hide their distress beneath a façade of normality—a common strategy—therapists often feel besieged by those patients' many symptoms and serious pain. Small wonder that many survivors of chronic traumatization have seen several therapists with little if any gains, and that quite a few have been labeled as untreatable or resistant.

In this book we share what we have learned from treating and studying chronically traumatized individuals across more than 65 years of collective experience. We have listened closely to our patients, struggling to understand their complex and sometimes astounding internal experiences, which they often find difficult and frightening to put into words. We have learned from practical, theoretical, and scientific reflection, and have been stimulated in these regards by the rich literature on traumatization from the 19th century, the first decades of the 20th century, and more recent years. A variety of concepts from numerous psychological theories have been most helpful in our quest, including learning, systems, cognitive, affective, attachment, psychodynamic, and object relations theory. Recent developments in evolutionary psychology and psychobiology, especially affective neuroscience and psychobiological trauma research, have been a major inspiration. All these sources have contributed to our understanding that the essence of trauma is *structural dissociation of the personality*.

We use this concept to reinstate the original meaning of the term *dissociation* as formulated by Pierre Janet (1859–1947), the French philosopher, psychiatrist, and psychologist, who is regarded as "one of the most seminal psychiatric clinicians and thinkers of the last two centuries" (Nemiah,

1989, p. 1527). His work is essential for the understanding and treatment of trauma-related disorders. Structural dissociation is a particular organization in which different psychobiological subsystems of the personality are unduly rigid and closed to each other. These features lead to a lack of coherence and coordination within the survivor's personality as a whole.

Our proposal of the term *structural dissociation (of the personality)* stems from an urgent need. There are currently so many confusing and often contradictory definitions of dissociation that the concept has become very problematic. For example, the term can represent symptoms, a conscious or unconscious mental activity or "process," a defense "mechanism," and still more. And the range of symptoms that are now described as dissociative has become so broad that the category has lost its specificity. Apart from the manifestations of structural dissociation of the personality, dissociative symptoms are also said to include a host of common and pathological alterations of consciousness. As we discuss in this book, we regard this extension as a serious miscategorization.

In this book we propose the theory of structural dissociation in combination with a Janetian psychology of action. This psychology of action, which has its roots in Janet's pioneering work, defines the nature of adaptive and thus integrative actions in which we as human beings must engage to function at our best. Such actions need to be promoted not only in our patients, but also in ourselves as therapists. Indeed, we have learned that the psychology of action is highly applicable to everyone. We discuss the way in which the personality of the traumatized individual is organized, and why many of his or her mental and behavioral actions are maladaptive. The theory of structural dissociation and the Janetian psychology of action presented in this book also detail the kind of integrative actions in which the survivor must engage in order to put his or her haunted past to rest and to make present life more successful.

This book is primarily intended for clinicians, but will also be of interest to students of clinical psychology and psychiatry, as well as to researchers. Therapists who treat adult survivors of chronic child abuse and neglect will find helpful insights and tools that may make the treatment more effective and efficient, and more tolerable for the suffering patient. And they may, as we did, rediscover an old truth that sometimes nothing is as practical as a good theory. We believe the theory and treatment approach presented in this book are also relevant to colleagues involved in the treatment of traumatized refugees, torture victims, and combat veterans, as well as those who mostly focus on therapy of adults traumatized by single events, such as rape, terrorist attacks, road accidents, and natural disasters.

This book will help prepare students of clinical psychology and psychiatry for the assessment, treatment, and scientific study of severely traumatized patients. Researchers can learn that the theory of structural dissociation is a strong heuristic: Many testable and refutable hypotheses can be derived from it. For example, the theory suggests how the mental and behavioral actions of survivors shift with the type of dissociative part that exerts executive control—a fact that has been largely overlooked in the field of traumatic stress studies.

Relatively short-term approaches have been recommended for single incident traumatization and posttraumatic stress disorder (PTSD; APA, 1994); for example, cognitive behavioral therapy and eye movement desensitization and reprocessing (EMDR; Foa, Keane, & Friedman, 2000; Foa & Rothbaum, 1998; Follette, Ruzek, & Abueg, 1998; Resick & Schnicke, 1993). There is no research showing that these approaches represent adequate treatment for survivors of chronic traumatization if they are applied outside of a phase-oriented treatment such as the one proposed in this book. In fact, severe comorbid psychopathology, a common feature of trauma survivors, emerged as the predominant reason for exclusion of participants across PTSD treatment efficacy studies (Spinazzola, Blaustein, & Van der Kolk, 2005). Furthermore, single traumatizing events in adulthood all too often reactivate earlier unresolved, traumatic experiences. Some survivors of chronic traumatization may have managed their difficult lives, albeit with much effort and in spite of their impaired integrative capacity, but develop a trauma-related disorder later in life when they become tested beyond their integrative limits. For these patients, relatively straightforward and short-term treatment is often not adequate. Patients with cumulative traumatization typically require more complicated and long-term treatments, and this book focuses on the treatment of these survivors.

Based on the theory of structural dissociation in combination with a Janetian psychology of action, we have developed a model of *phase-oriented treatment* that focuses on the identification and treatment of structural dissociation and related maladaptive mental and behavioral actions. The foundation of this approach is to support patients in learning more effective mental and behavioral actions. These will enable them to become more adaptive in life and to resolve their structural dissociation. This principle implies an overall therapeutic goal of raising the integrative capacity, or what we refer to as the *mental level* of the patient, first in order to cope with the demands of daily life and then to deal with the haunting remnants of the past, with "unfinished business," especially traumatic memories.

The introductory chapter provides a concise overview of the concept of dissociation and phase-oriented treatment, and basic concepts related to a Janetian psychology of action, all of which will be discussed in depth over the course of the book. The first five chapters of Part I present the clinical presentations of various levels of structural dissociation and open the door to explaining the theory of structural dissociation. Chapter 1 describes the most basic form of structural dissociation (i.e., primary structural dissociation), in which the personality of the trauma survivor is divided into one major dissociative part dedicated to daily life and avoidance of the traumatic memories, and one less complex dissociative part fixated in defense against threat. This chapter also describes the differences between narrative autobiographical memories and traumatic memories. Chapter 2 presents an in-depth analysis of the differences between these two prototypical dissociative parts. Chapter 3 deals with secondary structural dissociation; that is, the existence in trauma survivors of one dissociative part dedicated to daily life and more than one focused on defense against threat. This level of structural dissociation characterizes chronically traumatized individuals with complex trauma-related disorders. Chapter 4 describes tertiary structural dissociation, which basically pertains to patients with more than one dissociative part dedicated to daily life and more than one part focused on defense against threat. We propose that this is the exclusive domain of dissociative identity disorder. Chapter 5 proposes some solutions to the confusion in the trauma field about which symptoms are dissociative and which are not. Finally, Chapter 6 analyses how the theory of structural dissociation links to various trauma-related disorders—both DSM-IV (APA, 1994) and ICD-10 (WHO, 1992) dissociative disorders—as well as the many comorbid disorders so prevalent in chronic trauma survivors. This understanding provides essential points of application for treatment of these disorders.

Part II is dedicated to a Janetian *psychology of action* as it relates to structural dissociation, in which various maladaptive mental and behavioral actions, or lack of adaptive actions are analyzed in the chronically traumatized individual. These actions maintain structural dissociation once it develops, manifest in various symptoms, and constitute targets in treatment. More adaptive and integrative actions are also discussed. Chapter 7 presents an overview of the role played by particular mental and behavioral actions necessary for developing and maintaining an integrated personality, as well as for leading the most adaptive life possible. This chapter specifically focuses on synthesis, which is the most basic level of integration. Chapter 8 describes realization, with its components of personification and presentification, as a sophisticated and complex level of integration that requires higher mental functioning. This chapter also discusses the difficulties of survivors in perceiving reality. For example, they do not realize the past is not the present, and that the future is not a repeat of the catastrophic past, and their actions reflect their confusion. Distortions in reality cause problems in adaptation, but are also a reflection of survivors' low mental level in relation to the challenges they face. Chapter 9 describes a hierarchy of action tendencies; that is, various levels of increasingly complex actions that are necessary to adequately meet the challenges of everyday life, and which are often difficult for survivors to achieve. This hierarchy is a helpful instrument in assessing a patient's current level of adaptive functioning in terms of mental and behavioral actions. This chapter also deals with the maladaptive actions to which patients resort when their mental level falls short of that needed for adaptive action, as well the actions needed for healthy change. Chapter 10 presents an overview of various phobias that characterize chronically traumatized patients and that maintain their structural dissociation. This chapter extensively describes the learning principles involved in the maintenance of structural dissociation.

Part III presents a systematic application of both the theory of structural dissociation and the psychology of action in assessment of the patient's functioning in Chapter 11, and in *phase-oriented treatment* in subsequent chapters. Chapter 12 discusses general treatment principles that need to be applied throughout therapy. The overall aim of therapists' actions is to raise the patient's mental level, and to improve his or her mental and relational skills in this context. The next series of chapters deal with the objectives for the three treatment phases, in large part described in terms of overcoming specific phobias that maintain structural dissociation and hamper adaptive functioning. Chapter 13, the first of two that address treatment objectives for the first phase, discusses overcoming the phobia of attachment and attachment loss with the therapist. It thus focuses on establishing the therapeutic relationship with survivors who simultaneously approach and avoid attachment. Chapter 14 deals with the task of overcoming the phobia of trauma-derived mental actions (e.g., thoughts, feelings, memories, wishes), and Chapter 15 does the same with regard to overcoming the phobia of dissociative parts. Chapter 16 addresses the second treatment phase, notably overcoming the phobia of traumatic memories and related tasks. Chapter 17, about the third treatment phase, discusses overcoming the phobia of normal life and related phobias. The book ends with an epilogue.

Acknowledgments

W E WISH TO THANK THE MANY INDIVIDUALS who, directly or indirectly, have contributed to the ideas expressed in this book or in various other ways helped us during our writing project. We gratefully acknowledge the profound influence of teachers before our times, in particular Pierre Janet and Charles S. Myers. We thank our mentors who, over three decades, have taught us so much of great value for our clinical practice with chronically traumatized patients, for our evolving understanding of their plight, and for the development of our research: Bennett Braun, Catherine Fine, Erika Fromm, Richard P. Kluft, Richard J. Loewenstein, Steven Porges, Frank W. Putnam, Colin M. Ross, Roberta Sachs, David Spiegel, and Bessel A. Van der Kolk. We are very grateful to Martin Dorahy, Pat Ogden, and Yvonne Tauber, with whom we have discussed many issues presented in this book and who have helped us in rewriting various chapters. Pat Ogden deserves our special gratitude for her enduring and phenomenal support over the course of this entire project, both with regard to contents and emotionally.

We are grateful to Isabelle Saillot, President of the Institut Pierre Janet, Paris, for the fruitful discussions we have had on various aspects of Janet's theories. And we thank our many colleagues whose works have had a strong influence on our thinking and clinical approach or with whom we have had stimulating discussions. They include Jon Allen, Peter Barach, Ruth Blizard, Elizabeth Bowman, Steven Braude, Chris Brewin, John Briere, Danny Brom, Dan Brown, Paul Brown, Richard Chefetz, James Chu, Marylene Cloytre, Philip Coons, Christine Courtois, Louis Crocq, Constance Dalenberg, Erik de Soir, Paul Dell, Hans den Boer, Nel Draijer, Janina Fisher, Julian Ford, Elizabeth Howell, George Fraser, Ursula Gast, Marko van Gerven, Jean Goodwin, Arne Hoffman, Olaf Holm, Michaela Huber, Rolf Kleber, Sarah Krakauer, Ruth Lanius, Anssi Leikola, Helga Matthess, Francisco Orengo-Garcia, Laurie Pearlman, John Raftery, Luise Reddemann, Colin Ross, Barbara Rothbaum, Päivi Saarinen, Vedat Sar, Allan Schore, Daniel Siegel, Eli Somer, Anne Suokas-Cunliffe, Maarten van Son, Johan Vanderlinden, Eric Vermetten, and Eliezer Witztum. And most certainly there are more that we have inadvertently failed to mention.

We are especially indebted to our closest colleagues who have graciously and steadfastly supported us in our daily clinical practices. We collaborate with them on a daily basis, benefit from their clinical expertise and wisdom, and receive emotional support from them in difficult times. They include Suzette Boon (with whom one of us [OvdH] has done pioneering work in the Netherlands), Berry Cazemier, Sandra Hale, Steve Harris, Myles Hassler, Vera Mierop, Lisa Angert Morris, Janny Mulder, Kathie Thodeson, Herry Vos, and Marty Wakeland.

We thank our editors, Deborah Malmud, Michael McGandy, and Kristen Holt-Browning at Norton, and our Series Editor, Daniel Siegel, under whose expert guidance this project has been brought to completion, and Casey Ruble, for her essential help in shaping this book.

Finally, we thank our patients, from whom we learned most. It has been our privilege to join with them along part of their arduous journey, and we are grateful for the exceptionally valuable and impressive lessons they have taught us.

The Haunted Self

Introduction

Without realizing it, I fought to keep my two worlds separated. Without ever knowing why, I made sure, whenever possible, that nothing passed between the compartmentalization I had created between the day child and the night child.
                                    —Marilyn Van Derbur (2004, p. 26)

C HRONICALLY TRAUMATIZED INDIVIDUALS are caught in a terrible dilemma. They lack adequate integrative capacity and the mental skills to fully *realize* their horrific experiences and memories. But they must go on with a daily life that sometimes continues to include the very people who abused and neglected them. Their most expedient option is to mentally avoid their unresolved and painful past and present, and as much as possible maintain a façade of normality. Yet their apparent normality, their life at the surface of consciousness (Appelfeld, 1994), is fragile. Dreaded memories that are awakened by strong reminders haunt survivors, especially when they have exhausted their emotional and physical resources. And unfortunately, many survivors live their lives on the edge of exhaustion, and thus are more prone to the intrusion of traumatic memories. Survivors find it is beyond them to accept the painful realities of their lives, and they thus remain stuck in dread, hopelessness, and terror. They often struggle with deficits in skills to regulate overwhelming internal and relational experiences: These are skills that their caretakers failed to help them develop and that seriously limit their mental level (integrative capacity). They seem unable to achieve an adequate balance between their level of mental energy and the capacity to apply that energy to engage in adaptive mental and behavioral actions, which we call *mental efficiency*. They are beset by ineffective but repetitive actions and reactions that do not support a growing maturity and capacity to cope adequately with the vagaries and complexities of life.

TRAUMA-RELATED DISSOCIATION

We believe that *dissociation* is the key concept to understanding trauma-tization: This is a fundamental premise of the book. But we have not come easily to this appreciation, largely because many concepts in the trauma field need further clarification, and dissociation is chief among them. Virtually everyone in the trauma field uses the term *dissociation* in different ways, and there are many disagreements about its causes, its essential characteristics, and its role in the psychopathology of the traumatized individual. Often in a single discussion, the term *dissociation* can be used to denote a process, an intrapsychic structure, a psychological defense, a deficit, and a wide array of symptoms. And the symptoms considered to be dissociative vary tremendously from one publication to the next, and from one measurement instrument to the next. For example, even though phenomena such as intense absorption and imaginative involvement were originally distinguished from dissociation, they have now been subsumed under the concept of dissociation. Thus, *dissociation* is a much misunderstood, confusing, and sometimes maligned concept. Some have even suggested that the term be abandoned altogether. In the course of this book we will address these issues in depth.

Structural Dissociation of the Personality

Dissociation orginally referred to a *division of the personality or of consciousness* (Janet, 1887/2005, 1907; McDougall, 1926; Moreau de Tours, 1845; cf., Van der Hart & Dorahy, in press). More specifically, Pierre Janet noted that dissociation involved divisions among "*systems* of ideas and functions that constitute personality" (Janet, 1907, p. 332). He indicated that the personality is a *structure* comprised of various *systems*, as more contemporary definitions also assert. A system is an assembly of related elements comprising a whole, such that each element is a part of that whole in some sense. That is, each element is seen to be related to other elements of, or to the system in its entirety. The personality as a system can be understood as being comprised of various psychobiological states or subsystems that function in a cohesive and coordinated manner. For example, Allport (1961) proposed that personality is "the dynamic organization within the individual of those psychophysical systems that determine his characteristic behavior and thought" (p. 28). Likewise, systems theories (e.g., Benyakar, Kutz, Dasberg, & Stern, 1989) conceptualize personality as an organized or structured system comprised of different psychobiological subsystems, which are normally more or less cohesive, and function together as a whole in healthy individuals. Structure has been defined as "the composition of component parts, an organization of a complex whole . . . with reference to the positional and functional interdependence of their parts" (Drever, 1952, p. 285). Indeed, in terms of evolutionary psychology, humans are comprised of a number of psychobiological (sub)systems that have evolved by natural selection and that serve different functions; that is, that allow them to function at their best in particular environments (Buss, 2004, 2005; Metzinger, 2003; Panksepp, 1998).

As 19th century French psychiatrists have already noted, dissociation involves a particular organization of the psychophysical systems that constitute personality. In our view, this organization is not arbitrary or coincidental, but in traumatization it likely follows rather well-defined, evolutionary metaphorical "fault lines" in the structure of the personality. Based on this understanding of the personality, we have begun to use the term *structural dissociation of the personality* (Nijenhuis, Van der Hart, & Steele, 2002, 2004; Steele, Van der Hart, & Nijenhuis, 2005; Van der Hart, Nijenhuis, Steele, & Brown, 2004). Dissociative divisions do not just occur among mental actions, such as experiencing sensations or affects, but primarily take place between the two major categories of psychobiological systems that make up personality (Carver, Sutton, & Scheier, 2000; Gilbert, 2001; Lang, Bradley, & Cuthbert, 1998). One category involves systems that are primarily geared to approaching attractive stimuli in daily life, such as food and companionship. The other category of systems involves avoiding or escaping from aversive stimuli; for example, various threats. The purpose of these systems is to help us distinguish between helpful and harmful experiences, and to generate the best adaptive responses to current life circumstances. These situations encompass our interoceptive and exteroceptive worlds, our internal and external environments as we perceive them. We refer to these psychobiological systems as *action systems,* because each involves particular innate propensities to act in a goal directed manner (Arnold, 1960; Frijda, 1986).

Whereas different action systems can share action tendencies (e.g., speaking, walking), they also include their own action tendencies and related goals (e.g., attaching to one's mother, eating, drinking, flight, fight, playing with a friend, love making). The concept of action tendencies plays a major role in this book, and differs from the concept of actions. We tend to think of actions as being carried out or executed. *Action tendencies are not merely propensities to act in certain ways, but involve the complete cycle of action, including latency, readiness, initiation, execution, and completion* (Janet, 1934). Action tendencies involve adaptations to environmental challenges. Whereas many of these tendencies have been developed over the long course of evolution, thus are genetically transmitted, most of them still require maturation and adequate environmental stimulation to blossom. Each tendency comprises a more or less complex range of mental and behavioral actions. Action systems help us to behave, think, feel, and perceive in particular ways; that is, engage in certain action tendencies that are meant to be beneficial to us. Thus we may behave, think, feel, and perceive one way when we are hungry, and quite differently when we are curious about what has happened to a friend, or when we have a conflict at work.

The first category of action systems that make up personality involves action systems that support individuals in efforts to adapt to daily life; the second category pertains to the action systems for defense from major threat, and recuperation. Whereas evolution has prepared us both for tasks of daily living and for survival under threat, we are not able to engage with ease in both simultaneously. Thus when both are necessary, particularly for long periods of time, some individuals develop a rather rigid division of their personality to deal with these very discrepant goals and related activities. For example, Marilyn Van Derbur (2004), the former Miss America who was molested as a child, described her personality as being divided into a "day child," that was avoidant, numb, detached, amnesic, and focused on normal life, and a "night child" that endured the abuse and focused on defense.

The lack of cohesion and integration of the personality manifests itself most clearly in the alternation between and coexistence of the reexperience of traumatizing events (e.g., a "night child") and avoidance of reminders of the traumatic experience with a focus on functioning in daily life (e.g., a "day child"). This biphasic pattern is a hallmark of PTSD (APA, 1994) and is also observed in patients with other trauma-related disorders. It involves a division between action systems for defense, those which guide us to avoid or escape from threat, and for functioning in daily life—systems that are primarily for seeking attractive stimuli in life that help us survive and feel well. This division is the basic form of structural dissociation of the personality. *Trauma-related structural dissociation, then, is a deficiency in the cohesiveness and flexibility of the personality structure* (Resch, 2004). This deficiency does not mean that the personality is completely split into different "systems of ideas and functions," but rather that there is a lack of cohesion and coordination among these systems that comprise the survivor's personality.

We describe the division of personality in terms of *dissociative parts of the personality*. This choice of term emphasizes the fact that dissociative parts of the personality together constitute one whole, yet are self-conscious, have at least a rudimentary sense of self, and are generally more complex than a single psychobiological state. These dissociative parts are mediated by action systems. Moreover, traumatized patients generally find "parts of the personality" or "parts of yourself" an apt description of their subjective experience.

"Apparently Normal" and "Emotional" Parts of the Personality

In conceptualizing these prototypical dissociative parts of the personality, we begin with the important work of a British World War I psychologist and psychiatrist, Charles Samuel Myers (1916a, 1916b, 1940). He described a basic form of structural dissociation in acutely traumatized ("shell-shocked") World War I combat soldiers (cf., Van der Hart, Van Dijke, Van Son, & Steele, 2000). This dissociation involves the coexistence of and alternation between a so-called *Apparently Normal [Part of the] Personality* (ANP) and a so-called *Emotional [Part of the] Personality* (EP). Throughout the book we will refer to these prototypical parts as ANP and EP. Survivors as ANP are fixated in trying to go on with normal life, thus are directed by action systems for daily life (e.g., exploration, caretaking, attachment), while avoiding traumatic memories. As EP, they are fixated in the action system (e.g., defense, sexuality) or subsystems (e.g., hypervigilance, flight, fight) that were activated at the time of traumatization.

ANP and EP are unduly rigid and closed to each other, because they are constrained to some degree by the specific action systems by which they are mediated and by the level of action tendencies that they can attain. That is, survivors as ANP and EP exhibit their own relatively inflexible patterns of action tendencies, at least some of which are maladaptive.

Myers was not implying that emotion was only experienced by EP. Rather he was emphasizing the overwhelming or *vehement* nature of EP's traumatic emotions in comparison to ANP. *Vehement emotion differs from intense emotion in that it is not adaptive, is overwhelming to the individual, and its expression is not helpful.* In fact, the more it is expressed, the more dysfunctional and overwhelmed the survivor becomes. For example, this is commonly seen in "borderline" patients who express rage: The more they express, the more out of control they become.

Structural dissociation may also occur along the lines of particular emotions or beliefs that may be less obviously related to a particular action system or constellation of action systems. For example, a part may contain mental actions such as sadness, guilt, despair, or shame, and other parts may find those emotions intolerable. However, such emotions are very likely connected to action systems that help regulate our attachments and social positions. As Gilbert (2002) noted, individuals may be ashamed of certain actions when they fear that others will reject or despise them for engaging in those actions, and they may feel guilty if their actions have hurt others (such as giving up a caring role, harming children via divorce). They may thus avoid those actions in order to maintain the current status of attachments and social positions. These action systems for achievement of goals in daily life and for defense from major threat are thus insufficiently cohesive and coordinated.

Structural dissociation can range from very simple to extremely complex divisions of the personality, and these levels of complexity have implications for treatment. These levels represent a dimensional picture of dissociation and are merely prototypes of dissociative organizations. It is to be expected that the more complex structural dissociation becomes, the more there will be deviation from these prototypes. There can be infinite individual variations of the expressions of dissociation.

Primary structural dissociation. The most simple and basic trauma-related division of the personality is between a *single ANP* and a *single EP*. We have referred to this as *primary structural dissociation*. While ANP is the "major shareholder" of the personality, as described by incest survivor Sylvia Fraser (1987), EP usually is quite limited in scope, function, and sense of self. That is, the part of the survivor that is EP remains unelaborated and not very autonomous in daily life. More complex forms of structural dissociation that involve wider ranges of dissociative parts are variations on primary structural dissociation of the personality.

Secondary structural dissociation. When traumatizing events are increasingly overwhelming or prolonged, further division of EP may occur, while a single ANP remains intact. This *secondary structural dissociation* may be based on the failed integration among various kinds of defense that have different psychobiological configurations, including different combinations of affects, cognitions, perceptions, and motor actions. These involve conditions such as freeze, fight, flight, and total submission.

> Martha was a patient with the diagnosis of complex PTSD and borderline personality disorder. She had a childhood history of serious physical abuse and profound neglect. One part of her personality (EP) tended to become enraged at the smallest perceived slight, another (EP) froze in terror when she was triggered, a third (EP) was constantly on the lookout for danger, a fourth (EP) was always searching for somebody to take care of her, and a fifth (ANP) functioned quite well at work as long as relationships did not feel threatening to her.

Tertiary structural dissociation. Finally, division of ANP may occur, in addition to divisions of EP. This *tertiary structural dissociation* occurs when inescapable aspects of daily life have become associated with past trauma; that is, triggers tend to reactivate traumatic memories through the process of generalization learning. Alternately when the functioning of ANP is so poor that normal life itself is overwhelming, new ANPs may develop. In severe cases of secondary and in all cases of tertiary dissociation, more than a single part may have a strong degree of elaboration (e.g., names, ages, genders, preferences) and *emancipation* (Janet's [1907] term that denotes actual or perceived separation and autonomy from the influence of other dissociative parts). This is not commonly observed in primary structural dissociation, nor in many cases of secondary structural dissociation.

Levels of structural dissociation and DSM-IV diagnoses. In order to understand structural dissociation, it is essential to have a basic grasp of how the various levels fit with current diagnostic categories. Our basic premise is that all trauma-related disorders involve some degree of structural dissociation, with acute stress disorder and simple PTSD being the most basic, and dissociative identity disorder (DID) the most complex. Chronically traumatized survivors typically have a number of comorbid mental disorders that are related to traumatization and its neurobiological effects. The more extensive the dissociation, the more complex the disorders will be. Many survivors experience structural dissociation without the elaboration and emancipation of some dissociative parts found in DID. Table I.1 shows the proposed relationships between levels of structural dissociation and trauma-related disorders.

Developmental Pathways to Structural Dissociation of the Personality

In primary structural dissociation we have assumed that the personality was a relatively integrated mental system prior to traumatization. However, this is hardly the case in traumatized children. An integrated personality is a developmental achievement. The more complex levels of structural dissociation in adults who were chronically traumatized as children are thus developed within a personality that lacks the normal cohesion and coherence of the healthy adult. Children also lack the requisite skills to cope with difficult affects and experiences, and need much support to do so. Most chronically traumatized individuals were never taught those skills, nor did they have emotional support in times of stress (cf., Gold, 2000).

Structural dissociation involves hindrance or breakdown of a natural progression toward integration of psychobiological systems of the personality that have been described as discrete behavioral states (Putnam, 1997). It involves a *chronic* integrative deficit largely due to a combination of the child's immature integrative brain structures and functions (for reviews, cf., Glaser, 2000; Van der Kolk, 2003), and inadequate psychophysiological regulation by caregivers, such as insufficient soothing, calming, and modulation (Siegel, 1999).

STRUCTURAL DISSOCIATION VERSUS INTEGRATIVE ACTIONS

Actions shape our lives for better or worse. But actions are not exclusively about behavior; they are also essential *mental* endeavors. All but the most reflexive behavior is guided by a multitude of *mental actions*, such as planning, predicting, thinking, feeling, fantasies, or wishes. Behavioral ac-

TABLE I.1
Diagnoses and Structural Dissociation

Primary Structural Dissociation

> *One predominant ANP and one EP; the latter is often not very elaborated or autonomous*

Simple types of Acute Stress Disorder
Simple types of PTSD
Simple types of DSM-IV Dissociative Disorder
Simple types of ICD-10 Dissociative Disorders of Movement and
    Sensation

Secondary Structural Dissociation

> *One predominant ANP and more than one EP; the latter can be more elaborated and autonomous than in Primary Structural Dissociation, but is typically less elaborated and autonomous than in Tertiary Structural Dissociation*

Complex PTSD
Disorders of Extreme Stress Not Otherwise Specified (DESNOS)
Dissociative Disorder Not Otherwise Specified
Trauma-related Borderline Personality Disorder
Complex ICD-10 Dissociative Disorders of Movement and Sensation

Tertiary Structural Dissociation

> *More than one ANP and more than one EP; often several ANPs and EPs are more elaborated and autonomous (including the use of different names and physical features) than in SSD*

Dissociative Identity Disorder

---

tions include a synthesis of both mental and motor actions. Mental actions and behavioral actions may be adaptive or not. Our concern with survivors is in supporting their ability to raise the adaptive level of their actions.

Hierarchy of Action Tendencies

Janet (1926a, 1938) outlined various levels of low, intermediate, and high order action tendencies. These are referred to as the *hierarchy of action tendencies*. This hierarchy is useful in clinical practice, as it helps the patient and therapist understand which actions are in need of improvement and which are already at high levels.

Lower order action tendencies are automatic and relatively simple, often involving *reflexive actions*, those that are reactive and rather automatic instead of carefully considered. Reflexive actions are necessary in situations where more automatic behavior is useful (e.g., driving or getting dressed), but they do not make adequate substitutes for higher order actions (e.g, thinking through and deciding how to behave when one's feelings have been hurt). Modern life often involves complicated situations that require complex and flexible responses. Thus, higher order action tendencies are usually the most adaptive in these situations.

> Allison, a patient with a severe abuse history, hit her head or fist on the wall as soon as she felt intense emotion, unable to allow herself to feel and to think about those emotions. Higher order action tendencies are creative and often complex, requiring many mental actions. Over the course of therapy, Allison gradually was able to stop herself when she had the urge to hit the wall, would sometimes hit a pillow instead, and could allow herself to feel. Eventually she was able to talk about her feelings and resolve them, actions that were much more adaptive, and more complex and creative than hitting the wall.

Whatever their level of complexity, action tendencies have stages of activation, ranging from latency, planning, initiation, execution, to completion. Survivors often have trouble starting or completing actions, whether they are mental or behavioral. They can plan, but not begin; or they can begin, but not finish; or their actions may lack adequate quality. Such problems indicate that an individual does not have sufficient mental energy or adequate ability to focus that energy for successful completion of various mental and behavioral actions.

Mental Level

The highest level of action tendencies an individual can attain in a given moment is called his or her *mental level* (Janet, 1903, 1928b). One's mental level involves two factors that are in dynamic relation with each other, available mental (and physical) energy and mental efficiency (Janet called the latter *psychological tension*, a term that can be easily misunderstood because we associate "tension" with stress, which was not Janet's intention in using the term). Thus the term *mental level* indicates the ability to efficiently focus and use whatever mental energy is available in the moment. Mental efficiency includes the concept of integrative capacity. Thus being able to reach a high mental level is fundamental to one's capacity to integrate experiences. Many survivors have difficulty attaining and sustaining higher mental levels, regardless of how much mental energy is available to them. Traumatization involves fixation at or regression to unduly low levels of action tendencies, and by implication, low mental levels, for at least some parts of the personality.

There are three major problems related to mental energy and mental efficiency: (1) low mental energy; (2) insufficient mental efficiency; and (3) imbalances between mental energy and efficiency. Adaptive actions generally expend a lot of physical or mental energy. Many survivors function at a level of exhaustion that offers little mental energy because they try to do too much and are tired, or because they are too depressed to try to do anything. Physical illness, a frequent companion of many survivors, also lowers mental energy. In such cases, mental energy is insufficient, even though in principle individuals may have adequate mental efficiency to accomplish actions. A second problem is related to insufficient mental efficiency, even though the individual may have sufficient mental energy for a given task or action. In dissociative individuals, the mental level can vary to some degree for each dissociative part.

A third problem with adaptive actions is typically not only due to specific emotional and relational skills deficits, but involves a more pervasive impediment that generally is not recognized or treated explicitly in therapy. This is the problem of an imbalance between how much mental energy is available, *and* how well that mental energy can be utilized to engage in adaptive action in the present. There are various combinations of mental energy and mental efficiency (see Chapter 9).

Therapists often try intuitively, without much clarity, to help patients raise their mental efficiency so they can maximize their mental energy. Our focus to a large degree in this book will be on how to assess patients' mental levels systematically and improve and regulate their mental efficiency and energy, thereby helping them engage in more adaptive mental and behavioral actions. To this end the therapist encourages the patient to plan, begin, engage in, and complete various mental and behavioral actions at gradually higher levels.

Substitute Actions

Maladaptive mental and behavioral actions are implied in affect and impulse dysregulation, attachment problems, and other difficulties that plague survivors. Inadequate mental actions are also implicit in the ongoing maintenance of dissociation. Such actions are referred to as *substitute actions*, those that are less adaptive than required when the challenges of life exceed the mental level of the patient. For instance, when intense feelings are evoked, a patient may resort to cutting or purging as lower level substitutes for more adaptive actions such as journaling, thinking through, self-soothing, or other actions which would actually resolve the feelings rather than perpetuate them. People not only fall back on substitute actions when they are unable to engage in higher order adaptive actions, but also when integration is not yet attainable.

Substitute actions may vary in their level of adaptivity, with some reaching more adaptive and complex levels than others. Some substitute actions are behavioral, such as physical agitation, compulsions, and self-injury. But many substitute actions are mental in nature. There are times when emotions become overwhelming and intolerable. These are the *vehement emotions* to which we referred earlier, and they are in themselves substitute actions for other ways to cope with a situation. Individuals prone to vehement emotions may employ maladaptive mental coping strategies such as profound denial, disavowal, projection, and splitting.

Integrative Actions

Integration is a familiar term in the trauma field that implies patients must somehow assimilate traumatic experiences (and dissociative parts of the personality) in order to move forward with their lives. But integration is also an integral part of and necessary for adaptive living on a daily basis. The actions of integration require the highest degrees of mental energy and mental efficiency.

Integration is an adaptive process involving ongoing mental actions that help both to differentiate and link experiences over time within a personality that is both flexible *and* stable, and thus promotes the best functioning possible in the present (Jackson, 1931/1932; Janet, 1889; Meares, 1999; Nijenhuis, Van der Hart, & Steele, 2004). The capacity to be open and flexible allows us to change when required, whereas the capacity to stay closed allows us to remain stable, to act in preconceived ways. A mentally healthy individual is characterized by a strong capacity to integrate internal and external experiences (Janet, 1889).

What specific mental actions are involved in the process of integration, and how can they be achieved? It is helpful to understand two major types of integrative mental actions in order to effectively treat traumatized individuals: synthesis and realization.

Synthesis. A major integrative mental action is *synthesis*, in which we bind (link) and differentiate a range of internal and external experiences within a moment and across time. Synthesis includes binding and differentiating sensory perceptions, movements, thoughts, affects, and a sense of self. For example, we know how one person is like another (binding), but also the ways in which he or she is different (differentiation), and how our present situation is similar to but also different from our past. We also know that feeling mad and acting mad are similar in some ways, but also significantly differ from each other. Much synthesis occurs automatically and outside conscious awareness. Our capacity for synthesis fluctuates along with our mental level. For example, when an individual is fully awake, synthesis will be of a higher quality than when he or she is tired. Synthesis provides for the individual's normative unity of consciousness and history. Alterations of consciousness and dissociative symptoms can emerge when synthesis is incomplete.

Realization. A related, but higher level integrative mental action, *realization*, involves the mental actions of developing awareness of reality as it is, accepting it, and then reflectively and creatively adapting to it. Realization implies the degree to which closure of an experience is achieved (Janet, 1935a; Van der Hart, Steele, Boon, & Brown, 1993). It consists of two mental actions that are constantly maturing our view of ourselves, others, and the world (Janet, 1903, 1928a, 1935a). The first type of action involves integrating an experience with an explicit, personal sense of ownership: "That happened to *me*, and *I* think and feel thus and so about it." The second type of action is that of being firmly grounded in the present and integrating one's past, present, and future. It manifests in acting in the present in the most adaptive, mindful manner.

Both ANP and EP lack full realization of the present, are unable to live fully in the present. They also lack complete realization of their traumatization, that it is over, and often have been unable to realize a multitude of other experiences, leaving much unfinished business. With regard to traumatization, ANP lacks full realization of these experiences and their aftereffects. Thus ANP may deny or experience varying degrees of amnesia regarding the event(s). ANP perhaps acknowledges traumatic experiences but insists, "It doesn't feel like it happened to *me*." And EP does not experience that the traumatization has ended, is still immersed in it, and thus lacks the ability to be fully in the present. Restricted by their respective action systems and their limited coping skills, both ANP and EP selectively attend to a limited range of cues, such as those that are relevant for caretaking or defensive interests. This further reduces the capacity to fully realize and integrate traumatic memories and to be completely in the present.

MAINTENANCE OF STRUCTURAL
DISSOCIATION OF THE PERSONALITY

Structural dissociation has become chronic in those patients with trauma-related disorders. There are a number of interwoven factors that converge to maintain dissociation once it begins (which will be discussed in depth in Chapter 10).

The lower their mental level, the more individuals must rely on substitute actions that may protect against overwhelming emotions and thoughts, but that are at odds with integration of traumatic memories and associated dissociative parts. The mental level of survivors remains low when they have significant relational and emotional skills deficits. In many cases, these deficits are due primarily to a lack of adequate modeling and training by caretakers: many survivors grew up in environments in which these skills were never used. A low or modest mental level can be compensated for by social and relational supports that crucially assist a survivor in integrating traumatic experiences. However, many survivors have little to no support. They face the monumental task of integration alone and find it too overwhelming. Trauma-related changes in neurobiology also impede integration (Krystal, Bannett, Bremner, Southwick, & Charney, 1996; Krystal, Bremner, Southwick, & Charney, 1998; Nijenhuis, Van der Hart, & Steele, 2002; Perry & Pate, 1994; Vermetten & Bremner, 2002).

In these contexts, various trauma-related conditioning effects are also central to the persistence of structural dissociation. That is, survivors can develop conditioned fears of inner and outer cues (conditioned stimuli) when they have learned to associate these with the original traumatizing event (unconditioned stimuli), and which they will thereafter mentally and behaviorally avoid. Structural dissociation is specifically maintained when ANPs learn to phobically and chronically avoid intruding EPs with their traumatic memories and accompanying aversive sensations, emotions, and thoughts. The resolution of these phobias, briefly described below, is a major treatment focus.

Phobias That Maintain Structural Dissociation

Traditionally, phobias have been relegated to the category of anxiety disorders, and have been understood to be directed to external cues (e.g., spiders, heights, germs, social phobia), and to have psychodynamic meaning. However, phobias can also pertain to inner phenomena, to mental actions such as particular thoughts, feelings, fantasies, sensations, and memories (e.g., Janet, 1903; McCullough et al., 2003; Nijenhuis, 1994). Therapists who work with chronically traumatized individuals will readily recognize that such patients are often extraordinarily fearful of mental actions as well as external stimuli that remind them of the traumatic experience.

According to Janet (1904/1983b, 1935a), the core phobia in trauma-related structural dissociation consists of an avoidance of the synthesis and full realization of the traumatic experience and its effects on one's life; the *phobia of traumatic memory*. Behavioral and mental avoidance strategies which maintain structural dissociation, are needed to prevent what are perceived as unbearable realizations about one's self, history, and meaning. Subsequently, additional phobias ensue from the fundamental phobia of traumatic memory. Janet (1903, 1909b, 1922) stated that all phobias have in common fears of (certain) actions. Trauma-related phobias are thus treated in a specific order such that patients experience a gradually developing *capacity to engage in purposeful and high quality adaptive actions*, both mental and behavioral; that is, attain higher levels of mental efficiency. Increasingly more complex and difficult experiences (past and present) then can be tolerated and integrated, and improvement in daily living can be achieved.

When survivors associate an increasing number of stimuli with the traumatic experience and memory through stimulus generalization, they may start to fear and avoid more and more of inner and outer life. For example, when survivors as ANP have intrusive traumatic memories and associate this aversive intrusion with EP, they develop a phobia of this dissociative part. The survivor as EP can become phobic of ANP when that part is perceived as ignoring or harming (i.e., neglecting or abusing) EP in some way. In fact, survivors can become anxious and avoidant of any mental action, such as having particular feelings, sensations, and thoughts that are consciously or unconsciously associated with the original traumatic experience(s). Thus most survivors have some degree of phobia of trauma-derived mental actions (which we formerly called *phobia of mental contents*; e.g., Nijenhuis, Van der Hart, & Steele, 2002; Van der Hart & Steele, 1999). The phobia of trauma-derived mental actions evolves from the core phobia of traumatic memories, and involves the survivor's fear, disgust, or shame about mental actions he or she has associated with traumatic memories. As long as patients are afraid of their inner life, they cannot integrate their internal experiences, so that structural dissociation is ongoing.

Phobias of attachment and of attachment loss easily develop because chronically traumatized individuals have been hurt by other human beings, especially caretakers. Thus attachment is experienced as dangerous, but also, of course, as necessary. Phobia of attachment is often paradoxically accompanied by an equally intense phobia of attachment loss. It manifests in desperate feelings and behaviors that motivate the individual to connect to another person at all costs. Typically, different parts of the personality experience these opposite phobias. They evoke each other in a vicious cycle, with a perceived change in closeness or distance in a relationship resulting in the well-known "borderline" pattern of "I hate you—don't leave me," more recently described as disorganized/disoriented attachment (D-attachment, e.g., Liotti, 1999a).

Another manifestation of generalization is the *phobia of normal life*. Since normal life involves at least a basic level of healthy risk taking and change, many experiences of normal life also become vigorously avoided. Finally, more mature levels of attachment, such as intimacy, are avoided due to the plethora of phobias related to attachment and trauma-derived mental actions that have become conditioned stimuli, because most chronic traumatization is of an interpersonal nature.

PHASE-ORIENTED TREATMENT
OF CHRONIC TRAUMATIZATION

The theory of structural dissociation has major consequences for the assessment and treatment of chronically traumatized survivors (e.g., Steele et al., 2001, 2005). It is helpful for therapists to understand the implications of structural dissociation as an undue division of the personality, how it manifests, and how it must be treated. They should strive to understand the importance not only of psychodynamic, relational, and behavioral aspects of treatment, but also become proficient in assessing and working with the mental energy and mental levels of patients. Therapists need to analyze survivors' mental and behavioral actions for adaptivity. They will find it helpful to have a multitude of interventions at hand that transcend any given theoretical model, thereby maximizing the help they can offer in raising the level of action tendencies in each part of the personality over the course of treatment.

The major treatment approaches for complex PTSD and dissociative disorders are typically phase-oriented, are considered the current standard of care, and include the following phases: (1) stabilization and symptom reduction; (2) treatment of traumatic memories; and (3) personality integration and rehabilitation. Although the phases have been described in linear fashion, in reality they are flexible and recursive, involving a periodic need to return to previous phases (Courtois, 1999; Steele et al., 2005).

Each phase involves a *problem-solving and skills-building approach* within the broader context of a *relational approach* (D. Brown, Scheflin, & Hammond, 1998). The spiral course occurs as greater levels of mental efficiency are achieved, allowing previously intolerable dissociated material to become integrated, and more entrenched areas of dysfunction to be addressed. Phase-oriented treatment may be rather straightforward for relatively simple cases of traumatization. However, it may be much more complex, with more alterations among phases, and need to address multifaceted and chronic issues.

Assessment

Chronically traumatized patients often seek help during a crisis. Although they may need immediate assistance in this regard, it is essential not to forsake normal assessment procedures, including thorough diagnosis, psychological testing, and extensive history taking (including a possible trauma history and previous treatments). Serious comorbidity may occur in these patients. They may fulfill criteria for numerous diagnostic categories, which makes a cohesive explanation of extensive psychopathology virtually impossible.

Although systematic assessment of dissociative symptoms and dissociative disorders may not be part of a routine workup, it is indicated in patients who have complex comorbidity and symptoms, report traumatization, or who present with a history of "treatment failure." Here, we add the caveat that patients may have an underlying dissociative organization of their personality that is not reflected in a given DSM-IV dissociative disorder. For instance, a patient diagnosed with borderline personality disorder may well be characterized by secondary structural dissociation, and the same may apply to a patient with a somatoform disorder, as recognized in the ICD-10 diagnostic category of dissociative disorders of movement and sensation (WHO, 1992). However, it is usually only over time and with careful and extensive observation that the therapist develops a clearer picture of the complexity of the patient's structural dissociation.

In planning for an appropriate treatment trajectory, it is vital to assess a patient's unique strengths and weaknesses, such as functioning in terms of mental level (i.e., the highest level that can be attained in the hierarchy of action tendencies, along with available mental energy). Some patients may be high functioning in daily life, able to excel in a highly demanding profession, with occasional lowering of their mental level in situations that reactivate traumatic memories, or that require skills not yet mastered. Other patients may function at a low level, both in terms of the hierarchy of tendencies and available energy. Thorough assessment of the patient's mental level and its fluctuations should include a wide range of domains, including work, relationships, caretaking, play, sleep–wake and eating habits, potentially threatening situations, and proficiency in the mental actions that accompany behavioral ones. When a patient is assessed as being unable to adaptively deal with a particular issue or situation, the lower-order substitute actions that he or she is employing should be identified as potential treatment targets.

When structural dissociation of the personality is apparent, it is helpful in planning treatment to distinguish ANPs and EPs and their differences in mental level. While ANPs typically function at higher levels than EPs, they sometimes may be overwhelmed by the intrusion of EPs. A clear picture of the number and types of dissociative parts, and of their respective mental efficiency and energy may emerge only over time. However, a thorough assessment, such as briefly suggested here (more in Chapter 11), may provide sufficient information for an initial treatment plan.

Treatment Phase 1:
Stabilization and Symptom Reduction

Phase 1 is dedicated to raising the mental level and adaptive actions of ANPs and dominant EPs to allow for more effective functioning in daily life. This phase of treatment is directed toward helping patients achieve some measure of balance in mental and behavioral actions given the mental energy and efficiency that are available to them. Therapy is directed to raising the mental level of ANP and key EPs that are intrusive and interfering with therapy and safety. This implies that survivors must improve the reflective quality and sometimes quantity of their mental and behavioral actions. This is relatively straightforward in cases of primary structural dissociation within the context of short-term psychotherapy (Van der Hart, Van der Kolk, & Boon, 1998). However, in cases of secondary and tertiary structural dissociation, typically much more strenuous and long-term therapeutic effort must be invested.

It is important for patients to learn to work within the constraints of their energy at a given time, learn what improves or diminishes their energy, and reduce inefficient energy expenditures. Above all, they must begin to learn and experience the fact that well completed mental and behavioral actions raise their mental level. Some patients do too much, or push themselves beyond the energy available to them. They need to learn to simplify life and rest more. Reduction of an overly full schedule allows space and time to turn to the mental actions that are being avoided by too many behavioral ones. For other patients who are severely shut down and unable to get anything done, the need is to engage in more mental and behavioral actions, not less. For yet others who are entangled in endless obsessions and overthinking, the need is to simplify mental actions so that behavioral ones become more adaptive. In all cases, higher order actions that involve thoughtfulness and planning are necessary, and the need to improve or stabilize mental energy and mental efficiency is essential.

Low mental efficiency contributes to substitute actions that manifest as major and distressing symptoms, such as self-destructive behaviors. Promotion of daily life functioning in ANP involves decreasing or eliminating these debilitating symptoms, as well as those of depression, anxiety, and PTSD. Containment of traumatic memories is paramount. Patients may need to learn and repeatedly practice many emotional and relational skills, which will raise their mental level.

In order to systematically foster adaptive action, treatment in Phase 1 is directed toward overcoming particular trauma-related phobias: The phobia of trauma-derived mental actions, including the phobia of dissociative parts of the personality, as well as the phobia of attachment and of attachment loss must be worked through with the therapist. The phobia of change and of normal life will begin to be addressed, and will continue at more complex levels throughout the course of treatment. The presence of these phobias implies that patients have "unfinished business" and are expending energy to avoid or contain their unresolved issues. In response to phobias, survivors generally engage in lower order substitute actions that either further lower or prevent the raising of their mental level, so that integration is chronically out of reach. Treatment should address these serious problems with the employment of mental energy economy. The patient must gradually develop understanding and empathy for, and enhanced cooperation among all parts of the personality, without yet sharing traumatic memories. Thus, a more cohesive, stable, and flexible personality is already being fostered from the earliest phases of treatment.

Treatment Phase 2:
Treatment of Traumatic Memories

A major goal of Phase 2 is that of resolving the phobia of traumatic memories among various parts of the personality, so that structural dissociation is rendered unnecessary. This phase of treatment generally requires patients to sustain a higher mental level than the one that existed when they entered treatment. The careful pacing of therapy, including regulation of hyper- and hypoarousal will be crucial to success. Resolution of traumatic memory and related emotions and beliefs is a highly complex and difficult part of treatment (see Chapter 16).

Additional phobias to be addressed in this phase include those related to insecure attachment to the perpetrator(s). Patients are both strongly attached to and inherently avoidant of perpetrators, and this core approach–avoidance dilemma must be resolved. Various parts of the personality may express polarized and often unrealistic views of perpetrators (e.g., "He knows what I am thinking and will punish me"; "He can do no wrong"). These must be unraveled gently in the course of therapy. Survivors must ultimately grieve the loss of an ideal family and learn to appreciate functioning as an interdependent adult.

Occasional excursions into Phase 3 work may occur without much, if any resolution of traumatic memories. However, Phase 2 work is generally necessary, because resolution of the unfinished business of trauma helps raise an individual's overall mental level, and removes the chronic obstacles of traumatic reenactments and reactivation. Typically there is rather spontaneous movement back and forth between Phase 2, and Phases 1 and 3.

Treatment Phase 3:
Personality Integration and Rehabilitation

Phase 3 may contain some of the most difficult work yet (Van der Hart, Steele et al., 1993). It involves painful grief work that is necessary for deepening realization to occur, relinquishment of strongly held substitute beliefs, and the struggle to engage in the world with new coping skills that require high degrees of sustained mental efficiency and energy. Even though begun in the early phase of treatment, ongoing resolution of the phobia of change and normal life must continue in Phase 3. Finally, overcoming the phobia of intimacy is perhaps the pinnacle of successful treatment, and is essential for patients to move forward with a high quality of life. Patients who cannot successfully complete Phase 3 work often continue to have difficulty with normal life, despite significant relief from traumatic intrusions. But the quality of life for those who do well in Phase 3 work can be remarkably improved.

SUMMARY

This chapter has provided a synopsis of what is to come in this book regarding the understanding and treatment of chronic traumatization and structural dissociation.

PART I

Structural Dissociation
of the Personality

CHAPTER 1

Structural Dissociation
of the Personality

Basics

*I have another self . . . weltering in tears . . . I carry it deep inside me
like a wound.*
                                            —Michel Tournier (1972, p. 21)

THERE IS OFTEN CONFUSION about what kind of events and personal characteristics can be associated with dissociation, and what, in fact, is dissociated in a traumatized individual. This chapter addresses these issues,
which are essential to the understanding of structural dissociation.

THE TRAUMATIC ORIGINS OF STRUCTURAL
DISSOCIATION

The term *trauma* is used often and loosely, so we begin by setting the
parameters of the term *traumatization* as we use it, specifically in relation to structural dissociation of the personality. Trauma essentially
means "wound," "injury" (Winnik, 1969), or "shock." The word was first
applied to the psychological impact of stressful events by a German neu-
rologist, who introduced the term *psychic trauma* (Eulenburg, 1878;
Van der Hart & Brown, 1990). In the clinical and scientific literature the
term *traumatic event* is common, and the term *trauma* is often used as
a synonym for such events (Kardiner & Spiegel, 1947). However, events
are not traumatic in themselves, rather, they may be so in their effect on
a given individual. Thus not every individual who experiences an extremely stressful event will actually be traumatized. So when we speak in

this book of *trauma*, we do not refer to an event, but only to those individuals who have developed a trauma-related disorder, a degree of structural dissociation.

The extent to which an individual will become traumatized is due to two sets of interacting factors; the objective characteristics of the event and the subjective characteristics that define the individual's mental energy and mental efficiency (components of integrative capacity). Here we focus on general vulnerability factors inherent in both adults and children.

CHARACTERISTICS OF POTENTIALLY TRAUMATIZING EVENTS

Some events have more potential to be traumatizing than others. They include experiences that are intense, sudden, uncontrollable, unpredictable, and extremely negative (Brewin, Andrews, & Valentine, 2000; E. B. Carlson, 1997; E. B. Carlson & Dalenberg, 2000; Foa, Zinbarg, & Rothbaum, 1992; Ogawa, Sroufe, Weinfeld, Carlson, & Egeland, 1997). Events that are interpersonally violent and involve physical harm or threat to life are more likely to be traumatizing than other kinds of highly stressful events such as natural disasters (e.g., APA, 1994; Breslau, Chilcoat, Kessler, Peterson, & Lucia, 1999; Darves-Bornoz, Lépine, Choquet, Berger, & Degiovanni et al., 1998; Holbrook, Hoyt, Stein, & Sieber, 2002). Events that are not literally life-threatening but which include attachment loss (Waelde, Koopman, Rierdon, & Spiegel, 2001) and betrayal by an important attachment person (Freyd, 1996) also increase the risk of traumatization. Child abuse often includes all of these event factors.

In children, interpersonal violence is usually accompanied by neglect (Draijer, 1990; Nijenhuis, Van der Hart, Kruger, & Steele, 2004). But neglect may also occur within adult relationships. Neglect is a form of traumatization in which there is an absence of essential physical or emotional care, soothing, and restorative experiences from significant others. In children these experiences are developmentally requisite, and in adults they may be needed under certain circumstances, such as the aftermath of potentially traumatizing events.

Recurrent exposure to major stressors over time, such as child abuse, appears to have the most pernicious effects on survivors. Chronic traumatization increases the risk for trauma-related disorders and for more severe and extensive symptoms including illicit drug use (Dube, Anda et al., 2003) and attempted suicide (Dube, Felitti et al., 2001). These include not only mental, but also physical symptoms because brain development and neuroendocrine function are compromised (Anda et al., 2006 and Dube et al., 2003; Breslau, Davis, & Andreski, 1995; Draijer & Langeland, 1999; Glaser, 2000; Hillis et al., 2004; Nijenhuis, Van der Hart, & Steele, 2004; Ozer, Best, Lipsey, & Weiss, 2003; B. D. Perry, 1994; Schore, 2003a,

2003b). Chronic traumatization is a major factor in the development of more complex forms of structural dissociation.

Lack of social support constitutes a major risk factor for the development of trauma-related disorders (e.g., Brewin et al., 2000; Ozer et al., 2003). This may be especially true for children because they are so completely dependent on adults for help in integrating difficult experiences. Comfort, support, and care are essential in maintaining and improving an individual's mental efficiency (e.g., Runtz & Schallow, 1997), in part because they have important physiological calming effects (Schore, 1994; 2003b), and favorable effects on the immune system (Uchino, Cacioppi, & Kieclot-Glaser, 1996). Supportive touch is a major stress reducer and can help modulate strong emotional reactions (Kramer, 1990; Nijenhuis & Den Boer, in press; Weze, Leathard, Grange, Tiplady, & Stevens, 2005).

INDIVIDUAL CHARACTERISTICS

Many adults experience acute distress and some intrusions in the aftermath of overwhelming events, but these phenomena usually dissipate over weeks or months and generally do not develop into trauma-related disorders (Kleber & Brom, 1992). These peritraumatic intrusions can be regarded as manifestations of a temporary and minor division of the personality prior to the complete integration of a stressful experience. But some individuals go on to develop trauma-related disorders. For example, research suggests that approximately 10 to 25% of adults who are exposed to an extreme stressor may develop simple acute stress disorder (ASD; APA, 1994) and PTSD (Breslau, 2001; Kessler, Sonnega, Bromet, Hughes, & Nelson, 1995; Yehuda, 2002).

Meta-analyses found several major predictors of PTSD in adults: prior (cumulative) traumatization, especially chronic child maltreatment, prior psychological adjustment, family history of psychopathology, perceived life threat during the traumatization, peritraumatic emotional responses, peritraumatic dissociation, lack of social support, and gender (Brewin et al., 2000; Emily, Best, Lipsey, & Weiss, 2003; Holbrook, Hoyt, Stein, & Sieber, 2002; Ozer et al., 2003). Maltreated children often have virtually all of these risk factors.

Gene–Environment Interaction

Personality is defined in part by the interaction between our environment and our genetic makeup. Genetic factors may contribute to vulnerability to stressful situations and to personality characteristics that influence the person's risk for entering into potentially hazardous situations (Jang et al., 2003). However, a direct genetic link to traumatization is far from clear (Brewin et al., 2000; Emily et al., 2003; McNally, 2003).

Mental Efficiency and Mental Energy

A high level of mental efficiency is needed for an individual's personality to remain relatively unified after exposure to extreme stressors. Structural dissociation occurs when an individual's mental efficiency and mental energy (discussed in depth in Part II, and Chapter 12) are too low to fully integrate what happened. Mental efficiency varies from person to person, increases with age (but generally decreases with old age), and tends to change with variables such as physical and mental energy level, physical and mental health, mood and emotion, and stress exposure. The mental efficiency and mental energy of mentally healthy individuals are balanced (i.e., a high mental level), which allows them to integrate mental events relative to their developmental level (Jackson, 1931–1932; Janet, 1889; Meares, 1999; Nijenhuis, Van der Hart, & Steele, 2002).

Integration is prevented when an individual avoids traumatic memories, suppresses thoughts about the traumatic experience, has a negative interpretation of intrusive trauma-related memories, or is exhausted. These reactions predicted PTSD in both children (Ehlers, Mayou, & Bryant, 2003) and adults (Laposa & Alden, 2003; Marmar et al., 1996). We suggest that individuals are likely to engage in mental actions such as avoidance, suppression, or negative cognitions when their mental efficiency is low. This is particularly true of the apparently normal part of the personality (ANP), the dissociative part of the personality which avoids traumatic memory. However, the emotional part of the personality (EP), fixated in traumatic memories, can also avoid ANP as well as the present reality.

Age

The presence of trauma-related disorders has been linked to the age of the individual at the time of traumatization. The younger the person, the more likely a trauma-related disorder will develop. This has been found with PTSD, complex PTSD, trauma-related borderline personality disorder (BPD), dissociative disorder not otherwise specified (DDNOS) subtype 1, a lesser form of dissociative identity disorder (DID; APA, 1994), and DID (e.g., Boon & Draijer, 1993; Brewin et al., 2000; Herman, Perry, & Van der Kolk, 1989; Liotti & Pasquini, 2000; Nijenhuis, Spinhoven, Van Dyck, Van der Hart, & Vanderlinden, 1998b; Ogawa et al., 1997; Roth, Newman, Pelcovitz, Van der Kolk, & Mandel, 1997). Chronic traumatization that begins in childhood stands apart from other types of traumatization because of a child's immature mental efficiency and psychobiological development, and his or her special needs for support and care (see Chapter 5).

Peritraumatic Dissociation

Symptoms of dissociation during and after a traumatizing event indicate that the individual's capacity to integrate at least some of the experience around the time of the event is insufficient. The presence of these and other peritraumatic symptoms such as severe alterations of consciousness are highly correlated with the eventual development of serious trauma-related disorders (e.g., Birmes et al., 2003; Gershuny, Cloitre, & Otto, 2003; G. N. Marshall & Schell, 2002; Ozer et al., 2003).

Vehement Emotions and Hyperarousal

Psychic trauma is related to the presence of "vehement" emotions, such as panic and emotional chaos, during and after overwhelming events (Bryant & Panasetis, 2001; Conlon, Fahy, & Conroy, 1999; Janet, 1889, 1909a; Resnick, Falsetti, Kilpatrick, & Foy, 1994; Van der Hart & Brown, 1992). This hyperarousal probably manifested in elevated heart rate shortly after the overwhelming event (Shalev et al., 1998) and exaggerated startle (Rothbaum & Davis, 2003), two predictors of PTSD. Vehement emotion involves maladaptive substitutes for adaptive action (Janet, 1909a; Van der Kolk & Van der Hart, 1989); that is, reactivity rather than reflective thinking through and careful action.

Hypoarousal

Although the literature has stressed the presence of hyperarousal as a major diagnostic criterion, it has been noted more recently that hypoarousal is also a significant problem (e.g., Lanius, Hopper, & Menon, 2003; Nijenhuis & Den Boer, in press). Not all individuals become hyperaroused during overwhelming events, or they may be hyperaroused at first and then experience a serious and involuntary drop in level of consciousness (hypoarousal). When individuals are extremely hypoaroused they may not encode much of what is happening, may feel the event is not real, and may experience emotional and bodily anesthesia. To the extent that individuals nonetheless recall the events, all of these experiences make it more difficult for them to eventually fully integrate the experience.

Meaning

The meaning individuals assign to an event (e.g., an act of God, a punishment, one's own fault) is significant in the development of PTSD (e.g., Ehlers et al., 2003; Koss, Figueredo, & Prince, 2002). Children typically believe abuse and neglect is their own fault, because perpetrators and others often blame them, and because they may not know how else to understand why caretakers hurt them (Salter, 1995). Belief that an event is physically threatening has been linked to dissociation (Marmar, Weiss, Schlenger et al., 1994; Marmar, Weiss, Metzler, Ronfeldt, & Foreman, 1996).

Previous Training

The way in which people respond to an event depends to some degree on their level of preparedness for such an experience (e.g., Janet, 1928b; Morgan et al., 2001). Although it is hard to imagine how a child could be prepared for (further) chronic abuse, resilience studies may help us gain more insight into how children learn to cope adaptively with adverse experiences (Berk, 1998; Caffo & Belaise, 2003; Henry, 2001; Kellerman, 2001; McGloin & Widom, 2001). This knowledge may be of eventual help to children who have lower integrative capacities.

In conclusion, whether or not an event has been traumatizing can only be inferred from the effects it has on the individual, and therefore can only be determined after the event. The psychological and biological factors discussed above are known to lead to increased vulnerability to traumatization; that is, development of structural dissociation of the personality.

DISSOCIATIVE PARTS OF THE PERSONALITY

The idea that it is the personality that can be dissociated is certainly not a new one. In the 19th century, dissociation originally denoted a *division of the personality* (Azam, 1876; Beaunis, 1887; Binet, 1892–1896/1997; Breuer & Freud, 1893–1895/1955b; Ferenczi, 1932/1988; Janet, 1887/2005; Prince, 1905; Ribot, 1885; Taine, 1878; cf., Van der Hart & Dorahy, in press).

Dissociation as Division of the Personality

More specifically, dissociation is a division among "systems of ideas and functions that constitute the personality" (Janet, 1907, p. 332). When Janet spoke of "ideas," he meant not only thoughts, but psychobiological complexes (systems) that included thoughts, affects, sensations, behaviors, memories, what we refer to as *mental actions*. And he implied that those systems of ideas and functions have their own sense of self, even if it is an extremely undeveloped one. For example, if affect or sensation are dissociated, they are still within the context of an "*I*:" "*I* am terrified;"

"*I* feel pain in my stomach." This sense of *I* may be quite discrepant with another sense of *I* that exists simultaneously: *I* am not terrified; *I* do not feel pain; *I* feel nothing." Sense of self may then be quite limited and restricted to awareness of only a small part of experience.

The original idea that dissociation divided the personality has been carried forward to the present day. For example, Putnam (1997) has noted that dissociation involves the division of "discrete behavioral states" that are normally linked together, forming a "behavioral architecture." This "architecture," or structure, defines "an individual's personality by encompassing both the range of the behavioral states available to the individual and the sum of prior experiences that have created distinct, stable states of mind" (p. 157).

Dissociation as a division of the personality has been noted in acutely traumatized adults. For example, during World War I, dissociation of the personality was viewed as the explanation for alternations between intrusions and avoidance (e.g., W. Brown, 1919; Ferenczi, 1919; Horowitz, 1986; McDougall, 1926; Myers, 1940; Simmel, 1919; cf., Van der Hart, Van Dijke et al., 2000) in which what would now be called PTSD or simple dissociative (conversion) disorder of movement and sensation (WHO, 1992). Clinicians noted that in such disorders dissociative mental actions, such as traumatic memories, do not exist in a vacuum, but are always a part of "*some* personality" (Mitchell, 1922, p. 113), "not . . . something that can be adequately described as an idea or group or train of ideas, but rather as a self-conscious purposive thinking of a [part of the] personality" (McDougall, 1926, p. 543). Dissociative mental actions thus involve cognitive and other actions exerted by a survivor in a particular dissociative part of the personality that regards him- or herself as the *agent* of these actions, and that also regards the related experiences as his or her *own* (Braude, 1995). For example, when a survivor reexperiences a traumatizing event, there is an EP that maintains: "*I* ran away (EP as the agent of the flight) because *I* was afraid" (EP as the part that owns the fear). The criteria of agency and ownership distinguish structural dissociation from other manifestations of insufficient integration such as intruding panic attacks in panic disorder or intrusions of negative cognitions in major depression.

Dissociative Parts of the Personality

Even though Mitchell and McDougall spoke of "personalities," close examination of their writing reveals that what they actually had in mind were dissociative *parts of a single* personality. The essence of their contributions is the idea that dissociative "systems of ideas and functions" are self-conscious and involve their own sense of self in patients with PTSD and other trauma-related disorders.

Dissociative parts are components of a single personality. Even parts that only encompass few experiences still have stable features. In this sense, all dissociative parts have their own "enduring pattern of perceiving, relating to, and thinking about the environment and self." This is the DSM-IV criterion for dissociative identity or personality state (APA, 1994, p. 487), *as well as* the definition of personality traits (APA, 1994, p. 630). There is no qualitative principle in the current literature that distinguishes dissociative parts of the personality in DID from dissociative parts of the personality in other trauma-related disorders such as PTSD. We propose the difference is essentially one of degree of complexity and emancipation of the parts of the personality. Several psychoanalytically oriented authors (Ferenczi, 1926; Joseph, 1975; Rosenfeld, 1987) have also used the term *parts of the personality* to describe structural dissociation without implying undue reification.[1]

Even though dissociative parts have a sense of self, no matter how rudimentary, they are not separate entities, but rather are different, more or less divided psychobiological systems that are not sufficiently cohesive or coordinated within an individual's personality. Inspired by Charles Myers (1940), we have chosen to use "apparently normal part of the personality (ANP)" and "emotional part of the personality (EP)" to denote these different kinds of psychobiological systems. These systems are part of a single human being, so we have chosen to refer to the entire individual when he or she is directed by one of those unintegrated systems. Thus we say "the survivor *as* ANP or EP," and when we speak about ANP or EP, this is what we have in mind.

Apparently Normal Part and Emotional Part of the Personality

These parts of the personality have been recognized by many who have used a number of different terminologies (e.g., Brewin, 2003; Figley, 1978; Howell, 2005; Kluft, 1984; Laufer, 1988; Putnam, 1989; Tauber, 1996; Wang, Wilson, & Mason, 1996). For instance, Figley and others contrast the dissociative "survivor mode" (i.e., EP), in which the traumatized individual is trapped in traumatic memories, with a mode of "normal personality functioning" (i.e., ANP). With regard to traumatized Vietnam veterans, Laufer (1988) speaks of a "war self" and an "adaptive self." And in Holocaust child survivors, Tauber (1996) contrasts, in Holocaust child

1. In the clinical literature many different constructs are used to denote what we prefer to call dissociative parts of the personality, such as ego states, dissociative or dissociated states, dissociated self-states, dissociative identity states, dissociative personality states, alter personalities or alters, dissociative or dissociated selves, dissociative identities.

survivors, the "child component [or self]" with the "chronologically appropriate adult component [or self]."

ACTION SYSTEMS: MEDIATORS OF DISSOCIATIVE PARTS

These consistent clinical observations suggest that the survivor's personality does not become divided in a random fashion in trauma but has a consistent basic structure from which countless variations can emerge. The most simple division of personality in trauma involves *primary structural dissociation*, in which there is one ANP and one EP.

In the Introduction, we proposed that structural dissociation comprises a division of the survivor's personality into two (in primary structural dissociation) or more (in secondary and tertiary structural dissociation) self-conscious psychobiological systems. What lower level psychobiological systems mediate ANP and EP? These systems should minimally meet a range of criteria. First, they must be self-organizing and self-stabilizing within windows of homeostasis, time, and context to control and integrate all the rather coherent complexes of psychobiological phenomena exhibited by ANP and EP. Second, they should be functional systems that have been developed in the course of evolution, and should be analogous to mammalian biological systems. Clinical observations suggest that the survivor as ANP typically engages in tasks of daily life such as reproduction, attachment, caretaking, and other social action tendencies, and avoidance of traumatic memories, which support a focus on daily life issues. In contrast, the survivor as EP primarily displays evolutionary defensive and emotional reactions to the (perceived) threat on which he or she seems to be fixated. Third, survivors should be very susceptible to classical conditioning, because, as we discuss below, EP and ANP strongly respond to unconditioned and conditioned threat cues. Fourth, these systems should involve stable characteristics, but also allow for case-dependent variation as well, as ANP and EP exhibit both invariant and idiosyncratic variations. Finally, these systems should be available early in life, since dissociative disorders can manifest from a very early age. Action systems meet all of these requirements: they are organizational, evolution derived, functional, flexible within limits, and inborn but epigenetic.

The various types of action systems were mentioned briefly in the Introduction, and include two major categories: approach to the rewards and responsibilities of daily life, and avoidance and escape from physical threat (Carver, Sutton, & Scheier, 2000; Lang, 1995). These psychobiological systems are sometimes referred to as motivational (e.g., Gould, 1982; Toates, 1986), behavioral (e.g., Bowlby, 1969/1982; Cassidy, 1999), or emotional operating systems (Panksepp, 1998). We have called them *action systems,* because they help us to meet adaptive challenges through mental and behavioral action. In mentally healthy adults action systems of daily life and defense are integrated. For example, most people live daily life while also being aware of potential dangers: They drive defensively, avoid walking alone at night, and seek shelter during a major storm.

The Normal Functions of Action Systems

Action systems are the basic elements that shape personality. They are present in every individual. Ideally, integration occurs within and among action systems as a result of a developmental course, allowing us to live in the most adaptive way possible. They regulate and guide action tendencies (Bowlby, 1969/1982; Cassidy, 1999; Damasio, 1999; Gilbert, 2001; Gould, 1982; Lang, 1995; Lang, Davis, & Öhman, 2000; Panksepp, 1998; 2003; Timberlake, 1994; Toates, 1986). Over the course of evolution, these primitive action systems have become linked with higher cortical functions, enabling us to engage in complex action tendencies, including complex relationships.

Action systems define to a large degree what we find attractive or aversive, and then generate tendencies to approach or avoid, accordingly (Timberlake, 1994). Each action system allows us to filter stimuli in or out according to the relevant biosocial goals of that action system. They direct us to learn what is relevant for adaptation (Timberlake & Lucas, 1989), and in turn, these systems are modified by that learning (Timberlake, 1994).

For example, the defense action system and related feelings of fear help us know that there is danger, and prompt us to act in our own defense. The combination of sexual and attachment systems helps us move toward both attachment and reproduction, both of which provide meaning, support, and pleasure in our lives, and are ultimately necessary for the survival of our species. Action systems that concern forms of social engagement such as attachment, caretaking, and reproduction can involve self-conscious emotions of shame, guilt, and embarrassment, which prompt us to withdraw from others, preventing potential rejection or criticism. However, they also motivate us to conform to social norms to ensure we are an accepted part of the group. The exploration system activates our curiosity to learn more about our world, and in the process we become more adept at managing our environment, which helps us survive more effectively. The energy regulation system prompts us to respond to experiences of fatigue and hunger: necessary actions to survive and maintain homeostasis.

Individuals must meet a range of biosocial goals in daily life (e.g., taking care of children, socializing, competing with others, playing with friends, exploring their outer and inner world). To meet these complex goals, individuals must integrate action systems, which can be a daunting task because combining action systems is more challenging than engaging in a single one. Indeed, many common psychological conflicts involve difficulty in balancing such different interests. For example, working all the time is less complex than balancing work, relationships, and recreation, but being able to balance all those activities is more adaptive and healthy. The balance of action systems requires higher mental efficiency than engaging in a single one. When an individual has structural dissociation, a dissociative part of the personality will be directed by the particular goals of the action systems that motivate that part, and will inhibit or avoid other goals related to action systems that are dissociated in other parts of the personality. For example, one dissociative part focuses on staying safe, and thus tends to avoid people and social situations, and does not speak up. Another part of the same person finds people stimulating and interesting, feels safe with them, and wants to spend time with friends.

Components of Action Systems

Action systems are quite complex, each consisting of at least two levels of components, with their own goals, motivations, and related action tendencies (Fanselow & Lester, 1988; Timberlake, 1994). We distinguish action subsystems, and within these subsystems, modes or motivational states. For example, the action system of energy regulation includes *subsystems* such as eating and sleep, each of which involves different goals toward the common end of maintaining energy.

Action subsystems guide individuals to notice and be drawn to particular kinds of stimuli, and shape the action tendencies in which they engage. In this way, subsystems determine to a large degree what individuals will integrate of their experiences. Hungry people will try to find food and eat, sleepy ones will try to find a quiet place and sleep, frightened ones will try to avoid a threatening situation and seek safety, while angry ones may argue or fight. In other words, subsystems restrict an individual's field of consciousness to relevant stimuli (e.g., particular aspects of eating, safety, relationship, work) and promote certain action tendencies, while inhibiting others. Individuals must nonetheless integrate and balance these subsystems if they are to adapt.

Each subsystem is comprised of a range of modes or motivational states that are designed to help an individual reach particular goals via various action tendencies. For example, the energy regulation system includes a subsystem of eating, which involves much more than eating alone: it includes buying food or going out to eat, preparing it, eating, and digesting food. The action system of caretaking involves subsystems of protecting, nurturing, teaching, disciplining, and loving one's child. Within the subsystem of protecting a child, a parent might engage in many different actions if she briefly lost a child in the mall. She would frantically search, ask others for help, call out, think where he was most likely to go, and inhibit other action tendencies, such as freezing because she is frightened or sitting down to rest because she is tired from a long day. She would retract her field of consciousness as much as possible only to stimuli related to finding her child as quickly as possible.

Action subsystems and modes and dissociative parts. The distinction of these various levels of action systems—subsystems and modes—is highly relevant to our understanding of the functions and dysfunctions of dissociative parts of the personality. In the Introduction we stated that these parts are primarily defined by specific action systems. But they may be even more restricted to the confines of particular subsystems or even modes, which further limits their ability for adaptive change. If dissociative parts are fixated in particular action systems or subsystems, they may be unable to accurately perceive and cope with their situation because their perceptions are colored by the goals, and their field of consciousness will be restricted to stimuli relevant to that particular subsystem.

For example, as ANP, Miriam was constantly terrified of losing her child, and was overprotective in the extreme. When she went to the mall with her son, she could not focus on what she needed to buy, but only on watching him. She perceived every approaching stranger as a threat, and insisted on holding her son's hand tightly, even though he was 9 years old and terribly embarrassed by his mother's behavior. Her mind was filled with the urgent need to protect her child at all cost, and nothing else.

It should be noted that most action tendencies are not specific to a given action system or its components, but can be modified and "plugged in" to achieve a variety of goals. For example, different action systems can promote running to achieve a goal. An individual can run from threat and toward a safe place (defense), run in a race toward the finish line (play), and run toward a loved one (attachment). In the same way, sexual behavior may achieve different goals. Individuals may engage in sex for recreation, pleasure, procreation, and healthy intimacy. In some situations sex can be used as protection from threat (submitting to rape to save one's life), or as barter (exchanging sex for basic needs, such as food, shelter, or nurturing). Sex can also be used as a substitute action tendency to avoid feelings or traumatic memories.

In dissociative individuals this means the same action tendency may involve discrepant goals. While ANP may be involved in running as a sport, EP has only experienced running as a flight from danger. While ANP experiences sex as intimate and pleasurable, EP experiences it as coercive and frightening. The risk then is that the action of ANP (e.g., running, sex) may reactivate EP's traumatic memories and related actions (running away from threat or having to submit to sex in order not to be beaten), which may be quite maladaptive in the present.

Dissociative Division of Action Systems

In trauma-related structural dissociation of the personality, the coordination and cohesion of action systems appears to be disrupted. Normally, action systems are neither completely open nor closed to each other, as this would yield chaos or complete rigidity, respectively (Siegel, 1999). They need to function interdependently with each other, with one being more dominant than others at a given time. They thus involve boundaries such as stimulus filters and degrees of reciprocal inhibition (e.g., attachment and defense inhibit each other). But in structural dissociation these boundaries become too rigid and closed between various action systems. Each dissociative part of the personality thus will be limited to a great degree by the constellation of action systems (or subsystems) by which it is mediated. Thus, a part mediated primarily by defense has great difficulty engaging in close connection with another person (social engagement action system) because those goals are incompatible with those of defense. And such a dissociative part will tend to perceive far too many experiences as threatening because the defense system filters stimuli according to perceived threat, not potential reward.

In primary structural dissociation, division of the personality seems most often to occur between the two major categories of action systems, those of daily life and of defense. In some cases of more complex forms of dissociation related to chronic childhood traumatization there are reasons for these two types of action systems to become mixed in maladaptive ways in various parts of the personality.

Action Systems That Mediate ANP

Action systems that guide functions in daily life typically belong to ANP, particularly in primary structural dissociation. These systems primarily involve approach to attractive stimuli, although gratification may sometimes be delayed or seem rather indirect. They include exploration of the environment (including work and study), play, and energy management (sleeping and eating), attachment, reproduction/sexuality, and caretaking—especially rearing children (cf., Cassidy, 1999; Panksepp, 1998). Attachment is central to the context in which all other action systems mature. If attachment is disrupted early in life, it may lead to maladaptive functioning in various areas of life because the most basic action systems do not function well. Attachment relationships assist individuals in regulating their emotions and physiology, providing basic internal and relational stability.

Adaptive functioning in daily life also requires awareness of potential physical threat. But on a much more complex level, we must also deal with social and relational threats in daily life, and with internal threats to the integrity of our sense of self. ANP engages in these kinds of defenses, which may become more pronounced and chronic following traumatization.

Social defense. We are vulnerable to abandonment, aloneness, and rejection in social and relational contexts. These represent particularly unbearable threats to those who have endured chronic childhood abuse and thus have not experienced many secure attachments and safe social situations. Such chronic threats lead to phobias related to attachment and other forms of social engagement, which manifest in particular kinds of defense within the context of the social engagement action system. When a significant other or social group is rejecting, hostile, or unpredictably absent, actions in the traumatized individual are set in motion to protect him or her from a sense of abandonment or rejection (Gilbert & Gerlsma, 1999; Sloman & Gilbert, 2000). These actions include the general management of perceived distance and closeness in relationships, but also involve specific responses to relational threat.

Social defensive action tendencies are linked with physical defenses, and may have evolved from these action tendencies (Gilbert, 1989, 2001). Many action tendencies of social defense involve psychophysiological conditions quite similar to action tendencies of physical defense: hypervigilance, flight, fight, freeze, and submission. For example, actions related to shame and guilt such as gaze aversion and literal or emotional hiding share similar mental and behavioral characteristics with submission and flight. The concealment of one's true self and feelings may be related to early forms of camouflage that have evolved with self-awareness and the need to be socially acceptable. The expression of intense negative emotions, such as extreme jealousy, anxiety, and anger can be damaging to one's social reputation, and therefore must be modulated or concealed. Denial is a way to avoid and defend against aversive stimuli (e.g., realization that a partner is emotionally abusive) and reinforces trauma-related phobias.

Social submission is likely related to the total submission of physical defense. For example, the abused child's efforts to please and appease abusive caretakers, or the traumatized adult's effort to please her therapist involve forms of social submission that have perceived survival value. In sum, the action systems of daily life—hence ANPs—not only involve approach to attractive stimuli, but include impression management and other forms of social defense that have as a goal the protection of one's attachments and social status (Gilbert, 2000).

Interoceptive defense. There is a third type of defense, beyond physical and social defense. This is defense against intrapsychic threats, *interoceptive defense* (Goldstein & Chambless, 1978). These defenses are manifestations of the phobia of mental actions. As noted in the Introduction, they are known as psychological defense mechanisms in the psycho-dynamic literature, such as splitting, narcissism, or projection. They not only protect against one's own intolerable emotions, thoughts, or fantasies, but also serve as social defenses against attachment disruptions and perceived loss of social status.

ANP will thus avoid or escape from intruding traumatic memories, associated EPs, threatening thoughts and fantasies, and feelings or sensations that are linked with traumatic experiences. That is, these defenses are manifestations of trauma-related phobias of trauma-derived mental actions and traumatic memories. Like social defenses, interoceptive defense may have evolved from basic physical defenses such as flight (e.g., denial, splitting, suppression, motivated forgetting), and total submission (e.g., retraction and lowering of consciousness). These kinds of mental actions maintain or elaborate structural dissociation. In sum, ANPs are primarily mediated by (some constellation of) action systems of daily life, and in this context they also engage in social and intrapsychic defense. These latter systems can be seen as evolutionarily more advanced forms of the more basic physical defense action system.

Action Systems That Mediate EP

In primary structural dissociation, the action system of *physical* defense (e.g., Fanselow & Lester, 1988; Misslin, 2003) is primarily the domain of the EP, and has several subsystems that are important to consider. First, there is the separation cry, which is a young mammal's distressed vocalization when separated from a caretaker. This cry is actually an attempt to regain attachment upon separation, and thus we call it the *attachment cry*. Other defensive subsystems include hypervigilance and scanning the environment, flight, freeze with analgesia, fight, total submission with anesthesia, and recuperative states of rest, wound care, isolation from the group, and gradual return to daily activities (i.e., to the action systems of daily life) (Fanselow & Lester, 1988; Nijenhuis, 2004). EP typically will be fixed in one or more of these subsystems of physical defense.

Several authors have observed that humans share similar defense responses to stressful events with many other mammals and have related this to evolutionary parallels (e.g., Rivers, 1920). A link between mammalian defensive reaction patterns and physical manifestations of dissociation such as analgesia, anesthesia, motor inhibitions, and motor paralysis has been demonstrated (Nijenhuis, Vanderlinden, & Spinhoven, 1998; Nijenhuis, Spinhoven, & Vanderlinden, 1998; Nijenhuis, Spinhoven, Vanderlinden et al., 1998; Waller et al., 2000).

Each defensive action subsystem controls a pattern of psychobiological reactions that is adapted to meet a particular degree of threat imminence; that is, how close the threat is perceived to be (Fanselow & Lester, 1988).

This degree can be expressed in terms of the time and space that separate the individual from the threat (i.e., the distance between perpetrator and victim), as well as in terms of an evaluation of the defensive abilities of the individual (e.g., psychosocial influence and physical capabilities). However, if the perpetrator is a parent who is always there, it is possible for these defensive action systems to be evoked simultaneously with normal life action systems in chronically abused children.

Preencounter defense involves an apprehensive state with increased arousal. It is evoked when individuals find themselves in a situation of potential danger, such as being alone in an unfamiliar place. They will immediately interrupt daily life behaviors (and action systems of daily life), and focus on potential threat cues. At this point they may have a sense of impending threat from an undetermined source. When individuals spot a cue that they interpret as concrete threat, they often startle. *Postencounter defense* includes several subsystems: (1) flight and (2) freeze with associated analgesia. *Circastrike defense* involves fight, often a last ditch effort to escape from attack. *Poststrike (attack) defense* involves total submission and anesthesia. If one survives an attack, one's recuperative subsystem is activated. This subsystem allows for a return of affective awareness and body sensations such as pain, which motivate wound care and rest through social isolation and sleep. Upon recovery, there will be a reactivation of systems that control normal daily life interests such as eating, sex, caretaking, and attachment.

TRAUMATIC MEMORY VERSUS AUTOBIOGRAPHICAL NARRATIVE MEMORY

Traumatized individuals have both traumatic memories and autobiographical narrative memories (Janet, 1928a; Van der Kolk & Van der Hart, 1991). Autobiographical narrative memory is derived from our personal history and is able to be placed in a symbolic, verbal form that is personalized. The two types of memory cannot always be neatly categorized, but are sometimes mixed. For example, an EP may have a traumatic memory that has at least some verbal narrative that is not traumatically reexperienced.

The personality of traumatized individuals includes disruptions and discontinuties because the traumatic experience cannot yet be integrated fully as part of the person's own experience. As EP, individuals typically remember too much too intensely, and as ANP they remember too little of the traumatizing event (cf., Breuer & Freud, 1893–1895/1955b; Janet, 1889, 1904/1983b). The quality of traumatic memory is quite different from autobiographical narrative. It is typically ANP's function to hold and integrate most of an individual's autobiographical memory to the extent possible, while EP holds the traumatic memory. The survivor as ANP usually has extensive autobiographical narrative memory, but such memory may not include (parts of) traumatic experiences, so there are sometimes peculiar holes in the memory of ANP. In any case, the memory of the traumatizing event—to the extent it exists—may be quite depersonalized for ANP. In these cases, ANPs may recall as much of the traumatizing event as EP, but lack the emotional and physical feelings that belong to the memory, and the sense that it happened to them personally. On the other hand, EPs experience these traumatic memories far too intensely, as "too real" (Heim & Buhler, 2003; Janet, 1928a, 1932a; Van der Hart & Steele, 1997). This is certainly not normal memory.

Clinicians have long observed the fundamental differences between traumatic memories and autobiographical narrative memories (e.g., Breuer & Freud, 1893–1895/1955b; Janet, 1889, 1898a, 1928a; Myers, 1940; Roussy & Lhermitte, 1917; Van der Hart & Op den Velde, 1995; Van der Kolk & Van der Hart, 1991). Researchers have confirmed these findings (e.g., Brett & Ostroff, 1985; Brewin, Dalgleish, & Joseph, 1996; Cameron, 2000; Kardiner, 1941; Nijenhuis, Van Engen, Kusters, & Van der Hart, 2001; Van der Hart, Bolt, & Van der Kolk, 2005; Van der Kolk & Fisler, 1995; Van der Kolk, Hopper, & Osterman, 2001). It is most important to understand the nature of traumatic memories, because effective treatment, regardless of the techniques utilized, places an emphasis on the transformation of traumatic memory into a symbolic narrative. This requires a substantial degree of integration of ANP and EP.

Charlotte Delbo (1985), a survivor of Auschwitz, recounted the differences between the depersonalized memory of ANP and the traumatic memories of EP. She had recurrent intrusive nightmares in which EP relived the traumatizing event:

> . . . [I]n these dreams, there I see myself again, *me*, yes *me*, just as I know I was: scarcely able to stand . . . pierced with cold, filthy, gaunt, and the pain is so unbearable, so exactly the pain I suffered there, that I feel it again physically, I feel it again through my whole body, which becomes a block of pain, and I feel death seizing me, I feel myself die. (p. 13)

Upon awakening, her ANP would struggle to regain emotional distance from EP:

> Fortunately, in my anguish, I cry out. The cry awakens me, and I [ANP] emerge from the nightmare, exhausted. It takes days for everything to return to normal, for memory to be "refilled" and for the skin of memory to mend itself. I become myself again, the one you know [ANP], who can speak to you of Auschwitz without showing any sign of distress or emotion. . . . I feel that the one who was in the camp [EP] is not me, is not the person who is here, facing you

[ANP]. . . . And everything that happened to that other, the Auschwitz one [EP], now has no bearing upon me, does not concern me, so separate from one another are this deep-lying [traumatic] and ordinary memory. (pp. 13–14)

Characteristics of Autobiographical Narrative Memory

Autobiographical narratives occur when an individual has a sense of personal ownership of the memory and the events conveyed by the memory—this applies both to ANP and EP. Narrative memory or episodic memory (Tulving, 2002) has been described as "a function of the living personality" (Schachtel, 1947, p. 3). Thus autobiographical narrative memory adds cohesion to our personality across time and contexts.

Narrative memories have specific characteristics (Janet, 1928a; Van der Kolk & Van der Hart, 1991). They can be intentionally retrieved, and are not especially dependent on situational triggers to be evoked. They convey a narrative to the listener, stories that are flexible, and adapted to a particular audience. One might tell a personal story at a party in a quite different way from the way one would tell it when relaying it with more affect to a close friend. Memories are reexamined from new perspectives from time to time. Narrative memories are verbal and time-condensed—a long event can be told in a short time. Narrative memory is certainly not like a videotape of events, but rather is reconstructive in nature. Reconstructed memory is condensed and symbolized. For example, a woman may have a clear memory of being in labor, but does not reexperience the hours of labor, nor the physical pain. She can tell the story in a few moments of time, without including every detail. Some ANPs cannot deviate from a pattern of telling a story about themselves. They may be quite overgeneral in their narrative, have peculiar lapses in narrative, with unusual syntax and sequencing and use of pronouns. They may recount horrible events in a depersonalized manner, without any affect.

Narrative memory has social and relational functions. It serves as a connection between human beings; a way for an individual to become known to others, as well as a way to gain personal insights. For ANP, social isolation and lack of self awareness can occur partly because there are simply no words to tell the story.

Janet (1919/1925) noted that an autobiographical "memory, like all psychological phenomena, is an action; essentially, it is the action of telling a story" (p. 661). The creation of autobiographical memory consists of two types of mental actions (Janet, 1928a): (1) perceiving, encoding, and storing mental and behavioral actions during the original event, and (2) a parallel accounting (narrative) of what happened. These are the mental actions that relegate experience and meaning to memory: "such and such happens, and I feel this, and I think that, and it means such and so to me as a person, and it affects my behavior in such and so ways." When we remember our personal experiences, we more or less engage in both types of mental actions.

Characteristics of Traumatic Memory

Traumatic memories, which are characteristic of EP, are different from narrative memory. They are hallucinatory, solitary, and involuntary experiences that consist of visual images, sensations, and physical acts which may occupy the entire perceptual field, and are terrifying to the individual (Janet, 1928a; Van der Kolk & Van der Hart, 1991). Although traumatic memories are experienced as reliving traumatic events, they are still not reproductions but rather representations of such events.

As EP, survivors have been unable to create a complete personal story and are unable to share the original experience verbally and socially. They are stuck in the traumatic experience where they relive rather than retell their terror. Traumatic memories are sensorimotor and affective experiences rather than "stories" (e.g., Van der Kolk & Fisler, 1995; Van der Hart, Nijenhuis, & Steele, 2005).

Traumatic memories are subjectively characterized by a sense of timelessness and immutability (Modell, 1990; Spiegel, Frischholz, & Spira, 1993; Van der Hart & Steele, 1997). And although traumatic memories do indeed have behavioral content, they are primarily mental actions, as Janet noted of memory. These actions are quite different in nature from those of the abstract, verbal mental actions of narrative memory, however. The mental actions involved in creating a narrative cannot be completed. As Janet (1919/1925) observed, traumatized individuals (as EP) "are continuing the action, or rather the attempt at action, which began when the thing happened; and they exhaust themselves in these everlasting recommencements" (p. 663).

For example, George S., a Holocaust survivor, continually reexperienced fighting the Germans in his nightmares, unable to realize he was now safe (Langer, 1999). The frightened child EP of an incest survivor continually experienced herself as lying in bed frozen as she heard the footsteps of her father approach her room, unable to realize she was grown and the incest was no longer about to happen. When traumatic memories are reactivated, access to other memories is more or less obstructed. EP often seems unaware of much, if anything, about the present, and does not necessarily have access to skills and factual knowledge that are available to ANP (Van der Hart & Nijenhuis, 2001).

Evidence shows that many traumatic memories are accurate and can be corroborated. Nevertheless, there is also evidence that traumatic memories should still be considered as reconstructions rather than reproductions, as is true of *all* memory. For example, individuals who reexperience a traumatic memory adjust their behavior to some degree to the present social and environmental circumstances, thus indicating it is not an exact replica of the traumatizing event. When a survivor freezes in a therapy session, she adapts the position of her body to the chair in which she is sitting, or when engaged in fight behavior, does not actually hit the therapist, but rather a pillow.

At times, traumatic memories can blend with fantasies or dreams related to the traumatic experience. Charcot (1887) presented a classic case. His patient, LeLog, was struck by a wagon and became unconscious. Upon awakening he was paralyzed from the waist down, but examination showed no neurological cause. Some time after the accident, LeLog was able to report dreams and images of being run over by the wagon wheels, a fearful expectation that had occurred just before he lost consciousness, and was the cause of his paralysis.

Sometimes patients may report traumatic memories of events that they have not actually experienced themselves. Van der Hart and Van der Velden (1995) reported the case of a woman who had nightmares of being tortured in a Nazi concentration camp. She had not been in such a camp, but had heard terrible stories from her mother, who had. Sometimes patients may be unsure whether events happened to them or to someone else. Joe reported severe physical abuse from his childhood and adolescence, but was confused as to whether some events had happened to him or to his brother.

Automatic reactivation of traumatic memory. Traumatic memories are automatically reactivated by specific stimuli; these stimuli are known as *triggers, reactivating stimuli*, or *conditioned stimuli* (see Chapters 9 and 10). They include (1) various sensory experiences; (2) time-related stimuli (e.g., anniversary reactions); (3) daily life events; (4) events during a therapy session; (5) emotions; (6) physiological conditions (e.g., hyperarousal); (7) stimuli recalling intimidation by perpetrators; and (8) current traumatization (Morgan, Hill et al., 1999; Van der Hart & Friedman, 1992). Therapists are well aware of the rather common occurrence of reactivation of traumatic memories from apparently innocuous statements. Glenda went into a full reexperience when the therapist said, "We will do our best to be open with each other." The simple word, "open" evoked for the patient her perpetrator's violent demand of her: "Open your legs, bitch." When such reactivation takes place, the traumatized individual often is unable to suppress the intrusion of EP with its traumatic experiences.

Pathogenic kernels. Not all parts of traumatic experiences are equally threatening or overwhelming. We have called the most threatening parts *pathogenic kernels,* and the related cognitions *pathogenic kernel statements* (Van der Hart & Op den Velde, 1995). Brewin (2001, 2003) and Brewin and colleagues (Grey, Holmes, & Brewin, 2001) have called these *hot spots.* These cognitions or beliefs are embedded in extremely threatening and overwhelming experiences, and thus highly resistant to purely cognitive therapeutic interventions.

Because of the vehement emotions associated with these pathogenic kernels, or even amnesia, trauma survivors may be very reluctant or unable to report them initially. Sonja, a 22-year-old young woman, sought treatment for her PTSD symptoms related to a vicious rape at age 15. When the treatment of this traumatic memory was apparently completed, she became more anxious than ever. Eventually Sonja became aware of a particularly threatening aspect of her experience that she had not previously recalled: During the rape, the rapist put his knife against her throat and she believed he was going to kill her. Once this pathogenic kernel could be integrated, her anxiety abated, and her ANP and EP fully integrated.

SUMMARY

Structural dissociation occurs during confrontations with overwhelming events when mental efficiency is too low. In this condition, the individual tends to experience vehement emotions (hyperarousal) as well as states of hypoarousal which augment dis-integrative tendencies. The origins of traumatization offer insights into the vulnerabilities of the individual and into factors that have a negative effect on his or her integrative mental efficiency. Childhood abuse and neglect are major factors in the development of trauma-related disorders in adults following their exposure to extremely stressful events in adulthood. Early traumatization is a major risk factor for more severe symptoms that persist over time. Thus childhood traumatization plays a central role in the development of trauma-related disorders in children and adults.

CHAPTER 2

Primary Structural Dissociation

Prototypes of the Apparently Normal and the Emotional Parts of the Personality

Who was my other self? Though we had split one personality between us, I was the majority shareholder. I went to school, made friends, gained experience, developing my part of the personality, while she remained morally and emotionally a child, functioning on instinct rather than on intelligence.

—Sylvia Fraser (1987, p. 24)

IN TRAUMATIZED INDIVIDUALS the most simple dissociative division of the personality is primary structural dissociation. It consists of a single apparently normal part of the personality (ANP) and a single emotional part of the personality (EP). This division of personality seems to evolve most often in relationship to a single traumatizing event, although it can be seen in childhood abuse survivors in the form of the "inner child" phenomenon or what is sometimes referred to as an "ego state." We propose that primary structural dissociation characterizes simple trauma-related disorders, such as simple forms of PTSD, some "conversion disorders," and some ICD-10 diagnoses of dissociative disorders of movement and sensation.

CHARACTERISTICS OF THE "APPARENTLY NORMAL" PART OF THE PERSONALITY

ANP is by far the "major shareholder" of the personality (S. Fraser, 1987) in primary structural dissociation. That is, the survivor as ANP comprises the vast majority of the personality, except for that which is dissociated in EP. EP's domain is far smaller in primary structural dissociation than in more complex levels of dissociation, but varies relative to the number of traumatic experiences that ANP has not integrated.

Mental Efficiency in ANP

ANP can bear resemblance to the pretraumatic personality in some cases, and in others be quite different. One factor that influences the degree to which ANP exhibits differences from the pretraumatic personality relates to the survivor's mental efficiency and thus to his or her mental level. The mental efficiency of ANP is generally higher than that of EP. However, it is lower than the level developed by the survivor prior to traumatization, because incompleted trauma-related actions lower the mental level. The inability to integrate EP and associated traumatic memories constitutes incompleted action tendencies (see Chapter 9). Moreover, the degree of adaptive functioning of ANP can vary. The survivor's mental efficiency as ANP may be too low to organize adequately different action systems and their components. The lower this efficiency, the more likely it is that a survivor will engage in substitute actions rather than in action tendencies that demand high mental efficiency.

The patient as ANP consciously and unconsciously avoids stimuli related to traumatic memories (i.e, ANP is phobic of traumatic memories and related stimuli; see Chapter 10). This evasion maintains or strengthens amnesia, anesthesia, and emotional constriction. This avoidance is not a goal in itself, but assists the survivor as ANP to engage in daily life by excluding what seems too difficult to integrate. However, this mental avoidance also interferes with ANP's ability to organize, coordinate, and engage in the action tendencies that have become core features of EP.

Some traumatized individuals succeed in functioning in a rather normal fashion for years as ANP, with EP relatively dormant or latent. These survivors appear to have a relatively high mental efficiency, with the exception of being unable to integrate traumatic material. Such ANPs have a strong ability to inhibit EP. They presumably have the skills, energy, and opportunity to avoid some reminders of unintegrated experience and to inhibit emotional reaction to reminders they are unable to evade. However, other survivors may reach an advanced stage of posttraumatic decline (Janet, 1909a; Tichener, 1986), in which EP chronically intrudes on ANP, or dominates consciousness, and the functioning of the survivor as ANP more generally deteriorates as well. Some people tend to vacillate over time among various stages of decompensation (Wang et al., 1996), which may partly relate to normative oscillations of mental efficiency. Janet (1904/1983b) noted that many survivors lose their "capacity to assimilate new experiences . . . as if their personality has definitely stopped at a certain point, and cannot enlarge any more by the addition or assimilation of new elements" (p. 532). Thus, the survivor's capacity to learn from experience and to adapt may be limited to some degree for all parts of the personality.

A major challenge for ANP in primary structural dissociation is to integrate action tendencies within and across all daily life action systems. This challenge may pertain to the integration of two or more different action tendencies, but it also can concern a single action tendency that belongs to different action systems (e.g., running can be part of defense, play, or attachment). When a particular action tendency is associated with traumatic memories, this tendency may be avoided within all action systems because it becomes a reminder of traumatic experience and can activate EP.

> Hilda had been strangled to the point of unconsciousness and had raised her hands to her neck to pull off the hand of the man who was choking her. Subsequently she avoided putting her hands to her neck for any reason, and thus had trouble washing her neck or putting on necklaces or scarves. The very simple and innocuous action of putting her hands to her neck became almost impossible for her, evoking fear that she did not understand.

In this way, compromised action tendencies can affect the survivor's functioning within more than one action system.

Some actions in which we engage in daily life involve an integrated range of lower-order action tendencies that belong to a range of different action systems. For example, eating in company is more complex than eating alone. When in company, we must integrate components of the action systems of energy management, social engagement, and play. Some situations in life only require relatively automatic and simple action tendencies. However, adaptation to other situations such as living in a complicated social environment require complex perceptions, feelings, thoughts, and behaviors. Such complex action tendencies involve creative, higher-order integration of various lower-order action tendencies and (components of) action systems (Cosmides & Tooby, 1992; Hurley, 1998). Complex action tendencies may demand conscious awareness, but can also flow rather unconsciously, as sometimes happens in artistic expression. They can help us adapt to multifaceted environments, to improve our lives, and to expand our knowledge and awareness. An infinite range of mental and behavioral actions can be understood from this perspective, ranging from complex social, relational, and affect regulation skills, to skills such as operating a computer and driving a car, to sophisticated capacities to analyze, to countless expressions of creativity, to finding spiritual meaning. The lower the mental efficiency, the less the survivor as ANP will be able to accomplish such complex integrative tasks. For example, ANP may engage adequately in the tasks of daily life, but feels life is meaningless, and is unable to enjoy previous creative expres-

sion. Or the survivor as ANP can function well with a limited life, but becomes overwhelmed when life becomes more complicated.

Negative Symptoms in ANP

The survivor as ANP is sometimes able to present a façade of normalcy because the predominate symptoms of ANP are negative. That is, they are
losses of function that often result from dissociation and mental avoidance of perceived threat. Losses can sometimes be more easily disguised,
hidden, or ignored than positive symptoms. Dissociative losses may include a degree of amnesia (loss of memory), subjective detachment from
reality (with intact reality testing), various forms of sensory anesthesia (e.g.,
loss of smell, hearing, sensation), loss of affect that results in emotional
numbness or shallowness, and others that are discussed in Chapter 5.
These functions can be more or less profoundly dissociated and to some
extent can be found in EP; for example, recall of traumatic memory and
related cognitions, sensations, and affect.

In single event traumatization, the lowered mental level of ANP may
result in other functional loss or diminution of skills that are not necessarily dissociative in nature, but rather involve substitute actions for
higher level skills. For example, the survivor as ANP may lose the capacity
to regulate affect (e.g., to self-soothe) in the wake of traumatic experience, or lose social support because relationships become threatening or
too taxing for the survivor's limited mental level.

ANP's difficulty in regulating emotions includes problems with arousal
states. Some survivors as ANP experience chronic numbness (*hypoesthe-
sia*), a shutting down of emotional and physical feelings and awareness,
particularly in regard to traumatic events and relationships. Emotional
numbness and life lived "at the surface of consciousness" (Appelfeld, 1994,
p. 18) are characteristic of PTSD and other trauma-related disorders, and
inhibit enjoyment of life. Nancy Raine described it in her own life following rape:

> The numbness . . . seemed to spread out over the entire emotional
> landscape, like fog. Not only is pain blunted, but pleasure as well.
> Of all the consequences of the rape, this was the hardest to perceive
> and the hardest to endure. It was living with novocaine in the heart,
> condemned to life on the glassy surface of the emotional latitudes. I
> felt cut off from everything and, as the years passed, even from the
> memory of emotional life as I had once experienced it. (1998, p. 61)

However, to the extent that a survivor's mental avoidance is not effective, and mental efficiency remains insufficient to integrate traumatic

memories, he or she experiences chronic *hyperarousal*. In this case, the survivor may not feel numb, but instead may be overshadowed by a chronic dysphoria, a sense of urgency about tasks, generalized anxiety, depression, guilt, shame, frustration, irritability, or rage that prevents intimate relational feelings and enjoyment of life.

> Celia, a patient with complex PTSD, was chronically anxious and depressed, feeling constantly overwhelmed and stressed. When the slightest thing went wrong she became severely depressed and guilty, and was unable to function at work.

Most often, ANP will vacillate between extremes of hypo- and hyperarousal because of the inability to regulate affect.

Positive Symptoms in ANP

To the extent that the survivor as ANP cannot inhibit EP, he or she is plagued by recurrent intrusion of this part, with traumatic memories, such as flashbacks, body memories, and trauma-related nightmares. These intrusions are positive dissociative symptoms (see Chapter 5). They may consume a considerable amount of time and energy for ANP and can be very frightening (Engelhard & Arntz, 2005; Janet, 1904/1983b; Nijenhuis, 1994; see Chapter 10). ANP therefore becomes increasingly avoidant of anything that might potentially trigger intrusions of EP (e.g., Bucci, 2003; Clohessy & Ehlers, 1999; Nijenhuis & Van Duijl, 2001; Steele, Dorahy et al., 2005).

CHARACTERISTICS OF THE "EMOTIONAL" PART OF THE PERSONALITY

The survivor as EP is rigidly fixated in particular action tendencies that were part of traumatization. In primary structural dissociation, EPs are most often stuck in the various subsystems of the (physical) defense action system. However, EP also may be mediated by other action systems involved in traumatization, such as sexuality.

> Ina, who had PTSD, became sexually aroused during rape when her abuser incessantly stimulated her. As EP, she not only experienced fear and anger (affects related to the defensive system), but also engaged in compulsive masturbation (behavior related to the sexuality action system). No matter how much she hated herself for doing it, compulsive masturbation was a reexperiencing of rape for Ina. She repeated the actions of the perpetrator over and over to get rid of the sexual arousal that intruded as part of the traumatic memory.

Ferenczi, a therapist of both traumatized combat veterans and survivors of chronic childhood abuse, pointed to the defensive functions in which EP has become fixated. He stated that trauma involves an enduring division of the personality, in which one dissociative part manifests itself as "the guard against dangers, . . . and the attention of this guard is almost completely directed to the outside. It is only concerned about dangers, i.e., about objects in the outside world all of which can become dangerous" (1932/1988, p. 115).

Mental Efficiency in EP

The mental efficiency of the survivor as EP is more limited than that as ANP. The survivor as EP is dominated by traumatic memories, and has failed to integrate the whole of current reality, remaining fixated in past traumatic experience and in the action tendencies relevant to that experience. Thus, EP has involuntary and rigid retraction of the field of consciousness that is mainly focused on threat related to the experience of traumatization. The survivor as EP may be fearful, angry, ashamed, despairing, or disgusted, and does not realize the traumatizing event is over. Hence, such parts interpret the actual present in terms of the unintegrated past: EP is unable to adapt to the present without the help of ANP.

EPs tend to focus their attention on attachment loss and sources of actual or potential physical threat (e.g., Christianson, 1992; Kardiner, 1941). Once dissociated, defensive actions such as fight or submission may become repetitive, and never come to a conclusion (Janet, 1919/ 1925). EP can be stuck in one action system (defense), one particular subsystem (e.g., flight) or mode (e.g., moving away from a source of perceived threat, or hiding). For example, when Amanda, a rape victim, reexperienced oral rape as EP, she opened her mouth and gagged, actions that were not appropriate to the current situation, but were components of the traumatic experience which she could not complete. Action tendencies are only fully completed when individuals have *realized* that the experience is over (see Chapter 9).

> Margaret, a survivor of incest, described how as an adolescent she was easily startled, vigilant when she came into the house (hypervigilance), felt frozen and "like cardboard" when she heard her stepfather's footsteps on the stairs to her bedroom (freezing with analgesia), sometimes tried to push him away (fight), but ultimately would give up her futile resistance and "lie back and let him do what he was going to do" (total submission). She described curling up in bed for hours after the rapes, refusing to go to school, not eating, sleeping for hours on end (recuperative state), and being terrified and crying desperately if her mother left the house (attachment cry to evoke proximity of a caregiver). As an adult she often involuntarily engaged these defensive action tendencies over and over, for example, being easily

startled, feeling frozen, being inappropriately rageful, being unable to get out of bed and not wanting social contact, or obsessively calling her husband at work. Margaret as EP was fixated in these defensive action systems and was unable to bring those action tendencies to a close in the present.

Positive Symptoms in EP

In primary structural dissociation, the survivor as EP tends to experience representations of an entire traumatic experience rather than the fragmentary intrusions experienced as ANP. Janet's (1904/1983b, 1928a) term for this evocation of the entire memory was *reductio ad integrum* (to bring back as a whole). As each aspect of the traumatic memory is connected with the others, "one cannot excite the first without giving birth to the second, and the entire system [of traumatic memory] has a tendency to develop itself to the utmost" (Janet, 1907, p. 42). Joan was discussing her difficulties with flashbacks with her therapist: "It's the same thing every time. I just relive the whole thing and can't find a stopping place anywhere until it's over." Thus, EP will continue to repeat the actions related to the traumatic experience, such as cringing, fighting back, freezing in fear.

The "emotions" of the survivor as EP are usually not merely comprised of the normal range of affect, not merely intense, but rather tend to be the vehement emotions of trauma. These emotional changes influence the sense of self encompassed by EP. This sense of self encompasses the experienced history of that particular part of the personality, that is, an autobiographical self. The subjective *I* who (re)experiences traumatizing events is quite different from the *I* who lives out daily life, and survivors often cannot integrate these discrepant experiences of self, resulting in structural dissociation. In primary structual dissociation, such as simple PTSD, EP's sense of self is typically limited to the traumatic experience and no more. However, in some cases EP has developed more of a life of its own, and is characterized by secondary elaboration and some degree of autonomy.

> David is a patient with simple PTSD related to a particular combat experience. He has partial reexperiences in which he is aware of the present, but unable to respond to it, and feels as though he is back in battle. The EP of David that relives the traumatizing event does not have a separate name or experience beyond the period of time around the battle. David does not view this part of himself as a separate "person," yet feels like "I am watching someone else when it (a flashback) happens."

> Ray is a patient with complex PTSD related to childhood abuse and neglect who has a more elaborated and autonomous EP. One EP refers to himself "Raymond." He experiences himself as 6 years old, scared, and unable to be independent or engage in adult activities such as paying bills or cooking.

He is sometimes aware of the present when Ray is at home, but not when
he is at work. He takes control and sits in the closet for hours at a time. Little Raymond views Ray as another person who does not take care of him
and tries to ignore him.

EP may be latent, or dormant, for long periods of time, but can eventually be reactivated. This occurs when the traumatized individual is exposed to experience or to events that constitute a reminder of the traumatic experience—a "trigger" or rather, conditioned stimulus, and when
ANP can no longer inhibit EP's reactivation (Brewin, 2001; Gelinas, 1983;
Van der Hart & Friedman, 1992; Van der Kolk, 1994; see Chapter 10).
However, it is also possible that EP is sometimes reactivated and does not
intrude on ANP, but rather silently "observes" from an internal distance.

Once reactivated, EP becomes physiologically hyper- or hypoaroused,
relives catastrophic beliefs (e.g., "I am going to die;" "This is my fault"),
reexperiences the emotions of the traumatic experience, and has a tendency to engage in defensive behavioral actions such as running from
danger, warding off attack, or freezing. EP may intrude on ANP in forms
such as nightmares, or completely dominate consciousness and physically
enact the traumatic experience without awareness of ANP during the
night. EP also intrudes in the form of flashbacks, or so-called body or somatic memories. In our experience, these body memories not only pertain to sensations and body movements, but involve other features of EPs
such as thoughts, beliefs, feelings, and a particular body image.

Negative Symptoms in EP

The survivor as EP typically experiences positive dissociative symptoms.
The major exception is the case of an EP fixated in submission to major
threat, and that therefore experiences a severe reduction or even complete absence of aversive emotions. Such parts often also experience
some degree of hypoarousal, emotional and physical numbness (hypo-
esthesia), and lessening of pain perception (hypoalgesia). They are generally unresponsive to stimulation, and if present for an extended period
of time, such EPs when evoked may be mistaken for catatonia (it is not
uncommon in therapy sessions for these EPs to be evoked).

The Relationship between ANP and EP

Dissociative parts are not totally separated, but have certain dynamic relationships with each other, even if they are not consciously recognized.
Unraveling the interrelationships between ANP and EP is an essential part
of understanding the theory and treatment of structural dissociation. *The*

central relationship between ANP and EP involves avoidance of realization, primarily realization of traumatic experiences. The mutual non-realization and avoidance of ANP and EP are due in large part to conditioning effects, which will be discussed in detail in Chapter 10. Patients with PTSD are generally fearful of reliving traumatic memories and other intrusions, and thus try to avoid these experiences.

Survivors as ANP often note how extraordinarily difficult it is to manage daily life when they are overwhelmed with intrusions and hyperarousal, giving good reason for their avoidance strategies. Margaret, abused as an adolescent, spoke about it thus:

> Whenever something reminds me of what my stepfather did to me, I become freezing cold and my mind just turns itself off. If I think about it, I can't go on with what I am doing. I just stop. I guess I'm a coward, because I just can't think about it. But I can't do it and live my life at the same time.

Margaret had developed a number of phobias related to her traumatization. She was afraid of being close to others, afraid of her feelings, afraid of being sexual. Avoidance strategies are manifestations of these trauma-related phobias, and are discussed extensively in Chapter 10. The central phobia in traumatized individuals is the phobia of traumatic memories. Holocaust survivor and author Aharon Appelfeld provided an apt example of this phobia in himself and his group of survivors in the years directly following World War II. Notice the extreme degree of nonrealization that developed:

> How long did that violent oblivion continue? Every year changed its colors and every year obscured a different region of life. *The moment any memory or shred of a memory was about to float upwards, we would fight against it as though against evil spirits.* [Italics added] Our oblivion was so deep that when the day of our awakening came, we were thunderstruck and shocked: we were so far from ourselves that it was as if we had not been born in Jewish homes, and all that had happened to us was nothing but a kind of twilight whose source can no longer be reached. We spoke of the recent past from a strange distance. As if the things had not happened to us. (1994, p. 18)

This example demonstrates that without sufficient mental efficiency, traumatized individuals may find the past too painful to integrate, so that they continue to respond to potent reminders of traumatic experiences with alarm or other defensive reactions. In these circumstances, survivors as ANP use their energy and resources to rebuild and maintain a normal life following traumatization, and to evade EP and the traumatic memories associated with this part. Each inadvertent intrusion will strengthen ANP's fear of traumatic memories. In this way, the phobia of traumatic memories gains ascendancy over time, and for ANP the past becomes less and less "real," in the words of Appelfeld (1994), "as if the things had not happened to us" (p. 18).

The avoidance strategies of ANP may eventually become extreme, rigid, and unconscious (see Chapter 10), adding to a constricted lifestyle. Thus while the survivor as ANP directs conscious awareness to activities and goals of daily life (the action systems of daily life) he or she will also consciously or unconsciously avoid trauma-related stimuli. For example, ANP may avoid relationships that might serve as traumatic reminders and instead focus on work to the point of becoming a workaholic. As Nancy Raine said, "I was getting on with my life, and the busier it was, I thought, the better. . . . I was making a new life, one that left behind the woman who had been raped" (Raine, 1998, p. 175). In this example, note the increasing distance between ANP and EP ("the woman who had been raped") as ANP gets on with her life and is high functioning.

Some individuals can effectively avoid unwanted memories for a long time, particularly with practice (M.C. Anderson et al., 2004; M.C. Anderson & Green, 2001). It may be that those with higher IQs and capacities for working memory might be more successful in this regard (Brewin & Smart, 2005). But unfortunately for many survivors, the more avoidance is employed by ANP, the more frequent are intrusions from EP (M.I. Davies & Clark, 1998). These intrusions suggest that these survivors lack sufficient mental level required to successfully avoid traumatic memories that cannot yet be integrated.

Some of ANP's avoidance strategies involve behavioral actions such as self-harm and substance abuse, and avoidance of external reminders of traumatic experiences. Self-harm and substance abuse temporarily dampen emotional pain and block traumatic memories. However, these behaviors threaten ANPs' need to appear as normal as possible, so that survivors tend hide or minimize symptoms to belie their distress.

Interoceptive and social defenses in ANP are the particular avoidance strategies that emerge as part of phobias related to internal and relational threats. Interoceptive (intrapsychic) defenses, such as denial and retraction and lowering of consciousness, may become pronounced and chronic whenever more inner stimuli become associated with traumatic memories and EP due to recurrent intrusions (see Chapter 10). Entrenched, elaborate interoceptive defenses leave the survivor disconnected to varying degrees from inner life, from feelings, needs, and general self-awareness. This avoidance may also lead to increasing difficulties with relationships, including the relationship with oneself: It is nearly impossible for an individual to sustain intimacy with another in the absence of intimacy with self, and vice versa.

Particularly in the aftermath of interpersonal traumatization, the survivor as ANP may not only develop pervasive interoceptive defenses, but also social defenses that impair relationships. These avoidance strategies against attachment and intimacy, against being known by others, and against being triggered by social stimuli further reduce the survivor's capacity for trust and chances to receive needed support. For example, survivors may not share personal information when it might be appropriate to do so, or avoid situations in which they might be criticized or rejected, such as intimate relationships or social events.

Many survivors as ANP avoid physical and emotional feelings that remind them of traumatic experiences. However, these feelings are necessary: They motivate us to seek out what we need. In other words, they prompt us to engage in particular action tendencies that are part of a given action system, which has particular goals that serve survival and well-being. Survivors sometimes have difficulty identifying when they are tired, hungry, stressed, lonely, or sad. Unable to know, their experience prevents them from seeking out food, rest, relaxation, connection, or help with painful affects. Particularly when their own emotions and other internal states are reminders of traumatic memories, survivors as ANP avoid feelings about their relationships and daily life. They may also lose interest in themselves, and thus fail to engage in adequate self-care.

The survivor as ANP may have intense negative responses to reactivation of EP, including panic and depression, even if amnesia exists for EP.

Modai (1994) described a patient who had generalized amnesia for her childhood before and during the Holocaust. Her ANP appeared completely oblivious to her traumatic childhood, full of death, loss, and abandonment. However, when her EP was vigorously reactivated, ANP became extremely distressed, manic, and suicidal, while continuing to have amnesia for the past.

Survivors as ANP learn to fear, avoid, hate, feel shame or digust, or pity about themselves as EP (see Chapter 10). They cannot tolerate their view of themselves during traumatizing events. In more complex structural dissociation, elaborated EPs also develop avoidance of ANP. The clash between goals related to living daily life and goals related to defense can lead to conflicted and competing actions between EP and ANP in the same moment of time.

Marie often compulsively rubbed her lips until they were raw and bleeding, which was incongruent with her meticulous efforts to look attractive. It became clear in therapy that this was a repetitive action by an EP that was trying to rub off red lipstick that she had been forced to wear by a perpetrator to make her look "sexy." When this part of Marie could be introduced to present reality by the therapist, she wiped her lip with Kleenex and stared in wonder, "My lips are clean!" From that moment forward, Marie no longer felt the compulsion to wipe her lips, and was able to fully integrate the EP that contained painful memories of sexual abuse.

ANP may sometimes become fully deactivated with full activation of EP, a phenomenon that results in ANP's amnesia for the episode, and is typically called a *switch*. This term has been limited to the severe dissociative disorders, but is clearly observed in cases of simple PTSD as well. There are ample anecdotes of such experiences in acutely traumatized combat soldiers, for example. C.S. Myers noted the alternation between EP and ANP that manifested during the acute stage of traumatization in World War I combat veterans just out of battle:

> [T]he normal personality is in abeyance. Even if it is capable of receiving impressions, it shows no signs of responding to them. The recent emotional [i.e., traumatic] experiences of the individual have the upper hand and determine his conduct: the normal has been replaced by what we may call the "emotional" personality. . . . Gradually or suddenly an "apparently normal" personality usually returns—normal save for the lack of all memory of events directly connected with the shock, normal save for the manifestation of other ("somatic") hysteric disorders indicative of mental dissociation. Now and again there occur alternations of the "emotional" and the "apparently normal" personalities. . . . On its return, the "apparently normal" personality may recall, as in a dream, the distressing experiences revived during the temporary intrusion of the "emotional" personality. The "emotional" personality may also return during sleep, the "functional" disorders of mutism, paralysis, contracture, etc., being then usually in abeyance. On waking, however, the "apparently normal" personality may have no recollection of the dream state and will at once resume his mutism, paralysis, etc. (1940, pp. 66–67)

We reiterate that even though Myers speaks of "personalities," he clearly did not intend to reify these self-conscious psychobiological systems. And the complete amnesia of ANP described above is an overstatement in most cases, although it has been documented that PTSD involves memory problems, including degrees of dissociative amnesia for traumatic experiences (Bremner, Southwick et al., 1992; Bremner, Steinberg et al., 1993; Vermetten & Bremner, 2000). Nevertheless, it becomes clear from this quote that alternations between EP and ANP are manifestations of the failure to integrate traumatic experiences. And this description illustrates that the experiences and dissociative symptoms of ANP and EP differ in many respects, and that significant dissociative symptoms are experienced by both.

More often than a complete switch between ANP and EP taking place, there is a partial intrusion of traumatic memory, so that a survivor does not have amnesia, but rather some degree of awareness of sensations, visual images, of feeling compelled to behave or feel in a certain way. For example, ANP might feel compelled to cower in the corner or might have fight behavior and feelings that may or may not be under volutary control, but which are often not understood as flashbacks. Some intrusions may involve traumatic nightmares, in which EP is fully activated, and for which ANP has amnesia afterwards, as Myers noted.

Sometimes intrusion of EP is even less clear. Then ANP experiences bewildering nonspecific symptoms such as irritability, hyper- or hypoarousal, depression, anxiety, rage, sleeplessness, self-destructive urges, and unconscious reenactments of the trauma. ANP may find it very difficult to determine the underlying cause of these symptoms for long periods of time. However, sometimes they can be related eventually to intrusions of EP.

Apart from traumatic memories, other features of EP can intrude on ANP. Thus, ANP may have thoughts or images or sensory intrusions that may emanate from EP. At times ANP may hear the voice of EP as a dissociative form of auditory hallucinations (Brewin, 2005b). ANP often fears these symptoms, as there is usually little or no insight into why such experiences occur, and no control over them. Following some psychoeducation regarding dissociative intrusions, Susan, as ANP, expressed great relief and said, "I'm not afraid of all these things that happen to me now, because now I know I'm not crazy, and it all makes sense."

ANP and EP eventually must be integrated into a unified personality so that ANP realizes what has happened, and EP realizes traumatizing events have ended. Strenuous avoidance strategies are then less necessary, and survivors can engage in action tendencies that are more flexible and coordinated in daily life.

SUMMARY

Primarily mediated by action systems of daily life, the survivor as ANP is geared toward functioning in daily life with regard to maintaining relationships with others, being able to work and be productive, and completing other tasks and goals of life. However, ANP is unable to integrate traumatic experience(s). ANP may have initiated integrative action tendencies after the traumatizing events—it is the nature of the human mind to be integrative—but has been unable to engage in them adequately and completely. The survivor as EP is fixated in certain action tendencies evoked during traumatic experiences. In primary structural dissociaton these action tendencies are typically part of mammalian physical survival defenses, geared to protect the individual when he or she feels threatened physically. ANP engages in behavioral avoidance of external reminders of traumatic memories, and in mental avoidance strategies regarding EP and related traumatic memories, including feelings, thoughts, and wishes that pose a psychological threat.

CHAPTER 3

Secondary Structural Dissociation
of the Personality

*In general, observers have only noted two different conditions of
existence in their [dissociative] subjects; but this number is neither
fixed nor prophetic. It is not, perhaps, even usual, as is believed.*
— Alfred Binet (1892–1896/1977, p. 38)

A SINGLE, APPARENTLY NORMAL part of the personality (ANP) and a single
emotional part of the personality (EP) represent the basic prototype
of structural dissociation. However, the dissociative organization of the
personality can be much more complex, particularly in those who experienced chronic childhood abuse and neglect (Nijenhuis & Van der Hart,
1999a; Nijenhuis, Van der Hart, & Steele, 2002). In general, more severe
forms of traumatization involve greater levels of dissociative symptoms
(e.g., G. Anderson, Yasenik, & Ross, 1993; Butzel et al., 2000; Chu, 1996;
Draijer & Langeland, 1999; Irwin, 1996; Mulder, Beautrais, Joyce, & Fergusson, 1998).

Like the single EP in primary structural dissociation, EPs in secondary
structural dissociation are fixated in traumatic experiences and intrude on
ANP with reactivated traumatic memories that may involve feelings, various sensory perceptions, or strongly held beliefs related to traumatizing
events. In addition, many EPs related to childhood abuse and neglect have
insecure patterns of attachment that alternate with or intrude on the attachment pattern of ANP, creating conflicting relational patterns, known as
disorganized/disoriented attachment (e.g., Liotti, 1999a, 1999b; Main &
Solomon, 1986).

Adults may develop forms of complex trauma-related structural dissociation when their traumatization is prolonged and repeated. Such adult

trauma includes war, particularly involvement in atrocities; political torture; internment in concentration camps; prolonged captivity; and genocide. However, it may be that most adults who develop secondary structural dissociation do so because they have already been traumatized in childhood—research indicates that childhood traumatization is a major risk factor for the development of complex PTSD in adults (e.g., Donovan, Padin-Rivera, Dowd, & Blake, 1996; Ford, 1999).

CHARACTERISTICS OF SECONDARY
STRUCTURAL DISSOCIATION

Secondary structural dissociation of the personality has a wide range of complexity. The most simple form consists of two EPs, usually an experiencing and an observing EP, along with an ANP that involves the majority of the functioning of the personality. Other traumatized individuals become much more divided in their personality, with several to many EPs. These EPs may be present in various forms and sequences, and may have quite varied degrees of sense of separateness, autonomy, and elaborated characteristics such as name, age, and gender.

Those EPs developed in childhood may become more complex and autonomous than those developed in primary structural dissociation in adulthood. Their autonomy may allow them at times to completely dominate consciousness and behavior. However, the behaviors of these EPs are generally maladaptive in the present. Their core action tendencies are usually directed by specific subsystems of defense with respect to perceived bodily threat (especially threat from a person; e.g., flight, fight, submission) rather than by the action systems of daily life, and by overwhelming despair, rage, shame, childlike needs for care, and fear. They typically engage in primitive mental defensive action tendencies.

Once more than a single EP develops, different aspects of one traumatic experience or different sets of traumatic experiences tend to be contained in various EPs. Each EP may be mediated by particular animal defenselike subsystems, have specific insecure attachment styles, may engage in particular mental defense action tendencies (i.e., mental tendencies to cope with a variety of perceived inter- and intrapersonal threats), and may also be fixated in a particularly unbearable moment of the traumatic experience; that is, a pathogenic kernel.

Brenda, a patient with dissociative disorder not otherwise specified (DDNOS) had a single identifiable ANP and several EPs. (Note: when we use the term *DDNOS* in the remainder of this book, we have the diagnosis DDNOS, subtype 1 [APA, 1994] in mind, i.e., a lesser form of DID). She had been sexually and physically abused by her alcoholic stepfather from ages 8 to 14, and had witnessed her mother and older brother being battered. Her level of functioning was inconsistent; at times it was relatively stable when her ANP was in control. At other times it was chaotic when EPs intruded upon ANP with flashbacks and disorganized attachment patterns. Brenda had several distinct EPs. One often interfered with her job by becoming aggressive (fight action subsystem). As ANP, Brenda had fuzzy recall of these incidents, one of which included an attempted assault on a supervisor. Another childlike EP would sometimes become terrified of her husband when he wanted to be sexual. As this EP, Brenda would scream and run into the bathroom (flight action subsystem) and lock the door, begging in a childlike voice for "the bad man to go away." Again, Brenda as ANP had little to no recollection of these episodes. Brenda sometimes heard a third EP, who had her stepfather's voice, calling her a slut and saying "the world would be a better place if you were dead." On several occasions this EP made a suicide attempt. As ANP, Brenda was aware that she had taken overdoses, but felt she had no control over doing it, as though "someone was forcing me to swallow the pills." And she reported watching the suicide attempts from a distance.

COMPLEXITIES OF SECONDARY STRUCTURAL DISSOCIATION

Secondary structural dissociation can have many different configurations of EPs, and each EP may have a varying degree of secondary elaboration and autonomy. In addition, the ANP of a survivor of chronic childhood relational traumatization is more likely to have maladaptive coping strategies than that of patients whose personality functioning was relatively intact prior to a single adult traumatic experience.

Changes in ANP in Secondary Structural Dissociation

Chronic childhood traumatization can interfere with the functioning of ANP because its effects pervade the domains of various daily life action systems. For example, energy regulation and social engagement are often normally paired with eating. However, if the family dinner is a frequent battleground, disturbances in eating (energy regulation) and difficulty in sharing meals with others (social engagement) may become entrenched action tendencies. In the same vein, the action system of sexuality/reproduction may be profoundly disturbed following sexual abuse, resulting in extremes of promiscuity or complete avoidance of sexual behavior. If children are constantly punished for curiosity and exploration, and ridiculed as stupid when they do not know something, then the exploration action system may be inhibited or otherwise affected. Caretaking may take on exaggerated proportions in the child who learns to caretake an abusive or neglectful parent, leading to an inability to set interpersonal boundaries. Some of the most pervasive difficulties for ANP following chronic relational traumatization are those related to the attachment action system (see section below on origins).

A patient with a single ANP must cope with several other dissociative parts of the personality (EPs), and is thus at a disadvantage in comparison to a patient with primary structural dissociation. Increased structural dissociation results in more possibilities of intrusion of EPs, as more EPs tend to make the patient susceptible to more reactivating stimuli. If some EPs gain more autonomy and secondary elaboration, the single ANP may have increasing difficulties in managing intrusions and the various internal interactions that may occur among other parts of the personality.

Emotional Parts of the Personality and the Mammalian Defense Action System

In primary structural dissociation, the single EP's attention is narrowed to the traumatizing event. In secondary structural dissociation, various EPs are more tightly focused on specific stimuli or specific parts of a traumatic experience, and each EP is mediated by different defensive subsystems. Some parts may be fixed in a particular traumatic memory, while others may be fixed in mental defenses that prevent realization of traumatic memories. For example, a childlike EP may make up innumerable stories about what happened, using fantasy as a substitute action for realization of what actually happened.

Although EPs in secondary structural dissociation are primarily guided by mammalian defensive subsystems (e.g., flight, freeze) they may also incorporate certain elements of other daily life action systems. For example, some EPs engage in action tendencies related to play, exploration, or caretaking, but these are easily and quickly deactivated by physical defenses that are prone to be triggered by reactivating stimuli. Many such EPs perceive themselves as children rather than adults, and find daily life daunting. They may not gain full executive control except in the privacy of the patient's home or in therapy, or during a reexperience of a traumatizing event. In some cases they may operate only through passive influence; that is, the internal influence of one dissociative part on the mental and behavioral actions of another part without gaining executive control (Kluft, 1987a; see Chapter 5). They may pair daily life action systems with both mammalian defenses and mental avoidance, such as when a childlike EP insists on "playing" instead of talking about relevant issues in therapy, and if pushed to stay on task, may resort to switching or to other avoidance strategies. But overall, EPs are typically geared toward common mammalian defense behaviors such as flight, fight, freeze, and submission. Any reminders of their traumatic experiences may evoke these action tendencies.

EPs and Trauma-Related Pathogenic Kernels

Some EPs contain the subjectively most unbearable aspects of traumatic experiences—aspects we have referred to as *pathogenic kernels* or *hot spots,* which other EPs were unable to bear, and have thus avoided.

> Reggie, a patient with DDNOS, was sadistically molested by a teenage neighbor as a child. Overall, he seemed over time to resolve the memory except for one EP that continued to be mutely terrified. After two years of slow work, the therapist was finally able to help the EP express his fear by drawing. He drew a beheaded puppy: The neighbor had killed Reggie's puppy as a threat of what would happen to Reggie if he did not comply. Following the resolution of this pathogenic kernel and the associated EP, Reggie found his generalized anxiety decreased tremendously and his functioning improved.

EPs and Double Emotion

In some patients secondary structural dissociation may develop when an acute traumatic experience in adult life simultaneously reactivates old unresolved traumatic memories. The acute current traumatic response then become a mixture of reactions to both the new and the old traumatizing events. Janet (1903, 1928a) called this "double emotion." It was observed in traumatized combat soldiers during various wars (e.g., Rows, 1916; cf. Shephard, 2000, pp. 81–82; Witzum, Margalit, & Van der Hart, 2002). We have also noted this phenomenon in patients who have accidents, attachment losses such as death or divorce, medical procedures, and rape or assault civilian trauma survivors (e.g., Van der Hart, Boon, Friedman, & Mierop, 1992; Van der Hart, Witztum, & Friedman, 1993). Double emotion may reevoke existing EPs, or may precipitate development of further EPs, or both together.

> Marcelle, a 26-year-old woman cut her head during an accident. She was hospitalized with a concussion, but subsequently developed amnesia for her entire life, and did not recognize her husband or other family members. This amnesia could not be explained neurologically. She was referred to psychotherapy and during therapy she recalled a violent rape at age 15, which she had never revealed to anyone. The combination of the accident, the blood from her head, the pain, and the subsequent examination in the emergency room, where her arms and legs were restrained and her clothes removed, reactivated the experience of rape at age 15. The "double emotion" of both traumas was so overwhelming that Marcelle as ANP, already amnesic for the rape, developed a more extensive amnesia. In therapy Marcelle manifested an EP that contained the memory of the ac-

cident and subsequent emergency treatment, as well as another EP that held traumatic memories of the rape (Van der Hart, Boon et al., 1992, pp. 26–27).

Multiple Groups of EPs

It is not uncommon to hear that chronically traumatized children have been abused by more than one person, and in different contexts, such as sexual abuse by a grandfather at his home, sadistic physical torment by a sibling or neighbor while playing outside, and sexual abuse by a religious authority in the church. This is often due to lack of supervision and adequate protection, as well as the vulnerability of traumatized children to repeated victimization (Boney-McCoy & Finkelhor, 1996; Craine, Henson, Colliver, & MacLean, 1988; Kellogg & Hoffman, 1997).

Various traumatizing events may induce different sets of EPs. Each group of EPs usually experiences and contains traumatic memories related to a specific cluster of traumatic experiences. Groups of EPs are most often seen in tertiary structural dissociation, as DID patients tend to have experienced the most severe and multiple traumatizing events, but may also be found in secondary structural dissociation as well. Lena had a single ANP, but three sets of EPs: One related to her father's physical and mental torment of her as a child, another related to a single rape by a neighbor when she was around 4, and another related to her mother's extreme neglect.

Layering of traumatic memories and EPs. Traumatic memories, and thus the EPs that contain them, may manifest in a stratified manner: When one layer of traumatic memory has been integrated, another layer may present itself, along with their attendant EPs (Janet, 1889, 1894/1989d, 1898a; Kluft, 1988; Van der Hart & Op den Velde, 1995). This succession is highly characteristic of patients with a history of chronic childhood abuse and neglect.

Layering may also be related to different traumatic memories: Following completion of one traumatic memory, another traumatic memory comes forward, along with different EPs. Such EPs may be linked together in different ways. They may be chronological, following each other in time (see below, "Sequential Dissociation"). That is, one EP follows another in time throughout a traumatic memory. Léonie first processed a traumatic memory of being raped by her father at age 8 through one EP, and only afterwards another EP was activated that had made a suicide attempt shortly after the rape because she erroneously believed she had become pregnant. Other EPs may share a common emotional theme, such as rage or shame or sexual feelings. At times, a certain EP may be the sequential link among traumatic memories; for example, an EP that is sexualized may be present across time in several different experiences of sexual abuse.

Finally, the link may be between an EP related to the original traumatic memory and an EP that holds an extremely upsetting fantasy or hallucination, which was evoked by the traumatic experience. In therapy, the experiences of one or the other EP may come first (Janet, 1898a).

> Naomi was 3 years old when her baby sister died, which was traumatic for her and her parents, who were unable to comfort her. Having a fundamentalist religious background, the parents felt extremely guilty about the death of their daughter and were unable to provide sufficient emotional safety and care for their other children. Naomi also felt guilty, and subsequently developed a fantasy in which she was condemned for the death of her sister by being sent to hell where she was punished by the devil—in fact, an EP—and would burn forever. Later in life, whenever she experienced situations of abandonment, such as the death of another family member or a breaking off of the engagement with her fiancé, she would suffer from burning pain and from nightmares of burning in hell.

When such a terrifying experience dominates consciousness, the diagnosis of a dissociative psychosis could be made (see Chapter 6).

Dissociative Parts of the Personality and Maladaptive Mental Defense Action Tendencies

Dissociative parts of the personality often contain various mental defensive action tendencies, so-called psychological defenses, which range from normal to quite primitive and pathological. These mental defensive action tendencies are actually remarkably similar to the mammalian physical defenses in response to bodily threat, because they involve various forms of hyperarousal, freeze, flight, fight, and submission (collapse). For example, they may include projection, identification (with the aggressor), which typically involves EPs engaged in fight strategies of anger and hostility and flight from disowned experiences such as vulnerability. Splitting, in which one dissociative part views a person as "good," while another part perceives the same person as "bad," can be seen as an attempt to identify predators (e.g., "bad mother") versus those who will be accepting (e.g., "good mother"). Denial by various parts is an extreme form of mental flight, such as when an EP of an adult woman denies she has breasts or that she is married.

Maladaptive mental defense action tendencies are *attempts* to protect oneself from further relational trauma and from overwhelming internal states when adequate coping skills are not available. However, such tendencies are not only eventually ineffective in providing protection, they can actually lead to further relational difficulties and internal turmoil.

When such defensive action tendencies become entrenched, the result is enduring maladaptive personality changes for the whole human being, and many of these strategies will be directly related to certain ANPs and particularly to EPs.

ANP "uses" EPs as mental protection, in that these EPs contain emotions, thoughts, fantasies, wishes, needs, and sensations that ANP believes to be unbearable or unacceptable. For example, extreme sadness and loneliness are often found in childlike EPs that also display freeze, flight, or submission. ANPs may disown dependency needs through EPs that are commonly fixed in the attachment cry and desperately seeking attachment (Steele, Van der Hart, & Nijenhuis, 2001). They have attachment insecurity, which promotes the use of further psychological coping strategies that may become more rigid and involuntary over time. ANP usually feels ashamed of, has little empathy for, or tolerance of, dependency needs that can overwhelm daily life if dependent EPs strongly intrude or dominate consciousness. ANP mentally avoids accessing and integrating these parts of the personality in one way or another; for example, by inhibiting the normative access to the action systems that mediate the avoided EPs, by retracting their field of consciousness, and by devaluing, hating, or fighting with these parts, and by avoiding attachments (see Chapter 10). Patients who were traumatized as children maintain structural dissociation when as ANP they continue to mentally avoid EPs. This may protect them as ANP from the horrific experiences that dominate their consciousness as EPs. But the drawback of this organization of their personality is that they cannot consistently engage in mental and behavioral coping because these actions are not always accessible; being contained in various parts that are closed to each other.

> Sally, a patient with complex PTSD, sometimes made emergency phone calls to her therapist. At first, she could not articulate why she had called, and would feel puzzled and ashamed about it. Gradually it became clear that a young EP was urgently seeking contact with the therapist, while Sally was doing her best to avoid any semblance of need for her therapist.

Parallel and Sequential Dissociation

More than one EP can simultaneously experience the same moment of a traumatizing event, but may contain different aspects of it. For instance, one of Sally's EPs experienced her father's sexual abuse, but without hearing associated unpleasant noises, while a second EP experienced the noises in the same moments of such traumatizing events. We have called this phenomenon *parallel dissociation* (Van der Hart, Steele, Boon, & Brown, 1993). Different EPs may also experience successive episodes of

trauma over time, as when the first two of Sally's EP experienced her father's advances, but a third one experienced the next event in time, the
actual rape. We call this *sequential dissociation* (Van der Hart et al., 1993).

Both parallel and sequential dissociation may involve pathogenic kernels, discussed above. Thus, a single part of the personality may be able
to tolerate certain experiences, but not others. This could lead to both
parallel and sequential dissociation.

> Meredith had one EP that experienced the physical sensations of engaging
> in forced fellatio, but without affect or awareness that it was her father who
> was the perpetrator, while another EP realized it was her father and experi-
> enced terrible loneliness, betrayal, and terror. Meredith also had one EP that
> experienced the physical abuse that preceded sexual abuse, and another EP
> contained memories of the sexual abuse, but not of the physical abuse. The
> EP that remembered the sexual abuse blamed herself and was found to be
> disgusting and weak by other parts of the personality because they had never
> been able to realize that a severe beating had occurred to force her to be sex-
> ual against her wishes, and that was why she had not been able to say no.

Parallel and sequential dissociation are likely related to fluctuations in
mental level during the course of a traumatic experience. Development
of more than a single EP, each of which contains various aspects of a particular time during traumatization, theoretically indicates precipitous
drops to an especially low mental level during the event. Development of
EPs over the course of time in chronic traumatization perhaps indicates a
lowering of mental level for the previous part of the personality, such that
another dissociative part is formed.

However, there still remains the issue of what is dissociated in a given
part and how that relates to action systems and tendencies, mental defensive strategies, and various intrapsychic functions such as cognitions, affects, and sensations. During traumatization there may be sequences of
action tendencies that are evoked, such as hypervigilance, freeze, flight,
fight, and submission. Dissociation among these different action tendencies may result in the sequential dissociation of various EPs that contain
one or more of these tendencies. However, there are often times during
traumatization in which there may be simultaneous conflicting tendencies present in the victim. For example, the tendency to fight may coexist
with the tendency to run or to submit. In such cases, parallel dissociation
may occur within a given moment of traumatization, such that one EP may
attempt to engage in flight, while another may engage in fight. In reality,
during the traumatizing event some of these action tendencies could not
actually occur, but had to be suppressed or suspended (e.g., the victim
had to avoid the tendency to fight, but rather had to submit, as this had
the greater survival value). Thus, EPs fixated in particular mammalian defenses may have never actually engaged in the behavior during the traumatic experience, and it thus remains a simulated action.

Types of parallel dissociation. Noyes and Kletti (1976) observed that "in the face of mortal danger we find individuals becoming observers of that which is taking place, effectively removing themselves from danger" (p. 108). Effectively but not completely, we add, because one dissociative part continues to experience the traumatizing event as another part watches. Probably the simplest form of parallel dissociation during traumatization is this division between an EP that experiences the traumatic experience at sensorimotor and affective levels, an *experiencing* EP, and an *observing* part of the personality that is subjectively out-of-body and looks upon the experiencing EP from afar, as though there is a spatial distance between the two. This is a well-documented phenomenon, previously described as a dissociation between an experiencing and an observing part of the ego (Fromm, 1965). It has been reported by victims of childhood sexual abuse (Braun, 1990; Gelinas, 1983; Putnam, 1997), combat veterans (Cloete, 1972), and motor vehicle accident victims (Noyes, Hoenk, Kupperman, & Slymen, 1977; Noyes & Kletti, 1977). The fact that motor vehicle accident victims also report this type of parallel dissociation indicates that people undergoing a single traumatic incident also may experience this basic type of parallel dissociation and thus develop a very simple and perhaps temporary form of secondary structural dissociation.

> Joyce, a patient with complex PTSD, had this simple type of secondary structural dissociation. She had a single childlike EP who experienced abuse by her brother, and a single observing EP that "watched from the ceiling" as she was being hurt, and an ANP that functioned well in daily life and was relatively amnesic for the abuse.

H. L. Schwartz gives an example of an observing EP in a survivor of chronic abuse, in this particular example, organized sexual abuse:

> When they made me dance in front of all those men I just took three steps backwards, and then there was some girl there and she was dancing for them, and I was watching her from far away . . . she was not me, but I could see her. I didn't like her and I didn't like what she was doing. Even though I know she is me, she isn't really me. (2000, p. 40)

In many instances, the observing EP is described by ANP as a passive, unfeeling part that merely watches the trauma. Margaret, a 32-year-old patient with DDNOS, first told her story of abuse from that perspective: "I watched it happen from the doorway. I was just looking and didn't feel anything about that child and what was happening to her." This is an indication of nonrealization for the observing EP. Certainly, there is a psychological advantage for the observing EP, who does not have to realize the abuse is happening to *her*. It is possible that a prototype of this type of observing EP has been described by Hilgard (1977) as the "hidden observer," which is found in some normal subjects under hypnosis. It involves a monitoring function of the brain that is readily available to be dissociated and can develop some degree of a sense of self.

However, some EPs appear to be fixated in a hypervigilant defensive subsystem, and they can easily be mistaken for observing EPs. Hypervigilant parts do much more than merely passively observe; their focus is exclusively on the environment, which they actively scan, looking for danger signals, and they often have a feeling of alarm or even of fear. But generally such hypervigilant parts are not observant of other parts of the personality, as observer EPs may be. Some observing EPs seem to develop more secondary elaboration, and appear highly intellectualized, nonfeeling, but sometimes quite insightful parts of the personality, and have much more memory than only of traumatic experiences. A few do report feeling, but it is usually very limited and mild. As integration of the personality begins to occur, these parts generally develop more feeling and less psychological distance from their personal experiences. But until that time, they may recognize mental and behavioral actions of other parts and interpersonal relationships to a degree that is not present in other parts of the personality.

A few observing EPs appear to involve some level of caretaking, such as directing ANP to stay safe, and containing destructive EPs. They typically do not act externally in the world, but can be quite active internally. They are usually seen in DID patients, but not exclusively.

Lisette, a 27-year-old patient who was chronically traumatized as a child, was hospitalized for surgery, and developed acute respiratory distress on the ward. As some parts panicked and struggled to breathe, and the medical staff was frantically working to help Lisette, an observing EP came into existence. This EP "watched from above" and was later able to accurately report what was happening in the room. At some point Lisette lost consciousness, and thus this part did as well. Immediately prior to losing consciousness, the EP feared she would die. When Lisette was subsequently revived, the EP believed she had indeed died, but because she seemed to have conscious awareness, she believed herself to be a ghost. She developed a caretaking tendency as she watched the medical personnel deal with Lisette's body too harshly as they tried to save her. In her imagination she commented to them from her position above the body that they should take more care and be aware that they were dealing with a human being. Subsequently, she went on to take care of Lisette internally over time, all the while retaining the belief that she was a ghost and could not be seen.

This is an example of trance logic, in which the EP did not recognize the obvious: if Lisette survived, so did she. Trance logic is a form of extremely concrete thinking accompanied by extreme narrowing of attention, a severe retraction of the field of consciousness, in which there is an acceptance of experiences that would normally seem incompatible (Orne, 1959), and it can be seen as a lack of reflective thinking and a lapse into reflexive beliefs.

Therapists should be cautioned that such observing EPs have not necessarily observed everything, and may be amnesic for certain crucial parts of a traumatizing event, and what they report they have observed may not necessarily be accurate. Their insight into the individual's needs and psychological processes may also be quite flawed. Thus the wise therapist can appreciate the helpfulness of these parts in some patients with complex dissociation, but without being overly reliant on them.

More complex parallel dissociation involves additional EPs that simultaneously experience different aspects of the traumatizing event. These might include further subsystems of mammalian defense.

> Margaret experienced a documented and brutal group rape at age 5 by two of her adolescent brothers and their friends. She developed several EPs that experienced the entire rape (i.e., parallel dissociation). One was angry (fight), one was terrified and crying for her mother (attachment cry), one watched from the doorway, and stated she couldn't tolerate being in the body (flight), one EP experienced unbearable physical pain, one squeezed her eyes shut and pretended to be somewhere else, and one EP was completely still and silent, though terrified, reenacting one of the boys holding his hand over her mouth to keep her quiet (freeze).

Types of sequential dissociation. Sequential dissociation refers to several EPs experiencing successive episodes of the traumatizing event. As stated above, unbearable moments of the traumatic experience, or pathogenic kernels, may be the "breaking points" that precipitate another dissociative division.

> John had several EPs that appeared in succession when his uncle became violent. First was an EP that froze. This EP became so afraid that he "disappeared," lost mental efficiency, and an angry EP would then appear and yell at the uncle (fight). When the uncle began to beat him more than he could bear, the angry EP would "disappear" because he could not tolerate the pain, and a numb EP, without emotional or physical feeling, would appear (anesthesia and total submission) and wait for the beating to be over. This EP would become "tired" immediately after the beating, and a new EP would come forth that hid underneath the front porch of the house and went to sleep (recuperation).

"Rapid switching" (Putnam, 1989) among EPs is a commonly reported phenomenon that seems to occur in particularly terrifying or unbearably painful events.

Etty, a patient who experienced much childhood trauma, including physical abuse, illustrates "rapid switching" among EPs that may take place during excruciating pain. When traumatic memories of physical torture needed to be treated in therapy, one dissociative part said that in order to survive the ordeal without screaming—as demanded by the perpetrators—all of the EPs involved had to briefly feel and see everything and then to feel and see nothing. In other words, rapid switching among EPs was necessary to deal with the unbearable pain: "Away in the head, everybody in turn knowing/ seeing/feeling something, faster and faster and faster in order to be little and much."

Combinations of parallel and sequential dissociation. Most commonly, secondary (and tertiary) structural dissociation includes combinations of both parallel and sequential dissociation, particularly in relation to chronic childhood abuse. The various factors that contribute to a child's vulnerability to dissociate presumably make it more likely that dissociation will occur both within a moment of a traumatic experience, as well as across time with additional traumatization. In Margaret's case above, which illustrates sequential dissociation, there was also an observing EP that watched the entire scenario as other parts "came and went."

SUMMARY

Chronically traumatized individuals may experience more division of their personality, resulting in a single ANP and more than one EP. These EPs may be more elaborated than those in primary structural dissociation, and take on not only physical defensive characteristics, but also contain rigid and maladaptive mental defensive action tendencies. The ANP may be characterized by maladaptive mental defensive action tendencies as well. EPs may be related to pathogenic kernels within a given traumatic experience. Traumatized individuals are characterized by secondary structural dissociation when there is a single intact ANP and two or more EPs as a result of division among action (sub)systems of mammalian defense and attachment patterns involving approach and avoidance.

CHAPTER 4

Tertiary Structural Dissociation
of the Personality

Louis Vivet . . . has six different existences. Each of them is characterized, first, by modifications of the memory affecting now one period, now another; secondly, by modifications of character; in one state he is gentle and industrious, in another he is lazy and irascible; thirdly, by modifications of sensibility and motion; in one state he is insensible, and paralyzed in his left side; in a third he is paraplegic, etc.

—Pierre Janet (1907, pp. 83–84)

T ERTIARY STRUCTURAL DISSOCIATION involves not only more than one emotional part of the personality (EP), but also more than one apparently normal part (ANP; Nijenhuis & Van der Hart, 1999a; Van der Hart et al., 1998). We propose that tertiary structural dissociation is characteristic of dissociative identity disorder (DID), a disorder primarily related to severe, prolonged traumatization in childhood (Boon & Draijer, 1993; Kluft, 1996a; Putnam, 1989, 1997; Ross, 1989). In such cases, the action systems of daily life, such as exploration, attachment, caretaking, and sexuality, which are found in a single ANP in primary and secondary structural dissociation, are now divided among several ANPs. And as in some cases of secondary structural dissociation, some EPs may be more complex and autonomous, appear in daily life, and take on features of other action systems in addition to defense. While these EPs can thus take on some characteristics of ANP, they are still largely mediated by mammalian defense.

DISSOCIATIVE PARTS IN DISSOCIATIVE
IDENTITY DISORDER

The DSM-IV diagnostic category of DID is limited in its description of "identities" or "personality states." It states that "[e]ach personality state may be experienced as if it has a distinct personal history, self-image, and identity, including a separate name" (APA, 1994, p. 484). However, in our clinical practice we often encounter parts of the personality in DID patients, in particular some EPs, that do not have a name or other strongly defining characteristics. In DID, there is a requirement for amnesia and for alternation between at least two "identities," but the range and characteristics of dissociative identities are not specified. Furthermore, the DSM-IV discerns different types of dissociative parts of the personality in terms of being passive, dependent, guilty, depressed, hostile, and controlling, but does not describe how dissociative "identities" of patients with DID differ from those of patients with DDNOS. On a clinical level, therapists have tended to use the diagnosis of DDNOS when the emancipation and elaboration of dissociative parts of the personality (see below) are limited, although the DSM-IV offers no guidance.

We propose that secondary and tertiary dissociation differ along several lines. In secondary dissociation (and DDNOS) there are less profound amnesic boundaries among parts of the personality. ANP is by far the most extensive part of the personality, the "major shareholder." EPs tend to emerge in daily life less often, and tend not to be mediated by the action systems of daily life. Thus EPs in secondary structural dissociation are more likely to be mediated by defense only, and there is more tendency to have only a single ANP. When EPs emerge in daily life, it is usually related to reliving a traumatic memory or because there is a stimulus that evokes a part's defensive function. For example, a survivor may have an EP that emerges to fight with a partner whenever sex is initiated, perceiving it as rape. These parts generally have limited functions and often do not have a full awareness of the present. In principle, the number of parts of the personality in a given individual has little bearing on whether dissociation is at the secondary or tertiary level. A patient with secondary structural dissociation may have many EPs, while a patient with tertiary structural dissociation may only have two ANPs and two EPs. However, in general, more divisions relate to less mental efficiency and more likelihood that a traumatized individual will have tertiary structural dissociation.

On the other hand, patients with tertiary dissociation have more than one part of the personality that is active in daily life. They are not evoked by traumatic memories, as are EPs, but by the specific functions and goals involved in various areas of the patient's current life. For example, some parts are focused only on work, some on being a parent, some on sexual activity.

We hypothesize that the origins of the divisions among ANPs lie in the inability of an unsupported, emotionally neglected, and abused child to integrate emerging action systems of daily life when various aspects of daily life themselves are chronically traumatizing.

> Tracy, a 34-year-old patient with DID, had several distinct ANPs, all with different names. "Betty" went to work (which includes the exploration action system) and functions well in her job as a computer software engineer. When Tracy was a child, "Betty" was the part that went to school. "Betty" solved technical work problems, but did not relate well to others. This task (involving action systems that involve social engagement such as attachment) was left up to "Theresa," who was charming and outgoing, although irresponsible, and experienced herself as a teenager. Tracy herself (also an ANP) was depressed, suicidal, and withdrawn, did not enjoy her work, and avoided relationships. "Beppy" was an ANP that cared for "little" EPs internally (caretaking action system). Beppy did not function externally in daily life. There was one EP that tended to dominate time when Tracy was alone at home: "Little Tracy" cried, rocked herself, and seemed to be in severe physical pain, though she could not articulate what was wrong. Most of the ANPs did not like "Little Tracy," and avoided her as much as possible. A second rather elaborated EP was experienced as male, believed he was muscular and strong, was called "the Terminator," and frightened all the other parts. This EP interfered with any intimate relationships that "Tracy" attempted to develop, cursed men and wanted to rape them, and threw away the bed linens by trying to stuff them in garbage bags while muttering angrily immediately after sex while the man was still in the bed. Tracy reported other EPs as being internal, "living in a big room," and they did not appear to function externally, but were in continual chaos and pain, loudly screaming in her head.

DID patients may continue in adulthood to develop more ANPs to cope with events that they cannot integrate. In addition, ongoing reactivation of EPs and their traumatic memories also impede the functioning of ANP, making the survivor more vulnerable to dissociation—a deficit and defense that is quite entrenched by adulthood.

> Etty, a DID patient with a history of childhood sexual abuse, became pregnant and needed prenatal examinations by an obstetrician (Van der Hart & Nijenhuis, 1999). These exams caused reactivation of her sexual trauma. To evade these reactivations, she developed a new ANP which was able to tolerate the physical examinations without intrusion of traumatic memories.

> Lena developed an ANP that was present only for sex, because she could not tolerate having sex with her husband, but did not feel she could say no to him. She also created a very limited part of her personality whose sole function was to wash dishes.

These are examples of how structural dissociation begins as a deficit during traumatization, but can become a mental defense and way of coping with the mere unpleasantness of life. Such division in daily life is particularly likely to occur when the mental level of the individual is very low, as was the case with Lena.

In tertiary structural dissociation each ANP is restricted to the functions and needs of the particular action system(s) by which this part is mediated. Tracy's "Betty" focused only on working. Etty's new ANP only dealt with gynecological exams. Of course, therapists encounter many combinations of ANPs and action systems, with some encompassing a range of action systems for functioning in daily life, and some encompassing only a single one. Division of ANP can ensue when normal life becomes overwhelming to the individual, who then uses dissociative parts of the personality to cope with daily living.

EMANCIPATION AND ELABORATION OF DISSOCIATIVE PARTS OF THE PERSONALITY

There are two qualities of dissociative parts in complex forms of structural dissociation that generally evolve over a period of time. The first is the degree of *emancipation* (Janet, 1907), of separation and autonomy one dissociative part has developed from other parts of the personality. The second is the degree to which a dissociative part develops complexity and scope of the "ideas and functions that constitute personality" over time (Janet, 1907, p. 332). This we refer to as *elaboration*. Although emancipation and elaboration have tended to be associated with DID in the literature, these processes can also occur to varying degrees in secondary structural dissociation, and sometimes in primary structural dissociation as well.

Emancipation

Emancipation involves the degree to which one part of the personality is able to act on its own outside the control of other parts, including gaining full, or executive control. Other parts may be amnesic for the part in control, or be aware of and unable to control that part. Interactions among parts that avoid integration contribute to their emancipation. Fearful and shaming internal interactions, such as with a part that screams "Slut!" would foster emancipation because parts become ever more avoidant of each other, hence more divided.

The degree of emancipation of parts varies. Some have a depersonalized awareness that they are part of a larger personality: "I know I'm part of him, but it doesn't feel like it." Others realize this only vaguely, and a few regard themselves as an entirely separate person, even when confronted with obvious evidence to the contrary. This can lead to serious problems for survivors.

> As EP, Lena tried to kill herself by cutting her wrists. This EP could not understand that if Lena died, she would also die, that is, that they shared the same body and that they were parts of the same personality. The EP's intent was to get rid of Lena, a very inhibited ANP, so that the EP could finally do what she wanted, which was to go out with other men, be sexual, and drink and party. Thus, there is not only a profound lack of integration in this case, but also a very narrow field of attention and focus on specific action systems (sexuality and play) to the exclusion of others. It is also clear that Lena had disowned unacceptable impulses in this EP.

Emancipation is most obvious when ANPs and EPs exert executive control in the external as opposed to the inner world, with or without the conscious awareness of other parts. This degree of emancipation of parts is a common phenomenon in DID. For example, Lena's "Grandma" took care of her actual children, and Etty's new ANP was present during her obstetrical examinations.

The most commonly reported symptoms in complex dissociative disorders pertain to parts influencing each other internally (Dell, 2002). For example, one EP beats another. An ANP tries to take care of terrified internal children parts. Another EP frequently makes nasty comments on the behavior of an ANP. A small child EP lies in the closet and cries internally. This active, and sometimes elaborate internal life among parts is also quite common in DID, and often involves tormenting reenactments of abuse. Some dissociative parts that influence other parts seldom if ever act in the external world. The internal world, usually one of desolation and terror, can be as real to these parts as the external one, or even more real (see Chapter 8). In a few cases, it involves richly populated fantasy worlds (e.g., "fairyland") that allow the individual to have artificial relief from the daily vicissitudes of life as a severely traumatized human being.

Elaboration

Elaboration is concerned with the complexity of a dissociative part's repertoire of actions, including memory, skills, and sense of self. It is developed when a dissociative part is regularly exposed to external reality or a rich internal reality. Recurrent interactions of dissociative parts with other people or among themselves extend their life history and repertoire of mental actions, whether they occur in the context of daily life or traumatization. Thus, these interactions elaborate their existence. Some exhanges are benign or even supportive, but other contacts evoke fear, disgust, or shame.

Elaboration on the sense of self such as names, ages, and other identifying features are far less important than the lack of realization that causes the elaboration in the first place. Janet termed these elaborations, and the accompanying degree of emancipation, *substitute beliefs*, which occur when one cannot integrate a situation. The form of the substitute belief (e.g., "I am a child; I am an animal; I am deaf; I am a demon; I am my father") is not important:

> We must not attach too much importance to all these substitutions. We must find underneath them the non-realizations which are the essence of the illness and which often are more or less dissimulated. It is on these non-realizations, on their psychological importance, that often the seriousness of the illness depends. (1945, p. 187)

Braun (1986) suggested a continuum of elaboration. At one end is a very limited EP that contains a small aspect of a traumatic experience (which he referred to as a "memory trace fragment"), and much more complex EPs at the other. He described a very limited EP as "a fragment that has only a minimal set of response patterns to stimuli, life history, and range of emotion/affect but has knowledge for a short period of time" (p. xiii). Some of these EPs have a very specific purpose during traumatization. For example, the function of one EP in a DID patient was only to perform fellatio; this was in response to the patient's being whipped and forced to perform fellatio on her brother for child pornography. Another named Melody expressed the thoughts of other parts through music. Each EP experiences the traumatizing event from its own perspective, depending on the perceptual window and focus of the action systems by which they are mediated.

Elaboration may also be shaped by sociocultural influences, such as EPs that are modeled on television or movie characters. One male patient had an elaborate group of EPs all of whom were based on *Star Trek* characters. "Mr. Spock" served as the consummate intellectual but emotionally devoid ANP. However, there is absolutely no evidence that dissociative disorders are themselves *caused* by social role enactment (Gleaves, 1996).

Mixtures of ANP and EP

There may be complex mixtures of ANP and EP in very fragmented patients. Children who are abused and neglected by their caretakers in early childhood, with maltreatment constituting a substantial part of daily life, will probably have particular difficulty in developing normative daily life systems. This is a common experience of DID patients. These children must alternate so quickly and frequently among emerging defensive and daily life action systems that these systems, hence their EPs and ANPs, can become mixed in quite chaotic manifestations.

In very low functioning DID patients, many ANPs and EPs may seem to be virtually indistinguishable from each other. However, on closer scrutiny, some dissociative parts—"ANP-biased"—appear to be more oriented to functioning in daily life, while other parts—"EP-biased"—seem more oriented to defense. These patients are the most difficult to treat because their mental level is exceptionally low, and defensive systems are consistently operating in normal life, leading to paranoia, aggression, hyperreactivity to relational fluctuations, and general inability to engage in normal life activities. They generally have chronic and debilitating flashbacks, and are easily and frequently reactivated by conditioned stimuli (see Chapter 10). For such patients, daily life itself is overwhelming.

> The main dissociative part of Etty, a DID patient, was severely traumatized and could function at a low level only with much effort and much suffering. This part, although mediated by various major daily life action systems, also held many traumatic memories related to intense verbal abuse by her mother. Other EPs held other types of severe trauma.

When traumatizing events chronically invade the daily life of a child, EPs may take on particular action systems that would normally be a part of daily life, but instead, become an essential component of the trauma. The most common example is that of the sexuality action system. While this action system typically belongs to ANP as a part of normal life, it may become associated with EPs which must deal with sexual abuse. For example, perpetrators can stimulate teens to orgasm. Or they stimulate a younger child's awakening sexuality action system so frequently and intensely that this system develops prematurely in the context of abuse. Some EPs are developed as a defense against realizing sexual abuse. For example, some insist that they "seduced" the perpetrator, and thus were in control and not hurt, which implies activation of the sexuality system. Others believe they are homosexual, even though ANP claims to be heterosexual, or that they are of the opposite sex than other parts of the personality. When the child matures, such EPs may act out sexually, and cause significant confusion about sexual identity or gender. These EPs may have a prominent role in dealing with the patient's sexuality throughout his or her development.

Types of ANPs and EPs

In the literature on DID, various types of dissociative parts of the personality (that are not necessarily mutually exclusive) have been described (e.g., Boon & Van der Hart, 1995; Kluft, 1984, 1996a; Putnam, 1989; Ross, 1997). These include (1) host parts; (2) child parts; (3) protector and helper parts; (4) internal self helpers; (5) persecutor parts, based on introjects of perpetrators; (6) suicidal parts; (7) parts of the opposite sex; (8) promiscuous parts; (9) administrators and obsessive–compulsive parts; (10) substance abuse parts; (11) autistic and handicapped parts; (12) parts with special talents or skills; (13) anesthetic or analgesic parts; (14) imitators and imposters; (15) demons and spirits; (16) animals and objects such as trees; and (17) parts belonging to a different race. Some of these types of parts, such as child, persecutor, and suicidal parts are common, while others are not. All these parts can be regarded as more or less elaborated ANPs or EPs whose characteristics are defined by the action system(s) which mediate their functioning and which involve particular psychological defenses.

"Host Personality"

The literature on DID often mentions the existence of a so-called "host," the ANP that is "out" or in executive control most of the time (Braun, 1986; Kluft, 1984a; Putnam, 1989). It has also generally been referred to as the "original" personality. However, in tertiary structural dissociation no such original personality exists, nor is the host a nondissociative part of the personality. Instead, the personality is divided in two or more dissociative parts, one or more of which may be considered the "host." We prefer the term *ANP*, because the host has the function of living normal daily life, and has not, or not fully, realized the traumatization. Some DID patients may have several dissociative parts which have key positions in daily life, and therefore could be called "hosts," even though they may not be in executive control more often than others.

In some patients, several dissociative parts may form a social "façade" that attempts to hide many deficits and overt evidence of DID (Kluft, 1985). Lena had ANPs like these, all of whom had slight variations of the same name, and who functioned as a team to prevent others from becoming aware of the profound dissociation that existed. In others, the "host" may be an ANP with features of EP(s), resulting from early and extensive neglect and abuse that precluded the formation of parts that only involve action systems of daily life, and that thus are not "contaminated" by action systems of defense.

Most often, the "host" has some recognition of other parts of the personality, although a degree of amnesia may be involved. However, occasionally, the "host" does not know about the existence of other dissociative parts of the personality, and loses time when others dominate executive control (Putnam, Guroff, Silberman, Barban, & Post, 1986). As C. R. Stern (1984) pointed out, it is more often the case that the "host" actively denies (active nonrealization) evidence of the existence of other dissociated parts of the personality rather than dissociative parts "hiding" themselves from the host. This nonrealization may be so severe that when presented with evidence of other dissociative parts, the host may "flee" from treatment.

Child Parts of the Personality

Aside from persecutory parts, child parts are probably the most common EPs to be found in cases of chronic childhood abuse and neglect, both in secondary and tertiary dissociation. They are EPs that are often frightened and untrusting, and many are also clingy and needy. These latter are based on the defense action subsystem of attachment cry, with maladaptive dependency and insecure attachment (Steele, Van der Hart, & Nijenhuis, 2001). The focus of attention in "child" EPs is generally restricted to threat or attachment cues, thus the therapist may be perceived as a potential perpetrator, but one who may also provide comfort. Usually "child" EPs are fixated in the time of traumatization, and are more numerous than ANPs. Nonrealization may be severe and pervasive enough that they may literally experience themselves as actual children. Child parts may idealize the perpetrator, demonstrating extreme nonrealization of their history. Sometimes they deny they have the same parents as other parts of the personality. They often lack the judgment or skills necessary to cope with daily life situations.

Other child parts of the personality may actually be ANPs, mediated by action systems such as play, exploration, or attachment, who have been fixated in early development of these action systems. These action systems would normally direct an individual to grow and develop mentally and physically. However, some ANPs of survivors of chronic childhood traumatization may not have experienced mental growth, but rather have become fixated in time and development to a greater or lesser degree once daily life began to include ever more neglect and abuse. These ANPs involve the comforting, avoidant illusion that life did not proceed to harsher realities, and that all is good. Thus, they may only want to play, or be social to the point of naivete.

> Frances had a part called "Play" that loved to play games, chatted incessantly in an excited, childlike manner, and hated when other parts had to work, which she found boring. "Play" could not at all acknowledge that she had been abused, and if the subject was ever raised, she only increased her talkativeness about fun things. It was quite clear that she had a high degree of nonrealization, and that her function of play was not only a sequestering of an action system, but had also become a psychological defense against realizing her traumatization.

Sometimes parts that "play" may constitute not only the play action system, but also a reenactment of sexual abuse, which was presented to them by a perpetrator as "playing games."

> Lily had a child EP that only wanted to play games in therapy. Her rigid action tendencies and actions had a double function. First, it was her way of having some pleasure in life. The patient had been severely neglected, in-

cluding during a long hospitalization as a young child. One male nurse took her out of her bed to play. This play had initially been pleasurable and benign from Lilly's perspective, but eventually it involved sexual abuse. The EP's second and more hidden agenda was to keep the nurse interested in real play, so that she could prevent him from being sexual. This was the pattern that she reenacted with the (male) therapist.

Protector Parts

There are two related types of EPs that attempt to "protect," albeit in often extremely self-destructive ways: fight and persecutory dissociative parts of the personality. A third type is more directly helpful, supporting the individual in more mature and functional ways to adapt to daily life, often with a strong degree of observing wisdom. However, it usually has not personalized much of the patient's life.

The first two types are both defensive in nature, fixated in the protective "fight" defensive subsystem, and attempt to manage the difficult emotions of rage and anger and to avoid feelings of hurt, fear, or shame (Van der Hart et al., 1998). Within their specific action system these EPs have a narrowed attention to anything that they regard as a threat. However, they are often unable to differentiate what is threatening and what is not. They have such generalized conditioning that a host of stimuli evoke a rigid defensive reaction. Contact with the therapist will evoke these EPs because they are conditioned to avoid attachment, dependence, and emotional needs (Steele et al., 2001).

Fight EPs are part of the fight defensive subsystem, and have the explicit function of protecting the survivor, both internally and from perceived external threat. They have defensive substitute beliefs, such as the idea that they are strong, unhurt, and capable of carrying out strong actions of rage and revenge. Often these parts view themselves as a "tough" child or teenager or a large, strong man, and present with bravado in therapy: "I don't need anything from you; they (other parts) don't need you either. You'd better leave them alone!"

Persecutory EPs tend to experience and present themselves as the original perpetrators engaged in the original traumatic actions. This nonrealization may reach delusional proportions, but it is merely another type of substitute belief. Persecutory EPs are often more inner directed, responding not only to external, but also internal perceived threat (e.g., the crying of an EP fixated in traumatic memories). Without the ability to mentalize perpetrators, to create symbolic representations, children may "take in," introject, the "bad" object of the perpetrators. Thus, as EPs they claim they *are* the abuser, and not the abused, and have the affects and behaviors of a perpetrator to varying degrees. In this sense, these EPs often cannot distinguish internal reality from external reality. Many traumatized individuals are tormented by these internal perpetrators as though the abuse were continuing. Persecutory EPs also may enact representations of the traumatic experience from the child's perception of the perpetrator's viewpoint (e.g., "I will act and think in the manner in which I perceived my father to act and think") (cf., Ross, 1997). H.L. Schwartz offers an example:

> When they were fucking me I became them and it stopped the hurting. And it felt good to be the one hurting me, in charge of all that, instead of them. Now, even though I know it's me and that this belief isn't real, I cannot find my way back to that little boy who was hurt. I haven't felt even sorry for him. (2000, p. 41)

In this case, there is some realization that the victim is not really the perpetrator, but rather was himself the one who was hurt. Yet full realization cannot occur ("I cannot find my way back to that little boy who was hurt"). Like their actual perpetrators, these EPs do not have regulatory skills to manage anger and rage, or the pain, shame, needs, and fear that underlie much of their hostility. They must learn alternative ways to cope with rage and to cope with intense feelings over the course of treatment.

Both fight and persecutory EPs may intrude forcefully on ANP with self-destructive actions such as cutting or purging, and may dominate consciousness. They may act out toward the therapist or others in the patient's life while the ANP is amnesic of such behaviors, or has awareness but no behavioral control.

Other protectors are mediated by the action system of caretaking, or are more simply the elaboration of a peritraumatic observing part. Caretaking parts are more actively involved in managing the system of dissociative parts of the personality, though their ability may be more or less limited. Although these parts are primarily mediated by the caretaking system, they usually have a lack of awareness of self-care, and become easily depleted. Their awareness is limited to the needs of others internally or externally, and thus they have little ability to play, explore, or socialize. It is imperative that the therapist not rely too heavily on such dissociative parts, as it will only reinforce their retracted field of consciousness to caretaking and not to other action systems.

ORIGINS OF SECONDARY AND TERTIARY STRUCTURAL DISSOCIATION

More complex and chronic structural dissociation (i.e., secondary structural dissociation and tertiary structural dissociation), occurs with early, severe, and chronic traumatization. Theoretically, the various levels of structural dissociation of the personality are linked to a complex interaction among (1) the developmental level and related mental level of the individual; (2) the severity and duration of traumatization; (3) genetic factors that promote either vulnerability or resilience; (4) degree of social support, including attachment relationships; (5) disruption of the normal integration of the child's action systems that requires a secure attachment relationship; (6) and the interruption or regression of the child's development of mental and behavioral skills repertoire to cope adaptively and flexibly with the vicissitudes of daily life and relationships and other stressors.

Personality Development in Young Children and Immature Integrative Brain Structures

The young child's personality is relatively unintegrated, and integrative structures of the brain are still immature (Perry & Pollard, 1998; Teicher, Anderson, Polcari, Anderson, & Navalta, 2002). The quality of the first years of life, particularly secure attachment, is instrumental in laying the groundwork of a personality organization that is rather cohesive across contexts, such as action systems, place, time, and sense of self. With regard to primary structural dissociation, we have assumed that the personality was a relatively integrated mental system prior to traumatization. However, this is hardly the case in young children.

We hypothesize that secondary structural dissociation is likely to occur as a result of the intersection of a number of factors, such as age, degree and severity of traumatization, lack of social support, relationship to perpetrator, tendency to avoid traumatic memories, and possibly genetic factors (Becker-Blease et al., 2004). The older the child is prior to abuse and neglect, the more likely action systems of daily life have become more cohesive, and thus it is less likely that more than a single ANP would develop. Tertiary dissociation is much more likely to develop in earlier childhood traumatization (prior to age 8) that is an ongoing part of daily life, so that ANP also becomes structurally dissociated.

Intensity, Duration, and Repetition of Traumatization, and Developmental Level

Janet (1909a) stated that "[traumas] produce their disintegrating effects in proportion to their intensity, duration and repetition" (p. 1558). Like Janet (1909a), Ferenczi observed that severe and chronic traumatization in childhood induced more complex division of the personality:

If the shocks [i.e., traumatizing events] increase in number during the development of the child, the number and the various kinds of splits in the personality increase too, and soon it becomes extremely difficult to maintain contact without confusion with all the frag-

> ments, each of which behaves as a separate personality yet does not
> know of even the existence of the others. (1949, p. 229)

Even though Ferenczi overstated the lack of conscious awareness among different dissociative parts of the personality for each other, his clinical observations indicate that early onset and number of highly stressful events are major factors in inducing complex structural dissociation. Several studies with severely traumatized patients (Chu & Dill, 1990; Draijer & Boon, 1993; Nijenhuis, 2004; Nijenhuis, Spinhoven, Van Dyck, Van der Hart, & Vanderlinden, 1998b; Ogawa et al., 1997; Saxe et al., 1993), and with patients presenting in medical care (Nijenhuis, Van Dyck et al., 1999), have provided supportive evidence that severe and chronic dissociation is related to early and persistent traumatization. It has been additionally hypothesized that young children are particularly prone to peritraumatic dissociation and other trauma-related psychopathology (e.g., Kluft, 1991; Putnam, 1989; 1997). Thus, severe traumatization in early childhood tends to be associated with more severe forms of dissociation, which we describe in terms of secondary and tertiary structural dissociation of the personality.

The deleterious and chronic effects of emotional neglect and abuse have been widely documented (Cohen, Perel, De Bellis, Friedman, & Putnam, 2002) and include manifestations of structural dissociation. Thus, the severity of dissociative symptoms is linked with sexual and physical abuse, neglect, as well as the severity and chronicity of this maltreatment, and with maternal dysfunction (Draijer & Langeland, 1999; Macfie, Cicchetti, & Toth, 2001a, 2001b).

Attachment Disorganization in Chronically Traumatized Children

Severe disruptions in the early development of attachment patterns between children and their caretakers seem to be precursors of dissociative pathology, including more complex structural dissociation of the personality. Although the attachment system is only one of the action systems that motivate human action tendencies, it is indeed the sine qua non that promotes the development and cohesiveness of other action systems. In particular, it regulates threat responses that would interfere with enhancement of daily life action systems. According to Lyons-Ruth,

> the quality of regulation of fearful affect available in attachment relationships is foundational to the developing child's freedom to turn attention away from issues of threat and security toward other developmental achievements, such as exploration, learning, and play [action systems of daily life]. (2003, p. 885)

Thus, neural networks related to daily life systems become increasingly more complex and interactive through constant and consistent use, leading to a more cohesive personality and an individual who is well adapted to life with others.

However, what happens when caretakers manifest frightened, hostile, or helpless behavior toward their children? When such behavior is a pattern, a particular attachment style develops in infants (i.e., disorganized/disoriented attachment or D-attachment; Howell, 2005; Liotti, 1992, 1995, 1999a, 1999b; Lyons-Ruth, Yellin, Melnick, & Atwood, 2003, 2005; Main & Morgan, 1996; Schuengel, Bakermans-Kranenburg, & Van IJzendoorn, 1999). D-attachment describes the unusual approach–avoidance response patterns of an infant toward a caregiver who should be the source of safety and security, but is also simultaneously the source of fear and threat. Prospective, longitudinal research has demonstrated that even apart from gross childhood abuse and neglect, a parental relational style that induces D-attachment in the child is highly predictive of dissociative symptomatology at various developmental stages, up to adolescence or young adulthood (E. A. Carlson, 1998; Lyons-Ruth, 2003; Lyons-Ruth, Yellin, Melnick, & Atwood, 2003, 2005; Ogawa et al., 1997). Although such parental behavior may not be objectively considered abusive, it overwhelms the mental efficiency of the child, hence is traumatizing.

According to Liotti (1992, 1999a), the contradictory behaviors that represent the infant's D-attachment are indicative of the existence of multiple and incompatible "internal working models" (IWMs) of self and the attachment figure, implying an integrative failure of memory, affect, cognition, and identity. Indeed, Liotti (1999a) stated that these working models become dissociated from each other because the child has "no possible organized way of construing such a situation" (p. 304). In the language of this book, these internal working models are represented by dissociative parts of the personality.

Young children's innate attachment system evokes mental and behavioral approach when they are separated from their caregiver. However, when a child approaches an attachment figure who is also neglectful, abusive, or otherwise frightening, an increasing degree of threat occurs, and evokes defensive subsystems (flight, freeze, fight, submission, and total collapse). We argue that disorganized attachment actually is not entirely disorganized. The conflict between approach and avoidance that cannot be resolved by the child promotes a structural dissociation between the various action tendencies that are evoked by insecure attachment and the defensive system mobilized against threat. In themselves, each part of the personality is quite organized with very specific but limited action tendencies restricted to defense against threat and to particular insecure attachment styles. At times, alternation between or intrusion of such conflicted parts is not voluntarily and consciously coordinated, and thus behavior appears disorganized and disoriented. Another way to say this is that attachment and defense systems are organized within individual parts of the personality, but are not cohesive across parts.

In chronic childhood traumatization, the action system of defense contained in EPs does not occur in a relational vacuum, but rather in the context of primary and necessary relationships. Thus, attachment may manifest in different insecure and even secure patterns across dissociative parts of the personality. We have observed that some ANPs may develop quite secure attachments, while other parts of the personality continue to have quite insecure styles, in line with the literature that states a single individual may have a secure attachment with one person, but an insecure style with others (Main, 1995). Although EPs seem to be predominately focused on defense, it is highly likely that most or *all* parts of the personality display underlying, if not overt, attachment patterns. EPs are then not only shaped by defense, but also by insecure attachment action tendencies that are compatible with defense; for example, attachment cry and desperate (insecure) seeking of attachment; fight and resistant attachment that involves chronic anger and distress at separation (Hesse, 1999); or flight and avoidant attachment that involves little to no contact with others (Hesse, 1999). The attachment action tendencies of EPs related to interpersonal trauma may well distinguish them from EPs formed outside the context of relationship; for example, due to a natural disaster. Whereas the former display insecure attachment tendencies along with defensive strategies, the latter may be entirely focused on defense.

Careful observation of the sequences and repetitions of alternations of dissociative parts and of the particular behaviors related to specific attachment styles may reveal an underlying organization of variable attachment patterns that are often also correlated to defense action tendencies. For example, a fight EP that is resistant to attachment may consistently follow an EP that is needy and searching desperately for attachment, in order to protect it, or a flight EP may avoid attachment when ANP, who is more securely attached, attempts to deepen a relationship.

Inadequate Mental and Behavioral
Skills Repertoire

Individuals who grow up with chronic abuse and neglect often have profound deficiencies in the ability to regulate affect, physiology, sense of self, and other aspects of functioning that require regular modulation, coordination, and cohesiveness (Siegel, 1999; Solomon & Siegel, 2003; Van der Kolk, McFarlane, & Van der Hart, 1996; Van der Kolk, Pelcovitz, Roth, Mandel, McFarlane, & Herman, 1996). They lack skills such as mindful awareness; interpersonal relatedness; affect regulation; distress tolerance;

ability to tell the difference between internal and external reality; tolerance of aloneness; ability to self-soothe; regulation of self-hatred and
other self-conscious or social emotions (e.g., shame, guilt, embarrassment, and humiliation); the capacity to reflect rather than merely react;
and the ability to mentalize, imagine how others might think or feel, and
that such thoughts and feelings may be different from one's own (Fonagy
& Target, 1997; Gold, 2000; Linehan, 1993; McCann & Pearlman, 1990;
Van der Kolk, Pelcovitz et al., 1996). In addition, survivors have difficulties with physiological dysregulation, with basic problems of hypo- and
hyperarousal (Ogden & Minton, 2000; Ogden, Minton, & Pain, 2006; B. D.
Perry, 1999; Van der Kolk, 1994).

Secure attachment in early life is the foundation for self-regulation
skills (Cassidy, 1994; Fosha, 2001; Schore, 2002; Siegel, 1999). It appears
that primary caregivers provide regulatory functions for the infant's immature neural system (Polan & Hofer, 1999). Loss of attachment (proximity) to mother (Bowlby, 1969/1982), and the loss of (physiological) regulatory functions provided by the caregiver for various developing neural
systems in the infant, both elicit a separation response that is mediated
by panic (Polan & Hofer, 1999). When panic is regularly evoked, it is a
disorganizing factor in the developing personality of the young child.
Chronic absence of external regulation, coupled with the experience of
overwhelming events and the fear evoked by threat, leaves the child vulnerable to vehement emotions without needed help to regulate and
process them (Van der Kolk, 2003).

SUMMARY

Tertiary dissociation is the most complex level of structural dissociation,
and is typical for many cases of DID. Although the DSM-IV states that "dissociative identities" are rather elaborate and autonomous, even the most
complex cases of DID include some rather restricted EPs that are similar
to the usually more rudimentary EPs in primary and secondary structural
dissociation. Each ANP is restricted to the functions and needs of its particular action system(s) in tertiary structural dissociation, so that continuity and cohesion are difficult to achieve in daily life. In chronically traumatized young children whose personality has never integrated, ANPs
may be the manifestation of dissociated action systems of daily life. DID
patients may continue to develop additional ANPs because daily life may
be overwhelming due to a difficult environment, internal chaos from conflicts among dissociative parts of the personality, chronic reactivation of
traumatic memories, and low mental level. The more complex structural
dissociation is, the more likely that one or several parts of the personality
will emancipate and act autonomously.

CHAPTER 5

Trauma-Related Symptoms in Light of Structural Dissociation

The evidence of fragmentation may seem strongest in the case of those minor dissociations that result in such disabilities as an anaesthesia of a limb. But, when we obtain evidence of a secondary consciousness in such cases, we seem to encounter, not a mere aggregate of sensations but a thinking purposive agent, a self. . . .
—William McDougall (1926, p. 543)

MOST TRAUMA SURVIVORS have a plethora of symptoms. Even patients with "simple" PTSD often have symptoms that extend far beyond the well-known PTSD triad of numbing/avoidance, reexperiencing, and hyperarousal (Kessler et al., 1995). Some prominent authors in the trauma field have proposed that the multitude of symptoms in trauma patients do not comprise comorbid diagnoses, but rather reflect a wide range of complex somatic, cognitive, affective, and behavioral effects of psychological trauma (e.g., Van der Kolk, McFarlane, & Van der Hart, 1996; Van der Kolk, Pelcovitz et al., 1996; Van der Kolk, Roth, Pelcovitz, Sunday & Spinazzola, 2005). There is more likely a dimension of trauma-related disorders that involves ever more complex and elaborate symptomatology (Bremner, Vermetten, Southwick, Krystal & Charney, 1998; Moreau & Zisook, 2002).

There has been little in the way of theory development to explain the common threads of diverse trauma-related symptoms. The lack of theoretical clarity regarding the effects of traumatization makes a coherent diagnostic taxonomy difficult to achieve.

CONFUSION ABOUT DISSOCIATIVE
SYMPTOMS

Currently in the trauma field dissociation is viewed as merely one of many symptoms, rather than as an underlying organization of symptom complexes. Thus, many clinicians dismiss dissociation as "mild" in some patients, and may fail to understand that other symptoms, such as more complex behaviors that include recurrent substance use, affect dysregulation, or chronic difficulties in relationships may well have an underlying dissociative nature. After all, one of the hallmarks of dissociation is that some symptoms are not immediately obvious and may even be intentionally hidden or dissimulated by a frightened or ashamed individual (Kluft, 1987b, 1996b; Loewenstein, 1991; Steinberg, 1995).

There is confusion in the literature about which symptoms are dissociative, and whether the term *dissociation* has the same meaning across diagnostic categories (Van der Hart, Nijenhuis, Steele, & Brown, 2004). This confusion is due to three problems: (1) the addition of symptoms of alterations of consciousness to the concept of dissociation; (2) the relegation of structural dissociation of the personality solely to the diagnostic category of dissociative identity disorder (DID); and (3) the difficulty in determining whether a symptom is indicative of structural dissociation or not. First, symptoms of alterations in level and field of consciousness were only recently added to the concept of dissociation, which was originally and strictly meant as a division of the personality. For example, alterations of consciousness such as "spacing out" and absorption are described as dissociative, although they occur nearly universally, are perfectly normal when transient and mild, and often do not involve structural dissociation of the personality (Steele, Dorahy, Van der Hart, & Nijenhuis, in press). This confusion opens the door to lack of consensus as to which symptoms and disorders belong to the domain of trauma-related dissociation and which do not (cf., Brunet et al., 2001; Cardeña, 1994; R. D. Marshall, Spitzer, & Liebowitz, 1999).

The second problem is the arbitrary relegation of dissociation as a division of the personality only to some dissociative disorders, in particular DID. Dissociation found in other disorders, such as PTSD or borderline personality disorder, seems to mean something entirely different in the literature from that described in DID. Already the normal–pathological dissociative continuum has been challenged (e.g., Waller, Putnam, & Carlson, 1996), but it remains for the field to agree that all dissociative symptoms are manifestations of some degree of structural division of the personality.

The third problem is that it can be difficult to assess whether or not a phenomenon is a manifestation of structural dissociation, that is, a dissociative symptom, or whether it is something else. For example, abnormal levels of forgetfulness may be a manifestation of dementia, a brain tumor, exhaustion, intoxication, or structural dissociation. Similarly, a different sense of self may be due to major depression, exhaustion, intoxication, or structural dissociation. The proof that symptoms are manifestations of structural dissociation lies in demonstrating that one part of the personality recalls a memory or has experiences that another part does not.

DISSOCIATIVE SYMPTOMS

Symptoms of dissociation proper have been inconsistently charted in the current literature. Many modern discussions of dissociative symptoms, in particular in the PTSD literature, only refer to *negative dissociative symptoms*, those related to loss of mental actions such as perceptions, affects, memories, and loss of mental functions such as the ability to focus on the present or the ability to control one's behavior. Their counterpart, *positive dissociative symptoms,* such as intrusions of traumatic memory and voices, are rarely mentioned, with a few exceptions related to DID patients. Negative dissociative symptoms denote mental and physical phenomena that are *not* available to one or more parts of the personality, but are available to others. These symptoms thus are not *absolute* losses, because a complete loss, such as complete forgetting, would occur across the entire personality, not just in certain parts of the personality. Rather, in the case of dissociative amnesia, one part does not have access to a particular memory, while another part does.

Positive and negative dissociative symptoms have been clearly recognized throughout the history of psychiatry and psychology (Janet, 1901/ 1977, 1907, 1909b; Myers, 1916a, 1916b, 1940), up until the past few decades when they became less acknowledged and even forgotten (Nijenhuis & Van der Hart, 1999b; Van der Hart & Friedman, 1989; Van der Hart et al., 2000). Janet (1901/1977) observed that *negative* symptoms are more persistent and permanent over time. In our language, this observation is from the perspective of the apparently normal part of the personality (ANP), which has executive control most of the time.

Positive symptoms tend to come and go with intrusion of the emotional part of the personality (EP) into ANP. However, in more complex cases of dissociation, EPs may also intrude into each other, and one ANP may also intrude into another ANP in cases of DID. One dissociative part, say an EP, can gain full executive control from another, say an ANP. This constitutes an extreme level of positive symptoms. Thus, positive symptoms can be generally described as mental and physical or behavioral phenomena that intrude or interrupt one or more parts of the personality, and that represent features of one or more other parts of the personality. Positive symptoms might include memories available to these parts, their "voices," intentions, perceptions, emotions, cognitions or behaviors.

Some authors recognize the dissociative nature of intrusions and inter-ruptions of executive control (e.g., Butler, Duran, Jasiukaitis, Koopman, & Spiegel, 1996; Nijenhuis & Van der Hart, 1999a; K. S. Pope & Brown, 1996; Spiegel, 1993; Van der Hart et al., 2000; Van der Kolk & Van der Hart, 1991). The DSM-IV also notes that reexperiencing trauma can occur in a "dissocia-tive state" (APA, 1994, p. 424), and mentions "dissociative flashback episodes" among the diagnostic criteria of PTSD (p. 428). However, many authors do not seem to acknowledge positive dissociative symptoms, such as intrusions of traumatic memories (e.g., Harvey & Bryant, 1999a; R. N. Marshall, Spitzer, & Liebowitz, 1999; B. D. Perry, 1994, 1999; Schore, 2002).

While symptoms of structural dissociation may be understood as positive or negative, they also may be understood as symptoms that manifest mentally (i.e., *psychoform dissociative symptoms*), and in phenomena that manifest in the body (i.e., *somatoform dissociative symptoms*; Nijenhuis, 2004; Nijen-huis, Spinhoven, Van Dyck, Van der Hart, & Vanderlinden, 1996). Psychoform and somatoform dissociation are highly correlated phenomena (Dell, 2002; El-Hage, Darves-Bornoz, Allilaire, & Gaillard, 2002; Nijenhuis et al., 1996; Ni-jenhuis, Van Dyck et al., 1999; Nijenhuis, Van der Hart, Kruger & Steele, 2004; Şar, Kundakci, Kiziltan, Bakim, & Bozkurt, 2000; Waller, Ohanian, Meyer, Emerill, & Rouse, 2001). Both psychoform and somatoform dissociative symptoms are manifestations of structural dissociation because one part of the personality may experience the symptoms, while other parts do not.

In short, dissociative symptoms have not been accurately described in the current literature. A more consistent and comprehensive understand-ing of dissociation can occur when both positive and negative symptoms are taken into consideration; that is, symptoms of intrusion and symp-toms involving losses.

Negative Psychoform Dissociative Symptoms

The category of negative psychoform dissociative symptoms includes loss of memory (amnesia); loss of affect (numbing); loss of critical function and difficulty thinking things through; loss of needs, wishes, and fantasies; and loss of previously existing mental skills. The PTSD condition of de-tachment, numbing, and avoidance often pertains to negative dissociative symptoms. This condition also appears in other trauma-related disorders and constitutes symptoms in ANP. Negative dissociative symptoms can also be dominant in certain EPs that are fixed in freeze or total submis-sion. These parts can experience emotional (and sensory) anesthesia, loss of critical thinking, loss of skills, and loss of motor function (a somato-form dissociative symptom discussed below).

Dissociative amnesia. In order for amnesia to be considered disso-ciative, there must be some indication of structural dissociation: Information must be available to one part, but not to another part of the personality. Some evidence suggests that dissociative amnesia is particularly characteristic of survivors of chronic childhood abuse and neglect, and perhaps even more so in patients who were abused by close relatives and caretakers (Freyd, 1996). It is a major symptom of children and adults with DID (Boon & Draijer, 1993; Dell, 2002; Hornstein & Putnam, 1992; Steinberg, Cicchetti, Buchanan, Rakfeldt, & Rounsaville, 1994), but also may characterize patients with DDNOS (Boon & Draijer, 1993; Coons, 1992), complex PTSD (Pelcovitz et al., 1997), and "simple" PTSD (Bremner, Steinberg et al., 1993). Some individuals develop instant dissociative amnesia after their traumatic experiences (Van der Hart & Nijenhuis, 2001): in some it occurs after a delay, and in still others the symptom may wax and wane, perhaps due to alternations among amnesic and non-amnesic parts of the personality.

Dissociative amnesia occurs in varying degrees. For example, individuals may be unable to recall certain parts of a memory, or may know what happened, but not recall the episode with a sense of personal ownership ("It happened, but not to *me*"). Dissociative amnesia is a disorder in its own right (APA, 1994; Loewenstein, 1996; Van der Hart & Nijenhuis, 2001). The DSM-IV (APA, 1994) classifies types of dissociative amnesia based on the works of Janet (1901/1977). These categories include localized, selective, generalized, continuous, and systematized amnesia.

In *localized amnesia* the individual fails to recall events that occurred during a circumscribed period of time, usually the first few hours following a profoundly disturbing event (APA, 1994). After Sandy was raped when she was 19, she could not remember how she got away from her perpetrator, or how she got home, though she remembered most of the rape itself. Localized amnesias may pertain to events of short duration (e.g., one traumatizing event).

In *selective amnesia*, the individual call recall some but not all of the events during a circumscribed period of time (APA, 1994). It is not uncommon for a survivor to remember large portions of traumatizing events, but be unable to recall a pathogenic kernel, or "hot spot" (Brewin, 2003). Tina recalled that her uncle had often molested her, but it was only late in therapy when she remembered that he had killed her pet to threaten her not to tell.

Systematized amnesia is loss of memory for certain categories of information, such as all memories relating to one's family or to a particular person (APA, 1994). In *generalized amnesia*, the failure of recall encompasses the person's entire life (APA, 1994; Van der Hart & Nijenhuis, 2001). This is the "John Doe" version of amnesia where individuals have no idea who they are, where they are from, or any other generalities of their lives. This type is rare. Finally, the DSM-IV defines *continuous amnesia* as the inability to recall all events subsequent to a specific time up to and including the present. This is an extremely rare form of dissociative amnesia that may be related to events that have overwhelmed the individual (Janet, 1893/1898e, 1901/1977).

Patients with dissociative amnesia may be unaware of their amnesia, so-called "amnesia for amnesia" (Culpin, 1931; Janet, 1901/1977; Kluft, 1988; Loewenstein, 1991). It is only on close and careful questioning or full recovery from their disorder (Nijenhuis, Matthess, & Ehling, 2004) that they begin to realize how much of their memory is missing. Many of our patients have realized the serious degree of their amnesia only in retrospect.

Loss of critical function. Critical thinking requires recognition of details and nuances, and this ability is often impaired in trauma survivors. They tend to have more global responses and thoughts than nonabused individuals (e.g., Wenninger & Ehlers, 1998). These inclinations may be found in one or more dissociative parts of the personality. Some dissociative parts have difficulty thinking rationally, logically, and clearly. Others may have excellent critical faculties in relation to certain issues such as work, but cannot apply the same logic and rationality in their approach to other parts of their personality, or to a particular behavior such as self-injury. Critical faculties can be available to certain parts of the personality, such as a wise, objective part (Krakauer, 2001), but far less so to other parts.

Loss of mental skills. Cognitive impairments in traumatized children (Moradi et al., 1999) and traumatized adults (Jenkins, Langlais, Delis, & Cohen, 2000; Vasterling, Brailey, Constans, & Sutker, 1998) have been reported, and include problems with memory, concentration, attention, planning, and judgment. Frank cognitive impairments can occur in up to a third of chronically traumatized individuals (e.g., Golier et al., 2002). Whereas these losses may sometimes relate to impaired brain functioning in trauma-related disorders, they generally are independent of intellectual functioning (Buckley, Blanchard, & Neill, 2000; Vasterling et al., 2002).

The marked fluctuations in knowledge and skills displayed by many traumatized children (Putnam, 1997) and adults (Boon & Draijer, 1993; Steinberg et al., 1994), and their difficulty in learning from experience (Putnam, Helmers, & Trickett, 1993), often relate to alternations among dissociative parts. For example, many ANPs but not EPs have a degree of depersonalization. This symptom is associated with attentional problems (Guralnik, Schmeidler, & Simeon, 2000).

Loss of affect. Affect dysregulation is a common difficulty in mental health populations, particularly in traumatized individuals (Ford, Courtois, Steele, Van der Hart, & Nijenhuis 2005; Van der Kolk, 1996; Van der Kolk, Van der Hart, & Marmar, 1996). Affect dysregulation may occur because of switching among parts of the personality that experience diverse affects that are not integrated with each other, and that thus remain un-modulated (Van der Hart, Nijenhuis, & Steele, 2005). The diminution of affect in traumatized individuals is prominent, and can often be traced to structural dissociation. There is a degree of emotional numbing in the present, so that patients as ANP complain of feeling two dimensional, or like zombies, one-dimensional cardboard figures, or robots. There also may be a marked absence of emotion regarding the traumatic experience (e.g., in total submission).

Dissociation between observing EP with loss of affect and an experiencing EP has been described as one form of depersonalization, which is very common in individuals with different types of traumatization (e.g., Cardeña & Spiegel, 1993; Carrion & Steiner, 2000; Darves-Bornoz, Degiovanni, & Gaillard, 1999: Harvey & Bryant, 1998) and with major trauma-related disorders (Boon & Draijer, 1993; Bremner, Steinberg et al., 1993; Dell, 2002; Harvey & Bryant, 1998; Steinberg et al., 1994).

Loss of needs, wishes, and fantasies. In their numb and detached condition, survivors as ANP often have dissociated not only painful emotions, but also painful needs, such as for attachment, or wishes, such as the yearning for good parents. Many traumatized individuals experience tremendous ambivalence regarding attachment and dependency. These needs are often kept by childlike EPs, enabling survivors as ANP to believe that they have no desire to be dependent (Steele, Van der Hart, & Nijenhuis, 2001).

Negative Somatoform Dissociative Symptoms

Original 19th- and early 20th-century clinical sources strongly suggest that structural dissociation also manifests in physical symptoms and functions (e.g., Janet, 1889, 1901, 1909b; McDougall, 1926; Myers, 1940; Nijenhuis & Van der Hart, 1999b; Van der Hart et al., 2000). Modern empirical evidence supports this (El-Hage et al., 2002; Nijenhuis, Spinhoven et al., 1996; Nijenhuis, Quak et al., 1999; Şar, Tutkun et al., 2000; Waller et al., 2001). Some somatoform dissociative symptoms can be found in the ICD-10 diagnostic category of dissociative disorders of movement and sensation (WHO, 1992). However, the ICD-10 emphasizes negative somatoform dissociative symptoms, and ignores positive dissociative symptoms such as dissociative pain and tics (Nijenhuis et al., 1996; Van der Hart et al., 2000).

Negative somatoform dissociative symptoms occur in survivors as ANP, but also may be seen in EPs fixated in freeze or total submission. They include symptoms of loss of motor functions, including motor skills, and sensations that should normally be present or available.

Loss of motor function. Temporary or more permanent loss of motor control includes partial or total paralysis of limbs or the entire body, contractures, physical lack of coordination, cataplexy (i.e., a sudden and general loss of muscle tension), and loss of hearing, smell, taste, vision, or speech. These symptoms are often dissociative in nature and can be trauma related. For example, dissociative contractures were frequently observed in traumatized World War I combat soldiers (cf., Van der Hart et al., 2000), and may also be seen in survivors of chronic child maltreatment.

> Mary (ANP), a 24-year-old woman with DID, was highly suicidal and self-harming. She had a severe contracture of the right hand that emerged when she injured her right wrist in a car accident at age 17. The therapist wondered if there existed "a part of her mind" (i.e., dissociative part) that for some reason felt the need to keep the hand in this position. As ANP, Mary thought this might be a possibility. The therapist invited the presumed dissociative part of the personality to come forward. A sad and depressed looking part (EP) appeared that had wanted to kill herself. Unbearably lonely, this EP had thrown herself in front of a car. It kept the hand in that painful position because then there was a part of herself already dead, and because the distracting physical pain was more bearable than the loneliness.

Loss of motor function and sensation also occurs in survivors as EP that are fixated in freeze or in total submission. With regard to freezing, patients report being unable to move while still feeling extremely fearful and hypervigilant. This freeze condition should be distinguished from total submission, in which patients find themselves in a condition of extreme "shut-down," disengaged from the environment, feeling nothing emotionally or physically, and lacking any drive to move or think. In this condition survivors' muscles become flaccid and sometimes they temporarily may remain in fixed positions. The somatoform dissociative symptom cluster that includes bodily anesthesia, analgesia, and motor inhibitions predicted the presence of complex dissociative disorders extremely well, better than any other somatoform dissociative symptom cluster (Nijenhuis, Spinhoven, Vanderlinden, Van Dyck, & Van der Hart, 1998).

Loss of skills. Loss of skills not only involves the absence of certain mental actions, but also of behavioral actions. When EP has complete executive control, the daily life skills of ANP are often missing. Thus, survivors as EP commonly report that they have no idea how to cook, take care of children, or perform work duties, and generally feel inadequate and overwhelmed with the tasks of daily life because they do not have access to needed skills for periods of time.

Loss of sensation. The loss or diminution of sensation is a common occurrence in traumatized individuals. Varying degrees of anesthesia may occur—more or less profound loss of bodily feelings including the sense of touch, pressure, temperature, pain (analgesia), movement, arousal, including sexual arousal, and other physical signals such as hunger or fatigue. These losses may induce certain symptoms of depersonalization, such as experiencing (parts of) the body as a foreign object. Other manifestations of the loss of sensation include partial or complete loss of hearing, vision (e.g., tunnel vision), taste, and smell.

Positive Psychoform Dissociative Symptoms

Whereas negative dissociative symptoms involve experiencing and knowing "too little," positive psychoform dissociative symptoms are manifestations of experiencing and knowing "too much" (Janet, 1904/1983b, 1911/1983c). Positive symptoms include the intrusion symptoms of PTSD and other trauma-related disorders. They typically represent intrusions of EP into ANP, as well as full alternations among ANP and EP. For example, when survivors as EP are fixated in a particular traumatic memory, this part may intrude into ANP. Survivors as ANP then may experience the same memories and emotions as the EP, but without clear understanding of what they are. At all levels of structural dissociation, ANP and EP can intrude into each other's domain.

Schneiderian symptoms. Mental intrusions of one dissociative part into another part are often interpreted by clinicians as evidence of many of the 11 Schneiderian first rank symptoms of schizophrenia (Boon & Draijer, 1993; Ellason & Ross, 1995; Kluft, 1987a; Loewenstein, 1991a; Ross & Joshi, 1992; Ross et al., 1990). They include hallucinations, such as voices arguing or commenting, and images of traumatic experiences; thought insertion and thought withdrawal; and delusional thinking. Other Schneiderian symptoms are better categorized as positive somatoform dissociative symptoms, as described below. Schneiderian symptoms are usually experienced as ego dystonic, and as emanating from inside, rather than outside. Dissociative voices can generally carry on a conversation with the therapist and with other parts of the patient, while the voices of schizophrenia have a rather fixed and repetitious pattern, and cannot be engaged relationally.

In relatively simple cases of structural dissociation, voices may only be limited to something that occurred during the traumatizing event (e.g., the sound of a baby crying, or the voice of a child saying, "Please don't hurt me anymore," or the voice of a perpetrator saying, "If you tell, I'll kill you"). As the complexity of structural dissociation increases and as various parts of the personality develop more relationships among themselves, the quality of "voices" may change to include topics in the present. For example, an EP may have a running commentary on the actions of ANP: "Why can't you ever do anything right?" Or various EPs may talk with each other, resulting in a sense of chaotic background "chatter" for the ANP that can be quite distracting. Or certain parts may interfere with work by saying things like, "This is boring!" And some ANPs may be helpful: "Come on, you can do it!"

A common experience of dissociative patients is the sense that thoughts have been "put in" or "pulled out" of their mind (thought insertion and withdrawal). Generally, this is the experience of the part of the personality in executive control at the time (e.g., ANP), while the insertion or withdrawal is controlled by another part. Sophie said, "Thoughts plop into my head like somebody just laid an egg; I don't know what I'm supposed to do with them. I just get left to deal with whatever is put there, and they aren't even my thoughts!"

Delusional thinking may occur in dissociative individuals, but more often the actual difficulty is other types of disturbed cognitions related to dissociation.

Cognitive appraisals. Dissociative parts may have quite different worldviews, sense of self, and systems of beliefs. Thus, there may be confusing alterations between very discrepant cognitive appaisals and perceptions of people and situations, and self.

Fantasies and daydreams. Fantasy *proneness* involves a lack of critical function, which could be considered a negative dissociative symptom when it pertains to one or some dissociative parts but not to others. The presence of fantasy may sometimes constitute a positive symptom. For example, an ANP may fantasize a happy childhood, even though the contrary was true.

Alterations in relations with others. Dissociative symptoms may appear in survivors in the context of interpersonal relationships. For example, as ANP a survivor may feel connected with and think highly of a close individual, and treat that person well. However, an EP may feel very threatened by closeness with the same person and treat him or her with suspicion and hostility. When such ANPs and EPs intrude into or alternate with each other, traumatized individuals may exhibit a disorganized attachment style (Liotti, 1999a; Main & Morgan, 1996).

Alterations in affect. Mood swings and affect dysregulation are common in complex PTSD (Chu, 1998a; Ford et al., 2005; Schore, 2003b; Van der Kolk, Pelcovitz et al., 1996) and dissociative disorders (cf., Cardeña & Spiegel, 1996; Chu, 1998a). These alterations may relate to structural dissociation. For example, affect that is generally not present in the survivor as ANP may suddenly and unexpectedly intrude into daily life from an EP in which the vehement emotions related to traumatization are reexperienced (Chefetz, 2000). Discrete alternations of affect (as well as accompanying thoughts, sensations, and behavior) may accompany switches among various dissociative parts of the personality because they may each encompass different affects and impulses. In addition, alternations of affect may also occur within one part (or more parts) of the personality when this part has a limited window of psychophysiological stress tolerance (Nijenhuis et al., 2002).

Positive Somatoform Dissociative Symptoms

Positive somatoform dissociative symptoms involve specific sensations, other perceptions, and motor or behavioral actions of various dissociative parts of the personality that do not occur in other parts (Janet, 1907, 1909b; Butler, Mueser, Spock, & Braff, 1996; Nijenhuis & Van der Hart, 1999b; Van der Hart et al., 2000). These include pain; intentional behavior; repetitive, uncontrollable movements such as tics, tremors, and palsy; and sensory perceptions (vision, touch, hearing, taste, and smell) that may or may not be distorted. Revictimization is a positive dissociative symptom when dissociative parts of the personality fixated in total submission are reactivated and take full control of consciousness and behavior.

Schneiderian symptoms. Positive somatoform dissociative symptoms include Schneiderian first rank symptoms of somatic passivity, such as the sense that the body is being controlled by someone else, and that impulses and actions intrude on one dissociative part of the personality from other parts. Intrusions of traumatic memories generally have a sensory component. For example, individuals may have the sensation of a hand around their neck, or of their hands tied, or of someone sneaking up behind them. Some visual disturbances involve an aspect of reexperiencing, such as seeing the perpetrator's face superimposed on the therapist's face, and seeing specific images of traumatic experiences. Other perceptual alterations may also be positive somatoform dissociative symptoms, including sensory hallucinations related to traumatic experiences (the smell of alcohol or semen).

THE INTERPLAY BETWEEN VARIOUS DISSOCIATIVE SYMPTOMS

While we have distinguished negative and positive, and somatoform and psychoform symptoms for purposes of clarity, in practice many symptoms involve all of these forms of dissociation. Positive and negative symptoms may alternate with each other, or may simultaneously coexist. Thus, alterations in affect may involve positive symptoms in one part of the personality (presence of a strong affect), while another part exhibits negative symptoms (loss of this affect). And since affect is related to behavior, dissociated affect may well involve somatoform dissociative symptoms. For instance, a dissociative part of the personality who is rageful may hit the wall (positive somatoform symptom). Another dissociative part does not feel the rage (negative psychoform symptom) and says, "I did not hit the wall, and my arm feels numb" (negative somatoform symptom).

The enduring nature of negative symptoms is commonly related to the more usual executive control of the survivor as ANP, which has only sporadic intrusions of EP. However, positive symptoms may sometimes become more persistent in daily life. When this happens, ANPs become less functional, and EPs become intrusive more frequently. Also, during the course of therapy, as more safety in the present is experienced by all parts of the personality, there may be increased intrusions as more EPs begin to engage with the therapist.

Table 5.1 presents an overview of various dissociative symptoms, including negative and positive, psychoform and somatoform dissociative symptoms.

ALTERATIONS OF CONSCIOUSNESS

With the rediscovery of dissociation in the 1970s and 1980s (e.g., Hilgard, 1977), additional symptoms have been added to the domain of dissociative symptoms. These symptoms particularly include those of attentional phenomena that were seen in hypnosis, such as absorption, daydreaming, imaginative involvement, altered time sense, trancelike behavior, and so-called highway hypnosis (e.g., Bernstein & Putnam, 1986; Hilgard, 1977; Ray & Faith, 1995; Ross, 1996; Putnam, 1997). Alterations in consciousness include a wide range of experiences and symptoms that are ubiquitous among normal and clinical populations (e.g., E. B. Carlson, 1994; Coons, 1996), unlike structural dissociation, which is unique to traumatized individuals.

Some degrees of alterations in consciousness are necessary for adaptive functioning. Normal alterations happen every day in every person. All action systems require an adaptive retraction of the field of consciousness, or narrowing of attention, to focus on specific action tendencies, such as work or caretaking. Some systems, such as energy regulation, require a lowering of the level of consciousness, so that an individual may rest and sleep.

We return to Janet's (1907) definition of *hysteria*, the old term for generic dissociative disorders, to better clarify the difference between structural dissociation and alterations in consciousness. He defined hysteria as "a form of *mental depression* characterized by the *retraction of the field of personal consciousness* and a tendency to the *dissociation and emancipation of the systems of ideas and functions* that constitute personality" (p. 332; italics added). (By "mental depression," Janet did

TABLE 5.1
A Phenomenological Categorization of Dissociative Symptoms
(Adapted from Nijenhuis, 2004; Van der Hart et al., 2000)

	Psychoform dissociative symptoms	Somatoform dissociative symptoms
Negative dissociative symptoms	Loss of memory: Dissociative amnesia Depersonalization involving a division between experiencing and observing part of the personality Loss of affect: emotional anesthesia Loss of character traits	Loss of sensations: Anesthesia (all sensory modalities) Loss of pain sensivity: Analgesia Loss of motor actions, i.e., loss of the ability to move (e.g., catalepsy), speak, swallow, etc.
Positive dissociative symptoms	Psychoform intrusion symptoms (Schneiderian symptoms), e.g., hearing voices, "made" emotions, thoughts, and ideas	Somatoform intrusion symptoms, e.g., "made" sensations and body movements (e.g., tics) Pseudoseizures
	Psychoform aspects of re-experiencing traumatizing events, e.g., particular visual and auditory perceptions, affects, and ideas	Somatoform aspects of re-experiencing traumatizing events, e.g., particular trauma-related sensations and body movements
	Psychoform aspects of alternations between dissociative parts of the personality	Somatoform aspects of alternations between dissociative parts of the personality
	Psychoform aspects of dissociative psychosis, i.e., a disorder involving a relatively long-term activation of a psychotic dissociative part	Somatoform aspects of dissociative psychosis

not mean emotional depression, but rather a lowering of mental efficiency.) Clearly, Janet distinguished between dissociation and alterations
(retraction) in consciousness, but also noted that they both occur in traumatized individuals.

The Field of Consciousness

The *quantity* of stimuli that are held in conscious awareness at a given
time is referred to as the field of consciousness. This field can range from
very wide to extremely narrow (retracted), so that an individual can be
aware of a lot in a given moment, or very little. Not all perceived information will be available for recall, because it is impossible and quite maladaptive to remember every perceived stimulus (Luria, 1968). Yet, sometimes we are able to "take in" more than others, depending on the width
of our field of consciousness. Sometimes this is a voluntary process, in
the form of intentional concentration, guided imagery, and meditation.
Other times it is not, taking the form of inability to concentrate and focus
when tired or stressed; excessive fantasy life; staring at the wall for hours,
unaware of the passage of time.

Retraction of the field of consciousness, or narrowing of attention, is
characteristic of both ANP and EP. However, even though retraction and
other alterations in consciousness may accompany structural dissociation
and integrative failure, they can also occur apart from structural dissociation. The point is that the underlying mental actions are fundamentally
different from structural dissociation. In structural dissociation, dissociative parts recall at least some experiences and facts, creating episodic and
semantic memories that may or may not be accessible to other dissociative parts. Alterations in consciousness generally involve a *failure* to create such episodic and semantic memories in *any* part of the personality
(Holmes et al., 2005; Janet, 1907; Myers, 1940; Steele et al., in press; Van
der Hart et al., 2000).

The Level of Consciousness

Alterations of the *level* of consciousness range from very high to very low
levels. A high level may pertain to hyperalertness, such as when an individual (or part of the personality) is intensely searching for threat cues.
Lowering of the level of consciousness denotes impaired *quality of mental and behavioral action*, a failure to adequately perceive and remember experiences and facts of importance no matter how wide or narrow
the field of consciousness. Lowering of consciousness can manifest in
common phenomena such as concentration problems due to fatigue, anxiety, or illness, as well as symptoms of depersonalization, such as feeling

unreal, spacey, foggy, detached or strange, derealization, and time distortion (J. G. Allen, Console, & Lewis, 1999; Van der Hart & Steele, 1997). Serious forms progressing to stupor and coma may occur with some neurological diseases and injuries, and also sometimes in conjunction with other serious physical disorders (e.g., hepatic failure). Organic causes should always be ruled out when significant lowering of the level of consciousness is persistent.

The field and level of consciousness work in tandem at all times. Focused attention involves a combination of voluntary retraction with a high level of consciousness. Mindfulness can involve a wide or narrow field and a high level. Low levels of consciousness along with a wide or narrow field of consciousness result in conditions of spaciness or drowsiness, trance or unresponsiveness.

Normal versus Pathological Alterations in Consciousness

Alterations in consciousness have typically been described in the literature as "normal dissociation," "nonpathological dissociation," "mild dissociation," or "minor dissociation" (Bernstein & Putnam, 1986; E. B. Carlson, 1994; Prince, 1927; Putnam, 1991). However, these alterations do not need to involve structural dissociation, thus belong to a different category. Both high and low levels of consciousness can be quite pathological when they are excessive, frequent, rigid, and inflexible. For example, during threat, a high level of conscious awareness and retraction of the field of consciousness to threat cues are adaptive. But these types are maladaptive when exclusive focus on perceived danger occurs in everyday life when no threat exists, as in survivors who are constantly hypervigilant and suspicious. On the other hand, if a person is not able to achieve a high level and field of consciousness during threat, such as in a state of total submission, then potential ways out of the situation may not be noticed. At work, it is desirable to have a generally high level of consciousness and relative retracted field of consciousness focused on the task at hand.

Some people need to "stare at the wall" for a few minutes before they can get going in the morning. It is part of a normal transition to have a rather low level of consciousness and retracted field of consciousness just before and after sleep. But if "staring at the wall" goes on for hours, or recurs for long periods during the day, or cannot be voluntarily interrupted, it is pathological. Daydreaming is healthy and normal to a degree, but not if an individual is lost in a world of rich fantasy for hours at a time, instead of dealing with daily life (Somer, 2002). Normal attention waxes and wanes over the day; periods of high alertness may be punctuated by periods of drowsiness or fatigue. It is adaptive to intentionally enter trance states for healthy relaxation, whereas spaciness is generally maladaptive, though it often occurs when one is tired, sick, or stressed, and is so common that it is the subject of much humor. But a more serious lowering of consciousness in the sense of being in a kind of trance or "in another world" is a common experience in adult survivors of childhood abuse and neglect.

The failure of people to recall experiences and facts in any part of their personality under conditions of abuse and neglect has been described as "dissociation of context" (L. D. Butler, Duran, et al., 1996) or "dissociative detachment" (J. G. Allen, Console, & Lewis, 1999; Holmes et al., 2005). This so-called dissociation is attributed to an individual being too overwhelmed, preoccupied, or spacey to perceive and recall. Yet, as noted above, structural dissociation does not need to exist for failures of memory to occur. This failure can sometimes be adaptive, in that it helps an individual cope with stress or traumatic experience in the moment.

> Mary, a woman with a history of child abuse and neglect, had very large gaps in memory of her childhood. She had been characterized by secondary structural dissociation, but even after all parts of her personality were integrated many of these memory gaps remained. When she described her attempts to cope with the unrelenting stress of daily life as a child, it was clear that much of her childhood was simply never recorded. She noted, "People thought I was a space cadet. I kept my nose in a book. I tried not to pay attention, but just to stay focused on what was in front of me. I could never remember the details of things. Sometimes when I watched TV or read a book, I could almost feel this wall coming between me and the rest of the world. I didn't have to know about things that way."

Alterations in Consciousness in ANP and EP

Different dissociative parts can exhibit varying degrees of alterations in field and level of consciousness at a pathological level, particularly survivors as EP. While one part may be unresponsive, another part can be quite responsive and alert. While one part is only aware of a traumatic memory, another is quite alert and focused on a wide variety of activities of daily life. ANPs and EPs may have some awareness of each other, but may nevertheless assiduously avoid any reminders of each other, retracting their fields of consciousness to exclude each other (see Chapter 10).

> Etty, a patient with DID, was plagued by persecutory voices of EPs, and attempted to drown them out and ignore them by turning on the TV, radio, and CD player at the same time, and then attemped to pick out the sounds of one instrument on the CD: an example of a deliberate, extreme retraction of the field of consciousness.

Peritraumatic Alterations of Consciousness

During traumatic experiences, involuntary and severe alterations in consciousness are typically present at some point. These phenomena may be related to the development of structural dissociation in some way, but they can also occur without it. Instruments designed to measure peritraumatic dissociation (e.g., Marmar et al., 1994) include retraction and lowering of the level of consciousness as core symptoms. As detailed above, it is difficult to ascertain whether these symptoms indicate that structural dissociation has occurred.

The hyperalertness and hyperarousal during traumatic experience may exhaust the individual and manifest in a significant drop in level of consciousness in survivors during or immediately after the event. This phenomenon was frequently observed in "shell-shocked" combat veterans during World War I (e.g., Culpin, 1931; Léri, 1918; Myers, 1940). Myers, for instance, noted that immediately following the traumatizing event there is "a certain loss of consciousness. But this may vary from a very slight, momentary, almost imperceptible dizziness or 'clouding' to profound and lasting unconsciousness" (1940, p. 66).

Similar to the descriptions of traumatized World War I combat soldiers, many survivors of chronic childhood maltreatment in our clinical practices report that they experienced a severe drop of consciousness in the immediate wake of episodes of childhood abuse. They often report such experiences as hiding in a closet or other "safe place," getting into bed and pulling the covers over their head, "zoning out," being "unable to think," unable to concentrate, getting "lost in my head," "sinking into darkness," "closing off from my body," and feeling spacey.

Alterations of Consciousness and Dissociative Symptoms: Research Findings

Research findings support the idea that retraction and lowering of consciousness differ from, but often accompany dissociation. Thus, on the Dissociation Questionnaire (DIS-Q; Vanderlinden, Van Dyck, Vandereycken, & Vertommen, 1993), there tended to be a lower correlation between absorption—an alteration of consciousness—and other factors that are more directly indicative of structural dissociation, such as amnesia, identity fragmentation, and loss of control, than the correlations among these three factors. And the scores of patients with dissociative disorders on the Somatoform Dissociation Questionnaire (SDQ-20; Nijenhuis et al., 1996) also had a lower correlation with absorption on the DIS-Q than with the other three factors.

The Dissociative Experiences scale (DES; Bernstein & Putnam, 1986) includes items that address "nonpathological" and "pathological" dissoci-

ation (Waller, Putnam, & Carlson, 1996). As we have argued, "nonpathological" items such as absorption and imaginative involvement do not
stem from structural dissociation, but the "pathological" items of the DES
do represent symptoms of structural dissociation. Waller and colleagues
(1996) discovered that a subset of eight items that measure "pathological"
dissociation are better able to predict individuals who have chronic dissociation than the DES as a whole. These items, called the DES-T(axon), include those that would indicate severe dissociation, and do not include
any "nonpathological" items related to alterations in consciousness. The
DES-T not only predicts DDNOS and DID better than the DES, but also is
a better predictor of depersonalization disorder (Simeon et al., 1998).
Waller and colleagues (1996) concluded that these results support Janet's
original view "that there are two types of individuals: persons who experience chronic dissociative states and persons who do not" (p. 315). Although the DES-T assesses manifestations of structural dissociation somewhat better than the DES, DES-T scores may still be influenced by
self-reported alterations of consciousness (Levin & Sprei, 2003).

Other studies have suggested that alterations in consciousness are not
unique to traumatized individuals, but are prominent in patients with all
kinds of mental disorders. Leavitt (2001) documented that alterations of
consciousness were very prominent among patients with all kinds of mental disorders, not only trauma related. He also found that the severity of
alterations of consciousness seem to be associated with more general psychopathology, not with dissociation per se. Thus, most individuals who
experience alterations of consciousness do not have structural dissociation, but most individuals who have developed structural dissociation also
have pathological alterations of consciousness. Alterations of consciousness are thus *sensitive but not specific* indicators of structural dissociation, that is, their presence may hint at the presence of structural dissociation, but they are not a direct indication of it. And at least one study has
shown that symptoms of structural or "pathological" dissociation have
been associated with traumatization, but alterations in consciousness or
"nonpathological" symptoms have not (Irwin, 1999).

In conclusion, alterations of consciousness occur in patients with a
wide range of mental disorders. They are not necessarily manifestations
of structural dissociation, but occur along with structural dissociation.
Their persistent presence, especially in pathological forms, should alert
the clinician to the possibility of structural dissociation.

Depersonalization and Derealization

There are particular difficulties in determining whether the symptoms of
depersonalization and derealization are those of structural dissociation
or not because these labels are generally applied to a variety of phenom-

ena. We have described the existence of an observing EP and experiencing EP: This is clearly a manifestation of structural dissociation that has been called depersonalization (cf., Putnam, 1993; Steinberg, 1995). However, the current literature describes various other phenomena that are also labeled as depersonalization, but which may only involve the presence of alterations in consciousness, and thus may not denote structural dissociation. Such symptoms may include feelings of strangeness or unfamiliarity with self; a sense of unreality, such as being in a dream; and perceptual alterations or hallucinations regarding the body (Spiegel & Cardeña, 1991; Steinberg, 1995). Derealization involves a sense of unreality and unfamiliarity with one's environment, and distortions of space and time (Steinberg, 1995). Because these alterations of consciousness may occur independently of structural dissociation, they should not necessarily be categorized as dissociative without further study.

Depersonalization and derealization are ubiquitous phenomena found in many psychiatric conditions, and are reported by a substantial proportion of the general population (Aderibigbe, Bloch, & Walker, 2001). They are so prevalent that they are the third most common complaints in psychiatric patients, following anxiety and depression (Cattell & Cattell, 1974). Mild to severe forms are found in anxiety disorders, depression, schizophrenia, substance abuse disorders, borderline personality disorder, and seizure disorders, as well as dissociative disorders (Boon & Draijer, 1993; Dell, 2002; Steinberg, 1995). They may occur in normal individuals under conditions of mild stress, hypnagogic states, fatigue, illness, medication effects, and alcohol and drug intoxication. Generally, people find experiences of depersonalization and derealization unpleasant.

Obviously, depersonalization symptoms are the essence of depersonalization disorder (Guralnik et al., 2000). Depersonalization is very common in traumatized individuals with different types of traumatization (e.g., Cardeña & Spiegel, 1993; Carrion & Steiner, 2000; Darves-Bornoz et al., 1999; Harvey & Bryant, 1998), and with disorders ranging from ASD (Harvey & Bryant, 1998, 1999) and PTSD (Bremner, Steinberg et al., 1993), to complex dissociative disorders (Boon & Draijer, 1993; Dell, 2002; Steinberg et al., 1994). Many dissociative parts of the personality experience symptoms of depersonalization (Van der Hart & Steele, 1997).

Hanny had experienced depersonalization symptoms for as long as she could remember, and she thought these experiences were normal. There was no evidence that her personality was structurally dissociated. Her depersonalization disorder proved refractory to long-term psychotherapy until the existence of a "little girl" EP became evident. When the therapist invited Hanny as ANP to be very mindful of her bodily sensations, she noted that her pelvic area felt cold and very distant. The therapist suggested that Hanny could perhaps warm this body area, and connect to it more. When she did, images of a little girl popped up. This EP initially stared at Hanny with a rejecting look. Later she accused Hanny of having forgotten her and of not wanting to know about abuse and neglect. The "little girl" recalled a one-time incident of incest committed by her father and general emotional neglect by her self-centered mother. Hanny overcame her depersonalization when she eventually accepted and later integrated the little girl and her recollections.

Clinically, it is imperative to note whether depersonalization and derealization phenomena occur without structural dissociation, or are a manifestation of structural dissociation, because treatment interventions will be different depending on whether dissociation is present or not (Allen et al., 1999).

SUMMARY

Nonrealization of trauma, more specifically structural dissociation of the personality, tends to manifest in a spectrum of mental and physical symptoms whose diversity is more apparent than real. Structural dissociation can be categorized as negative and positive symptoms, and further understood as being psychoform or somatoform. These symptoms are different from alterations of consciousness, such as "spacing out," but pathological alterations often accompany structural dissociation. Numerous symptoms not typically considered dissociative can be rather specific for particular parts of the personality, but not for others. Symptoms such as suicidality, substance use, self-harm, and promiscuity may all manifest in one part, but not in another dissociative part of the personality. While theory provides a clear way to discern dissociative symptoms from nondissociative ones, in actual practice it can be quite difficult to assess the status of a particular symptom. A symptom can only be said to be dissociative if there is clear evidence of dissociative parts of the personality, and the symptom can be found in one part, but not in others.

CHAPTER 6

Structural Dissociation and the Spectrum of Trauma-Related Disorders

[H]istories of childhood trauma are often found in patients who are diagnosed with borderline personality disorder, affective disorders, somatization disorder, dissociative disorders, self-mutilation, eating disorders, and substance abuse. . . . [O]ne central element that all these conditions have in common is the high prevalence of dissociation.
—Alexander McFarlane & Bessel Van der Kolk (1996, p. 570)

UNDERSTANDING THE ROLE of structural dissociation of the personality in trauma-related disorders can assist clinicians and researchers in making sense of the possible links among the wide variety of symptoms and so-called comorbid disorders that are found in many survivors. Traumatized individuals typically have serious and complicated comorbidity. It is doubtful that so many comorbid symptoms and disorders are not part and parcel of *one* posttraumatic syndrome, provided they did not already exist prior to traumatization. We propose that a common major factor is *structural dissociation*.

Some experts in the trauma field more generally believe that DSM-IV and ICD-10 are inadequate in their classification of trauma-related disorders. As a result, a new diagnostic category (i.e., complex PTSD) as well as a spectrum of trauma symptoms (Van der Kolk, 1996) and trauma-related disorders have been proposed (Bremner et al., 1998; Moreau & Zisook, 2002). The complexity of structural dissociation can constitute an important organizing principle of a spectrum of trauma-related disorders.

TRAUMA-RELATED DISORDERS

There is a range of trauma-related mental disorders. Even though few mental disorders are overtly linked to traumatization in DSM-IV, empirical data indicate that among patients with a wide range of mental disorders, many, and in some cases practically all of them report traumatization. Many of these disorders include prominent comorbidity, described in DSM-IV as additional descriptive features and disorders. Commonalities among the trauma-related disorders can be explored both in terms of comorbidity and of structural dissociation.

Acute Stress Disorder

There are only two diagnoses in the DSM-IV that have a criterion requiring the individual to have experienced or witnessed a traumatizing event. These include acute stress disorder (ASD) and posttraumatic stress disorder (PTSD). Like PTSD, ASD is listed as an anxiety disorder (Bryant & Harvey, 2000). ASD lasts from two days to four weeks, and begins no more than four weeks after the traumatizing event. When the symptoms exist beyond these time limits, the diagnosis becomes PTSD. Some authors therefore argue that ASD should be considered as PTSD (e.g., R. N. Marshall, Spitzer, & Liebowitz, 1999). Regardless of whether ASD ultimately stands on its own as a diagnosis, it strongly predicts subsequent PTSD (Brewin, Andrews, Rose, & Kirk, 1999; Classen, Cheryl, Hales, & Spiegel, 1998; Grieger et al., 2000; Harvey & Bryant, 1998).

Even though ASD is listed as an anxiety disorder, its diagnosis is partly made on the basis of having three or more so-called *dissociative* symptoms, including numbing, reduction in awareness of surroundings, derealization, depersonalization, and dissociative amnesia. However, as noted in Chapter 5, reduction in awareness of surroundings is essentially related to alterations in the level and field of consciousness, and thus may not necessarily be dissociative in nature. This is also true for a number of the symptoms that are typically labeled as depersonalization and derealization. Thus, although the diagnosis of ASD is made on purported negative dissociative symptoms, some of these may not be dissociative. In fact, the diagnosis of ASD has opened the door in the trauma field to discussions about confusion regarding definitions of dissociation (e.g., Harvey & Bryant, 1999b; Holmes et al., 2005; R. N. Marshall et al., 1998). Nevertheless, DSM-IV indicates that the presence of (negative) dissociative symptoms is essential to the diagnosis, thus it seems reasonable that dissociation be viewed as an underlying mechanism of the disorder.

Other criteria for ASD should also be met: *persistent reexperiences*, *marked avoidance of trauma-related stimuli*, and *marked hyperarousal or anxiety*. We have made a case for intrusions as positive dissociative symptoms, and for the possibility that hyperarousal may have its origins in dissociative parts of the personality. *The diagnosis of ASD thus requires the presence of both negative and positive dissociative symptoms.*

Simple cases of ASD likely include a very rudimentary EP along with an ANP that encompasses the individual's personality prior to the trauma. Over the course of a few weeks, some traumatized individuals go on to integrate these two parts of their personality, and their ASD resolves. But a significant number do not and subsequently develop PTSD. Nonrealization of traumatic experience can also be at the heart of several associated features of ASD, including feelings of despair, guilt, and hopelessness (e.g., EP stuck in grief that obstructs recuperation), and impulsive and risk-taking behavior (e.g., positive dissociative symptoms of EP).

Complicated cases of ASD likely involve more than one rudimentary EP. In our terms, simple cases of ASD are associated with primary structural dissociation, and complicated cases with secondary structural dissociation. For example, in complicated ASD, a survivor may have developed two EPs that operate in parallel (e.g., one experiencing EP and one observing EP), or two or more sequential EPs, each with its own features (e.g., one fixated in freeze, and another in total submission). In some cases, an individual may manifest the symptoms of ASD in response to a potentially traumatizing event, in which the reactivation of already existing traumatic memories (related to the phenomenon of "double emotion" described in Chapter 5) plays a dominant but often unrecognized role. Then the trauma disorder is actually more complex that ASD.

Posttraumatic Stress Disorder

PTSD is acute when the duration of symptoms is less than three months, is chronic when the symptoms last three months or longer, and has a delayed onset when at least six months have passed between the traumatizing event and the onset of symptoms. In addition to exposure to a potentially traumatizing event, PTSD requires *persistent reexperiences* (Criterion B), *persistent avoidance* (Criterion C), *persistent hyperarousal* (Criterion D), and duration of symptoms for more than one month (Criterion E) (APA, 1994). We consider reexperiences, some avoidance, and hyperarousal to be dissociative in nature, so PTSD can thus be regarded as a dissociative disorder, as has been proposed before (Brett, 1996; Chu, 1998a; Van der Hart et al., 2004).

According to the theory of structural dissociation of the personality, the severity and extent of dissociative symptoms in PTSD should be less than in complex PTSD and DID. Dissociation scores of patients with PTSD are indeed less than those in individuals with DSM-IV dissociative disorders, but significantly greater than in individuals without PTSD (e.g., Bremner et al., 1992; El-Hage et al., 2002).

Most patients with PTSD (about 80%) have comorbid symptoms in addition to reexperiencing, avoidance, and hyperarousal, or they qualify for the diagnosis of additional mental disorders (e.g., Van der Kolk, Pelcovitz, Mandel, Sunday, & Spinazzola, 2005). These include (symptoms of) anxiety, mood, and substance abuse disorders (McFarlane, 2000), dissociative disorders (e.g., Johnson, Pike, & Chard, 2001), somatic complaints (e.g., Van der Kolk, Pelcovitz et al., 1996), attention deficit/hyperactivity disorder (Ford et al., 2000), and personality changes and personality disorders (Southwick, Yehuda, & Giller, 1993). These associated symptoms and disorders may be so prominent that they can divert the clinician's and researcher's attention from the patient's coexisting traumatization (Van der Kolk & McFarlane, 1996).

Complex PTSD

Many of the DSM-IV "associated descriptive features" of simple PTSD involve complex PTSD symptom clusters. Complex PTSD (Herman, 1992a, 1993), also known as disorders of extreme stress not otherwise specified (DESNOS; Ford, 1999; Pelcovitz et al., 1997; Roth et al., 1997; Van der Kolk et al., 2005), was originally formulated as a disorder of prolonged and extreme stress, particularly childhood abuse. Some authors have used the term *chronic PTSD* when the term *complex PTSD* is more likely applicable (e.g., Bremner, Southwick, Darnell, & Charney, 1996; Feeny, Zoellner, & Foa, 2002).

Most individuals with complex PTSD have experienced chronic interpersonal traumatization as children (Bremner, Southwick et al., 1993; Breslau et al., 1999; Donovan et al., 1996; Ford, 1999; Ford & Kidd, 1998; Roth et al., 1997; Zlotnick et al., 1996). Consistent with the theory of structural dissociation, they have severe dissociative symptoms (Dickinson, DeGruy, Dickinson, & Candib, 1998; Pelcovitz et al., 1997; Zlotnick et al., 1996). However, assessment of somatoform dissociation and more precise assessment of psychoform dissociative symptoms in complex PTSD is needed.

Apart from the symptoms of PTSD (Ford, 1999), patients with complex PTSD have characterological disturbances and a high risk of revictimization (Herman, 1993; Ide & Paez, 2000). The proposed criteria for complex PTSD include the following symptom clusters: (1) *alterations in regulation of affect and impulses*; (2) *alterations in attention or consciousness*; (3) *alterations in self-perception*; (4) *alterations in relations with others*; (5) *somatization*; and (6) *alterations in systems of meaning* (Pelcovitz et al., 1997; Roth et al., 1997; Van der Kolk et al., 1993, 2005). There is a strong potential for these symptom clusters to be dissociative (cf., Chapter 5; Van der Hart, Nijenhuis et al., 2005).

We have proposed that complex PTSD involves secondary structural dissociation—a single ANP and two or more EPs (Van der Hart, Nijenhuis et al., 2005). The presentation of these EPs tends to be more subtle in complex PTSD than in DID. In other words, these parts are usually not very elaborated or emancipated.

Borderline Personality Disorder

In a majority of cases, borderline personality disorder (BPD) is associated with traumatic experiences, dissociative symptoms, and other trauma-related disorders (e.g., Herman & Van der Kolk, 1987; Laporte & Guttman, 1996; Ogata et al., 1990; Zanarini et al., 2000). In a longitudinal study of individuals with various personality disorders, patients with BPD reported the highest rate of traumatic exposure (particularly to sexual trauma, including childhood sexual abuse), the highest rate of PTSD, and the youngest age of first traumatic event (Yen et al., 2002). Many studies suggest a specific relationship between BPD and sexual abuse (e.g., Zanarini et al., 2002; McClean & Gallop, 2003). Other studies also report very high rates of childhood neglect (Zanarini et al., 1997), and more severe BPD is associated with more severe traumatization (Yen et al., 2002; Zanarini et al., 2002).

Many patients with BPD fear abandonment and intimacy. Their fear of abandonment and intense anger may relate to actual abandonment, maltreatment, and deprivation. The continuing expectation of being victimized and the recapitulation of abusive and failed relationships leads to a growing reservoir of bitter disappointment, frustration, self-hate, and rage (Chu, 1998a, p. 46). These vigorous emotions dominate the patient's personal and therapeutic relationships. They are linked with unresolved, preoccupied, or disorganized/disoriented attachment that is related to traumatic experiences (Agrawal, Gunderson, Holmes, & Lyons-Ruth, 2004; Buchheim, Strauss, & Kachele, 2002). Disorganized attachment is a strong vulnerability factor for and predictor of (chronic) dissociation (Ogawa et al., 1997; cf. Chapter 4), and its symptoms are, in fact, those of dissociation (Barach, 2004). Disorganized and other forms of insecure attachment are predominant in abuse survivors, and attachment theory goes a long way in explaining and describing the enduring characterological difficulties in traumatized individuals (Alexander, 1992; Alexander & Anderson, 1994; Blizard, 2001, 2003; Lyons-Ruth, 1999, 2001; Schore, 2003a). Although disorganized attachment is usually, but not always associated with abuse, it is always associated with a caretaker's responses that are outside the range of normal inattention or misattunement, and this may explain why some patients with BPD do not report traumatization per se.

Given that BPD is associated with severe and early traumatization and with disorganized attachment, one would expect that patients with BPD have many psychoform and somatoform dissociative symptoms. This has been confirmed by various research studies (e.g., G. Anderson, Yasenik, & Ross, 1993; Chu & Dill, 1991; Gershuny & Thayer, 1999; Stiglmayr, Shapiro, Stieglitz, Limberger, & Bohus, 2001; Wildgoose, Waller, Clarke, & Reid, 2000).

The diagnosis of BPD is based on a pervasive pattern of instability of interpersonal relationships, self-image and affects, and marked impulsivity beginning in early adulthood. It must include five of the following symptoms: (1) *frantic efforts to avoid real or imagined abandonment*; (2) *pattern of unstable and intense interpersonal relationships characterized by alternation between extremes of idealization and devaluation*; (3) *identity disturbance; markedly and persistently unstable sense of self or self-image*; (4) *impulsivity in at least two areas that are potentially self-damaging* (spending, sex, substance abuse, reckless driving, binge eating); (5) *recurrent suicidal behavior, gestures, or threats or self-mutilating behavior*; (6) *affective instability due to a marked reactivity of mood* (a few hours to [rarely] a few days); (7) *chronic feelings of emptiness*; (8) *inappropriate, intense anger or difficulty controlling anger*; and (9) *transient, stress-related paranoid ideation or severe dissociative symptoms*.

It may be difficult to make a differential diagnosis between BPD, complex PTSD, and DSM-IV dissociative disorders, given extensive overlap between the core and additional symptoms of these disorders. There is a remarkable parallel between the symptom clusters of BPD and complex PTSD. Both disorders include affect dysregulation, disorders of self, suicidality, substance abuse, self-harm, and relational difficulties (APA, 1994; Driessen et al., 2002; Gunderson & Sabo, 1993; McLean, & Gallop, 2003; Yen et al., 2002), and both involve very similar psychobiological deficits and features (Driessen et al., 2002).

Dissociation is strongly related to self-harm (Noll, Horowitz, Bonanno, Trickett, & Putnam, 2003), which is common in patients with BPD (Brodsky, Cloitre, & Dulit, 1995). Approximately half of DID patients also have BPD (Boon & Draijer, 1993; Chu, 1998b; Dell, 1998; Ellason, Ross, & Fuchs, 1996), and many have a combination of features of borderline, avoidant (76%), self-defeating (68%), and passive-aggressive personality disorder (45%) (Armstrong, 1991; Dell, 1998). However, patients with BPD have lower scores for dissociative amnesia on the Dissociation Questionnaire (DIS-Q) than patients with DID, and lesser degrees of identity confusion and alteration (Vanderlinden, 1993). These differences distinguish BPD from DID.

Based on the data, it seems likely that a majority of patients with the diagnosis of BPD can be understood and treated as traumatized individuals who have experienced early abuse and neglect, while a small subset may have other etiological factors associated with their personality disorder.

We propose that BPD involves secondary structural dissociation. Consistent with this, Golynkina and Ryle (1999) found that patients with BPD encompassed a dissociative part of the personality that seems to represent an ANP (a coping ANP) and more than one EP (abuser rage, victim rage, passive victim, and zombie). Some patients with BPD have severe dissociative symptoms, and may actually border on DDNOS or DID. Our clinical observations suggest that dissociative parts in BPD patients have less emancipation and elaboration, and less distinct sense of self than in DDNOS or DID.

Alternations among dissociative parts in BPD occur between a typically depressed, empty ANP, and enraged or overwhelmed EPs that are fixated in past trauma, which may account for affective instability and reactivity. The disorganized attachment that occurs in most patients with BPD is associated with dissociative relational alternations (e.g., Blizard, 2001, 2003; Lyons-Ruth, 1999, 2001). Some dissociative parts of the personality will approach and idealize others, while other parts of the personality will avoid and devalue the same individuals, resulting in intense and unstable relationships. Thus, different dissociative parts of the personality compete with contradictory needs: Some are driven to attach and to desperately maintain attachment, while others are driven to avoid attachment.

Dissociative Disorders

The DSM-IV dissociative disorders include dissociative amnesia, dissociative fugue, depersonalization disorder, dissociative disorder not otherwise specified (DDNOS), and dissociative identity disorder (DID). These disorders, particularly DID, have long been shown to be associated with prolonged, severe, and early childhood trauma (Chu, Frey, Ganzel, & Matthews, 1999; Coons, 1994; Draijer & Boon, 1993; Hornstein & Putnam, 1992; D.O. Lewis, Yeager, Swica, Pincus, & Lewis, 1997; Nijenhuis, 2004; Ogawa et al., 1997; Putnam et al., 1986; Ross et al., 1991). The vast majority of patients with DID (85–97%) have experienced severe forms of abuse, and a minority of cases may relate to severe neglect without physical or sexual abuse, and highly abnormal parental approaches that induce disorganized attachment in the child (Blizard, 1997, 2003; Draijer & Langeland, 1999; Liotti, 1999a, 1999b).

Many authors have pointed out that DID is the most complex form of PTSD (e.g., Bremner et al., 1996; Dell, 1998; Loewenstein, 1991; Spiegel, 1984, 1986, 1993). Consistent with this, PTSD symptoms are highly prevalent in patients with dissociative disorders, and 60% of patients with DDNOS, and 89% of patients with DID meet full criteria for PTSD (Boon & Draijer, 1993).

Dissociative amnesia. The main DSM-IV criterion for the diagnosis of dissociative amnesia is the *sudden inability to recall personal information that is too extensive to be explained by ordinary forgetfulness.* The diagnosis also requires that no other dissociative disorder be present. The memories that the patient cannot retrieve are often of a traumatic nature, but may also pertain to conflicts or other causes (APA, 1994; Van der Hart & Nijenhuis, 2001). Dissociative amnesia disorder has been reported with regard to combat trauma, Holocaust-related traumatization (Van der Hart & Brom, 2000), traumatic loss, robbery, torture, physical abuse, as well as suicidal acts and criminal acts (see for reviews Brown, Scheflin, & Hammond, 1998; Van der Hart & Nijenhuis, 1995). A history of childhood trauma also has a strong relationship with the disorder of dissociative amnesia (Coons & Milstein, 1989; Loewenstein, 1993).

DSM-IV states that additional features of patients with dissociative amnesia disorder include other psychoform dissociative symptoms such as spontaneous age regression and trance states, analgesia (a somatoform dissociative symptom), self-mutilation, aggressive and suicidal impulses and acts, and impairment in work and interpersonal relationships. All of these features may imply structural dissociation. Thus a more complex dissociative disorder may exist and supercede dissociative amnesia disorder (e.g., Coons & Milstein, 1989; Loewenstein, 1993). Additional co-morbid disorders include conversion disorder (i.e., somatoform dissociative disorder), mood disorder, and personality disorders. In our view, dissociative amnesia suggests the dominance of ANP, whereas occasional positive dissociative symptoms suggest intrusion by EP.

Dissociative fugue. The main DSM-IV criterion for dissociative fugue is *sudden, unexpected travel away from home or one's customary place of work, with an inability to recall the past* in the absence of another dissociative disorder. The associated features and disorders include depression, guilt, aggressive and suicidal impulses, mood disorder, PTSD, and substance-related disorder. Patients who have dissociative fugue (as a symptom or as a disorder) typically have a history of severe childhood abuse (Berrington, Liddel, & Foulds, 1956; Loewenstein, 1993; Kirshner, 1973), but fugues can also be related to intense conflicts or otherwise stressful situations such as marital discord, financial difficulties, and war events (Kirshner, 1973; Kopelman, 1987). The patient's conscious awareness seems to be dominated largely by a pathogenic kernel statement or idée fixe, such as "I need to get away from it all!" (Janet, 1907, 1909b; Van der Hart, 1985).

While dissociative amnesia is a *negative* symptom, dissociative fugue involves not only amnesia, but very complex *positive* dissociative symptoms of behavior. In fugues, another part of the personality takes complete control of behavior and consciousness from the usually present

ANP, travels to a different place, and often engages in behaviors that are not typical for the individual as ANP.

Some patients experience complete amnesia for their former identity during the fugue, indicating a strong division between parts of the personality. Most have some idea of their identity, but cannot recall important aspects of their lives. Fugues may indicate a temporary dissociative division among parts of the personality, but often they are a manifestation of another part of the personality that is generally not active in daily life, but rather more internal until the time of fugue.

In some cases, patients with fugues involve an ANP that continues to function in daily life, although they may take on a different kind of work and display a rather abnormally retracted field of consciousness. In other cases, the part that engages in the fugue is best understood as an EP. For example, sometimes they act in a childlike manner or engage in aggressive or fearful and confused behaviors. Often patients initially diagnosed with dissociative fugue eventually show indications of a more complex set of dissociative symptoms (Boon & Draijer, 1993, 1995; Steinberg, 1995).

Depersonalization disorder. Symptoms of depersonalization are common among many mental disorders. Generally these symptoms are transient. When symptoms are primary and chronic, and occur in the absence of other major mental disorders, the diagnosis of depersonalization disorder can be made. The criteria include *persistent or recurrent episodes of feeling detached from one's mental processes or body*, while *reality testing remains intact*. This disorder has significant comorbidity with anxiety, depression (Baker et al., 2003), and substance-related disorder (APA, 1994). Among different types of traumatization, depersonalization as a disorder and as a symptom cluster are most strongly associated with emotional abuse (Simeon, Guralnik, Schmeidler, Sirof, & Knutelska, 2001).

Baker and colleagues (2003) found that earlier onset of the disorder was related to significantly higher levels of dissociation as measured with the DES. In Chapter 5 we discussed the specific symptoms of depersonalization and questioned whether some of the major symptoms might be more accurately catergorized as alterations in consciousness rather than as dissociative symptoms. Nevertheless, some symptoms are clearly dissociative, such as out of body experiences, indicating an observer and an experiencing part of the personality. Other symptoms of unreality can occur when one part of the personality is intruding into another, or when a switch among parts is imminent.

In some cases, depersonalization may be a prominent symptom that leads to a diagnosis of DID following careful diagnostic assessment.

> Martha, a young doctoral candidate, entered therapy because of confusion, difficulty in completing her dissertation, and a persistent feeling of being unreal following unexpected major surgery. Organic causes were ruled out.

Over several sessions it became clear that she was rapidly switching from one part to another, and the depersonalization was secondary to the rapid switching and the confusion of parts as they gained executive control ("How did I get here? This isn't my life.").

Dissociative disorder not otherwise specified. The DSM-IV diagnosis of DDNOS comprises six categories. Here we focus exclusively on the first category, namely, the clinical presentations similar to DID that fail to meet full criteria for this disorder. Clinically, it is the diagnosis of choice when an individual has symptoms consistent with DID, but parts do not exhibit extreme elaboration and autonomy, and may not be as active in daily life as some parts of the personality in a patient with DID (Boon & Draijer, 1993; Steinberg, 1995). Patients with DDNOS do indeed have a specific profile of dissociation that is distinct from DID. This profile includes somewhat less severe dissociative symptoms, prominence of intrusion of parts that result in positive dissociative symptoms instead of parts that completely gain executive control, and a less severe level of personality disorders (Boon & Draijer, 1993; Dell, 1998, 2002; Steinberg, 1995). These research findings should inspire a reformulation of the criteria for DDNOS to improve diagnostic accuracy. In our consistent clinical experience, most patients with DDNOS have developed secondary structural dissociation.

Dissociative identity disorder. The DSM-IV criteria for DID include the *presence of two or more distinct identities or personality states*; *at least two of these identities or personality states recurrently take control of the person's behavior*; and *amnesia*. These criteria present serious problems in diagnosis. For example, what is the range of what is considered to be a dissociative identity or personality state? How much amnesia must be present? Must a part take complete control, or does passive influence sufficiently meet the criterion of taking control? What about dissociative identities that act in the present, but do not have a particular name or other defining characteristics? The DSM-IV criteria for diagnosing DID are sufficiently unclear as to present serious clinical problems in making accurate diagnoses, particularly for the majority of DID patients who do not present with flamboyantly different "identities."

Experts therefore urge clinicians to administer reliable and valid diagnostic instruments such as the Structured Clinical Interview for DSM-IV Dissociative Disorders (SCID-D; Steinberg, 1994), or the Multidimensional Inventory of Dissociation (MID, Dell, 2002; Dell, 2006a, 2006b; Somer & Dell, 2005) a relatively new instrument. The SCID-D constitutes a valuable diagnostic tool (Boon & Draijer, 1993; Kundakci, Şar, Kiziltan, Yargic, & Tutkun, 1998; Steinberg, 1995, 2000), but clinical experience and substantial training is required for its accurate administration and for the interpretation of the patient's responses (Draijer & Boon, 1999).

The long list of DSM-IV additional features and disorders that are co-morbid with DID include symptoms of PTSD, self-mutilation, aggressive, homicidal (Nijenhuis, 1996), and suicidal behavior, impulsivity, repetitive relationships involving physical and sexual abuse, conversion (i.e., somatoform dissociative) symptoms, as well as mood, substance-related, sexual, and eating disorders, and personality disorders.

Increasing severity of dissociative phenomena occurs along the trauma disorders continuum, with DID patients manifesting the most severe levels of dissociative symptoms. For example, DID patients score highest of all populations on self-report dissociation questionnaires, including the DES (Boon & Draijer, 1993; Nijenhuis, Van Dyck et al., 1999; Van IJzendoorn & Schluengel, 1996), DIS-Q (Vanderlinden, 1993), MID (Dell, 2002/ 2006), and SDQ-20 (Nijenhuis et al., 1996; Nijenhuis, Matthes et al., 2004). They also have the highest scores on the SCID-D (Boon & Draijer, 1993; Steinberg, 1994), MID (Dell, 2006; Somer & Dell, 2005) and the Dissociative Disorders Interview Schedule (DDIS; Ross, 1989).

Psychosis and Traumatization

Traumatizing events are reported by a substantial majority of individuals with "serious mental illness," a rather indistinct category that includes schizophrenia, bipolar mood disorder, and psychotic disorder NOS (Goodman, Rosenberg, Mueser, & Drake, 1997; Goodman, Thompson, Weinfurt, Corl, Acker, & Mueser, 1999; Mueser et al., 1998; Read, Van Os, Morrison, & Ross, 2005). Many psychotic patients indicate a history of childhood abuse (Holowka, King, Saheb, Pukall, & Brunet, 2003; Janssen et al., 2005; Read, Perry, Moskowitz, & Connolly, 2001, Read & Ross, 2003; Read et al., 2005), and chronically traumatized individuals may be particularly vulnerable to psychosis (J. G. Allen, Coyne, & Console, 1996, 1997; Hamner, Frueh, Ulmer, & Arana, 1999).

None of the definitions of psychotic symptoms in DSM-IV (APA, 1994, p. 273) provides a clear demarcation between psychotic symptoms and a considerable number of intrusion symptoms of PTSD and dissociative disorders. This lack of clarity compromises the differential diagnosis between psychosis and dissociative disorders and PTSD. According to the narrowest DSM-IV definition, psychotic symptoms include delusions and prominent hallucinations, with hallucinations occurring in the absence of insight into their pathological nature. A less restrictive definition of psychosis includes prominent hallucinations that the individual recognizes as hallucinatory experiences. A definition that is still broader includes positive symptoms of schizophrenia such as disorganized speech, and grossly disorganized or catatonic behaviors.

Many traumatized patients, with disorders ranging from PTSD, BPD, to DID, have psychotic symptoms as defined by DSM-IV (R. W. Butler et al.,

1996; David, Kutcher, Jackson, & Mellman, 1999; Miller, Abrams, Dulit, & Fyer, 1993; Ross, 2004). A proportion of these patients qualify for a comorbid DSM-IV psychotic disorder (Bleich & Moskowits, 2000; Hamner, Frueh, Ulmer, & Arana, 2000; Sautter et al., 1999; Tutkun, Yargic, & Şar, 1996). However, most studies are not clear on whether such psychotic symptoms or disorders have a dissociative basis or not. We propose that in most traumatized patients, these symptoms are indicative of structural dissociation.

Psychotic and dissociative symptoms. Chronic PTSD patients with comorbid psychotic features have positive and negative symptoms of psychosis in a range of severity that approaches that of patients with schizophrenia (Hamner et al., 2000). Still, psychotic symptoms may be under-recognized in traumatized patients with chronic PTSD because such patients "are reluctant to report these symptoms and because they may not have overt changes in affect or bizarre delusions characteristic of other psychoses, e.g., schizophrenia" (Hamner et al., 2000, p. 217).

There is a phenomenological overlap between psychotic symptoms and dissociative symptoms. For example, many patients with complex dissociative disorders and schizophrenia hear voices, and both types of patients can have difficulty with reality testing. This overlap contributes to theoretical confusion regarding the nature of psychotic and dissociative symptoms, and to lack of diagnostic accurary of dissociative disorders and psychosis (C.A. Pope & Kwapil, 2000). Patients with DID or DDNOS are often misdiagnosed as suffering from schizophrenia or other psychotic disorders, mostly because they report hearing voices and other Schneiderian first rank symptoms (Boon & Draijer, 1993; Ross, Norton, & Wozney, 1989). Many psychotic patients have dissociative symptoms (Ross, 2004; Spitzer, Haug, & Freiberger, 1997). For example, Haugen and Castillo (1999) found that patients diagnosed with paranoid or undifferentiated schizophrenia experienced symptoms of severe amnesia, depersonalization, and identity fragmentation based on the SCID-D. They conclude that a "probable factor underlying the nonrecognition of severe dissociative disorders in patients diagnosed with psychotic disorders is the great overlap of Schneiderian first rank symptoms in both types of disorders" (p. 753). The phenomenological overlap also exists for negative symptoms; that is, negative symptoms of schizophrenia, avoidance symptoms of PTSD, and symptoms of depression (Kuipers, 1992). However, Ellason and Ross (1995) found that DID patients had more positive, but less negative symptoms of schizophrenia than those with schizophrenia.

It is not always clear how one should discriminate between psychotic and dissociative symptoms. For example, dissociative parts may fail to perceive particular parts of the body, hallucinate a different body size, or believe that they are of a gender different from the patient's actual gender, or are not even human. These negative and positive hallucinations that are so common in complex dissociative disorders, perfectly fit the definitions of psychosis described above. However, in patients with dissociative disorders these symptoms are manifestations of dissociative parts, and over the course of therapy, their reality testing usually improves significantly, if not completely. These dissociative symptoms are also refractory to antipsychotic medication.

The presence of Schneiderian first rank symptoms in both dissociative and psychotic patients should not be underestimated. The MID (Laddis, Dell, Cotton, & Fridley, 2001; see Chapter 5) discriminates well between patients with DID and those with schizophrenia, taking these symptoms into account. Items that were very indicative for DID were "not feeling together, not feeling one whole"; "feeling that there is another person inside you who can come out and speak if it wants"; and "your mood changing rapidly without any reason." About 80 to 98% of DID patients endorsed items that tap voices arguing, conversing, or commenting, "made" feelings, "made" impulses, and "made" actions, influences on the body, thought withdrawal, and thought insertion. Items that were endorsed more often by patients with schizophrenia included, "Your thoughts being broadcast so that other people can actually hear you"; "Feeling that your mind or body have been taken over by a famous person" (e.g., Elvis Presley, Jesus Christ, Madonna, or President Kennedy); and "Hearing voices that come from unusual places (e.g., the air conditioner, the computer, the walls) that try to tell you what to do."

Patients with DID had *higher* scores for seven of eight Schneiderian first rank symptoms than patients with schizophrenia (see also Ellason & Ross, 1995; Kluft, 1987a; Ross, Miller, Reagor, Bjornson, Fraser, & Anderson, 1990; Ross, 2004; Yargic, Şar, Tutkun, & Alyanak, 1998). Other distinctive features of DID include hearing child voices and more persecutory voices than reported by schizophrenics. The abundant presence of Schneiderian first rank symptoms in DID suggests the possibility of a complex dissociative disorder, and indicates that schizophrenia should not be diagnosed on the basis of these symptoms alone. The overlap also suggests that findings regarding the prevalence of traumatization and the nature of the symptoms in alleged ly psychotic patients must be interpreted with caution if these patients have not been systematically interviewed with diagnostic instruments for dissociative disorders.

Dissociative psychosis. A diagnostic category of dissociative psychosis has been proposed in those cases where the psychotic disorder is trauma related and clearly dissociative in nature—embedded in structural dissociation of personality (Graham & Thavasothby, 1995; Van der Hart, Witztum, & Friedman, 1993). Dissociative psychosis has been documented in a number of traumatized patients with diagnoses ranging from PTSD to DID (Graham & Thavasotby, 1995; Tutkun et al., 1996; Van der Hart & Spiegel, 1993; Van der Hart, Witztum et al., 1993). The disorder was originally called hysterical psychosis (Hollender & Hirsch, 1964; Moreau de Tours, 1865). The following diagnostic criteria have been suggested for dissociative psychosis (Van Gerven, Van der Hart, Nijenhuis, & Kuipers, 2002; Van der Hart, Witzum et al., 1993): (1) psychoform or somatoform dissociative symptoms are prominent; (2) the psychosis can be understood as a dissociative condition; (3) structural dissociation exists; and (4) there are meaningful behaviors in the psychosis that the patient cannot control. These four criteria address the dissociative character of the psychosis, but what defines the psychosis as such? In cases of dissociative psychosis, typically a part of the personality, notably an EP, has lost all contact with present reality and is flooded with terrifying hallucinations. The hallucinations, in some cases persisting for weeks or months, are mostly of a visual or auditory nature, and they may pertain to extremely intense reexperiences of actual trauma or to extremely threatening symbolic experiences derived from the primary traumatization (Van der Hart, Witzum et al., 1993). Antipsychotic medication is not always helpful in such cases, and psychotherapy is the treatment of choice. It involves rest, reduction of stress, education of the survivor as ANP about the psychosis, and if possible, the establishment of contact with the EPs caught up in the terrifying hallucinations, followed by transformation and resolution of these hallucinations and related traumatic memories.

Psychosis in BPD and DDNOS. "Transient psychotic episodes" have also been observed in patients with BPD, but their potential dissociative nature is not commonly considered. Lotterman (1985) nevertheless noted that these episodes are characterized by psychoform and somatoform dissociative symptoms. He also reported that many patients in his sample were traumatized. The psychotic symptoms in BPD may last for weeks to months, but are generally short-lived. These symptoms are often refractory to medical treatment, including ECT, but respond to psychotherapy. These combined features are suggestive of dissociative psychosis.

> Dissociative psychosis can also manifest in patients with DDNOS. Anja, diagnosed with DDNOS and dissociative psychosis, walked around for days in an apparent haze, making tiny steps, feet and knees turned inward, and uttering in a childlike voice, "All red, everything is red." Medication, rest, and time did not relieve this condition. When the therapist joined her and agreed that everything was red in her world, he suggested that some places perhaps might be more or less red than other places. This approach eventually helped Anja to relate that the most red place was her underwear. It was blood after anal rape at a young age by a man who had club feet, and whose gait she had apparently imitated. This revelation, together with the therapist's empathic responses, ended the psychotic episode within a few hours.

In Anja's case, the contents of the dissociative psychosis pertained to an aspect of a traumatizing event as experienced by a very young EP. However, as mentioned above, the contents can also involve extremely anxiety-provoking fantasy experiences—with hallucinatory qualities—that are derived from a real-life traumatic experience. Such secondary experiences may involve guilt-induced visions of being persecuted by a devil or demon, or of being tortured in hell (Janet, 1894–1895/1898b, 1898a; Van der Hart & Spiegel, 1993; Van der Hart, Witzum et al., 1993).

Somatoform Disorders

The DSM-IV recognizes two major disorders involving physical complaints and difficulties that have no organic cause. Both *somatization disorder* and *conversion disorder* are associated with a history of traumatization and dissociation.

Somatization disorder. Somatization is found as part of general psychopathology in many psychiatric patients, but it is especially prominent in chronically traumatized individuals (e.g., Andreski, Chilcoat, & Breslau, 1998; Atlas, Wolfson, & Lipschitz, 1995; Dickinson, DeGruy, Dickinson, & Candib, 1999; Nijenhuis, 2004; Roelofs, Keijsers, Hoogduin, Naring, & Moene, 2002; Van der Kolk et al., 2005). The severity of somatization generally correlates to the severity of the trauma-related disorder and dissociative symptoms.

DSM-IV somatization disorder requires the presence of *multiple physical complaints before age 30* and all the following criteria over the course of the disorder: (1) *four pain symptoms*; (2) *two gastrointestinal symptoms*; (3) *one sexual symptom*; (4) *one pseudoneurological symptom*; (5) *the symptoms are found to be functional, or when there is a medical condition, the symptoms cause distress and impairment in excess of what would be expected.* Neither the DSM-IV nor the ICD-10 points out that somatization can involve somatoform dissociation, and that the symptoms can be trauma related. For example, the pseudoneurological symptoms of DSM-IV conversion symptoms are dissociative in nature. The additional features and disorders of somatoform disorder include anxious and depressed mood, impulsive and antisocial behavior, suicide threats and behavior, chaotic lives, as well as substance-related disorders and BPD, all of which may be linked to structural dissociation in at least some cases.

Little is known about the severity of psychoform dissociative symptoms in somatization disorder. Relative to medical comparison subjects, patients with somatization disorder had more dissociative amnesia (R. J. Brown, Schrag, & Trimble, 2005). The two groups reported similar levels of depersonalization, derealization, identity confusion, and identity alteration. We are not aware of studies of somatoform dissociation of somatization disorder.

It is essential for clinicians to explore the possibility that a medically unexplained somatic symptom has an underlying dissociative nature, because treatment of somatoform disorders depends on the underlying causation. The dissociative nature of a somatoform symptom is only ascertained when it is demonstrated that the symptom specifically relates to a dissociative part (Nijenhuis, 2004).

Conversion Disorder/Dissociative
Disorders of Movement and Sensation

According to DSM-IV (APA, 1996, p. 452), the essential feature of conversion disorder is the presence of symptoms or deficits affecting voluntary motor or sensory function that suggest a neurological or other general medical condition. The DSM-IV does not categorize conversion disorders as somatoform dissociative disorders, and states that "if conversion and dissociative symptoms occur in the same individual (which is common) both diagnoses should be made" (APA, 1994, p. 456). Thus, DSM-IV considers conversion symptoms to be different from dissociative symptoms. However, based on theoretical and empirical grounds, the fundamental nature of conversions should be regarded as dissociative (Bowman, 2006; Kihlstrom, 1992; McDougall, 1926; Nemiah, 1991; Nijenhuis, 2004; Spitzer et al., 1999; Van der Hart & Op den Velde, 1995). The ICD-10 (WHO, 1992) label of *dissociative disorders of movement and sensation* is an improvement in this regard. The category encompasses *dissociative motor disorders, dissociative convulsions, dissociative anesthesia and sensory loss, mixed dissociative (conversion) disorders,* and *other dissociative (conversion) disorders.* However, ICD-10 fails to recognize that the category of *somatoform disorders* can involve profound somatoform dissociation. A category of somatoform dissociative disorders should be seriously considered for the next editions of the DSM and ICD.

High rates of somatoform and psychoform dissociation, as well as a history of traumatization and recent stressful life events are found in patients with DSM-IV conversion disorders (Moene et al., 2001; Nijenhuis, Van Dyck et al., 1999; Roelofs et al., 2002; Roelofs, Spinhoven, Sandijck, Moene, & Hoogduin, 2005; Şar, Akyuz, Kundakci, Kiziltan, & Dogan, 2004). Patients with the somatoform dissociative symptom of pseudoepileptic seizures (i.e., dissociative convulsions), have elevated scores for psychoform and somatoform dissociation, and a substantial number of them report a history of traumatization (Bowman & Markand, 1996; Kuyk, Spinhoven, Van Emde Boas, & Van Dyck, 1999; Prueter, Schultz-Venrath, & Rimpau, 2002).

The DSM-IV criteria for conversion disorder include the following: (1)*one or more symptoms suggesting a neurological or other medical condition*; (2) *initiation or exacerbation of symptoms is associated with psychological stressors or conflict*; (3) *symptom is not intentionally produced or feigned*; (4) *symptoms are not limited to pain or sexual dysfunction*, which would indicate somatization. Comorbidity of conversion disorders includes so called nonconversion somatic complaints and dissociative disorders, major depressive disorder, and particular personality disorders.

Somatoform dissociative symptoms are manifestations of dissociative parts of the personality, no matter how rudimentary. Thus those patients with somatoform dissociative disorders will have a level of structural dissociation, and should be assessed for the existence of another trauma-related disorder such as PTSD, DDNOS, or DID.

COMORBIDITY OR SPECTRA OF SYMPTOMS AND DISORDERS IN TRAUMATIZED INDIVIDUALS?

There is ample evidence that many traumatized individuals have a wide range of symptoms and meet criteria for a range of mental disorders, particularly when their traumatization began early in childhood, was of an interpersonal nature, involved threat to the integrity of the body, and was severe and chronic. Many additional descriptive features of trauma-related disorders were described above. They include depressive mood, anxiety and panic, sexual dysfunction, sleep disturbances, self-mutilation, somatoform symptoms, aggressive impulses, suicidal impulses, and impairment at work and in interpersonal relationships. Additional or comorbid disorders for PTSD, BPD, dissociative disorders, schizophrenia, and somatoform disorders include *major depression* (e.g., Brady, Killeen, Brewerton, & Lucerini, 2000; J.C. Perry, 1985; Şar, Kundakci et al., 2000); *anxiety disorders* (J. G. Allen, Coyne, & Huntoon, 1998; Brady, 1997; Breslau, Davis, Andreski, & Peterson, 1991; Lipschitz, Winegar, Hartnick, Foote, & Southwick, 1999; Stein et al., 1996); *substance abuse disorders* (e.g., Brady, 1997; McClellan, Adams, Douglas, McCurry, & Storck, 1995; McDowell, Levin, & Nunes, 1999); and *eating disorders* (Brady et al., 2000; Darves-Bornoz, Delmotte, Benhamou, Degiovanni, & Gaillard, 1996; Lipschitz et al., 1999; Vanderlinden, 1993).

The DSM-IV dissociative disorders, especially severe DDNOS and DID, tend to involve the most substantial and extreme comorbidity (Boon & Draijer, 1993; Şar & Ross, 2006; Steinberg, 1995; Steinberg et al., 1994). However, as noted above, even patients with PTSD often have additional disorders (APA, 1994; Breslau et al., 1995; Kessler et al., 1995; McFarlane & Papay, 1992; Van der Kolk, Van der Hart, & Marmar, 1996). Future studies should explore the degree to which this comorbidity relates to trauma-related structural dissociation of the personality

Comorbidity, Affect Dysregulation,
and Structural Dissociation

The profound range and overlap of symptoms and disorders that characterize survivors of traumatization, particularly when this traumatization was severe and chronic, suggest that the different symptoms and disorders are intimately linked. Faced with the diversity of symptoms and disorders, and ensuing difficulties in accurate diagnosis, specialists in the trauma field have raised the question as to whether we should think of trauma-related problems along a continuum (e.g., Allen, 2001; Van der Kolk, 1996). Van der Kolk and colleagues (1996) suggested a spectrum of trauma-related *symptoms*, including symptoms of PTSD, dissociative symptoms, affect dysregulation, somatization, depression, and problems at work and in interpersonal relationships. Others have proposed a spectrum of trauma-related disorders ranging from PTSD to DID (Bremner et al. 1998; Moreau & Zisook, 2002). Although these views indicate that a variety of symptoms and mental disorders relate to each other, they do not seem to provide common substrates that explain the links between them. Presenting their ideas of a spectrum of trauma-related symptoms, Van der Kolk et al. (1996), referred to the work of both Janet and Nemiah (1998) who believed that it is critically important to pay attention to the role of dissociation. However, Van der Kolk and colleagues did not explain how dissociation may relate to all symptoms of the proposed spectrum.

Schore (1994, 2003a, 2003b) regarded affect dysregulation as the common substrate of trauma-related symptoms and disorders. We concur with Schore that affect dysregulation is a major feature of all trauma-related disorders, but add that this dysregulation in traumatized individuals typically occurs in a context of structural dissociation. The same goes for the more encompassing lack of self-regulation that Van der Kolk (1996) regarded as "the most far-reaching effect of psychological trauma in both children and adults" (p. 187). Thus, affect regulation in traumatized individuals is associated with particular dissociative parts of the personality (Van der Hart, Nijenhuis et al., 2005). Certain parts of the personality may be depressed and suicidal, whereas others have different moods. One study points to this possibility in noting that although patients with PTSD experience similar levels of depression as patients with major depression disorder, PTSD patients have a much wider range of mood variability (Golier, Yehuda, Schmeidler, & Siever, 2001). The EP in PTSD can be fearful, experience panic, or engage in substance abuse (to ward off traumatic memories or other distressing positive dissociative symptoms), bulimic or anorectic behavior, and aggressive acts, or experience somatoform symptoms such as bodily anesthesia, localized pain, or bodily paralysis. Some symptoms and disorders pertain to dysregulation and conflict among these parts and the action systems mediating their functioning.

For example, dysregulation may result from conflicts between parts that are aggressive, parts that are fearful, and parts that seek attachment. Some such parts seem to be strongly mediated by the sympathetic nervous system, and other parts by the (dorsal vagal component of) the parasympathetic nervous system, again resulting in psychophysiological dysregulation (Nijenhuis & Den Boer, in press). The sympathetic nervous system primes the body and mind for action, thus mediates active defense such as flight and fight. It increases heart rate and stimulates the secretion of *catecholamines* (acetylcholine, epinephrine, norepinephrine). The parasympathetic nervous system conserves energy as it slows the heart rate, increases intestinal and gland activity, and relaxes sphincter muscles in the gastrointestinal tract. It thus acts to reverse the effects of the *sympathetic nervous system.*

In short, we propose that structural dissociation of the personality constitutes the common psychobiological substrate, or at least a major substrate of symptoms and disorders of traumatized individuals. Our theory suggests that the spectrum of trauma-related disorders involves different degrees of structural dissociation. This hypothesis is open to empirical test.

SUMMARY

The DSM-IV and the ICD-10 include disorders that are related to traumatizing events by definition (ASD and PTSD) or that have been related to such events through research and clinical experience. However, criteria for these disorders involve only a small subset of a wide range of symptoms in traumatized individuals. The DSM-IV sometimes labels these other problems as additional features and disorders of the trauma-related disorders. But such vague categorization fails to highlight consistent findings of significant correlations among a range of trauma-related symptoms, and considerable overlap among the various trauma-related disorders. There exists a wide range of trauma-related mental disorders such as, ASD, PTSD, complex PTSD, BPD, DSM-IV dissociative disorders, psychotic disorders, and somatoform disorders. We proposed that each of these disorders involve degrees of structural dissociation. Understanding this substrate has major implications for treatment.

PART II

Chronic Traumatization and a Janetian Psychology of Action

Introduction to Part II

*[I]n [structural dissociation], the functions do not dissolve entirely
. . . they continue to subsist. . . . What is dissolved is personality,
the system of grouping of the different functions around the same
personality.*
                                                          —Pierre Janet (1907, p. 332)

*[W]hat is altered in both neurological disconnection syndromes and
dissociative disorders is not so much the degree of activity of a brain
area or a psychic function, but the degree of interactivity between
such areas or functions.*
                                          —Gerald Edelman & Guilio Tononi (2000, p. 67)

THE THEORY OF TRAUMA-RELATED structural dissociation includes three basic tenets. The first is that chronically traumatized individuals engage in a range of substitute mental and behavioral action tendencies (Janet, 1919/1925, 1928b). These action tendencies are survivors' efforts to adapt to their inner and outer worlds, but are unequal to the task. Thus, every dissociative part of the personality is directed, from his or her limited perspective, toward achieving adaptive goals with the inadequate resources at hand. Second, survivors' limitations often involve a lack of regulatory skills, sometimes a lack mental or physical energy, and always a lack of mental efficiency, an insufficient ability to utilize mental energy to best advantage. Third, these deficiencies cause and maintain a degree of structural dissociation of the personality and a number of related symptoms.

Based on these three tenets, this part of the book will take our understanding of structural dissociation from Part I and focus on the specific mental and behavioral actions involved in structural dissociation and in integration. Our ideas regarding survivors' actions are strongly inspired by Janet's *psychology of action* (Janet, 1919/1925, 1926a, 1928a, 1928b, 1934, 1938), and serve as a theoretical basis for clinical assessment and treatment of chronically traumatized patients. The inclusion of Janet's work here is not a romantic flight into history: His ideas on actions are most helpful and practical in understanding the plight of trauma survivors, and his perspective is currently undergoing a major revival in psychology, albeit in frequent ignorance of his work (e.g., Berthoz, 2000; Carver et al., 2000; Hurley, 1998; Llinás, 2001).

CHAPTER 7

Synthesis and Its Limitations in Trauma Survivors

Our ability to act coherently in the presence of diverse, often conflicting, sensory stimuli requires a process of neural interaction across many levels of organization without any superordinate map to guide the process. This is the so-called binding problem. . . .
—Gerald Edelman & Guilio Tononi (2000, p. 106)

MENTAL HEALTH IS CHARACTERIZED by a high capacity for integration, which unites a broad range of psychobiological phenomena within one personality (Edelman & Tononi, 2000; Fuster, 2003; Janet, 1889; Stuss & Knight, 2002). When individuals have the (very high) mental level needed to integrate shocking events, they do not develop structural dissociation. We each have a limit as to what we are able to integrate under extreme or enduring stress. When major organizers of our personality, such as action tendencies and action systems, are sufficiently integrated within and among themselves, our mental and behavioral actions can be coordinated and flexible, allowing us to adapt in complex and creative ways. And in turn, these action tendencies and action systems determine to a large degree what we will integrate in a given moment or situation and over time.

However, sometimes an individual's mental level is so low that various action systems (and action tendencies) become dissociated from each other within the personality, with a limited or more extensive sense of self organized around each constellation. To some degree, these self-conscious systems take on a life of their own, or these action systems were never well integrated in the first place in those who experienced early and chronic neglect and abuse.

Integration is the result of both lower and higher order actions. A Janetian psychology of action is useful in understanding normative integration and its failures. Integration involves two major mental actions, *synthesis* and *realization* (Janet, 1889, 1907, 1935a). In synthesis we perceive, link or *bind*, and *differentiate* (components of) our experiences (Edelman & Tononi, 2000; Fuster, 2003; Metzinger, 2003). For example, we must differentiate between what stimuli are relevant and irrelevant for our current interests in order to function adaptively. *Binding* different perceptions into a smooth whole includes lower order mental actions. Thus, binding different components of visual perception such as color and shape of an object, as well as the results of visual, auditory, and kinesthetic perception are commonly unconscious and automatic. These lower order actions require low levels of mental energy and efficiency. However, in order to direct one's field of attention to cues that really matter in a complex situation and to bind these together while ignoring irrelevant cues, one must engage in higher order mental actions that are conscious, voluntary, and complex. Higher order mental actions require high levels of mental energy and efficiency. Thus, synthetic actions occur on a continuum of complexity.

Realization (Janet, 1903, 1928a, 1935a; Van der Hart et al., 1993; Steele et al., 2005) involves meaning making and the creation of a continuous sense of self across time and experience, including a cohesive autobiographical narrative or episodic memory. Realization generally is a more complex action than synthesis. Synthesis can occur without full realization: a common problem for survivors. However, the actions of synthesis are the foundation for realization, and thus cannot be completely separated from it. The emphasis in this chapter is on synthesis, while realization will be discussed in more detail in the following chapter.

THE RELATIONSHIP BETWEEN MENTAL AND BEHAVIORAL ACTIONS

Much integration occurs instantly and automatically, and is generally outside of our conscious awareness. But it takes time and conscious as well as complex mental work to integrate certain experiences such as major changes in our belief system, our sense of self across time and diverse situations, experiences that are painful or at odds with our values, and certainly, traumatic experiences. And traumatic experiences have the capacity to alter any or all of the former.

We must synthesize (bind and differentiate) our perceptions, affects, cognitions, and body movements in a given moment and across time in order to engage in adaptive action according to the goals we wish to achieve. Synthesis is typically thought of as a "process." But this process is actually composed of a series of specific actions, both mental and behavioral, that can be understood and promoted in survivors. Actions are often understood as what we do and say in the external world to achieve an effect. But actions do not merely involve our movements and behavior, they include mental actions such as sensory perceptions (including body sensations), emotional feelings, thoughts, memories, fantasies, plans, and judgments (Janet, 1926b, 1928a,b, 1929b). Mental actions can exist without body movements (Janet, 1927). However, behavioral actions depend on the dynamic integrative interaction of perceptive, affective, and cognitive and motor actions that are geared toward attaining specific goals.

Recent neurobiological findings indicate that mental and behavioral actions have much in common. For example, mirror neurons are activated not only when we are engaged in behavioral action but also in the mental action of observing the same behavioral action by someone else, or by imagining and recognizing the behavioral action (e.g., Garbarini & Adenzato, 2004; Stamenov & Gallese, 2002). Whether we are experiencing pain ourselves or watching someone we love in pain, the same mirror neurons fire in the insula (Singer et al., 2004), a part of the brain involved in emotion, pain perception, and motivation. These and related findings indicate that mirror neurons help us *simulate* the experience of others in our minds more generally, contributing to our capacity for empathy and mentalization (Gallese, Keysers, & Rizzolatti, 2004), two important mental action tendencies that are sometimes deficient in trauma survivors. In addition, they assist learning through imitating someone's behavior by mental simulation (Rizzolatti & Craighero, 2004).

Mirror neurons also help us predict the effects of our behavioral actions. Indeed, the mental action of perception involves far more than a monitoring of events. It involves *prediction* of what will happen next because it involves *mental simulation* of behavioral action (Berthoz, 2000; Llinás, 2001). Our perceptions and cognitions are embodied, i.e., rooted in our bodily interaction with the world, and mirror neurons play an important role in this regard (Garbarini & Adenzato, 2004; Smith & Gasser, 2005; M. Wilson, 2001, 2002). This insight was previously formulated by Janet (1935a), who noted that an individual's perception not only stimulates an immediate action in response to the situation, but also includes an appraisal of potential future perceptions. For example, when a patient perceives the therapist as being angry, he or she is also predicting how the therapist will behave next, such as yelling or hitting. And the patient will respond behaviorally to that prediction, perhaps by freezing. All this occurs in milliseconds.

We cannot separate our mental actions from our behavior in the world: They are synergistic partners, each shaping the direction of the other toward adaptation. The mental actions of perception, including the perception of bodily and affective feelings, cognition, and behavioral actions do not operate independently, but comprise a whole complex, each constantly dependent on the others for input and output (Barkow, Cosmides,

& Tooby, 1992; Buss, 2004; Hurley, 1998). This feedback loop is called a *dynamic perception–motor action cycle* (Hurley, 1998). Perception–motor action cycles must have organization and focus, otherwise they would be a chaotic tangle of mental and behavioral actions (Edelman & Tononi, 2000). In fact, they are coordinated by our goals that emerge from action systems, and include ongoing evaluation of progress toward goals. And our goals, whether they involve relating with others, playing, resting, working, solving problems, or being safe are largely determined by action systems that are activated during a given time. In other words, specific perception–motor action cycles—what we perceive, think, feel, and do—are organized and limited by the constraints of the action system(s) of which they are a part.

Trauma survivors, their dissociative parts, and the interactions among these parts can be understood in terms of these cycles and their goals. Because dissociative parts are relatively closed to at least some perceptions and goals that belong to the whole person, the perception–motor action cycles of such parts may be inappropriate to the situation. For example, a part focused solely on defense cannot accurately perceive and respond to complex social situations without perceiving threat and behaving accordingly.

An adaptive behavioral action generally depends on the mental action of accurately anticipating the outcome of this action. For example, a patient may predict that shaking hands warmly with the therapist will induce a good sense of connection. The handshake offers feedback to be perceived, such as movements of both people toward the handshake, and the length and strength of the handshake, whether it is combined with eye contact, and much more. Individuals must evaluate (one mental action) their behavioral actions as they unfold so that they can compare (another mental action) the results of a behavioral action with the goal of this action (Carver & Scheier, 2000; Hurley, 1998).

The maladaptive actions of survivors often emerge from inaccurate predictions of their own actions and those of others. Depending on the interplay of his or her perception, affect, cognition, and body movement, one patient (or one dissociative part of the personality) might find the handshake helpful and reassuring, while another might find it intimidating and withdraw his hand, and yet another feels the therapist did not really want to shake hands at all because her own perception of herself is that she is unlikable or dirty.

INTEGRATION AND THE GOALS OF ACTIONS

Our biopsychosocial goals range from the most basic, such as the need to eat, rest, and be safe, to existential and highly developed goals, such as the desire to improve the quality of our relationships, to achieve spiritual meaning, and to be ethical and productive human beings. All human goals can be understood as being strongly influenced by the basic action systems of daily life and defense, and the higher-order relations that we have developed among different action systems. These action systems and the higher-order relations that we create between them help us develop adaptive goals (e.g., to avoid what is aversive and approach what is help-ful). These goals are often related to values (e.g., what is attractive, good, important) that are intrinsic to action systems. They help us adjust our actions in response to significant internal and external changes. Action systems therefore strongly guide whatever we tend to perceive, ignore, feel, value, think, and do, hence what we consciously and unconsciously integrate. Survivors must learn to integrate accurate perceptions of the current situation with appropriate action systems and goals.

Trauma Survivors' Problems with Goals

As noted before, the first tenet of the theory of structural dissociation is that chronically traumatized individuals try to adapt to their inner and outer worlds, but they do not always have the mental level and the re-sources to engage in adaptive action. They resort to substitute mental and behavioral action tendencies that result from a lower mental level (Janet, 1919/1925, 1928b). The lack of integration in survivors unduly limits their ability to achieve goals, restricts the kinds of goals they are able to pursue in a given situation, and makes it less likely they will engage in adaptive actions to reach some of their goals.

> Alie, a 54-year-old woman diagnosed with DDNOS, thought that her thera-pist was angry at her when she witnessed during a session that he was an-noyed after he had just discovered that someone (not Alie) had stolen his fa-vorite fountain pen. As ANP, Alie understood the therapist's explanation of the real reason for his anger, which was not directed toward her. However, a scared EP was evoked. This EP correctly perceived the therapist was angry, but incorrectly evaluated the anger as a physical threat based on her experi-ences with her abusive father, and engaged in freezing behavior. As EP, Alie recalled physical abuse and little else, which strongly shaped the percep-tions, feelings, cognitions, body movements, and goals of this part. Further-more, Alie's EP was only able to synthesize the short-term benefits of her ac-tions, that is, of making herself safe, but not the long-term costs. There were very serious and negative long term consequences of her behavior for the EP and for Alie as a whole person: an increase in ANP's avoidance of this intru-sive EP; the persistence of maladaptive defenses in safe situations; lack of mentalization regarding other people's actions in the EP; remaining stuck in traumatic memories; and maintenance of structural dissociation.

Alie's case illustrates the difficulties that ensue when survivors do not re-alize that a goal has been achieved, so that the continued pursuit of the

goal becomes maladaptive. As EP, Alie was still engaged in defending herself against her father's abuse by freezing, not yet having realized that the
abuse had stopped long ago.

Sometimes we must adjust our goals: This often takes a relatively high
mental level. Survivors may not realize when "recalibration" of goals is
necessary and possible (Carver & Scheier, 2000). When a goal is beyond
reach, we must interrupt our actions until it becomes attainable. When a
goal can never be attained, we must permanently stop efforts to achieve
it. It takes a high mental level to realize that a core goal in which we have
invested much effort (e.g., the wish to be loved adequately by abusive
parents) is totally out of reach. Survivors may not have this level, so they
continue the actions to achieve an unrealistic goal.

> As EP, Alie desperately wanted the love of her parents, and was unable to
> realize that she had to grieve the loss of that possibility; she could not ac-
> cept that her goal was unattainable and thus not realistic to continue to pur-
> sue. She continued to be compelled toward winning their love, even while
> ANP avoided having contact with them and knew there was nothing that
> could change their attitude toward her. As ANP, Alie was avoidant of this EP,
> and did not realize that she (ANP) had developed a sufficient mental level
> to integrate this EP. She had therefore not adjusted her goal of avoiding this
> EP to a goal of stepwise integration.

Conflicts among dissociative parts involve conflicts among goals.
We all have conflicting goals at various times, but our ability to reconcile
them by prioritizing and considering our best options is a function of integration. The degree of mental efficiency needed to integrate conflicting
goals is compromised in trauma survivors who have, by definition, developed a degree of structural dissociation that renders inner conflicts relatively unavailable for reconciliation. They find it difficult or impossible to
acknowledge other parts or goals that may be quite discrepant. Dissociative parts may have divergent ideas of which values and goals are most
important in the life of the patient as a whole. Due to their rigidly retracted field of consciousness, they tend to evaluate actions only in light
of the specific action system(s) by which they are mediated.

Because dissociative parts of the personality can be unduly closed to
each other (Braude, 1995), they may experience partial or complete amnesia for other parts and their goals. Or they may be aware, but believe
the goals of other parts have "nothing to do with me." Some dissociative
parts may be empathic toward other parts. But many often resent, despise, or feel ashamed of what other parts want or need (i.e., their goals).
They lack understanding and empathy for goals that are not within their
limited range of experience. Parts tend to respond negatively to each
other because they have become conditioned to do so (evaluative conditioning; see Chapter 10). A survivor as ANP who prides himself on never

getting angry because he does not want to be like his abusive brother will have a most difficult time accepting an enraged part of himself whose goal is revenge. Or a survivor as EP who finds sex repulsive will be hard pressed to accept a part that seeks out and enjoys sexual encounters. A moralistic part may be ashamed of a part that drinks heavily, but cannot stop herself from doing so. The opposing tensions between dissociative parts and their goals can be compelling and sometimes overwhelming. However, reaching a point of acceptance of all parts and understanding the goals of each is essential in the course of therapy. As one survivor of incest noted:

> I [*ANP*] couldn't find a way to connect with the night child [*EP*] I had abandoned. I just hated her. I had no compassion for her at all. I was finally understanding that I would be stuck in the muck of dysfunction until I could find a way to stop judging her so unmercifully. (Van Derbur, 2004, p. 281)

PHASES OF GOAL ATTAINMENT

Our actions are designed to meet specific goals. We are most effective when we can prepare, initiate, engage in, evaluate, and complete actions in such a way that our goals are met successfully. These phases of goal attainment generally should blend seamlessly into actions that are well executed from beginning to end. But survivors sometimes become stuck in various phases of attaining goals—in different stages of action tendencies (see also Chapter 9).

Preparation

As discussed above, when we prepare ourselves for action, we simulate it in our mind. This simulation is an integrative mental action that involves planning and evaluation of the expected effects of the imagined actions. It can be conscious and volitional, or not. Preparation for action is only adaptive when there is a *need* for action, and when we have an opportunity to realize our goal. For example, being prepared for imminent defense is only adaptive when there is an immediate risk of attack. However, trauma survivors tend to prepare themselves for defense when they are perfectly safe. They (mis)perceive imagined threat more than actual safety cues, thus overpredict threat and underpredict safety. They may overpredict which people are likely to reject them and, underestimate the care people feel for them. On the other hand, survivors may be unprepared for particular actions. For example, as ANP they may underpredict danger because they do not sufficiently integrate actual threat signals. Or, they may not be able to prepare themselves for successful social interactions if they have been so neglected that they have no basis to simulate interpersonal situations in their minds.

Initiation

Making plans is far easier than putting them into behavioral action. It takes a certain mental level to get started, and when that is too low, we may not be able to implement these plans. Survivors can have the mental level to create the best of plans, but sometimes lack the level required to put them into action. Or they may start, but give up easily. They may become tired or bored, be unable to coordinate more complex actions, fear they will fail, or fear that they might be successful and as a result lose something essential (e.g., "If I get better I might decide I need to leave my partner").

Execution and Ongoing Evaluation of Actions

Action systems prompt us to evaluate the immediate effects of our behavioral actions in recurrent cycles of perception, feeling, thinking, and body movements (i.e., perception–motor action cycles). This evaluation involves weighing, and thus integrating, the costs and benefits of our ongoing actions as they relate to a set goal. Our recurrent perception–motor action cycles allow us to evaluate and thus adapt virtually any action, ranging from a simple body movement to highly complex mental actions of realization and creativity. Ongoing evaluation of the effects of our actions (a mental action in itself) tells us, for example, when to abandon a plan and create a new course of action. The more internal and external events we synthesize and evaluate that are relevant to the goals we wish to achieve, the more effective our actions will be. Goal-directed actions are efforts to reduce discrepancies between a desired and an actual state of affairs (Carver & Scheier, 2000). For example, within the confines of the defense system, our evaluations may tell us whether a particular defensive strategy is effective or whether we need to shift to another tactic (cf., Carver & Scheier, 2000). These flexible shifts are mediated by different subsystems or modes of defense and the links between them. However, such rapid and smooth transitions will only work if we have integrated the different components of the defense system. In the same way, all action systems require the challenge of integrating their various components (i.e., subsystems and modes).

The way in which we achieve a short-term goal must be considered within the context of long-term goals whenever possible. Mental and behavioral actions are only adaptive when we integrate the immediate present along with future consequences, an integrative action called *presentification* (Chapter 8). And we often need to consider one action in a broader context of many goals and our needs as a whole person. In other words, we must be able to appraise our actions in the context of most, if not all, action systems and their respective goals that comprise our personality. For example, a therapist may respond in kind to a patient who becomes enraged and calls the therapist names. The defensive actions of the therapist may stop the patient from continuing to be verbally abusive (defensive goal achieved). However, such action may damage the therapeutic relationship beyond repair (caregiving and attachment failed). Adaptive therapeutic actions, like many actions needed in daily life, require delicate and complex integration of a range of action systems and goals.

Dissociative parts may not attend sufficiently to feedback from their own actions or to those of other parts, so they cannot adequately evaluate the effectiveness of their actions. They may ignore or avoid their body and be unaware of physical cues of discomfort or pain; they may be unaware of or avoid other dissociative parts that could provide important feedback; and they may not attend to cues in relationships or in the environment. For example, some parts seem unaware of the harm or pain experienced when they cut or burn the body. Some parts do not integrate the fact that all parts share one body. When a survivor as ANP hears a terrified part begging for help internally, he or she may avoid the voice rather than being aware that something is wrong and doing something constructive about it. And when parts are stuck in traumatic memories, they are unable to take in feedback from the present that might change their fearful behavior to that which is more adaptive to current reality.

Completion and Realization

We complete our actions when we realize that our goals have been achieved. A major tenet of a Janetian psychology of action is that the well-executed and well-completed action improves our mental efficiency. However, this desirable effect will only emerge if we integrate the fact that we have indeed accomplished our goal; that is, we have completed our actions. We recognize and own (i.e., personify—an aspect of realization discussed in the next chapter) our successes when we engage in the *action of triumph* (Janet, 1919/1925, 1928b). This action of triumph manifests in the big smile on a child's face when she has managed to ride her bicycle for the first time, the ecstatic jumping of a football player who has scored a goal, or the joy of a patient who has managed to assert himself more.

It takes a degree of mental efficiency to realize our little and big successes. Survivors who engage in actions in a depersonalized or disinterested way may not appreciate their accomplishments enough, so their mental efficiency is not augmented by a sense of accomplishment. And they may minimize or discount their successes for various reasons.

Structural dissociation of the personality involves failure to complete major integrative actions, that is, the (re)integration of the dissociative parts. This deficiency is intimately related to survivors' experienced inability to complete the actions we describe as traumatic memories (Janet, 1919/1925, 1928a; Van der Hart, Steele, Boon, & Brown, 1993). As noted before, Janet observed that survivors

> are continuing the action, or rather the attempt at action, which began when the [traumatizing event] happened; and they exhaust themselves in these everlasting recommencements. . . . The [trauma survivor] remains confronted by a difficult situation in which he has not been able to play a satisfactory part, one to which his adaptation has been imperfect, so that he continues to make efforts at adaptation. The repetition of this situation, these continuous efforts, give rise to fatigue. . . . (1919/1925, p. 663)

This useless expenditure of effort to accomplish a goal that could not be achieved (e.g., fending off a perpetrator effectively, or securing the attention and love of a neglectful caretaker), characterizes traumatic memories and drains a survivor's energy and mental efficiency. It eventually leads to the condition of posttraumatic decline in which the survivor is unable to accomplish goals in life, and ultimately ends with a deep sense of failure and collapse. Survivors become more adaptive when they can invest their energy in realizing that the traumatizing event has happened. This goal requires the realization that nothing can be done to change what happened, that the event has deeply affected their existence, and that it is not now happening. The realization that the traumatizing event has happened is a most difficult action that requires a high mental level. It leads to painful mourning of all losses, which also calls for a high mental level. Much of the treatment of chronic trauma survivors is geared toward developing this mental level.

INTEGRATION IN MENTAL HEALTH AND TRAUMATIZATION

Integration, the combined actions of synthesis and realization, involves a series of ongoing actions, beginning at the most basic level with the organization of neurons into neural networks, to living adaptive and creative lives that meet the complex challenges of our world. Ultimately, integration provides us with the uniquely human capacity to create meaningful and cohesive experiences of our world and our sense of self across time (Janet, 1929a; Siegel, 1999; Tucker, Luu, & Pribam, 1995). As we have noted, what we integrate depends to a large degree on our innate action systems and their essential emotions, which serve major organizing functions. A healthy personality is characterized by a strong capacity to integrate a wide range of mental and behavioral actions tendencies (Janet, 1889), not only within the domain of a single action system, but also among action systems.

TRAUMA-RELATED STRUCTURAL DISSOCIATION AS A UNIQUE FORM OF INTEGRATIVE FAILURE

Integration is on a continuum, with everyone having some degree of integrative imperfection in life. However, not all integrative failure results in structural dissociation. As noted before, trauma-related structural dissociation specifically involves an undue division of or failure to integrate the psychobiological systems that together constitute personality. An essential element of this dissociation entails a fragmentation of the sense of self. We normally experience ourselves somewhat differently at work than at play, and very differently as a lover than as a mugging victim, and differently as a child than as an adult. We must integrate these discrepant experiences of ourselves and our world and fashion a rather unitary history from them: "*I* am the same person who works, plays, loves, and was mugged; *I* am an adult and am no longer a child, but am the *same* person: All these experiences are *mine*."

A dissociative person does not engage in this degree of integration, at least to an extent. Sometimes structural dissociation may be restricted only to a single traumatizing event, as in simple PTSD, with one extensive ANP and one very limited EP. But the integrative failure may be more extensive for those who were chronically traumatized as children. These children are often deprived of the very developmental tools necessary to develop self-coherence; namely, a sense of self that is unified and singular (D. Stern, 1985).

Generally we speak of our "self" as the active agent of integration: "*I* integrate my experience." But in fact, our "self" does not integrate experience, but rather is the *result* of integrative actions (Loevinger, 1976; Metzinger, 2003). A unified sense of self emerges when we have unconsciously and consciously integrated the many "selves" or "self states" that are a part of normal development (Harter, 1999; D. Stern, 1985), and which we suggest are based to a large degree on various (constellations of) action systems and their subsystems and modes. Patients with trauma-related structural dissociation have not been able to engage adequately in the integrative actions that generate and maintain one largely cohesive sense of self and a cohesive personality.

Synthesis

We must often engage in integrated series or "strings" of mental and behavioral actions in order to achieve our goals. The integration of these actions is a mental action in itself, which may or may not be conscious. *Synthesis* involves *binding together* and *differentiating* among a range of mental and behavioral actions that constitute our internal and external world at any given moment and across time. Thus, our experiential world is not a given but an ongoing personal construction based on our subjective appraisals. Synthesis is not an all or nothing phenomenon, but is rather on a continuum, and our capacity to synthesize oscillates. For example, when we are fully awake, synthesis will be of a higher quality than when we are tired. Synthesis provides the basic foundation for our normative unity of consciousness and history, which is further developed through higher levels of integration. Alterations of consciousness and dissociative symptoms can emerge when synthesis is incomplete. When an individual's consciousness is retracted or lowered, he or she may not adequately synthesize particular stimuli. He or she is not aware of a stimulus at all, or is only dimly aware of it. In dissociative patients, one part typically synthesizes certain stimuli that other parts do not. But when a dissociative individual also experiences a severe lowering or narrowing of consciousness, stimuli needed for adaptation will not be synthesized at all by any part of the personality. For example, Susan had DID, and also frequently spaced out as a whole person so that none of her dissociative parts attended to the present moment. Thus, at times, no part of her had any recollection of the present. Synthesis that occurs in a given moment or event is called *core synthesis*, while synthesis of experience over time is called *extended synthesis*.

Core synthesis. Core synthesis involves binding together sensations, emotions, thoughts, behavioral actions, and a sense of self within a given moment or situation, but also differentiating them. In other words, adaptive synthesis in the moment must include essential internal and external stimuli and appropriate perception–motor action cycles. On a broader level, it involves the immediate coordination and cohesion of action systems. Adaptive core synthesis provides the building blocks for synthesis over time (i.e., extended synthesis). Failures in core synthesis may manifest as symptoms of structural dissociation or maladaptive alterations in consciousness.

What we synthesize in a given moment or situation is strongly influenced by the action tendencies and action systems (and their modes) that are activated at the time. Synthesis of action systems and their components is a developmental task: Some people synthesize these systems more adequately than others, and our capacity to synthesize them may fluctuate according to circumstances. For example, we may synthesize action systems less well when our mental level is low, such as when we are extremely tired or ill, or when we struggle between highly conflicting interests of different action systems: "I have a deadline at work, but am very tired: Shall I work or rest now?"

Binding. Binding (or connecting) together aspects of our internal and external experiences is one aspect of synthesis in the moment. The first step in binding goal-directed actions together as a whole involves connecting related but different perceptual actions. Much of this type of synthesis occurs automatically and unconsciously. For example, we typically automatically and unconsciously bind together sensations of movement and touch, temperature, taste, smell, and sight into one whole and higher order perception. However, this is not always the case. For example, when we learn new skills, or focus consciously and with great effort on a paper we are reading, synthesis is far from automatic.

Survivors may have difficulties even at the most basic level of synthesis. While some parts may accurately perceive and bind certain stimuli, others do not. This failure to bind perceptions that belong together into a whole may produce a variety of symptoms, including negative somatoform dissociative symptoms such as analgesia or kinesthetic anesthesia.

> Alie, a survivor who was repeatedly raped as a child, was able to have pleas-
> ant sexual feelings as ANP. However when she initiated sex with her part-
> ner, an EP with no genital sensations became evoked, leading to sexual dif-
> ficulties. This part of her never fully synthesized pelvic sensations because
> that region of her body became numb in her efforts to defensively respond
> during the rape.

We must also bind perceptions with our motivations and goals, and link those with the appropriate actions to meet our goals. And of course, some of our most powerful motivations are emotions, which must also be bound together with our actions. Dissociative parts that do not bind feelings as part of their experience can be emotionally flat or numb. Without much feeling to direct and motivate them, they often have difficulty generating enough mental energy and efficiency to act adaptively.

Action systems must be linked together for synthesis to be adaptive. For example, dinner in company does not merely involve eating (a mode of the energy-regulation system), but also seamless integration of actions related to social engagement such as attachment, and sometimes play, exploration, or even sexuality (e.g., flirting). However, we must also be able to inhibit action systems that are not appropriate to the situation. For example, participation in a dinner should not include activation of the defense system if no threat exists, and should not include flirting as a general rule. If such action tendencies are dissociated, an individual will have less control over their activation and inhibition. The stronger the integrations among action systems and their related sense of self, the more flexible *and* stable the personality, which promotes the best possible functioning in the present (Jackson, 1931/1932; Janet, 1889; Meares, 1999; Nijenhuis et al., 2004).

> Mary, a patient with DDNOS, found it painful and frightening to eat in company and thus preferred to eat alone. When she did eat with others, she kept her eyes on her plate and did not join in conversation. She ate quickly and usually found an excuse to leave the table early. She had developed rigid and profound links between eating and defense because as a child meals were fraught with violent fights, vicious ridicule, and sarcastic verbal attacks. Her family did not chat amicably or have stimulating discussions or laugh together (social engagement, exploration, play), so Mary never learned how to integrate these action systems together with eating. It was adaptive for Mary to engage in defense at the dinner table with her family, but as an adult, it impaired her ability to be social with friends.

Our mental and behavioral actions must be linked with our awareness of ourselves (i.e., our sense of self). This sense is primarily dependent on developing feelings of what happens in or to our body in a given moment and situation (Damasio, 1999). Even in core synthesis (i.e., what occurs in a given moment), we draw upon our personal history and genetic heritage to some degree, including our previous sense of self (Fuster, 2003). Synthesis in the moment cannot exist without building upon some synthesis of the past that is at least held in implicit memory (Edelman & Tononi, 2000).

A major problem for survivors is that their sense of self is too restricted and rigid within dissociative parts, because it has been derived from a range of experiences and action systems that is too limited, and excludes too much of the survivor's history. When survivors are unable to bind actions adequately with a sense of self in the moment, they experience symptoms of depersonalization. For example, when Alie touched her abdomen or genitals it felt as though they belonged to someone else's body. She *knew* they were hers, but they did not *feel* that way.

In sum, when dissociative parts can perceive feelings, thoughts, memories, wishes, behaviors, and the sense of self of other parts, but do not regard these as their own, they have engaged in insufficient binding. The same goes for parts that fail to synthesize external stimuli that really matter. For example, a part may see the therapist shift in his chair and perceive this as a sign of rejection or disapproval, but fails to perceive other signals that indicate the therapist remains connected and empathic.

Differentiation. Adaptive core synthesis not only involves binding what belongs together in a given moment and context. We must also differentiate between what we perceive and what we actually do. Thus, it is important to know that our perceptions, affective feelings, thoughts, and movements relate to each other in a given moment, but still are different. For example, we must be able to distinguish between our own body and what is external to us ("The chair is not a part of me"; "You are a separate person from me"). This involves a very basic level of action tendencies (see Chapter 9).

Survivors sometimes lack such core differentiation. When they confuse thoughts and objective facts, they may wonder, "Am I really at work or am I dreaming?" Or they confused hallucinations with reality: "My mother is standing there; she wants to grab me!" They may also have difficulty knowing the difference between wishes and behavioral actions. For example, survivors as EP sometimes believe that they have actually killed their perpetrator, when in fact, they only fantasized doing so.

Attention. In addition to knowing how certain mental and behavioral actions are related but different from each other, we must be able to know *which* internal and external stimuli to synthesize and ignore in a given situation. This is a function of *attention,* and is a manifestation of the goal-directedness of adaptive (constellations of) action systems. Attention helps us focus on, synthesize, and react to what is essential, and exclude what is not. Attention is based on the action tendencies and action systems that direct us in the moment (Fuster, 2003). It thus includes an ability to ignore irrelevant stimuli that is essential to organizing our experience. This is a mental action itself, which Janet (1935a) referred to as our reaction toward the insignificant (*la réaction de l'insignifiant*). Some survivors are unable to engage in this important mental action of exclusion, and inappropriately focus on extraneous details, failing to grasp the essentials of an experience.

Healthy individuals can shift their attention as needed, and therefore change what they synthesize, depending on the demands of the situation. Survivors often cannot "shift gears" so easily. Dissociative parts tend to be fixed in a retracted field of consciousness, attending only to stimuli related to their action systems, such as defense. At other times, survivors shift their attention reactively and inappropriately, without conscious control. These shifts, which may or may not be adaptive, can occur when a particular dissociative part reflexively responds to powerful stimuli.

Some internal and external stimuli have a strong, natural, and universal potential to activate a particular action system, and are known as unconditioned stimuli. These stimuli can evoke an almost instantaneous and adaptive shift in our attention and goals. For example, a sudden, loud noise behind us will trigger an immediate defensive reaction. Survivors (as one or more dissociative parts) have learned to associate particular stimuli that were previously neutral to them with unconditioned aversive stimuli. Thus, these previous neutral stimuli become conditioned stimuli. Survivors overattend (and overrespond more generally) to conditioned threat stimuli (Izquierdo, Cammarota, Vianna, & Bevilaqua, 2004; Peri, Ben Shakhar, Orr, & Shalev, 2000). Some, but not all dissociative parts may have this attentional bias. Thus one part may be triggered by a stimulus, while another part is not.

> Pia, a patient with DID, had an EP who perceived herself to be 6 years old. This part of her was afraid of the sound of a door slamming behind her back because in the past it had consistently signalled the entry of a perpetrator who would subsequently beat and rape her. However, as ANP, Pia did not recall any abuse, and thus a slamming door did not have any special meaning. When the door to a room next to the therapist's slammed, Pia attended to it for a second and continued her session. However, she soon became restless. She did not know what was wrong, but remarked that it was as if there was a monster inside her. A moment later, Pia switched into a fearful EP, who was very afraid and focused on the door of the therapy room as though someone dangerous might enter. This EP's fear only gradually subsided when the therapist helped her inspect the empty hallway.

The degree to which survivors attend to a conditioned stimulus thus strongly depends on the probability that it signals an unconditioned stimulus. They can only estimate this likelihood by synthesizing and evaluating the conditioned stimulus in context (i.e., by knowing what is happening in the present). Survivors should learn to ignore irrelevant stimuli and stop a defensive reaction by inhibiting their defense system when the conditioned stimulus does not signal threat. With repetition, their attention for a conditioned stimulus should become minimal, while their defense system remains inhibited.

In general, some dissociative parts do not sufficiently attend to certain conditioned stimuli, and pay too much attention to irrelevant stimuli (i.e., they underengage in the reaction toward the insignificant). For example, as ANP, Carla talked in great detail about her work, but ignored scared parts internally. Other parts attend to particular conditioned stimuli and not enough to the context of the stimuli (the present situation), so that they find it very hard to ignore stimuli such as the normal sounds of the therapist's office. These attentional and synthetic differences for dissociative parts often explain sudden major shifts in attention in survivors (we revisit the topics of conditioning and context evaluation in Chapter 10).

Therapists should be aware of failures in core synthesis and help patients attend to, bind, and differentiate relevant stimuli in the moment, and ignore the irrelevant (i.e., engage in the action toward the insignificant). Patients can be helped to be more aware of current experience, to be mindful, and to accept sensations, emotions, and thoughts (Hayes, Folette, & Linehan, 2004). They can be encouraged to look at the therapist and read body cues more accurately, not focusing only on a single cue. Patients can be taught gradually to focus on the whole picture with the ability to exclude what is irrelevant.

Extended synthesis. Many goals are not achieved in a single moment but entail an extended series or string of actions that must be synthesized over time. We refer to this complex mental action as extended synthesis (i.e., binding and differentiating across time and situations). Extended synthesis involves creating associations between related events and experiences, as well as distinguishing between them. For example, we bind together the experiences of today and yesterday, but appreciate they are different. What we view as related events is affected by the constellations of action systems we have created. A major advantage of extended synthesis is that it allows us to learn from our experiences and evolve ever more complex and creative solutions to new experiences based on what we have learned.

It is easier to bind experiences that are similar than to bind those that are different in some way. Survivors, for example, may be more inclined to associate negative relational experiences with many different people across time, and thus are less able to notice the positive relational experiences that happen in the therapy session.

Our capacity to successfully attain different goals is at its best when we are continuously involved in extended synthesis of our different action systems, and when we synthesize these action systems with our ever changing internal and external environment (e.g., Borkovec & Sharpless, 2004; Hurley, 1998). In many cases, we cannot pursue different goals at the same time (e.g., rest and work). This is because very different action systems tend to exclude each other and because the capacity of our working memory is quite limited. Consequently, we cannot engage in a wide or complex variety of different actions at a time. Core synthesis involves relatively limited synthesis of different action tendencies and goals. In extended synthesis, we bind together and differentiate a much wider range of both similar and discrepant actions and goals over time.

We engage in simple forms of extended synthesis, such as listening to music, in which we synthesize long strings of notes into a melody over time, or planning our day while we drive to work. Extended synthesis also helps us engage in highly complex actions. It helps us create our life history and a consistent sense of self because we are able to bind, differentiate, and coordinate not only a single action system, but complex constellations of them over long periods of time. For example, we can synthesize our interests and experiences as a parent, partner, professional, and friend across time as aspects of our whole self.

Lack of synthesis explains to a large degree the survivor's seeming inability to learn from experience in various areas of life, because experience has not been adequately synthesized. Different parts synthesize different experiences and goals across time, so that they create not just a different view of the world in the moment, but also sometimes a different personal history, no matter how limited. And because dissociative parts are not totally separate from each other, they engage in conflicts that are fueled by the different goals they pursue, and their different perceptions and experiences that are based on their discrepant core and extended syntheses.

Insight into the survivor's problems with core and extended synthesis helps therapists understand and modify many dissociative symptoms and pathological alterations in consciousness.

SUMMARY

We all integrate our personality and our experiential world by engaging in a wide range of unconscious and conscious mental and behavioral actions. Janet's psychology of action supports our understanding of the specific actions of integration and their failure in structural dissociation. In this perspective, integration is not understood as an outcome of "mechanisms" and "processes," but emerges from specific and creative integrative actions. However, at least some forms of psychopathology, including structural dissociation, involve undue limitations of these integrative actions. The integrative mental and behavioral actions in which we engage in a given moment or situation, and across time are guided by (constellations of) action systems. These systems motivate us to engage in particular goal-directed cycles of perceptions, cognitions, and behavioral actions. Traumatized individuals have various difficulties within these cycles that make integration less likely to be achieved. Integration occurs at various levels, some more automatic and basic, others more conscious and calling for much higher mental functioning. The basic form of integration is that of synthesis.

CHAPTER 8

Traumatization as a Syndrome of Nonrealization

Every realization implies promises of action, either promises of accounts of past action or promises of future actions. In certain individuals, the thought of the execution of these actions provokes such anxieties that this representation become impossible.
—Pierre Janet (1945, pp. 181–182)

I NTEGRATION DOES NOT MERELY involve our capacity to synthesize experience. It includes the uniquely human ability to make meaning and create a cohesive sense of time, reality, self, and experience. Such complex mental actions, those of *realization* (Janet, 1903, 1928a, 1935a; Van der Hart et al., 1993), require a higher level of mental functioning than synthesis, needing the maximum amount of our mental energy and level of efficiency. It is these actions that are most difficult for survivors to achieve, at least in regard to their traumatic experiences. In fact, trauma-related dissociation of the personality is known as a *syndrome of nonrealization* (Janet, 1935a; cf., Van der Hart, Steele, Boon, & Brown, 1993). The core issue in traumatization is that survivors have been unable to realize fully what has happened to them and how it affects their lives and who they are. In other words, the inability to realize involves many ways of *not knowing* massive psychic trauma (Laub & Auerhahn, 1993). Actually, chronically traumatized individuals often have difficulties with realization not only in regard to their traumatic experiences, but also in daily life.

REALIZATION

We must engage in acts of realization, otherwise our attempts to adapt to our changeable world are not well grounded in reality, and thus run a higher risk of being maladaptive. Each act of realization involves two components (Janet, 1935a; cf., Van der Hart, Steele et al., 1993). The first action is to *formulate beliefs* about our experiences: what has happened, why, and to whom. The second is to *adapt our subsequent mental and behavioral actions* based on these beliefs. In other words, we rely on what we have synthesized to construct a worldview and act accordingly.

Realization runs from the mundane and practical, to ascribing philosophical and spiritual meaning to our lives. It can be instantaneous, or slowly and painfully earned over a long period of time, requiring a high mental level. Many realizations eventually involve conscious beliefs that can be verbalized. It is common for us to say, "I *realize* that: I must watch my expenses; I am a good person; my father is dead and can no longer abuse me; I am an adult and can be responsible for myself; my life and what happens to me has meaning." The beliefs that emerge from realization are not instantaneous, uncritical, and simpleminded, but are well contemplated. They thus involve *reflective* rather than *reflexive* action tendencies. Such realizations promote changes in our usual mental and behavioral actions that may be quite new and different for us (see Chapter 9).

Realization is more than an intellectual cognitive action; it also includes affect and behavior that accompanies knowing that an experience or fact is real, and that it has consequences for our personal existence. We thus accept all of our experiences for better and worse, rejoice in or resign ourselves to them, and reorganize our behavior accordingly (Janet, 1935a, 1945). In a word, the beliefs involved in realization are "hot" rather than "cold" cognition (cf., Abelson, 1963). Realization is about making connections between our world and our sense of self, and changing our selves and our world as a result. In this way realization plays a dominant role in the ongoing "construction" of our personality (Janet, 1929a).

Survivors and Social Nonrealization

Lack of realization is not a problem limited to survivors, but manifests to some degree in many ways in all individuals and societies. The more severe and pervasive nonrealization is, the more serious the consequences. There is a strong social component in realization. We often share significant realizations with others as a way to solidify our awareness and to create a narrative about how these realizations have affected our lives and our relationships. This social sharing allows for the possibility that changes based on realizations can affect ourselves, others, and our world. We also sometimes need social support to realize difficult issues, such as the loss of a loved one. Empathy, support, and caring from others can increase our mental energy and efficiency to a point where we can realize painful issues that might otherwise be intolerable. In fact, lack of social support is considered a major vulnerability factor for ongoing traumatization (Chapter 1). Indeed, survivors are often surrounded by people who are themselves unable or unwilling to realize the impact of abuse and neglect.

> Kelly, a patient whose father was severely physically abusive, recalled that her mother seemed not to notice when one of the children was bleeding or bruised, and once stepped over Kelly's brother who was unconscious on the floor after a beating, and continued with her housework as if nothing had happened. The fact that the father was abusive was never mentioned by anyone in the family until Kelly spoke of it for the first time after several years of therapy.

Serious forms of nonrealization not only occur in individuals and families, but in society at large. For example, there is much outrage expressed that abuse happens, but there is little treatment accessible to survivors, even though we know that childhood abuse often has devastating and life-long consequences. Our society seems to have a depersonalized awareness in which people can feel comfortable in being aware enough to acknowledge a problem, but not to the degree that they demand that difficult and complex social and interpersonal changes be made. Thus on both individual and social levels there is often virtually no support for survivors to realize their devastating experiences. As Van der Hart and colleagues noted, "In fact, there is often enormous pressure from perpetrators and families to continue the pattern of dissociation and denial that characterizes collective nonrealization" (1993, p. 175; cf. Herman, 1992b).

Realization includes two related major types of mental and behavioral actions that are constantly maturing our view of ourselves, others, and the world: *personification* (Janet, 1903, 1929a) and *presentification* (Janet, 1928a, 1935b). Both actions involve the ability to differentiate between what should be more real to us and what should be less real (Janet, 1928a; Van der Hart & Steele, 1997).

PERSONIFICATION

Personification is an essential component of realization that involves the capacity to take personal ownership of our experiences: "This is *my* experience." We become consciously aware that a particular event happens to *us*, that *we* have done or felt something, that an experience will affect *our* lives and we change our own actions accordingly (Janet, 1935a). Personification thus connects our sense of self with past, present, and future events, and with our own mental and behavioral actions, giving us a sense of agency.

As with realization in general, personification evolves from perception–motor action cycles; what we do (and do not) personify depends to a large degree on the continuous cycling of what we perceive and how we behave in the world. As noted previously, the focus of these cycles is dependent upon the types of action systems that are active. We strengthen our sense of ownership of our mental and behavioral actions when we give ourselves (and sometimes others) an account of them. In other words, we formulate beliefs about what is happening to us and within us. This account of personal ownership should be in the form of conscious and often verbalized thought and belief. Our owning of experience becomes stronger when we can make social statements about it than when we keep it to ourselves. When, for example, therapists remind themselves that they must be therapeutic with a patient who is lashing out, they are creating an account of their realization of the patient's behavior as it relates to them, and also of their own behavior in response. Because they have formulated a belief that the patient is in need of help with relational difficulties, and they *realize* their personal role as therapist ("*I* am this patient's therapist, not his adversary"), they are able to act reflectively and responsibly rather than defensively. And when they discuss their struggles in consultation or supervision (i.e., make a verbal account of them), they are better able to realize their personal role of therapist. In fact, making an account of our experience helps us become more aware, more mindful of what we are doing, and thus more responsible for how we respond to what is happening within ourselves, with others, and in the world. And when we share that account with significant others, our sense of responsibility to act mindfully based on what we have realized becomes even greater.

Recounting an experience to ourselves and others only once is often not sufficient for adequate realization. For example, therapists may need to remind themselves frequently that they must respond therapeutically to certain patients when they are inclined to do otherwise, and be responsible for engaging in practical action as an inherent part of this realization. The fact that we need to remind ourselves or talk repeatedly about unusual, difficult, or stressful events (to recount our reality), highlights the fact that personification is not always an easy task. And as with all forms of realization, it takes more mental energy and efficiency to personify experiences when they are outside the range of our normal experience or when they are overwhelming.

Like synthesis, personification can occur in a given moment or situation (core), or across time (extended).

Core Personification

Core personification is the ability to make experience our own in a present moment (cf., Damasio, 1999; Edelman & Tononi, 2000; D.N. Stern, 2004), which stimulates us to take responsibility for engaging in immediate mental or behavioral actions. For example, when we personify our current bodily or emotional feelings, we might say, "I feel tired," and take care of ourselves by resting. When we do not engage in core personification, we will not experience such feelings as our own, fail to act on them, or merely act reflexively. Many trauma survivors do not sufficiently personify their mental and behavioral actions, feelings, thoughts, and behavioral actions in a given moment. This leaves them depersonalized. For example, they may experience as ANP, "I am on an automatic pilot; I know I'm here, but it does not feel that way."

Extended Personification

Extended personification consists of mental activities by which we bind and differentiate experiences with our sense of self across time and situations. We construct our personality, including personal history and autobiographical self (Damasio, 1999), by connecting strings of core personified experiences and acting accordingly. To paraphrase Damasio (1999, p. 17), our autobiographical self depends on our systematized, personified memories of situations regarding the important or most invariant characteristics of our life: Who we were born to, where, when, our likes, dislikes, the way we usually react to a problem or a conflict, our name, significant life events we memorize, and so on. And so extended personification contributes to a cohesive sense of self and experience over time.

The various roles we have in life must be connected, at least to a degree, as a part of our whole self. For example, therapists should be able to personify their roles and experiences as a child, an adolescent, a student, a parent, a partner, a friend when they are in the role of therapist. Each of these roles and experiences likely has something helpful to offer in the therapeutic situation at one time or another. But at the same time, these roles are in the background, available to be drawn upon, but not dominant, because we realize that our primary role in this situation is that of therapist.

Difficulties with Personification in Trauma Survivors

Our personality involves not only a perception of who we are across time, our sense of self, but also particular skills, action tendencies, and combinations of action systems that we have learned or created. Survivors sometimes have problems in transferring skills from one area of life to another because they have not been able to personify the skills or action tendencies (action systems), across their different senses of self, whether that is a different role in life, or a different dissociative part of the personality. For example, they may be excellent at negotiating with and being empathic toward others at work, but are unable to do so in close personal relationships at home or internally with parts.

Survivors do not personify their actions in a given moment and across time under the umbrella of an integrated, unified personality. Their structural dissociation implies the existence of at least two "me's." In this organization, each dissociative part personifies some actions and experiences, but regards other actions and experiences as "not me" to some degree, including one or more other parts.

> As EP, Alie was unable to personify much about her present-day life. For example, she was absolutely disinterested in keeping up the house, which she did not view as her own. She did not believe she was part of Alie, and felt she did not need to respond to current life situations, such as working or being with friends. She was unable to personify some of her own body sensations, lacking feeling in her genitals, as though they did not belong to her. Alie had several parts, each of which had a relatively separate sense of self—one as a toddler, one as an older child, one as an adolescent. But she was unable to engage in extended personification to integrate these different senses of self into one whole. And as ANP, Alie was unable to personify her past abuse history as belonging to her, and was not motivated to integrate it and thus to function at a higher mental level.

Each dissociative part has personified at least some degree of sense of self: "*I* feel; *I* think, *I* hurt; *I* know." But personification may be extremely limited when a part has only realized a minimal amount of experience out of the individual's entire history, such as a few fragmentary moments within an extended traumatic event. Some parts have engaged in little more than core personification involving the short moments of time in which they are fixated, hence lack extended personification. Such parts have a small basis of realization and, accordingly, a small range of action tendencies. For example, in simple PTSD, a single EP may encompass little more than one (core) personified traumatic experience and memory involving synthesis of pain sensations and fear. The more experience a survivor has personified within a dissociative part of the personality across time, the more elaborate this part's autobiographical self will be and the more types of actions this part can engage in.

As essential as personification is, it can be carried too far when synthesis does not include adequate differentiation. For example, some survivors may come to believe that someone else's experience is their own. One patient was confused about whether a memory involved him watching his father beat his brother, or whether he had an out of body experience in which he was watching himself being beaten. Another patient reported that she felt physical pain if she was near anyone in pain. A more common problem is that of becoming overwhelmed by someone else's suffering as though it is our own: A difficulty perhaps not unfamiliar to many highly empathic therapists in response to their patients. In such cases we seem unable to "screen out" the experiences of other people and separate them from our own.

Survivors need much help in personifying their experiences, both in the moment and across time. This is a major component of realization that will be developed over time in therapy. All dissociative parts must be supported in raising their mental level to the degree that they can personify the experiences of other parts. Thus each part ultimately must be able to respond to the present moment and the history of the whole person and say, "This is *my* experience, *my* feeling, *my* body, *my* history."

Personification is necessary, but not an entirely sufficient part of integration to help us make enduring changes in the ways that we think, feel, and behave. Experience can be owned (personalized), but still may not induce an individual to be different as a result. Real and lasting change comes in the form of *presentification*.

PRESENTIFICATION

Presentification is that complex human endeavor of simultaneously *being* and *acting* in the moment in a highly reflective manner. This multifaceted action includes the experience of "being present" (i.e., *presentness*, or experiencing "the moment of subjective experience as it is occurring. . ." [D. N. Stern, 2004, p. xiii]). We are present when we synthesize and personify current internal and external stimuli that are critical for our current interests, and adapt our subsequent mental and behavioral actions accordingly.

Furthermore, when we experience ourselves as being present, we have connected our past and future to the here and now. Indeed, presentification is more than being aware of the present moment. It involves our creation of the present moment from a synthesis of personified experiences stretched over time and situations, from the past, the present and the projected future. Ultimately, presentification is our construction of the *context* and *meaning* of the present moment within our personal history.

Indeed, the function of presentification is to help us organize and change our actions and sometimes our sense of who we are. It allows us to form reflective beliefs and act with deliberation, conviction, conscience, and purpose, to grasp our reality to the maximum and act adaptively because of it (Janet, 1928a, 1935a; Ellenberger, 1970). In other words, we must engage in presentification to adapt and evolve and to achieve a complex balance between stability and flexibility within our personality.

> Jonathan, a patient with complex PTSD, was able to realize his painful, abusive history over time. In doing so, he felt more present in general, was more aware of himself, of others, and of his surroundings. He realized that because of his history he found it difficult to trust people, but also recognized that he no longer needed to always act on those distrustful feelings. He and his therapist worked out cues that he could use to help him know whether someone might be trusted, and he learned to move slowly forward with trust, taking each step at his own pace. He learned that most people

are not abusive, and he learned how to have friends who were good to him. Jonathan was more able to connect with people in the present. He also felt more positive about his future, no longer worried that he would fall apart and be unable to take care of himself.

As a most complex action, presentification requires our highest levels of mental energy and efficiency. Thus this action disappears easily and often when we are stressed or distracted. It is our highest achievement to sustain presentification both in the moment and over the course of life, and is an ultimate goal of therapy with traumatized individuals. Like the actions of synthesis and personification, we can also understand presentification as being in the moment (core) as well as across time and experience (extended).

Core Presentification

Core presentification is the action of being present in the moment. It includes making an account of our present action and experience (Janet, 1903, 1928a, 1935a) as being here and now, and as being real. Another component of core presentification involves adapting our immediate actions to this account. The account can be nonverbal, but putting it in words will give it a higher degree of reality. Our account of the present, a mental action in itself, is influenced by other mental and behavioral actions, and in turn, influences our behaviors in constant perception–motor action cycles. We do not then confuse the past with the present, or the internal with the external, but stay connected to the synthesis of our reality of the moment. It is often essential for patients to make conscious, verbal accounts of their core presentifications in therapy, because this helps solidify integration and thus stimulates higher level, more adaptive actions. For example, a patient might say, "I am sitting here on this blue couch in the therapy room and my therapist is sitting across from me, listening to what I'm saying. I am safe, and no one is going to hurt me."

Core presentification takes a lot of mental energy and efficiency. It is not easy to pay attention to the stimuli and actions that really matter to us in the present moment without wandering off into the past or future, or losing an adaptive balance between conscious awareness of our internal and external world. And being fully present requires that we have a sufficient mental level to sustain our attention and control serious maladaptive alterations in consciousness. It takes even more mental effort to concentrate reflectively on present action.

In core presentification, we immediately reflect on and accept our unfolding experiences (e.g., Hayes et al., 2004; Linehan, 1993), essential mental actions for integration. These actions have been described in terms of mindfulness, and primarily refer to observation of and reflection on our own actions (e.g., feelings, thoughts). In other words, core presentification requires our capacity to have a *theory of mind*, to know that we have a mind, that other people also have minds, and to be aware of how our minds work and what affects them, instead of merely reacting to internal experiences (Fonagy, Gergely, Jurist, & Target, 2002; Fonagy & Target, 1996). Core presentification not only includes self awareness, but heightened conscious awareness of what surrounds us, and ultimately involves our reflective *response* to our mindfulness.

Being present, the basic aspect of core presentification, does not imply that we are mindful of all stimuli; that would be impossible, overwhelming, and very maladaptive. We must adaptively select those experiences with which we are present. For example, it may be more adaptive in one moment to focus attention externally, and in another to focus internally on what we are thinking or feeling or remembering. But even in the moment of internal focus, we should retain enough conscious awareness of the external so that we could respond if necessary. Our focus in the moment is determined to a large degree by the combinations of action systems that are activated, by what is motivating us at the time.

Thanks to core presentification, we do not experience the ever changing present as a range of successive fragments but as a cohesive, personal experience that has meaning, and that involves our motivation to attain particular goals through mental and behavioral actions. This cohesion exists because we are continuously engaged in making accounts of our present. We are able to do so because of working memory. The capacity of working memory, even though limited in its extent, allows us to link the present and the immediate past and future so that we can engage in prospective actions on the basis of past experiences and current circumstances. In other words, working memory helps us to link predictions of the outcome of our actions with the past and the current moment, allowing us to better adapt ourselves to the present. Thus, working memory is referred to as the remembered present (Edelman, 1989), and as our active memory for the short term (Fuster, 2003).

Core presentification, our account of the present, thus, does not just involve the present alone, rather it is a synthesis of the memories and predictions we need to adapt to an immediate situation. For example, we include at least some of our autobiographical self and aspects of our personal history as part of being in the present, as well as previously learned skills and knowledge (Damasio, 1999; Fuster, 2003; D. N. Stern, 2004).

Extended Presentification

Extended presentification occurs across time and situations. It requires our highest mental energy and efficiency to sustain because we must integrate and condense massive amounts of experience from our entire life:

different memories, affects, beliefs, senses of self and various roles, relationships, action tendencies, and action systems. In extended presentification we coordinate our actions not only with the external world, but with the whole of our personality (Ellenberger, 1970).

Of course, our ability to be present naturally waxes and wanes: Even at best it is not a steady state over time. But we must be present enough of the time to be able to bridge those times when we are not very present. We thus link enough of our experience so that it is relatively cohesive to us, and as a result, our personality is cohesive. That is the function of extended presentification. It orients us in time and space, and to our personal existence. It is about knowing how our interoceptive and exteroceptive present, our perceived internal and external world, is embedded in our past and future. We thus make an account of ourselves and our history over time, and act accordingly. It is through both extended presentification and extended personification that we take responsibility for our past, present, and future actions.

As with synthesis and personification, the difference between core and extended presentification is not a categorical one, but a matter of degree. Core presentification pertains to a single situation, or at most a very limited range of contiguous situations. Extended presentification refers to the realization of far more elaborate strings of core presentifications. Extended presentification thus relates to anything from, say, 10 minutes of our existence to our complete life. It is through ongoing extended presentification that we expand our personality and the account of our life (i.e., our autobiographical memory and our autobiographical self).

Lack of Presentification and Personification in Survivors

Problems with presentification inherently involve problems with synthesis and personification, at least to a degree, as the latter two are necessary for the former to occur. A major obstacle to presentification is pathological or chronic alterations in the field and level of consciousness, a problem endemic to survivors. If survivors do not adequately synthesize and personify an experience, are not paying attention to the moment, are spaced out, depersonalized, foggy, or confused, it is impossible for them to be fully present. In other words, survivors often are unable to engage in the mental actions of core presentification, and thus to be adaptive.

It is also impossible to be present when survivors are fixated in the past. EPs often have such a severe lack of presentification that they are not even aware of the real present, much less able to act adaptively in response to it. They have their own, anachronistic sense of the present that involves too much of the past. Simultaneously, they also have a sense of self that excludes or only partially includes the sense of self experienced by other parts of the personality: A failure in personification. When survivors as EP reexperience a traumatic memory, they have a sense of personal existence across a limited stretch of time, fixated in the past that they perceive as the present. But neither that experience nor that sense of self is integrated with the present.

Survivors as ANP are often not able to fully be in the moment either, because they are avoiding internal and external reminders of trauma, again resulting in difficulties with synthesis. When intrusions of traumatic memories (and EPs) occur, their ability to be present becomes more limited. When survivors cannot tolerate certain stimuli, such as a feeling or memory, or the sight of someone who reminds them of their perpetrator, they will not be able to include these in their core and extended personification and presentification. Instead, these stimuli are avoided and survivors will engage in substitute actions to continue the avoidance: This is *nonrealization*.

Experiential avoidance (Hayes et al., 2004) can be distinguished in synthesis, personification, and presentification. In avoidance of synthesis, survivors as ANP or EP avoid including particular perceptions. For example, dissociative parts may believe "I do not have breasts"; "That never happened"; "I do not feel anger." When they avoid personification of what has been synthesized, they may say "These breasts exist, but they feel as though they are not mine"; "That happened, but not to me: It happened to someone else"; or "That anger exists, but belongs to that other part, not me." Avoidance of presentification, which includes failures in synthesis and personification, might lead them to say "Since I do not have breasts, or they are not mine, I do not need to have mammograms"; "Whether I was abused or not, it has no impact on me in the present"; "I am not responsible for hitting someone because anger doesn't belong to me."

REALIZATION AND SENSE
OF TIME AND REALITY

Realization depends upon our capacity to know what is real in the moment, and to distinguish the present moment in time and space; to tell the difference between the past, present and future. And we must also be able to distinguish the reality of internal experiences such as memories, fantasies, dreams, ideas, thoughts, and wishes, from external ones. Janet (1903) referred to this capacity as the function of reality (*fonction du réel*). A prerequisite for extended personification and presentification is knowing that the past and future are related to, but distinct from the present, which is our current reality. This capacity is often impaired in trauma survivors, both in terms of organizing a time line of their experiences, and in terms of knowing what is real in the moment (Janet, 1928a, 1932a; Terr, 1984; Van der Hart & Steele, 1997). Terr (1983, 1984) has noted that time sense is a relatively recent evolutionary acquisition, and as such, is readily disrupted by traumatizing experiences.

In order to adapt, we must organize our experience such that the actual present feels the most real and relevant in the moment, and the nearby past and future feel somewhat less real (Janet, 1919/1925, 1928a, 1932a; Van der Hart & Steele, 1997). This perception is most adaptive because we can only act in the actual present. Janet (1928a, 1932a) called this organization the *hierarchy of degrees of reality*, and observed that many difficulties occur in our adaptation to life when we cannot properly order our sense of reality in time and space.

The most common time distortion in survivors is the reexperience of the past as the present. Some patients may also distort present time so that it is condensed or expanded; for example, "I was working and thought only an hour had passed, but it was nearly all day." Some patients have no sense of time. One patient incessantly looked at the clock during the session and said, "I have no idea how much time is passing, whether it is a minute or an hour."

In order to know what is most relevant and real, we create syntheses of our experiences in the present, our recollections of the immediate past, and our ideas about the immediate future that include a stable sense of self: "I am all of me: my past, present, and future." However, core and extended personification may occur without core and extended presen-

TABLE 8.1
Pierre Janet's Hierarchy of Degrees of Reality

1. *The present reality,* which applies to our mental and behavioral actions, including our perception of internal and external reality.
2. *The immediate future,* which interests us almost as much as the present, though somewhat less vividly.
3. *The recent past,* which includes affective memories, with happy and unhappy recollections, illusions, and regrets.
4. *The ideal,* which we recognize as not being real, but which we wish to see realized.
5. *The distant future,* which we hope to see realized, but which is too remote to greatly interest us.
6. *The dead or distant past,* which has lost its affective character, but whose reality we still maintain as having occurred in time.
7. *The imaginary,* which we recognize as not being real. The dream, when it is recognized as such, is one example of the imaginary.
8. *The idea,* a verbal action whose reality we neither affirm nor deny.
9. *The thought,* a verbal action which we do not even question as real or unreal.

Source: Adapted from Janet, 1932a, pp. 148–149.

tification, without an accurate recognition of the (real) present. Indeed, as EP, survivors may engage in a limited degree of core and extended personification, but confuse the experienced and the real present. In other words, they confound the past and the present.

Table 8.1 displays the ideal hierarchy of reality that Janet proposed, and Figure 8.1 shows the curve that represents the ideal relationship between the course of time and degrees of reality. Being able to maintain this hierarchy of degrees of reality is an essential part of realization.

The degree of reality of particular inner and outer stimuli may shift. What we regard as more or less real in the moment depends on what seems to be most adaptive for us to attend to in a given internal and external environment, and is mediated by action systems. For example, a mother with a new baby is strongly mediated by attachment and caregiving. Her feelings of intense love and protection thus help her to perceive her baby's needs in the middle of the night as the most pressing, the most real, and her own need for rest as secondary, somewhat less real in the moment. Chronic activation of defense also shapes our view of reality. Once we have been exposed to major traumatizing events, the world never seems quite the same again, danger becomes more real and possible, and we may become more prone to engage quickly and easily in defense.

Although Janet presented this hierarchy of degrees of reality as rather fixed, it is actually much more flexible. Healthy people can voluntarily and temporarily change the sense of present reality in accordance with specific goals they have in mind. For example, when individuals choose to remember a difficult event, they may weave a narrative that evokes the reality of that past event to a greater or lesser extent. If they are relating the story to a relative stranger, a lower degree of reality would be more

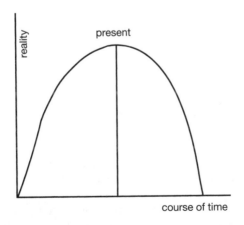

Source: Adapted from Janet, 1928a, p. 492.

FIGURE 8.1 Relationship between course of time and degrees of reality.

appropriate; they would choose to feel more emotionally distant from the experience. However, if they are relating the story to a therapist in order to resolve some unfinished business, a more intense and thus higher degree of reality would be appropriate. There is an element of conscious intent and manipulation inherent in this process, and a healthy individual rarely experiences confusion in time sequence, and does not, therefore, actually confuse the past and the present. Survivors, however, may be too depersonalized to experience something as real or may be too caught up in a past experience.

Placing Accounts of Reality Too High and Too Low

Janet distinguished two basic ways in which patients manifest their disturbance of time and consequently reality: They place their accounts of reality too high or they make them too low in the hierarchy of degrees of reality (Janet, 1928a, 1932a; cf., Van der Hart & Steele, 1997). For example, when a survivor incorrectly believes she is bad and dirty, this becomes her reality: She places this incorrect account of reality too high in her experience. She also believes no one likes her, despite the objective reality that people actually find her delightful: She places this account of reality too low. The example illustrates that when one account is too high (e.g., "I am bad"), it follows that another account (e.g., "I am likeable") will automatically be too low. And when one dissociative part places an account of an event too high (e.g., an EP who believes she is still in great danger), usually another part places an account of the same event too low in the hierarchy (e.g., an ANP who believes that she was not abused). Placing accounts of reality too low or too high are major forms of *nonrealization* (Janet, 1935a, 1945; Van der Hart, Steele et al., 1993).

   Misplaced accounts of reality in EPs. EPs typically place traumatic memories and related beliefs so high on the hierarchy of degrees of reality that these memories are far more real to them than the actual present, which they usually place too low in the hierarchy. They do not realize they are remembering the past, but rather experience internal reality as the present. They are often unable to distinguish between the reality of an internal experience (a flashback), and that of external reality, which involves a lack of differentiation (see Chapter 7).
   Misplaced accounts of reality in EPs relate to their limited mental efficiency, as well as a narrowed field of consciousness and the limited range of action systems that mediate their perceptions, emotions, cognitions, and behavioral actions. These restrictions impede the scope and quality of their perception–motor action cycles, and thus limit their capacity for presentification. Such parts may also confuse the reality of the imagined

future: It becomes a mirror of the past. Even when they no longer live with a perpetrator, or when the perpetrator is dead, fearful EPs tend to be focused on an imagined future that contains the past: "Daddy is going to hurt me!" Depressed EPs are typically focused on the miserable past, but do not envision much, if any future. Some EPs describe themselves as dying or dead—for them, a future cannot be imagined at all.

Many subjective physical and emotional characteristics of EPs are based on their misperception of reality. They experience themselves as how they were in the past; thus, they experience themselves as talking, behaving, thinking, looking, and feeling as they did in the past. Or they may experience themselves as being what they fantasized themselves to be: "I am Superman"; "I never get hurt." In short, dissociative parts commonly use these ideas and fantasies as substitutes for higher order actions that are beyond them, such as realization of trauma.

> Adeleide, a patient with secondary structural dissociation, had an EP with the identity of a teenager, who was convinced that she had long hair. This was true for the patient during her adolescence, but not in the present. The EP thus was unable to realize her short haircut in the present. When the therapist invited the EP to check the length of her hair, she was shocked and confused to see that her hair was short. When she talked about her sadistic perpetrator, she "saw" him in the therapy room and grew extremely anxious and believed it was 1964. As EP, Adeleide had an outdated account of reality that she placed far too high in the hierarchy of reality. When the therapist asked her to explain why she experienced herself as not growing older, she said, "I only exist for brief moments in time, I am not around much. When I have not been present for a week or longer, I have not grown any older. You are around all week, so you are one week older compared to last week. But not me."

This part of Adeleide did not realize that she was still affected by the long periods of time she was unable to realize (synthesize, personify, and presentify). She believed that what she did not fully perceive did not affect her, even though she was able to know that time was passing for others. So she believed she hardly grew older and brushed her long hair, engaging in imaginary substitute actions for realization of the present.

EPs that experience themselves as children may sometimes have a developmentally delayed sense of time, which may be pervasive in the survivor as a whole (Van der Hart & Steele, 1997). Thus they sometimes cannot tell time or have a sense of timelessness, such as an EP who experiences the time between sessions as interminable, and subsequently makes emergency phone calls to the therapist. Such EPs may also experience that the therapist has disappeared between sessions, lost in endless time. The ability to have a sense of time, and to organize their experiences in terms of the past, the present, and the future is an important component of developing object constancy in such patients.

Misplaced accounts of reality in ANPs. While EPs experience the past as too real, ANPs experience the past as not real enough. Patients' ANP may perceive the past as vague, fragmentary, or nonexistent, or as a history that does not pertain to *them*: They lack personification of their past. Janet described the quality of such nonrealized memories.

> [These] are only empty reports, with no imagery or attitudes surrounding them, calling forth no feeling of joy or of sadness; and arousing no interest or desire for action, in the way of either drawing them out or cutting them short. Sometimes these unreal reports are not even accompanied by belief, and the patient cannot affirm that these visions have had a real existence in the past. (1932a, p. 145)

Nonrealization of the past can take a number of forms, with the most severe and pervasive being complete amnesia: The past is not real because it does not exist (Janet, 1935a). A less extreme form characterizes many ANPs who experience their past as existing, but as not pertaining to them or as not actual reality: "I know it happened, but it doesn't feel like it happened to me"; "I don't feel anything about it"; "It seems like a dream." Thus they place accounts of their past, including the traumatic experiences, too low on the hierarchy of degrees of reality.

Clinical observations indicate that ANPs experience the present as being less real than when survivors are completely integrated and are *present*. This lack of presentification is especially strong when they have symptoms of depersonalization and derealization and lose a good sense of time: "I cannot remember if it is Tuesday or Saturday, and so I don't know if I should go to work or not." Many ANPs (and some EPs) experience themselves as not being real, or as living in a dream. One highly traumatized patient asked her therapist: "How can I know if this session is a dream or real? How do I know if what I am thinking is what is happening, or if I am just thinking it?" Several items on the DES reflect the tendency to place experience too low on the hierarchy: "Some people have the experience of not being sure whether they have done something or just thought about doing it" (Bernstein & Putnam, 1986). These items do not reflect dissociation per se; however, they often accompany structural dissociation, in particular when the survivor's mental level is low.

Many survivors have a sense of a foreshortened future. They lack the mental efficiency required for extended presentification. They cannot make accurate predictions regarding the near or more distant future. Some ANPs find it very difficult to plan their actions for more than a few hours ahead. Other ANPs cannot imagine a more remote personal future, and believe they will not live very long. For ANPs who frequently experience the intrusion of EPs, the future may feel dreadful or hopeless, indistinguishable from the traumatic past. This experience stems from a lack of differentiation of the current reality of the past, present, and future.

SUMMARY

Realization is a sophisticated level of integration that requires higher mental functioning. It involves mental and behavioral actions that help us create a cohesive and meaningful experience from our lives, and unify our personality into one whole. Because the actions of realization require the maximum level of mental energy and efficiency, they are often most difficult for survivors to achieve, particularly in regard to their traumatizing experiences. Traumatization is thus understood as a disorder of nonrealization. Not only individuals, but families and societies also engage in varying degrees of nonrealization, which makes it ever more difficult for traumatized individuals to receive the social support they need to realize their experiences. Realization includes two components. The first is personification: the capacity to take personal ownership of our experience and act accordingly. A prerequisite for engaging in action is synthesizing our experiences with our sense of self. In personification we do more: We take ownership and responsibility. Core personification is the ability to make experience our own in a given moment or situation, while extended personification is the capacity to personify actions and experiences across time and diverse situations. The second component of realization is presentification: the capacity to be in the present while connecting it to the past and future, thus embracing reality to our maximal ability, and acting adaptively in response to that reality.

CHAPTER 9

The Hierarchy of Action Tendencies

*The richest and most complex forms [of action tendencies]—for
the expression "higher type" means no more than this—perish more
easily: Only the lowest preserve an apparent indestructibility.*
—Friedrich Nietzsche (1901, p. 684)

THE THERAPIST NEEDS to understand action tendencies in which the patient can and cannot (yet) engage, which actions are needed to overcome traumatization, and know how to help survivors to develop these
tendencies in order to assist them in solving trauma-related problems and
improving daily life. Janet's hierarchy of action tendencies (Ellenberger,
1970; Janet, 1926a, 1926b, 1935b, 1936, 1938) serves as a useful guide in
this regard. It anticipates and relates to many modern insights in disciplines
that are relevant to action tendencies, such as developmental and cognitive psychology (Loevinger, 1976; Schore, 2003a, 2003b); learning theory
(Rescorla, 2003); psychoanalysis (Fonagy, Gergely, Jurist, & Target, 2002);
neurobiology (Berthoz, 2000; Damasio, 1999; Fuster, 2003; Llinás, 2001;
Panksepp, 1998); evolutionary psychology (Buss, 2005); and neurophi-
losophy (Metzinger, 2003; Noë, 2004). With Janet, we recognize that the
hierarchy proposes a somewhat arbitrary and selective but clinically con-
venient and instructive set of divisions of human action tendencies.

ACTION TENDENCIES AND ACTIONS

Action tendencies involve adaptations to environmental challenges. That
is, they have developed out of a long history of evolutionary selection and
are goal-directed (Buss, 2005; Janet, 1926a). Depending on their complexity, they encompass a range of different mental and behavioral ac-

tions that are realized in various stages: latency, readiness, initiation, execution, and completion (Janet, 1934). These actions foremost involve perceptions, including physical sensations, emotional feelings, thoughts, and movements. When we perceive the "right" kind of internal and external stimuli, and are in the "right" psychobiological state, we awaken a matching action tendency from latency and enter a stage of readiness. For example, when our blood sugar is low and we notice the accompanying sensation of hunger, we become ready to start looking for food. When we perceive a threat cue and feel scared, we are ready to defend ourselves. When we are alone but highly dependent on others, we are ready to cry out for help or support.

Whether we actually initiate one or more specific actions, and if so, how soon, often depends on the appearance and our perception of one or more additional stimuli that operate as "go" signals.

> Lara (DID, 33 years) did not dare eat food she liked, because her parents had severely punished her for doing so in her childhood. She only received leftovers. It was only when the therapist, whom she had learned to trust, offered her chocolate and reassured her that she would not be punished for accepting and eating it, that she initiated eating the "forbidden" food. She took the chocolate from the therapist's hand, and brought it, most hesitantly, to her mouth. Thus the therapist's offering of food in a safe environment, including relational support, allowed the patient to initiate the previously inhibited action of eating something she liked.

Initiation of an action is followed by a stage of *execution*, which involves carrying out the action, such a chewing and swallowing food after taking it in hand. The final stage of action tendencies is their *completion*. For example, Lara noticed and realized that she should not eat too much chocolate because her stomach was not used to it. This perception and realization constituted a "stop" signal for eating chocolate. Completion often involves conscious realization. In the case of automatic actions, completion involves rather unconscious awareness of what we have done, and that we have achieved the goal of the action tendency, or cannot achieve it. But important actions and their results must usually be realized consciously. To assist Lara in this regard, the therapist made sure that she was able to personify and presentify the fact that *she* had eaten chocolate (personification), that she had eaten it *a minute ago*, and that she had *subsequently* not been punished but praised for eating it. So she was safe in the *present* (core presentification), and would likely be safe on *future* occasions when she ate delicious food (extended presentification), at least when she was in the therapist's presence (an important contextual variable; see Chapter 10 regarding context evaluation).

Action tendencies require a combination of *mental energy*, physical energy when they involve movement, and the capacity to use these energies— *mental efficiency*. The more complex an action tendency is, the higher our mental energy and mental efficiency must be to initiate, execute, and complete it. Mental actions allow us to weigh the merits of alternative mental or behavioral actions, such as contemplating different therapeutic avenues to address the patient's presenting problem. In this sense, we can save time and energy. Perhaps even more importantly, by anticipating the effects of our actions we are able to select gainful actions, and prevent harmful ones. For example, the therapist prevents trouble when he or she accurately foresees how a particular (critical) remark will affect a patient with features of borderline personality disorder. Anticipating effects of actions involves presentification, and is the basis of human culture. However, mental actions can only affect the environment indirectly. For example, it is often far easier to *plan* certain behaviors, to make a promise to engage in behavioral actions, than to actually engage in them. Survivors may firmly promise, "I will get up early tomorrow and do my homework"; or "I will leave my abusive partner and live alone." Nevertheless, when it comes down to it, some survivors may be unable to carry these promises from the stage of readiness to the stage of initiation and beyond to completion. They stop before they have started, or they feebly or unenthusiastically initiate housework, or try to be present or tolerate their feelings, but may soon give up (Janet, 1903, 1934).

Action tendencies not only require energy and efficiency, but also regulation. One regulator of action tendencies is *effort,* because each action needs a particular, adaptive degree of force or dedication (Janet, 1932c). When we try too hard, or do not try hard enough to do something, our actions are likely to fail. It takes experience to know how much effort an adaptive action needs. Experience improves mental efficiency because it saves useless expenditure of energy and raises the probability of success. According to Janet (1929b, 1932c), as a regulator of action and action tendencies, effort is a secondary action that accompanies movement, which is the primary action. Another action regulator is success, which Janet called the action of triumph (Janet, 1919/1925, 1928b; cf. Chapter 7).

LEVELS AND COMPLEXITY
OF ACTION TENDENCIES

The hierarchy suggests that we can consider our personality to be a construction that involves different levels of action tendencies (Janet, 1929). In this sense, personality is a complex dynamic system with higher level tendencies that have emerged from but cannot be fully explained by lower level action tendencies. So each level of the hierarchy operates on its own set of principles (cf., G. R. F. Ellis, 2005). For example, tendencies that involve language, hence symbolization, are of a higher level than presymbolic action tendencies, and cannot be explained by these lower level action tendencies: Language has its own principles.

There is substantial contemporary evidence that supports the 19th-century idea (Bain, 1855; Jackson, 1931–1932; Janet, 1926a) that the development of our species (phylogeny) and our individual development (ontogeny) involve action tendencies of increasing complexity (e.g., Fuster, 2003).[1] Thus, the tendencies range from basic reflexes that are largely automatic and rigid, to highly reflective, voluntary, and creative actions. Janet (1926a, 1938) conveniently divided them into three main groups—lower, intermediate, and higher action tendencies. Each group includes several sublevels. See Table 9.1 for an overview in which we have adapted Janet's terminology of the hierarchy with his original terms in parentheses. The complexity of different action tendencies increases with the number of component actions that we must synthesize (i.e, bind and differentiate), and realize (i.e., personify and presentify). And the more complex an action tendency is, the more complex the perception-motor action cycles it involves.

The levels of action tendencies that constitute personality evolve with age and experience. This layering is adaptive because sometimes we need lower action tendencies such as reflexive movements to attain our goals (e.g., riding a bicycle, typing), and at other times intermediate or higher action tendencies are needed. Thus, higher action tendencies are not better or more adaptive in themselves than lower ones: It depends upon the situation. It is not adaptive to have to think too much about riding a bicycle, for instance—lower level action tendencies are the most efficient for these kinds of actions.

LOWER ACTION TENDENCIES

The lower action tendencies are the most simple. Many of them involve automatic and primary behaviors that we, as humans, have in common with other mammals. They primarily involve limited and nonverbal actions that serve very short-term goals. With the exception of disorganized movements, they require at least some degree of synthesis. Degrees of personification and presentification only emerge with basic symbolic action tendencies, which require simple language, and more thought and planning.

Disorganized Movement

In the absence of mental efficiency, mental energy is not used for any action tendency (i.e., adaptation). A complete lack of mental efficiency re-

1. Like Jackson, Janet also believed that our ontogeny recapitulates our phylogeny; that as we mature, we repeat the developmental steps of our species, and that these steps are captured in the hierarchy. In its literal form, this hypothesis is incorrect. For example, it is generally accepted that we have evolved from fish through reptiles to mammals, but our embryonal development does not precisely recapitulate these "fish," "reptile," and "mammal" stages. There are nevertheless important links between ontogeny and phylogeny, as contemporary evolutionary psychologists show (Buss, 2005; Panksepp, 1998).

TABLE 9.1
The Hierarchy of Action Tendencies

Lower level action tendencies
Basic reflexes
Presymbolic regulatory action tendencies
Presymbolic sociopersonal action tendencies
Basic symbolic action tendencies

Intermediate level action tendencies
Reflexive symbolic action tendencies
Reflective action tendencies

Higher level action tendencies
Prolonged reflective action tendencies
Experimental action tendencies
Progressive action tendencies

Sources: Ellenberger, 1970; Janet, 1926a, 1926b, 1938.

---

sults in disorganized movement rather than an effort to achieve a goal through purposeful action. For example, epileptic patients expend energy in undirected agitations when they have a seizure, patients with an anxiety disorder when they panic, and trauma survivors when they experience vehement trauma-related emotions.

Basic Reflexes

A basic reflex involves an adaptive, automatic, involuntary, and organized reaction to an attractive or aversive stimulus. At this level, we essentially synthesize one stimulus and one response that has proved advantageous from an evolutionary standpoint. For example, we automatically jerk our hand away from a hot stove, or reach out to catch ourselves when we start to fall. In Pavlov's terms, we respond to an *unconditioned stimulus* with an *unconditioned reflex*. This reflex can be a physiological response (e.g., sweating when we are afraid) or a motor reaction (e.g., startle reflex). Unconditioned stimuli may be positive or attractive, such as food, shelter, warmth, and gentle touch. Or they may be negative. For example, emotional abuse and neglect, and physical and sexual abuse include major aversive unconditioned stimuli such as pain and abandonment. These stimuli unleash defensive reflexes time and again in the survivor.

Typically, reflexes operate on a primitive on/off basis; that is, the unconditioned stimulus makes us either explode in action or it doesn't. For example, we either startle with full power, or we don't startle at all. This crude regulation of action can be adaptive, because we will instantly spend major energy only on reactions that are essential to our survival.

When we engage in these reflexes, we inhibit action tendencies that are irrelevant to the task at hand and that would interfere with the execution of the reflex. For example, when our hand touches a hot stove we do not continue to tend to the food we are cooking, or to the friend to whom we are talking. The downside of this primitive on/off regulation is that we cannot modulate or time the reflex. For example, if a survivor were better able to synthesize his or her defense system and exploration system, that person could initiate defensive actions at the best possible moment rather than only at the moment when the unconditioned stimulus appeared. Thus, the survivor would not cringe automatically when the therapist raised his hand while talking, but would wait to see what happened next before immediately reacting.

There are many shades of gray between the levels of the hierarchy. For example, a survivor may say, "I am a little jumpy." He or she feels apprehensive, is ready to startle, but does not engage in this reflex yet. So there is a double action: the inclination to startle, as well as the inclination to inhibit this reflex. Inhibition of reflexes involves regulatory action that appears at the next level of the hierarchy.

In addition to a single exteroceptive stimulus and a single response, perception–motor action cycles include a perception of our bodily condition. For example, our degree of attention and response to food depends upon how hungry or satiated we are. Because action systems are homeostatic and homeostasis essentially involves the body, we perceive our bodily condition in relation to most simple action tendencies onward. Action tendencies exist in the context of one or more action systems. These systems regulate our internal environment by means of equilibrium adjustments (e.g., temperature regulation; safety seeking). Awareness of our bodily condition is most important in that it allows us to select and engage in potentially adaptive reactions (Damasio, 1999), and then move on to the next action. Hence, the actual *condition of our body* influences how strongly we will be focused on a particular unconditioned stimulus, and how strongly we will respond. For example, survivors often feel fear. The related physical sensations of fear function as the equivalent of sensations of hunger: The more hungry we are, the more strongly we are compelled to seek food; the more fearful we are, the more we are compelled to seek safety and avoid danger. But survivors are often fearful regardless of whether they are actually safe or not. They respond to the sensations of fear with continued engagement of their defense action system and a narrowed focus on potential threat cues, which ultimately does not create homeostasis, but rather a serious imbalance.

Not all action is completely automatic at the level of the basic reflexes. We can still learn, create new syntheses, at this level. For example, we can learn to associate a particular stimulus (a certain sound) with an unconditioned stimulus (a blow to the head), which changes our original response to the stimulus. This synthesis, discussed further in Chapter 10, helps us navigate more efficiently in the world. For example, a survivor learned as a child to immediately engage in a defensive reflex when he or she heard footsteps coming from behind, because this usually preceded being hit. Unfortunately, such reflexes persist long after there is a need for them. A survivor who is now safe will still sometimes regress to this level of reflexes and startle or cringe when he or she heard footsteps coming from behind. This regression implies a major decrease of mental efficiency, which interferes with his or her ability to regulate the defensive reflex. Often an emotional part of the personality (EP) will react with a reflex to a stimulus, which cannot be stopped or modulated by the survivor as an apparently normal part of the personality (ANP) or by the therapist. This EP has retracted the field of consciousness to only a threat cue and an immediate reflexive response, and little more. EPs that engage in defensive reflexes may even begin to perceive the therapist as perpetrator, thus lose the ability to differentiate the therapist and their abuser(s). The dissolution of normal social contact when the defense system dominates is probably due to the concomitant inhibition of social action systems such as play, attachment, and reproduction.

Presymbolic Regulatory Action Tendencies

Presymbolic regulatory action tendencies (*perceptual–suspensive tendencies*; Janet, 1938) are those that involve waiting before acting, and thus represent our earliest attempts at affect and impulse control. They are actions in which we can engage even before we have language and the ability to symbolize, which involves higher level control. Thus, they are still very primitive action tendencies, not sophisticated impulse regulatory actions. But they are less explosive than reflexes because their full activation requires at least two steps. Once we perceive a stimulus (thirst), it evokes our readiness (impulse) to act (to drink). However, at this level of action tendency we can suspend this reflex when we also become aware that it would not adequately realize the goal (e.g., satiation of thirst). For example, the water may be too hot, or may be dirty. We thus *wait* for a second stimulus (e.g., cooling of the water) that launches the reflex from a stage of construction and readiness (Janet, 1934), and lets it run its full course. This regulation through simple impulse control has several advantages over basic reflexes. It allows us to adapt our actions more to what happens over time—they gain flexibility—and it marks the beginning of our ability to accumulate physical and mental energy. We accumulate energy as we postpone the motor action because we become more needful as we wait. For example, we can only postpone actions such as eating, drinking, and sleeping for so long, and then we must act. This buildup of impatience provides us with energy to execute the motor action(s) with physical force and mental dedication. It also helps us learn that we can receive gratification from actions that are delayed.

Presymbolic regulatory action tendencies include the tendencies of defense (e.g., flight, freeze), and basic action tendencies in relation to objects ("things"). Objects do not exist for us in a psychological sense until we *construct*, that is, detect how we can *use* them. For example, a safe place is not a given abused children, but only becomes a safe place when they discover that they can, for instance, hide in the closet and feel safe. In the same way, a survivor has to learn that the therapist's office is a safe place. Our use for an object depends on the action system(s) that is dominant in a given moment. Thus, depending upon whether a survivor is dominated by the action system of defense or one of daily life, he or she may perceive a chair as something to hide behind or to use as a weapon (defense), or as a reminder of being tied to a chair and abused as a child, or as something in which to sit and talk quietly and safely with the therapist (exploration). These different constructs mediate quite different behavioral action tendencies regarding an object (hiding, fighting, cringing, sitting). Hence, mental construction of an object in one way or another generates some flexibility of behavioral action, as long as our action systems are somewhat coordinated. This flexibility is an advance over the simple, unconditioned reflex in which the connection between stimulus and response is largely fixed. Thus, when a survivor is able to engage in presymbolic action tendencies, his or her action tendencies are slightly more flexible. That is, he or she can adapt more easily than when completely dominated by simple reflexes.

Presymbolic regulatory action tendencies also include the regulation of different action tendencies regarding a *situation*. A situation involves a combination of two or more different perceived stimuli that exist in close proximity to each other. For example, a child is thirsty and sees water in a glass, but also sees his or her abuser in the room. These different "objects"—water and abuser—can be relevant for different action systems (energy management and defense). To resolve potential conflicts, these action systems must be(come) integrated. Thus the child does better to suspend the wish to drink water if the abuser will punish him or her for drinking it.

Finally, presymbolic regulation involves managing needs that cannot be realized because a stimulus that would release the motor action does not occur. For example, Lara had no way to manage her desperate need for food, water, and warmth when her abusers locked her in a shed in winter for days at a time. Therefore, at that time she was unable to execute and complete the action tendencies of eating, drinking, and seeking warmth. In treatment it became apparent that Lara as EP continued to long for food, drink, and warmth in the present as though they were not available. She was so afraid that she would be denied these necessities that she avoided seeking them out or accepting them when they were offered. That is, the normal stimuli of food and drink, which would normally evoke behaviors to attain them, did not evoke Lara's action tendencies to fill her own needs.

Presymbolic regulation comprises the beginning of attention, because as we put our behavioral action on hold, we wait or search for the stimulus that tells us to release the suspended action. And waiting and searching involve emergent mental actions that generate the phenomena of memory and sense of time. Without these mental actions, we would lose the point of waiting and searching. Thus the perception–motor action cycles involved in this regulation are more complex than in basic reflexes.

The perception–motor action cycle at this level in the hierarchy also includes an idea of the body. As we mentally construct "objects," we experience a difference between external objects and our body. The idea of the body and its distinction from the external world marks a primitive idea of self (Janet, 1929a; Damasio, 1999; Metzinger, 2003). This sense of bodily self permits us to adjust our behavioral actions to our current environment, a possibility that hardly exists at the level of simple reflexes. Our behavioral actions become a bit more flexible.

Dissociative parts, particularly EPs, are sometimes dominated by presymbolic regulatory action tendencies. The term domination implies that the action tendency strongly mediates a survivor's functioning, but that it is not necessarily the only tendency that guides his or her actions.

> Petra (DDNOS) had strong urges as a child to hit her abusive father out of anger and a wish to fight him off. However, she would suspend this impulse until he had left after abusing her, and then hit a wall or herself. Her ability to suspend the action of hitting was adaptive at the time because she knew from experience that hitting her father would provoke a dreadful counterattack and more pain.

Hitting something other than her father constituted a substitute for the actual defensive actions that Petra could not execute, because as a child she still lacked the mental level and support to engage in higher level action tendencies, such as confronting her father with his behavior, or asking for outside help.

Lack of impulse control or affect regulation (i.e., basic regulation of action systems) is a notorious problem in trauma survivors. Particularly as EP, they engage in simple perception–motor cycles that preclude self-regulation that would be more adaptive. At times, their field of consciousness is so retracted that they do not synthesize vital stimuli, and their mental efficiency so low that they cannot control their impulses. For example, survivors as EP may hit their partner when they feel severely threatened or reexperience traumatizing events. They can be so "blind" in these instances that they hit a loved one, instead of a pillow or other object. However, given sufficient mental efficiency, they may suspend particular impulses for a long time, or may never (fully) execute them (Bailey, 1928; Janet, 1928b).

> Petra eventually furiously and desperately hit her father when he tried to rape her even after she was married and pregnant. The combination of her pregnancy and his attempted rape constituted the second stimulus compound that set her suspended defensive action free. She had accumulated so much energy that she hit and kicked him violently. In other words, hitting him had become a highly charged action tendency.

Presymbolic Sociopersonal Action Tendencies

In basic reflexes and presymbolic regulatory action tendencies, a single individual performs the complete action. In presymbolic sociopersonal action tendencies, which Janet (1938) more briefly refers to as *sociopersonal* action tendencies, a complication is added. Now the action of one individual must be completed by a complementary action from another individual. As Bailey (1928, p. 215), summarizing Janet's view, noted, "[a]n act is social when several individuals associate to perform different portions of the act. It is a suspended act in which the second stimulation comes from the action of our associates." At this level, our perception–motor cycles include a recognition of other people and their relevance to us, but still with little language. This recognition is the beginning of mentalization. The actions of mentalization involve the recognition that other people are not just "objects," as applies to the previous level of the hierarchy, but have their own minds, thus feelings, thoughts, and goals that may be different from ours (e.g., Rizzolatti & Craighero, 2004; cf., Chapter 7). Mentalization allows us to be empathic and to learn from others (e.g., skills) and to adaptively respond both to their actions and our own (Keysers & Perrett, 2004; Keysers et al., 2004).

Presymbolic sociopersonal tendencies are primarily nonverbal and can be divided into actions of imitation, subordination, and collaboration. Our exquisite ability for imitation is at the heart of human culture (Gallese, 2003; Rizzolatti & Craighero et al., 2004). Learning via imitation is far more efficient or *economical* (see Chapter 12) than learning by trial and error, because it saves energy, time, and error. Our ability to imitate is available early in life. For example, infants start to imitate the facial expression of their mother within 40 hours after birth (Berlucchi & Aglioti, 1997). Actions of imitation include the imitator and the imitated. Some individuals allow themselves to be imitated or stimulate others to imitate them, and take the risk of making mistakes (e.g., parents). Others (e.g., their children) willingly imitate these models. Janet (1926a, 1935b) maintained that the collaboration implied in imitation is the origin of a social hierarchy, of all social behaviors of subordination including actions such as giving and following commands. At this level of action tendencies in treatment, the therapist can serve as a model from which patients can imitate adaptive behaviors and learn by following directions. For example, the therapist can take a deep breath, and encourage the patient to imitate that behavior in order to teach breathing techniques.

The awareness of our own actions and those of others also involves the synthesis of our bodily and affective feelings (Damasio, 1999). These feelings tell us how our actions affect others, a major prerequisite for collaboration, and allow us to develop a relationship with ourselves, a form of inner collaboration (Janet, 1935b). Thus, collaboration with others is probably an important basis of our ability to relate to ourselves—self-consciousness (Barkley, 2001; Janet, 1929a). When we become aware of the impact we can have on other individuals and on ourselves, we develop an ability to regulate our relationships with others and with ourselves (Janet, 1928b, 1929b, 1932c).

Survivors sometimes lose presymbolic sociopersonal tendencies, such as when they reexperience traumatizing events, and thus lose contact with the present moment and with those around them. That is, they lose their social context and the basic behaviors that accompany it. For example, a therapist may make a simple command to a patient experiencing a flashback: "Open your eyes, please." But the survivor cannot (yet) follow the command. Survivors may have negative dissociative symptoms that disconnect them, as ANP or as totally submissive EP, from important bodily and emotional signals which might help them in a social context. The consequences of this loss are serious. Survivors lose the ability to feel empathy regarding others and themselves, and to imitate, follow nonverbal directions, and collaborate with the therapist or anyone else. Survivors as ANP are usually able to engage in sociopersonal action tendencies, but not necessarily in every circumstance. Some EPs can also minimally function at this level when they feel relatively safe. That is, they can relate to and imitate those whom they trust, such as the therapist, thus learn from them in *nonverbal* ways.

Basic Symbolic Action Tendencies

The basic symbolic action tendencies (*simple intellectual tendencies*; Janet, 1938) include the use of "tools" and simple language (Janet, 1935b) in our perception–motor action cycles. "Tools" are objects we use adaptively, such as a basket to carry apples (Janet, 1936), a stick to hit an adversary, a watch to track time. But most importantly, and most relevant to therapy, we use words and language as *symbolic tools*, based on our ability to relate one thing to another, which is the basis of intelligence (Janet, 1936). For example, at this level we understand that a command can result in an obedient reaction, and that we can use concrete objects to attain goals that would otherwise be out of reach (e.g., an ax to cut a tree). We now look upon objects and people in more than one way, which dramatically increases the flexibility of our actions. For example, a person can now be a "symbolic tool" whom we "use" to feel enjoyment, safety, care, relaxation, playfulness, as well as fear, shame, and embarrassment. Language is a huge step in our ability to symbolize, as words are symbols for a thing, person, experience, event, etc. And the use of verbal (and other tools) is highly economical. For example, now we can give someone or ourselves a command, which is fast and takes little energy: we no longer have to demonstrate how to do something. The drawback is that it is quite uncertain whether the command will be executed. Language also implies the ability to organize events in a space and time; that is, syntax ("He took a stick, hit me, and left"). Thus, it is a prime tool for personification, hence sense of self ("I'm John; I'm sleepy"), and for presentification, hence sense of time ("I saw Granny this morning, am alone now, but will meet her again tomorrow"). In other words, language is probably required for human self-consciousness and autobiographical memory. Emerging personification and presentification allow us to regulate our own actions more, because they allow us to imagine different courses of action based on prior personal experience and to anticipate their likely results.

When survivors engage in basic symbolic action tendencies, they can symbolize their experiences in a simple form, and use "tools" in simple ways. For example, they can make a drawing of their experiences and realize that the drawing is a representation of the experience (when very low levels of action tendencies are dominant, they may respond with fear and defensive reactions to a picture of a perpetrator as if it were the actual perpetrator). Survivors may also add a few words to the drawing, using a crayon to hit it, or say some simple words (e.g., "I don't like *that*"). At this level of the hierarchy, survivors can make simple promises (e.g., "I will make a drawing"; "I will do my homework"), which increases their self-control and social effectiveness. However, therapists should not be surprised that survivors may not always have the mental level to put these promises into behavioral action.

Basic symbolic action tendencies can be weak in subjectively very "young" EPs. For example, survivors as these EPs may not be able to tell the time, hold a pen and write, and they may only use and comprehend very simple language. These assets become even weaker when survivors become very afraid, angry, or ashamed. Even as ANP, survivors may find it sometimes difficult to put their feelings into words. Particularly when they become emotional, their active and passive command of language becomes simpler. Therapists should be aware of these limitations.

INTERMEDIATE ACTION TENDENCIES

Intermediate action tendencies involve the use of symbols, including language. Some intermediate action tendencies are reflexive, and involve impulsive beliefs. Others are more reflective. These more sophisticated action tendencies involve an ability to suspend immediate, uncritical beliefs.

Reflexive Symbolic Action Tendencies

Reflexive symbolic action tendencies (*reflexive beliefs and actions*; Janet, 1926a, 1926b, 1938) involve promises to perform particular (motor) actions that cannot be immediately executed because the stimulus (configuration) that releases the action is not yet present (e.g., "I will do my homework tomorrow"). These actions are symbolic because they are cast in a verbal formula. Reflexive promises vastly expand the power of commands, which is efficient. Janet regarded promises with deferred execution as a kind of *belief* (e.g., a survivor may say "Believe me when I say that I will never cut myself again"). Reflexive beliefs are often associated with equally reflexive motor actions that we can verbalize. For example, Janny with complex PTSD and DDNOS, rather obediently did her therapeutic homework. When her therapist asked what she learned from it, she said, "Well I don't know really; I do it because that is what you expect from me."

Indeed, the downside of reflexive symbolic beliefs is that they are often uncritically accepted and potentially unsustainable (e.g., "I believe that all delayed memories of child abuse are false, thus I will not accept them as real memories"). At this level, we thus synthesize and accept at face value, sensory input and verbal messages and thoughts, and act accordingly. The implied risk is that the beliefs and associated actions are based on feelings, prejudice, suggestion, and restricted views of ourselves and others. They often involve reductionistic, black and white thinking, thus involve a retracted field of consciousness that limits our realization of the past, present, and anticipated future. This low degree of extended presentification, and related problems with the hierarchy of degrees of reality (cf., Chapter 8), relates to weak autobiographical memory at this level that "ignores an accurate localization in time, and is the starting point of legends and myths" (Ellenberger, 1970, p. 391).

Reflexive beliefs are the focus of contemporary cognitive theories that concentrate on irrational beliefs (e.g., Kubany, Hill, & Owens, 2003; Ziegler & Leslie, 2003) and fixed cognitive schemas; that is, maladaptive core beliefs about self, others, and the world (Dutton, Burghardt, Perrin, Chrestman, & Halle, 1994; Galloucis, Silverman, & Francek, 2000). For example, our sense of self has not evolved to a true sense of personal identity at this level. We rather tend to follow the rules of the group (e.g., our family or peer group), do not distinguish ourselves much from other members of this group, are quite sensitive to disapproval from other group members, and are inclined to reject other groups (Janet, 1936; Loevinger, 1976).

Many survivors, both as ANP and as EP, have a plethora of trauma-related reflexive beliefs (e.g., "I am dirty"; "I don't deserve happiness"; "You will leave me sooner or later"). They have difficulty distinguishing between (subjective) feelings, fantasies, and more objective facts; they have problems with the hierarchy of degrees of reality. Feelings and fantasies can be as real to them, if not more so, than "objective reality." They often engage in reflexive beliefs and behavioral actions to avoid realizing painful facts. For example, survivors would rather believe that they themselves are to blame for the abuse and neglect characterizing their childhood than to realize that they were helpless.

Some reflexive beliefs and motor actions in survivors are based on malignant suggestion (Janet, 1910/1911, 1919/1925). Many perpetrators implicitly and explicitly induce false ideas in their victims. For example, perpetrators of childhood sexual abuse tend to say things like: "You made me do it because you are bad," so that EPs may believe "I deserve to be hit, I'm no good" (cf., Salter, 1995). Perpetrators also use this malignant suggestion when they make threats to prevent the victim's disclosure of the abuse— "If you ever talk about it, I will find out and hurt you."

Patients with trauma-related disorders tend to engage in reflexive beliefs centered around emotions (S. Epstein, 1991), hence action systems. For example, some dissociative parts believe that the world is dangerous, that they are weak and vulnerable, and that others are dangerous or unhelpful, so that they are wise to always run and hide (flight). Other dissociative parts regard the world as malevolent, themselves as exploited, and others as unjust and untrustworthy, so that they feel suspicious and are ready for impulsive counterattack (fight). The rigidity of their sense of self and of actions systems is perhaps most obvious and specific in traumatic memories. When a survivor as EP reexperiences traumatizing events, he or she is commonly stuck in the defense action system and in reflexive beliefs such as: "I'm helpless," "He will choke me," or "I'm dirty."

Reflective Action Tendencies

Reflective action tendencies (*reflective beliefs and actions*; Janet, 1938) are symbolic social action tendencies that involve deliberation (Janet, 1926a). At this level, we expand our perception–motor action cycles with outer and inner discussion and considered reasoning. We contemplate with others or ourselves whether or not we will make a promise; that is, subscribe to a belief that we will engage in behavioral action. We thus put our reflexive belief in a verbal formula and examine it critically ("Is it realistic to believe I can help my patient integrate this traumatic memory in one session, right before my vacation?"). At this level our field of consciousness is considerably wider, because we now synthesize a variety of positions (e.g., "This delayed memory of child abuse could be accurate"). We regard these positions as ideas or possibilities that we may, but need not act on, thus simulate different courses of action. In a word, we reflect more and act accordingly.

Reflective action tendencies can be more adaptive than the lower level action tendencies. For example, when the therapist is verbally abused by a patient, he or she has some choice about how to act instead of merely responding in kind. And a survivor can start to contemplate long held reflexive beliefs, and discover that these are not unwavering facts, but are ideas which may or may not be true. Reflection on our thoughts, feelings, and other mental actions allows us to infer intentions and motivations behind our own and other people's behavior. This aspect of mentalization (Fonagy et al., 2002) helps us predict the actions of others more accurately (Janet, 1938; Llinás, 2001) and to regulate our own. It frees us from blindly believing and doing what we are told but introduces doubt and uncertainty that are hard to resolve when the higher action tendencies are still beyond reach (e.g., "If I am not dirty and bad, then why was I beaten and raped?"). Survivors who function at this level, often as a result of Phase 1 work (Chapter 13), can use words to identify, modulate, and express their mental states. They can tell others and themselves what they feel, and so regulate their actions by social exchange and self-reflection. At this level, they may be able, often with the help of the therapist, to transform their traumatic memories into autobiographical, narrative memories.

The ability to engage in reflective actions constitutes the foundation for and precursors to the higher level action tendency of *realization*, including high degrees of personification and presentification. Reflection opens the door to discovery and understanding of our personal interoceptive reality and to the wider interpersonal world; that is, to the development of a "theory of mind" (Fonagy & Target, 1997). When survivors attain this level, they can evaluate how *real* phenomena and actions are (Janet, 1928a, 1932c; Metzinger, 2003). For example, they can now recognize that a thought or memory is less real than a motor action based on these mental actions, and that the present is more real than the past or future.

Personification has its roots in the sociopersonal action tendencies once we start to note differences between self and others. Basic symbolic action tendencies provide us with a primitive, verbalized sense of self that can evolve into a reflexive, confirmatory sense of self (Janet, 1929a; Loevinger, 1976). At the level of the reflective action tendencies, we start to reflect on who we are and recognize that our mental contents belong to us and that our life is different and separate from that of others. When survivors attain this level, they cease to experience themselves merely as the object of others' perceptions ("My uncle thinks I'm a slut, so I must be"), and develop a personified sense of self (cf. Loevinger, 1976). They start to doubt, for instance, that other people can read their thoughts, that a wish to hit somebody proves their badness, or that they must always be the person others say they are. But the ability to doubt has a downside. Survivors may become quite uncertain of themselves when they give up maladaptive reflexive beliefs, when they doubt new ideas ("I know I'm not bad, but don't know whether I can tolerate all the pain?"; "Won't you run when I show my deepest pain?"). New ideas initially make them vulnerable.

Reflection involves evaluating facts and experiences in the context of the past, the present, and the anticipated future—extended presentification. These mental actions are seriously compromised in trauma-related disorders. Once survivors are able to function more consistently at the level of reflective action tendencies, they gradually engage more in these actions.

HIGHER ACTION TENDENCIES

The higher action tendencies involve the ability to engage in long strings of action tendencies that serve long-term goals, the ability to engage in these tendencies in a deliberate and systematic way, and the ability to personify and presentify our existence at a high level of abstraction.

Prolonged Reflective Action Tendencies

Prolonged reflective action tendencies (*rational-ergetic tendencies*; Janet, 1938) involve the ability to invest in a long term goal, hence to distribute energy across complex actions, and sustain them over time. This ability allows us to put promises—to others and to ourselves—into major endeavors such as scholastic endeavors, formal education, and long-term psychotherapy. The goal of the venture may not be personal gain alone, but can pertain to a higher moral principle ("I am dedicated to assisting trauma survivors, although the work can be difficult and unrewarding at times"). Perception–motor action cycles now encompass long strings of actions, and include a synthesis of a sense of personal duty and ability, voluntary actions, initiative, perseverance, patience, and morality (cf. Loevinger, 1976).

Survivors who function at this level—typically as ANP—can engage in projects that serve a higher goal than immediate reward, even when the actions are unpleasant. They achieve a rather high degree of personification and an ability to envision realistic goals that may be quite far in the future. And so they can engage in the challenges of therapy that require major dedication and endurance. However, many ANPs and most EPs cannot attain these levels. Treatment of chronic traumatization is a major work for survivors and therapists alike that takes a wide range of small steps. Most survivors (and, for that matter, some clinicians) do not have the mental efficiency to realize the extent of the therapy upon which they are embarking, but can often meet the challenge of a limited number of treatment steps.

Experimental Action Tendencies

Experimental tendencies involve an ability to test systematically reflective ideas, including scientific hypotheses. They also encompass an ability to execute behavioral experiments—systematic testing by doing. At low levels of the hierarchy, we need to have demonstrated or be told what works, or learn from experiences from trial and error, or conditioning. However, from the level of reflective actions and notably at the current level, learning becomes self-initiated and explicit. We now accept that our ideas may be wrong or mistaken, and can admit and learn from our mistakes. Experimental tendencies require a high degree of personification and a keen appreciation of relevant aspects of the past, present, and anticipated future, hence a high degree of (extended) presentification.

Survivors need to learn to be more effective in dealing with their turbulent lives. Therapists should help them engage in important actions that involve systematically examining their inner and outer world, and adjust their actions to the results of this exploration (observing and use of "wise mind"; Linehan, 1993). Although many survivors are very scared to examine and realize their past, current, and future world, and to experiment with new mental and behavioral actions, this is what therapy is about. More precisely, treatment ideally assists survivors to reach this high level of functioning with respect to a wide range of action systems.

Progressive Action Tendencies

The progressive tendencies constitute our highest development and our most original actions. For example, functioning at this level, we grasp the ideas of coincidence (e.g., "It was bad luck that I was in the house when that man broke in and raped me."); chance (e.g., "The abuse I experienced could have happened to anyone; it's not my fault."); evolution (e.g., "Many of my reactions to the abuse may seem weird, but I have learned that they were useful actions that stem from our ancestors; anyone might have these reactions."); freedom (e.g., "There are many forces that affect my behavior, but that does not mean that I cannot make choices or change."); and relativity ("My mother abused and neglected me, and that has deeply affected me in many, but not all regards: I am more than a trauma survivor"). We now realize that life and experience evolve over wide stretches of time, and that we, like all human beings and events, are unique in spite of all shared features. This realization involves supreme presentification and personification.

In general, many individuals don't reach the level of the progressive tendencies. For survivors to be able to function at this level, they must have benefited considerably from Phase 3 work and have integrated the whole of their personality—all parts of it and their traumatic memories. Survivors eventually can develop a deep emotional understanding at this level that their traumatization was not due to them but to disturbed or irresponsible people. If applicable, they can also realize that some of those who harmed them were traumatized themselves, but unable or unwilling to overcome their condition.

MENTAL EFFICIENCY AND MENTAL ENERGY

There is an intimate and reciprocal relationship between mental efficiency and level of action tendencies (Janet, 1928b, 1934). To comprehend this relationship, it is important to refine our definition of mental efficiency. In the Introduction, we described mental efficiency as the ability to efficiently focus and use whatever mental energy is available in the moment. However, the concept, in fact, captures three different but related meanings. The first meaning is *the upper level of action tendencies on which we can spend our mental and physical energy, without undue loss or waste of energy.* That is, the higher our mental efficiency, the higher the action tendencies in which we can engage, provided we also have sufficient mental energy. As we mature biologically and psychologically, and receive the social and material stimulation we need, we increase our mental efficiency within the limits of our potential. Positive social stimulation involves actions such as social support and encouragement, and adequate material stimulation is provided by an environment that has neither too few nor too many stimuli.

However, our mental efficiency is not fixed. It oscillates between the window of our present lower and upper limits, and these limits can shift across time and situation (Janet, 1921–1922, 1934). For example, our mental efficiency diminishes, or its development becomes arrested, when we become traumatized. Mental efficiency also diminishes when we are tired or ill—when we have less mental and physical energy at our disposal. As noted before, ANPs have a higher level of mental efficiency than EPs, but the degree oscillates for both types of parts.

The second meaning of the term *mental efficiency* involves *the ability to select the level of action tendency that is required to adapt to a given situation.* This selection, this mental action, can be challenging, and thus requires a certain level of mental efficiency. When our mental efficiency is high, we select the level of action tendencies that fits the task at hand, but when this efficiency is too low, we are prone to select levels that are too high or too low. We should not engage in higher level action tendencies when automatic actions will do better. For example, a handshake should be meaningful, but also a rather reflexive action. Some survivors waste precious mental energy obsessing about whether other people will find their touch dirty and repulsive. This obsession prevents him from shaking a visitor's hand and compromises spontaneous, smooth action. On the other hand, we need to rely on our reflexes when we are physically attacked rather than on a reflective understanding of the assailant's emotional problems. But in many situations we need blends of lower and higher order action tendencies of one or a range of action systems.

Sometimes we have the mental efficiency to select the level of action tendency that is needed to accomplish a goal. However, we may not have the mental efficiency to engage in the tendency. For example, a survivor may have the mental efficiency to recognize that she has to integrate painful feelings. However, her mental efficiency may be too low to engage in this difficult integrative action.

The third meaning of mental efficiency denotes an inherent feature of action tendencies. *This feature involves the degree of mental efficiency that is needed to initiate, execute, and complete a particular action tendency* (Janet, 1934). The higher the action tendency, the more mental efficiency it takes to accomplish the tendency.

In sum, when our mental efficiency is high and our mental energy suffices, and when we firmly wish to attain a particular goal, we can select the level and kind of action tendency that is most adaptive to achieve this goal, and execute it with precision, dedication, and grace.

MOBILITY ALONG THE HIERARCHY OF ACTION TENDENCIES

We become traumatized when our mental efficiency or mental energy is too low to engage in the high level action tendencies required to integrate extremely aversive events. The combination of these events and low mental efficiency can lead to a developmental arrest at or regression to maladaptive low-level action tendencies.

This fixation or regression manifests in *substitutes* for adaptive action tendencies (Janet, 1928b; see Chapter 7). As Jackson (1931/1932) put it, "[d]issolution . . . is a process of undevelopment . . . from the least organised, from the most complex and most voluntary, towards the most organised, most simple, and most automatic" (p. 46). Dissolution (Meares, 1999; Meares, Stevenson, & Gordon, 1999) or regression need not involve a complete loss of more advanced action tendencies but nonetheless entails a major *shift in dominance toward lower level action tendencies* (Janet, 1903, 1909a, 1928b). For example, under major actual or perceived threat, survivors need not totally lose their command of language and their ability to engage in social interaction, but these resources certainly tend to become much weaker and simpler in these circumstances. When survivors have become fixated at low levels of the hierarchy, they will thus have difficulty in symbolizing their experiences in words, share these experiences with others, and realize what happened to them. They will rather engage in *substitute actions* (Janet, 1903).

Substitutes involve maladaptive shifts to lower level action tendencies, hence a qualitatively lower integrative level. In terms of nonlinear dynamic systems theory (Edelman & Tononi, 2000), they involve a fall to a lower level form of self organization. The term *nonlinear* means that a minor stimulus can have a major effect on a system, or that a major stimulus or set of stimuli may exert no effect on a system. That is, there is a disproportional relationship between input and effect. When survivors regress along the hierarchy, their actions will be guided by the self-organizing principles of a lower level action tendency. This shift, which may be caused by a minor incident, will manifest in qualitatively different action tendencies. For example, many trauma therapists have experienced that one "wrong" remark can cause a major crisis in a patient. Such a crisis involves one or more substitute actions such as self mutilation and a temporary rupture in secure attachment. And one faint reminder of a traumatic experience can cause complete reexperiencing of that event in the form of undue, painful sensorimotor and highly emotional actions that are accompanied by a loss of all sociopersonal action tendencies.

Excessive or vehement emotions (Janet, 1889, 1909a; Van der Hart & Brown, 1992) involve a particular class of substitute actions. Vehement emotions involve an excess of mental and physical energy, and insufficient mental efficiency to use these energies, leading to disorganized behaviors. They are thus different from intense emotions that may accompany and guide adaptive action (Janet, 1928b). Vehement emotions can emerge when our action systems are tested beyond our limits of functioning.

The therapist may also experience the dissociative parts, and the survivor as a whole operate as nonlinear dynamic systems. That is, there can be a highly disproportionate relationship between the therapist's input and the effects of this input on the survivor. For example, the therapist may invest much effort in pointing out to the survivor that she is not responsible for the abuse—to no avail. This expenditure of energy and time can be fully neutralized by the survivor's fear of letting go of the fantasy, the reflexive belief that the perpetrator would have loved her if only she had not been "so bad." At other times, the therapist experiences that survivors can have a "breakthrough," an abrupt lift in mental efficiency that manifests as a leap toward a higher action tendency: A sudden major insight or new, reflective idea, an unexpected fusion between two previously dissociative parts. In short, progression sometimes can be as swift as regression.

Regression and progression entail qualitative shifts in perception–motor action cycles. This idea is not new, but was already proposed in the 19th century. Thus inspired by Bain (1855), Jackson (1931/1932) suggested that there is continuity of sensorimotor function at all levels of the nervous system. The hypothesis of multilayered perception–motor action cycles receives major support from contemporary philosophical analysis (Hurley, 1998; see Chapter 7) and psychobiological research (Berthoz, 2000; Fuster, 2003). In psychobiological terms, the higher-order cycles involve neural networks that include higher cortical structures and functions, whereas the lower-order cycles are associated with subcortical dominance. Differences between survivors as ANPs and as EPs would thus involve different neural networks. Findings from recent neuroimaging research support this hypothesis (see Box 9.1).

INTEGRATION OF ACTION TENDENCIES AND ACTION SYSTEMS

Action tendencies and action systems are related phenomena. One connection is that a particular action tendency can be a component of more than one action system. For example, reaching for something attractive can be part of energy management, attachment, exploration, and play. Different dissociative parts thus may engage in action tendencies that seem very similar at first sight but that in fact serve different goals. For example, a survivor may encompass two EPs that do not eat. One EP may not eat because sitting at the table with other people is a conditioned signal for abuse for this part. Aware that fasting will eventually stop menstruation, the other EP does not eat in order to prevent pregnancy.

Another link between action tendencies and action systems is that each action system includes action tendencies that are specific for that action system. Thus the inborn links between unconditioned stimuli and responses seem to reside within action systems. For example, survivors' ability to engage in unconditioned startle or freeze belongs to the action system of defense, and their tendency to salivate when they have an appetite and see or smell food is an unconditioned response that belongs to the energy management system. Dissociative parts that are mediated by different action systems can thus have quite different reactions to a particular stimulus. The implication is that these different parts will not understand each other very well. Moreover, many other people, including therapists, will find it difficult to understand or relate to the patient's seemingly capricious responses that can involve remarkable shifts in the level of action tendencies (e.g., "Yesterday she loved me for telling her how fine she looked, and today it scares her. You never know how she will be").

BOX 9.1

Regression to and Fixation at Low-level
Action Tendencies in Complex Trauma:
Some Psychobiological Findings

Findings of psychobiological studies of PTSD (Liberzon & Phan, 2003), and trauma-related BPD (Schmahl et al., 2003), strongly support the hypothesis that traumatization involves a regression to or fixation at unduly low and rigid levels of perception–motor cycles. For example, when traumatized patients are exposed to an audio-taped description of their traumatic experiences, they have abnormal brain activity in prefrontal brain areas such as the medial prefrontal cortex and the anterior cingulate. These higher cortical structures are essentially involved in the regulation of emotions. Instead, trauma survivors have excessive activation of the amygdala and insular cortex when exposed to the trauma script. These lower-order, subcortical brain areas mediate the emotional reactions to internal and external real or perceived threat stimuli that go more or less unchecked by the higher cortical control.

Studies of ANP and EP in trauma-related DID in women suggest that ANP and EP engage different neural networks when they listen to trauma scripts that they perceive as a personal memory as EP, but not as ANP (Nijenhuis & Den Boer, in press; Reinders et al., 2003, in press). Cortical activation is associated more with ANP, and EP with subcortical activity. Compared with ANP, EP engaged the medial prefrontal cortex and anterior cingulate less, whereas the insula, somatosensory cortex, caudate, and amygdala were activated more. ANP displayed more activation in a wide range of brain structures than EP, including regions of the parietal (Brodmann areas [BA] 7/40) and occipital association (BA17/18) cortex. Because these brain areas were also highly activated in patients with depersonalization disorder (Simeon et al., 2000), Reinders and colleagues (2003, in press) suggested that ANP controls emotional reactions to the trauma-related script more than EP, but fails to personify the described trauma memory (see Lou et al., 2004).

These findings support the theory of structural dissociation of the personality. Participants as ANP entertained the reflexive belief that the trauma script did not pertain to an event that happened to *them*. They had not realized the traumatizing event as a personal experience. EPs lacked all presentification regarding the trauma script and engaged in low level conditioned defensive reactions when they listened to the audiotape.

A shared developmental aspect of action tendencies and action systems involves the integration of different action tendencies and action systems into the framework of our personality. How exactly action tendencies and action systems become integrated is currently unknown, although some theoretical hypotheses have been proposed (Edelman & Tononi, 2000; G. F. R. Ellis & Toronchuk, 2005). They involve the idea that higher level action tendencies and integration among action systems emerge from, but cannot be fully explained by lower level action tendencies and systems. In this view, each new, more advanced integrative step involves a new kind of self-organization. These nonlinear changes may correspond with the observation that progression, including progression in treatment, may at times unfold with leaps.

Advances in our understanding of the normative developmental integration of action tendencies and action systems, and of how childhood traumatization compromises this development are major themes for future study. A related challenge is to comprehend better how some survivors accomplish these integrative challenges despite significant childhood abuse and neglect (i.e., to learn more about their strengths). An essential concern of these studies is that important goals in life can only be achieved when we integrate two or more different action tendencies and systems. The hierarchy suggests that the higher the level of the action tendency is, the more action systems we must integrate, and the higher our mental efficiency must be to accomplish the goal of the tendency. Integrating an extensive history of childhood abuse and neglect is an extremely demanding action tendency.

SUMMARY

The hierarchy of action tendencies is helpful in assessing the level of action tendencies in which trauma survivors engage, and in understanding the level they must reach to overcome their traumatization. The hierarchy begins with the most simple and automatic actions that commonly emerge from one action system. It ends with the most difficult and creative ones that integrate many action systems. The complexity of synthesis, memory, action regulation, sense of self, sense of time, and realization increases with each next level in the hierarchy of action tendencies, and can be expressed in terms of increasing complexity of perception–motor action cycles. Traumatization involves fixation at unduly low levels of the hierarchy or a regression to such levels for at least some parts of the personality. These parts engage in low and intermediate action tendencies, when the action tendency that is needed to accomplish a goal is beyond their level of mental efficiency, energy, and effort. Such regression is often as sudden, as is therapeutic progression along the hierarchy.

CHAPTER 10

Phobic Maintenance of Structural Dissociation

The moment any [Holocaust] memory or shred of a memory was about to float upwards, we would fight against it as though against evil spirits.

—Aharon Appelfeld (1994, p. 18)

S TRUCTURAL DISSOCIATION of the personality can have adaptive value if survivors lack the mental energy and efficiency to integrate their traumatic experiences and dissociative parts. Survivors with such a limited mental level as the apparently normal part of the personality (ANP) may be more able to adapt to daily life if they can avoid traumatic memories associated with the emotional part(s) of the personality (EP). A number of factors continue to maintain chronic dissociation over time, even though survivors may have increased their mental levels, matured, have better social support, and are no longer traumatized.

PHOBIA OF ACTION

Traumatized individuals have a *phobia of action* that can be more or less complex, and that basically pertains to a set of trauma-related actions (Janet, 1903, 1922). That is, survivors are unable to complete particular trauma-related actions effectively because they fear, detest, or are ashamed of, and thus avoid these actions, such as having certain feelings or being sexual. Phobias of trauma-related actions are substitute actions that maintain structural dissociation because they interfere with integrative mental actions needed to (re)integrate survivors' divided personality. They also prevent behavioral actions that would enhance the survivor's adaptive capacities, such as being assertive or taking healthy risks (Janet, 1904/1983, 1919/1925; Nijenhuis, Van der Hart, & Steele, 2002, 2004; Steele, Van der Hart, & Nijenhuis, 2005; Van der Hart, Steele, Boon, & Brown, 1993).

The core phobia of action involves avoidance of complete synthesis and realization of traumatic experiences, the *phobia of traumatic memory* (Janet, 1904/1983; Van der Hart, Steele et al., 1993). Many survivors develop additional trauma-related phobias through generalization learning, when they associate the recall of traumatic memories with certain other mental and behavioral actions. For example, Mark was ashamed of feeling angry because he was afraid he would be just like his violent perpetrator. Sandy avoided eye contact because it brought up her acutely painful embarrassment as a child when she was ridiculed. Thus the actions of becoming angry or of making eye contact in the present also will be experienced as fearful or shameful, and subsequently are avoided. Survivors may avoid physical sensations, affects, thoughts, wishes, needs, behaviors, and relationships whenever these become associated with the actions of their traumatic memories. They thus tend to lead a "life lived on the surface of consciousness" (Appelfeld, 1994, p. 18).

Survivors become more restricted and avoidant as they generalize their phobia of traumatic memories to other trauma-related stimuli. For example, they can develop a phobia of dissociative parts, and of particular sensations, movements, emotions, and thoughts. Chronic childhood abuse and neglect furthermore elicit a phobia of attachment and attachment loss regarding abusive or neglectful caretakers, which can generalize to many other interpersonal relationships. In addition to all these phobias, survivors can become phobic of change and normal risk taking.

ORIGINS OF TRAUMA-RELATED PHOBIAS

The roots of trauma-related phobias involve multifaceted and interrelated phenomena. These include classical and operant conditioning of trauma-related stimuli and difficulties in integrating discrepant action systems that are activated chronically by unconditioned and conditioned stimuli. The origins of these phobias also include maladaptive action tendencies resulting from poor modeling, inadequate dyadic regulation, lack of basic emotional skills, and lack of reflective and other higher level action tendencies (Nijenhuis, Van der Hart, & Steele, 2004; Steele et al., 2005). Trauma-related phobias also evolve as a result of entrenched psychological defenses, maladaptive trauma-related cognitions, and social and relational deficiencies. For example, negative cognitive appraisals of experiences increase phobias. A survivor may believe he or she is crazy, dirty, weak, stupid, or shameful for having certain thoughts, feelings, or needs: Thus these experiences are avoided. Finally, there are trauma-related neurobiological factors that are likely to contribute to the maintenance of structural dissociation. These include dysregulation of the HPA-axis, insufficient integration of different components of the central nervous system, low EEG coherence, lack of prefrontal inhibition of the "emotional brain" in EP, and small volume of the hippocampus and parahippocampal gyrus (e.g., Bremner, 1999; Ehling, Nijenhuis, & Krikke, 2003; Kowal, 2005; Nijenhuis et al., 2002; Nijenhuis & Den Boer, in press; Schore, 2003a; Vermetten et al., 2006).

TRAUMA-RELATED PHOBIAS AND CLASSICAL CONDITIONING

The development and maintenance of trauma-related phobias can be explained to a great degree by the principles of learning theory. These involve classical, operant, and evaluative conditioning, generalization learning, and lack of context evaluation. With the exception of evaluative conditioning, insights from learning theory are incorporated in the literature on PTSD (Brewin & Holmes, 2003; Foa, Zinbarg, & Rothbaum, 1992; Peri, Ben Shakhar, Orr, & Shalev, 2000; Rau, DeCola, & Fanselow, 2005). Although learning theory is highly relevant for the understanding and treatment of all trauma-related disorders, these insights are largely missing in the dissociative disorders literature.

Like any phobia, trauma-related phobias involve two major components. One component is a *classically conditioned fear or other aversive emotion* (e.g., shame, sadness) toward stimuli that survivors have associated with their traumatic experiences. These conditioned stimuli include *exteroceptive*[1] stimuli that once signaled traumatization (e.g., "If a man looks at me that way [conditioned stimulus], he will hit me [unconditioned stimulus]"), or that strongly refer to it (e.g., "The smell of aftershave [conditioned stimulus] reminds me of the rape [unconditioned stimulus]"). Conditioned exteroceptive stimuli include social stimuli that survivors have associated with neglect or abuse. For example, they may perceive a friendly remark as an overture to abuse. Essential *interoceptive*[2] conditioned stimuli are those associated with synthesizing and realizing traumatic memories (e.g., "If I would fully realize what happened to me, I would go insane or kill myself"). The second component of the trauma-related phobias is *conditioned escape and avoidance*. That is,

---

1. Exteroceptive stimuli are those that individual perceives in his or her external world.

2. Interoception is commonly defined as sensitivity to stimuli originating from inside the body. Given the fundamental unity of the body and the mind, in our view, interoceptive stimuli not only include perceived sensations and movements, but also perceived mental action more generally, and the experiences these mental actions generate.

when survivors perceive conditioned trauma-related stimuli, they engage in lower levels of reflexive mental and behavioral avoidance and escape.

Classically Conditioned Stimuli

Classical conditioning (Pavlov, 1927; Rescorla, 1998, 2003) is pervasive in traumatization, and involves lower level action tendencies (Shalev, Ragel-Fuchs, & Pitman, 1992; Van der Kolk, 1994). This basic form of associative learning is particularly strong when we are exposed to stressful events. Such events are unconditioned aversive stimuli that are intense and recurrent (Brewin, Andrews, & Valentine, 2000), and occur in unpredictable or uncontrollable ways (Bolstad & Zinbarg, 1997; Buckley, Blanchard, & Hickling, 1998).

Conditioned trauma-related stimuli are those that signal or strongly refer to an unconditioned stimulus, e.g., a traumatic experience for a survivor. Generally, some stimuli are more likely to become conditioned than others. Thus, classical conditioning depends upon the intensity (salience) of the stimulus, and on the degree to which it predicts the unconditioned stimulus. Furthermore, we are biologically prepared to become conditioned to aversive stimuli that have been of significance to the survival of our species (Garcia, Forthman-Quick, & White, 1984; Mineka & Öhman, 2002). For example, we are naturally wary of angry faces because they signal potential harm. A survivor is thus prone to develop a classically conditioned fear of angry looking individuals if he or she was abused (a cluster of unconditioned stimuli) by someone with an angry face (a conditioned stimulus for abuse for the survivor). Childhood abuse and neglect involve a host of evolutionarily relevant stimuli because this mistreatment poses a threat to survival, thus it implies major classical conditioning.

However, we can also develop a classically conditioned reaction to stimuli that do not have particular survival value from an evolutionary perspective. Anne, a 37-year-old woman with DDNOS, was extremely afraid of getting into black cars. She developed a conditioned fear of them when her neighbor forced her into a black car as a young child and raped her. Thus the previously neutral stimulus of a black car became a conditioned trauma-related stimulus for Anne.

The difference between conditioned stimuli that *signal* and stimuli that *refer* to an aversive unconditioned stimulus is clinically relevant. Stimuli that signal a traumatic experience are those that indicate it is about to happen again. Stimuli that refer to a traumatic experience are those that remind the survivor of what happened.

Nell, a patient with a history of physical abuse, would duck and cover her head with her arms if someone unexpectedly raised his or her hand. The raising of one's hand is generally a neutral stimulus. But for Nell it *signaled* a beating. She had learned: "If someone suddenly raises his or her hand, I will be beaten." Previously neutral stimuli may also *refer* to a traumatizing event, and thus become conditioned stimuli. Nell became violently nauseated and panicked at the sight or smell of egg salad. At age 8, she had received a particularly brutal beating in the middle of lunch while she was eating egg salad. The perpetrator shoved it down her throat, choking her. Eating egg salad did not signal abuse, but strongly reminded her of it.

When survivors are repeatedly exposed to a conditioned *signal* in treatment such as a raised hand, and the expected outcome does not occur (e.g., being beaten), they can learn that this conditioned stimulus does not signal the unconditioned stimulus (i.e., actual threat), in the present situation. Thus they learn there is no need to engage in conditioned defense responses. In other words, their reflexive reaction has become a higher level action tendency involving reflection and presentification in the moment: "This person is raising his hand to express himself, and it does not mean I am about to get hit." Learning that the conditioned stimulus does not signal the unconditioned stimulus in the present situation is the working principle of all forms of exposure therapy. But when the therapist exposes trauma survivors to a conditioned stimulus that *refers* to or reminds them of their traumatic experiences, the exposure will not change the meaning of the stimulus. Rather, survivors will need some form of counterconditioning which changes the meaning of the conditioned referential stimulus. For instance, Nell would have to learn to associate egg salad with positive stimuli such as a safe partner and the joy of sharing a nice dinner together.

Classical Conditioning and Interoceptive Stimuli

The classical conditioned stimuli in the examples above (a raised hand, the smell and sight of egg salad) involve exteroceptive stimuli. Classical conditioning can also occur with the perception of interoceptive stimuli (Goldstein & Chambless, 1978; Nijenhuis et al., 2002). *Classical conditioning of interoceptive stimuli is key in the maintenance of structural dissociation.* This conditioning primarily occurs when the survivor as ANP experiences an unexpected intrusion of a traumatic memory. This intrusion—often experienced as confusing, overwhelming, and ego dystonic (Van der Hart & Steele, 1999)—involves three major series of actions. First, the survivor as EP relives a traumatic experience (one series of mental actions). Second, the survivor as ANP minimally synthesizes some aspect of EP's experience (i.e., becomes aware of it). This entails another series of mental actions without which ANP would not experience a (part of a) traumatic memory. However, the survivor as ANP does not go on to fully synthesize or realize the memory. The failure of these integrative actions relates to another action of ANP, that of mental flight. Thus, third, ANP takes mental flight from the traumatic memory and the associated EP, because experiencing the memory is inherently aversive. As a powerful sensorimotor and affective representation of the original traumatic experience, *the traumatic memory operates as an unconditioned stimulus for both ANP and EP.*

Fixated in traumatic memories, the survivor as EP cannot avoid or escape from them. However, given a sufficient mental level, the survivor as ANP *can* avoid them, at least some of the time, because he or she is guided by action systems of daily life that can inhibit the defense system, and may have the mental level to avoid traumatic memories. The actions of escape of ANP tend to become conditioned reactions to stimuli that saliently signal or refer to an impending intrusion of traumatic memories. These stimuli become conditioned interoceptive stimuli for ANP. For example, the survivor as ANP may notice that intrusions are preceded by anxiety. Impending anxiety becomes a conditioned signal that motivates the survivor as ANP to escape this emotion (e.g., by staying very busy at work, or by drinking).

In short, *exposure of ANP to EP's traumatic memories is functionally equivalent to exposure to the original traumatizing event when ANP does not have the mental efficiency to integrate these memories. In these circumstances, this exposure implies the survivor is retraumatized by these interoceptive stimuli, which serves to strengthen structural dissociation.* The theory of structural dissociation thus predicts that the division between ANP(s) and EP(s) will become more profound with recurrence of unmanageable traumatic reexperiencing. With recurrent intrusions, a host of interoceptive stimuli can become conditioned, trauma-related stimuli for the survivor as ANP. Thus ANP may fear and avoid the sound of EP's crying, the sensation of EP's racing heart, or a mental image of a perpetrator, if these stimuli saliently signal or accompany a traumatic intrusion. ANP may also start to fear EP generally, and eventually any stimulus that signals or refers to EP.

The survivor as ANP learns to avoid or escape EP's intrusions not only consciously but also preconsciously. That is, ANP may preconsciously synthesize a conditioned stimulus that signals an upcoming mental intrusion, and instantly avoid it by inhibiting further synthesis (e.g., by lowering or retraction of consciousness). Research indeed suggests that survivors as ANP can block further synthesis of traumatic memories that began at an earlier stage of information processing (see Chapter 9; Hermans, Nijenhuis, Van Honk, Huntjens, & Van der Hart, 2006; Reinders et al., 2003, in press). Thus survivors as ANP typically do not personify traumatic memories, and are not consciously aware that this lack results from their own inhibitory mental action. They may merely experience that "the memory is not mine." As Appelfeld (1994) noted about himself and other Holocaust survivors directly after World War II: "We spoke of the recent past from a strange distance. As if the things had not happened to us" (p. 18).

Variable Reactions to Classically
Conditioned Stimuli

Survivors can respond to a given conditioned stimulus with a variety of reactions that may or may not resemble the original defensive action. A conditioned threat stimulus will initially activate the complete defence system rather than only one particular defensive subsystem (e.g., flight) or mode (e.g., curling up in a corner). This relates to the fact that in many instances of classical conditioning, the conditioned stimulus (e.g., a man saying: "We're going to play a little game") reactivates a memory of the original unconditioned stimulus (e.g., childhood sexual abuse). In reaction to this memory and his or her perception of the present circumstances (e.g., awareness of current physical strength), the survivor will consciously or unconsciously select a particular response or pattern of responses from the reactivated defense system that fits the present circumstances best (e.g., defensive fight as an adult). Thus *the conditioned reaction is not an exact replica of the unconditioned reaction*. For example, Anne had submitted to her perpetrator and had gone limp when he pulled her into the black car to rape her. Thus her original response was one of submission. As an adult, however, she had a quite different response when she needed to be hospitalized because of a dissociative psychotic episode. A black taxi came to transport her, she vehemently fought two men to avoid getting in the car, as the car was a conditioned stimulus. Thus her response as an adult was one of fighting, not submission, but nevertheless was still a part of the defensive action system.

Classical conditioning is adaptive in principle. For example, we can better adapt to our environment when we are aware that one event (the conditioned stimulus) predicts another event (the unconditioned stimulus). This awareness helps us more easily find attractive unconditioned stimuli and avoid aversive ones. Furthermore, the flexibility of responses to conditioned stimuli is adaptive because the actual threat situation in the present can be different from the original threat situation. For example, a former escape route may be blocked and we must take another type of evasive action, which nevertheless is still flight.

However, we should also be able to know that the relationship between the conditioned and unconditioned stimulus does not apply in every circumstance; we should be able to *evaluate the context* in which a conditioned stimulus occurs (Bouton, 2004; Bouton, Westbrook, Corcoran, & Maren, 2006). This evaluation of context is lacking in survivors. So they continue to activate their defense system in reaction to a conditioned threat stimulus, and do not activate other action systems that may in fact suit the current context far better.

PHOBIAS AND OPERANT CONDITIONING

Reactions to (conditioned) stimuli can also be influenced by the effects of operant conditioning (Skinner, 1988). Classical conditioning involves the effects on actions from stimuli that *precede* those actions (e.g., an angry face that signals that abuse is about to occur). In contrast, operant conditioning involves learning from the *consequences* of one's actions. For example, when a therapist applies a new intervention and gets excellent results, he or she learns to apply this intervention more often, when the situation is appropriate. The consequence of the intervention is rewarding. If a child cries and gets hit for crying, he or she may learn not to cry. The consequence of crying is punishment; the consequence of not crying is avoidance of punishment.

There are different kinds of "reinforcers" of our actions. They include positive reinforcement (reward), negative reinforcement, punishment, and frustrative nonreward (i.e., expected reward does not occur). Of these, we focus on negative reinforcement given its important role in phobic avoidance. *Negative reinforcement* involves an increase in a particular behavior because it removes or prevents an aversive or unpleasant stimulus. Interoceptive stimuli (trauma-related emotions, sensations, images, thoughts, etc.) that are evoked by conditioned trauma-related stimuli ("triggers") are highly aversive to the survivor. Thus he or she seeks ways to avoid these stimuli. For example, a survivor learns that a particular action (e.g., staying busy, becoming spacy, avoiding thinking about the past) prevents or reduces painful feelings or memories, and thus he or she tends to engage in that action more often on future occasions. Escape and avoidance strategies are negatively reinforced on a regular basis in a survivor, and therefore gradually increase in strength and frequency.

Negatively reinforced actions are ubiquitous in traumatized individuals. For example, a survivor learns to be silent about the abuse when a perpetrator threatens him or her about reporting it. Or the survivor learns to appease people to avoid being hurt or rejected. These negatively reinforced responses are strong and difficult to overcome. They lead, for example, to great difficulty for the survivor in speaking in therapy about what happened, or being assertive, even when there is a strong need for assertiveness. Negative reinforcement may also lead survivors to accept their perpetrators' claim that they (i.e., the survivors) are crazy, disgusting, or guilty of the abuse. Realizing that these claims are false may be more painful for a child who has to continue to live with the abuser than adhering to the reflexive belief that the perpetrator is right. By the same token, a child may attach to an abusive and neglectful caretaker because the feeling of attachment offers some relief from the painful realization that the caretaker is and remains malicious. It may be less aversive to remain attached to an abusive caretaker than to experience the pain of abandonment.

The efforts of the survivor as ANP to evade synthesis and realization of traumatic memories may also be *rewarded* (i.e., *positively reinforced*), and thus increase in frequency and strength. For example, avoidance is usually socially rewarded: "It is indeed good to get on with your life and forget about what happened. You'll feel much better that way." This kind of recurrent social reward strengthens the survivor's avoidance of traumatic memories and leads him or her to believe it is wrong or bad to have serious unfinished business. That is, it enhances false reflexive beliefs.

Avoidance and Escape from Perceived Threat

A survivor can behaviorally avoid trauma-related stimuli. For example, Nell, who was once beaten while eating egg salad, avoided egg salad. The very sight of it made her sick. Other behavioral avoidance reactions to trauma-related stimuli include avoiding intimacy, sexual relations, interpersonal conflict, showers or bathtubs, looking at or touching one's own body, places where abuse occurred, and therapy.

Survivors can engage in behavioral avoidance or escape from their own feared mental actions. For example, they can temporarily evade traumatic memories by self-harming because this action generates endogenous opioids that temporarily block or impair their ability to reactivate these painful memories (Sandman, Barron, & Colman, 1990). Or survivors may take drugs or drink alcohol to cloud their consciousness (Southwick, Bremner, Krystal, & Charney, 1994), or stay too busy in order to prevent or block feelings and thoughts.

Survivors can also *mentally avoid or escape* from perceived external threat. We have already noted that they consciously or preconsciously avoid the integration of traumatic memories, dissociative parts, and other trauma-related actions. For example, survivors as ANP may know that they try to avoid their traumatic memories: *"The moment any [Holocaust] memory or shred of a memory was about to float upwards, we would fight against it as though against evil spirits"* (Appelfeld, 1994, p. 18; italics added). Avoidance actions that involve *lowering of the level of consciousness* include dizziness, absent-mindedness, confusion, fogginess, or depersonalization. Other substitutes for integration involve *retraction of the field of consciousness* such as obsessive focus on the mundane content of daily life, incessant joking or chatter, or fixation in negative emotions (e.g., shame) that are perceived as less threatening than other emotions (e.g., anger). We refer to avoidant lowering and retraction of consciousness as *phobic alterations in consciousness*.

The extreme of phobic alteration in consciousness is the complete deactivation of a dissociative part when survivors are confronted with stimuli that part cannot or does not wish to integrate. This substitute action involves a psychogenic loss of consciousness such that the patient as a whole is completely unresponsive, or a dissociative switch when a different part takes control of consciousness and action.

Another major conditioned mental escape and avoidance action involves treating significant stimuli as if they were insignificant. For example, an ANP may tell the therapist and herself that nothing is wrong, although she hears an EP crying in her head.

Context Evaluation and Generalization Learning

When a conditioned stimulus signals *real* danger, it is adaptive to act to make ourselves safe, to find ways to reduce or eliminate the threat. But such actions are maladaptive when the danger is a misperception and thus is not real. A conditioned stimulus does not necessarily evoke a conditioned response in every situation. But many survivors are especially prone to reflexive reactions to trauma-related stimuli, no matter the circumstances. That is, they often engage in conditioned responses irrespective of the context in which they find themselves. Adaptation, however, includes the ability to engage in *context evaluation*—the ability to distinguish one context from the other and to choose one's actions accordingly (Bouton, 2004; Bouton et al., 2006). This requires a higher level of action tendencies than reflexive ones. Instead, the survivor follows a reflexive belief or implicit rule in all situations: "If a man looks at me that way, he will abuse me." The inability to accurately read context is partly due to the fact that EPs filter everything through the lens of the defense action system. In addition, the survivor as ANP does not sufficiently appreciate that once his or her mental level has increased and social support is available, traumatic memories and associated EPs can be integrated. Lack of context evaluation from both ANP and EP maintains trauma-related phobias.

Trauma-related phobias can become elaborated through *generalization learning*. Survivors learn to respond in a similar way to stimuli that in some way resemble the original conditioned stimulus. Even though Anne was raped in an old black junk car without wheels, she generalized her fear to all black cars. Survivors can generalize their response to relationships as well. For example, Margaret is afraid of all men; Brett becomes panicked when he is kissed by a woman; Sandy has an immediate shame response when someone hugs her.

When survivors are unable to accurately perceive the present context and have generalized many stimuli in daily life such that they have inappropriate reactions, they are not able to be fully in the present. That is, they lack presentification. As noted earlier, presentification involves an accurate assessment of the present, past, and future, and how they are related, while recognizing that the present is the most real. When survivors unduly fear and avoid traumatic memories, dissociative parts, and other trauma-related actions, they are not sufficiently or accurately evaluating the present. Instead, they retract their field of consciousness to the past in which they were unable to integrate their traumatic experiences.

Evaluative Conditioning

Evaluative conditioning is the unconscious, automatic, and persistent transfer of our (dis)like of one stimulus to another. When we are simultaneously exposed to a neutral stimulus and a stimulus we naturally (dis)like, we will also start to (dis)like this previously neutral stimulus (Baeyens, Hermans, & Eelen, 1993). The neutral stimulus can become *inherently* (un)attractive after a single time of pairing it with the (dis)liked stimulus. For example, when an individual has sexual feelings during sexual abuse, experiencing sexual feelings can become inherently aversive.

Evaluative conditioning is not well known in the trauma field, but its effects are pervasive in traumatization and may remain treatment resistant when not recognized. Evaluative conditioning explains to a large degree how survivors learn to hate themselves when they are abused and neglected. When they inherently pair themselves ("I") with the maltreatment, they begin to negatively evaluate their very being (e.g., "I am bad"). For example, survivors associate their aversion, disgust, shame, and fear of sexual abuse with physical touch, body odors, sex-related sounds, their own body (e.g., "My body is revolting"), and physical reactions, sex in general, and even their view of themselves as a person (i.e., "I am dirty and disgusting"). They may learn to loathe their gender ("Girls are disgusting and weak").

Evaluative conditioning can occur in relation to dissociative parts. One dissociative part can develop a dislike of another part because that part has been associated with negatively evaluated stimuli. For example, when the traumatic experience involved shame, an ANP may learn to be ashamed of, or despise the EP involved in this traumatic experience. For example, as the day child (ANP), Marilyn Van Derbur (2004) hated the night child (EP) that endured sexual abuse: "I loathed, despised, and blamed her" (p. 191). Shame is a ubiquitous feeling in survivors, a result of evaluative conditioning of the self. It often remains silent and hidden, pervasively coloring the survivors' experience. Shame is overwhelming and entwined with fear and anger that obscure its presence. It can inhibit other affective mental actions, particularly in relationship with others (Nathanson, 1987; Tomkins, 1963). For example, shame can inhibit joy, sexual feelings, anger, sadness, and hurt. This aversive emotion can thus prevent the integration of other emotions.

Evaluative conditioning not only occurs with negative feelings in survivors; it can also relate to positive feelings. For example, a survivor may pair a positive feeling of closeness with sex and become promiscuous, constantly seeking sex as a maladaptive way to feel close. Others may pair a positive feeling of being in control and powerful with aggression or even sadism, and thus become perpetrators themselves.

Conditioned negative evaluations maintain structural dissociation. For example, a submissive EP will fear and avoid a fight EP that reflexively hates, insults, or hurts this submissive EP. Such unjustified but understandably harsh feelings and ideas are hard to change, because the effects of evaluative conditioning are impervious to extinction or cognitive correction (Baeyens, Eelen, Van den Bergh, & Crombez, 1989): Exposure to the conditioned stimulus and insight will not change the negative evaluation. For example, exposure of a fight EP to a submissive EP is not enough. Effective therapy involves *counterconditioning*. For instance, the therapist helps the fight EP associate the submissive EP (negatively evaluated stimulus) with a realization that submission had survival value (positively evaluated stimulus). Thus, the fight EP eventually learns to associate empathy and appreciation with the previously despised submissive EP. The same process can occur in reverse, with the submissive EP learning to appreciate the survival value of fight EP. In this way, survivors can be supported to accept all aspects of themselves; such as thoughts, feelings, wishes, and dissociative parts.

PHOBIAS OF TRAUMA-RELATED
STIMULI AND ACTIONS

Classical, operant, and evaluative conditioning, and lack of context evaluation are most helpful to understanding trauma-related phobias. These phobias play an essential role in the maintenance of structural dissociation, thus must be identified and overcome to resolve structural dissociation of the personality.

Phobia of Traumatic Memories

Referring to traumatic memories regarding combat, World War I veteran Erich Maria Remarque (1929/1982) believed that "It's too dangerous for me to put these things into words" (p. 165). He feared loss of control: "I am afraid they might become gigantic and I be no longer able to master them" (p. 165). The mental action of recalling traumatic memories is "dangerous" (i.e., overwhelming), for a survivor if his or her mental level is too low to integrate them, when social support is lacking, or when the threat still exists. But with sufficient mental energy, mental efficiency, support, and actual safety, with this change of context, survivors can gradually integrate traumatic memories and safely transform them into autobiographical narrative (episodic) memories. This demanding work, which implies giving the traumatic past a much lower degree of reality, is a core feature of Phase 2 treatment (Chapter 16). When survivors continue to believe, usually quite reflexively, that traumatic memories are inherently dangerous and that remembering leads to loss of control, they have a phobia of traumatic memories (Janet, 1904/1983b, 1919/1925; Van der Hart, Steele et al., 1993). This is the essential phobia of mental action in trauma survivors.

Phobia of Trauma-Derived Mental Actions

The phobia of trauma-derived mental actions evolves from the core phobia of traumatic memories, and involves the survivor's fear, disgust, or shame about mental actions he or she associates with traumatic memories. Thus, the survivor tends to fear and avoid physical and emotional feelings and self-reflection. Conditioned negative evaluations of mental actions and the contents they generate contribute to this phobia. For example, survivors may believe: "My uncle told me I am a piece of dirt; I am a piece of dirt"; "I had needs as a child that were denied; having needs is bad"; "I felt aroused when I was sexually abused; sexual feelings are disgusting." Once an intense affect, bodily feeling or need (e.g., wishes to be held) is labeled as "awful" or "bad," other experiences may be labeled in the same way through generalization learning.

Gradually overcoming the phobia of trauma-derived mental actions is a prerequisite for overcoming the core phobia of traumatic memory, a fact that is often overlooked in the treatment of traumatic memories.

Phobia of Dissociative Parts of the Personality

A specific phobia of trauma-derived mental actions is the *phobia of dissociative parts of the personality* (Nijenhuis, 1994; Nijenhuis & Van der Hart, 1999a). The fear, anger, disgust, or shame felt by one part for another is variable. For example, EPs that receive some support from a caretaking ANP will be far less avoidant of this ANP than of other dissociative parts. Actually, some trauma survivors have parts that already interact with each other in positive ways before treatment; for instance, two ANPs may collaborate in daily tasks. All things being equal, when such positive collaborative and empathic relationships exist among dissociative parts, integration of these parts probably will be easier than the integration of parts that do not cooperate with or like each other.

However, many dissociative parts fear, despise, and misunderstand each other. When they express their reflexive feelings and ideas while interacting, endless negative feedback loops may ensue that may lead eventually to posttraumatic exhaustion.

Sally, a graduate student with DDNOS, heard a critical voice that called her "stupid" each time she tried to finish a difficult research paper. The EP whose voice she heard was secretly afraid of failure (phobia of healthy risk taking), and therefore sabotaged the work of Sally as ANP. When ANP heard the EP's voice, which had become a conditioned interoceptive stimuli for her because it signaled and referred to fierce criticism, her reflexive substitute action was to drink heavily to drown out the voice. The result was that Sally became drunk and did not finish her paper. The feared and despised voice then returned with renewed vehemence, enraged at the failure that created intense shame. The more Sally as ANP heard the voice, the more depressed and worthless she felt. Needing to avoid these feelings, she continued to drink, which produced further internal berating from the EP. Sally was finally hospitalized for substance abuse and suicidality.

EPs' vehement traumatic memories remain unresolved as long as ANP is able to effectively avoid them. The chronic reactivation of these negative experiences intensifies them, which is known as *kindling* (McFarlane, Yehuda, & Clark, 2002). Thus, the more EPs are reactivated by conditioned stimuli, the more intense their emotional reactions tend to become. The more intense EPs' experiences become, the more ANPs will avoid and despise them. And the more avoidant ANPs are, the more EPs feel trapped in the past, fearful, rejected, or angry. In a word, such ANPs and EPs respond increasingly negatively toward each other and try to avoid or escape from each other more and more. This spiral of avoidance and sensitization prevents presentification in both ANPs and EPs, strongly contributing to the maintenance of structural dissociation of the personality.

In cases of tertiary structural dissociation, some ANPs may despise each other or are condescending, even if they are not afraid of each other. For example, a worker ANP may despise a caretaker ANP who has feelings and thus detracts from work that is the main purview of the worker ANP. This part avoids feelings, relational needs, and traumatic memories by working. Thus, underneath the disdain there is also fearful avoidance of feelings (i.e., the worker ANP has a phobia of mental actions). This is but one example of how various trauma-related phobias are intertwined with each other.

There are several specific types of dissociative parts that are especially avoided by other parts. These include fight EPs that are fixed in the fight defense subsystem and try, often inappropriately, to protect the survivor from a perceived threat. And most dissociative parts are even more phobic of persecutory EPs. These EPs are based on introjected perpetrators and typically direct rage inward and traumatic reenactments toward other parts. However, they may also direct rage outward toward other people.

In addition, EPs that contain unbearable traumatic memories or engage in other highly aversive mental or behavioral actions are avoided with special intensity. Many parts abhor or fear those that contain disavowed dependency needs, sexual feelings, terror, rage, shame, guilt, loneliness, despair, and suicidal thoughts. Not only are these feelings and wishes avoided because of their intensity and pain, but survivors often cannot make the distinction between *feeling* and *doing,* between mental actions and behavioral ones: a problem with the degrees of reality involving a lack of differentiation between the subjective and objective world. Thus survivors as ANP work ever harder to keep a distance from parts they fear may "take control" and act on unacceptable feelings or impulses. Along with overcoming the phobia of other trauma-related mental actions, the successful treatment of the phobia of dissociative parts is essential prior to overcoming the phobia of traumatic memories.

Phobias of Attachment, Attachment Loss, and Intimacy

Maltreated children tend to develop a phobia of attachment when the action of attaching to the caretaker has become associated with emotional and physical pain. Thus, proximity to an abusive and neglectful caretaker will activate survivors' defense systems, which includes distancing from the caretaker and often very low level action tendencies (i.e., simple reflexes and presymbolic regulatory action tendencies). However, survivors tend to activate the attachment system, hence social engagement action tendencies, once they reach a certain mental or physical distance from the caretaker (e.g., by reapproaching the caretaker and saying "Stay with me.").

Especially in chronic traumatization, the phobia of attachment and attachment loss regarding caretakers may generalize to anyone who attempts to become relationally close, including therapists. For many survivors, interpersonal relationships become conditioned stimuli that evoke parts fixed in attachment approach or avoidance. *Phobia of attachment* is often paradoxically accompanied by an equally intense *phobia of attachment loss* (Steele, Van der Hart, & Nijenhuis, 2001). Different parts of the personality typically experience these opposite phobias. They evoke each other in a vicious cycle, with a perceived change in closeness or distance in a relationship resulting in the well-known pattern of "I hate you—don't leave me." In psychobiological terms, the phobias of attachment and attachment loss deactivate the ventral vagal system. According to Porges (2001, 2003; see Nijenhuis & Den Boer, in press), this component of the central nervous system helps individuals regulate potent affects such as fear and anger through social interaction. This implies that *disrupted attachment and lack of social support lowers survivors' mental efficiency.*

When some dissociative parts avoid other parts that strive for attachment, again, structural dissociation is maintained. These avoidant parts can include any that are not mediated by attachment or attachment cry. On the other hand, parts fear and avoid attachment loss when they are fixed in attachment cry or driven by unmet dependency needs, sadness,

and loneliness (Steele et al., 2001). These parts may engage in indiscrimi-
nant or unhealthy relationships, desperate to prevent feelings of abandonment, raising the risk of relational hurt or betrayal. The ensuing relational difficulties only further confirm to the survivor that she or he is
unlovable, amplifying isolation and self-loathing.

The *phobia of (emotional and sexual) intimacy* is closely related. Unlike the biologically driven attachment of a child to a caregiver, intimacy is
more under volitional control, involving more choices about revealing aspects of one's self and one's needs. Attachment provides the general framework for all relationships, while intimacy is the deepest and most satisfying
form of attachment, found in only a few relationships over the course of a
lifetime. Many survivors can form more superficial and social attachments,
but they often cannot be fully intimate because of the fear of being known
and being hurt or betrayed. Yet, there is a human drive to be known, understood, and loved, and in survivors this is almost always expressed by
some dissociative parts. The tension between the risks of intimacy and the
yearning for intimacy serves to maintain structural dissociation.

Phobia of Normal Life

The phobia of trauma-derived mental actions can become so generalized
that for some survivors life becomes increasingly restricted. For others,
life runs amok as they constantly react to conditioned stimuli and remain
in the familiar world of hyperarousal and chaos. The chronic activation of
the defense action system precludes activation of daily life action systems
that can lead to a more normal and balanced life. And even when daily
life action systems are activated, the actions tendencies of survivors are
often not developed adequately to ensure healthy functioning in normal
life. A *phobia of normal life* ensues (Van der Hart & Steele, 1999), as the
survivor feels increasingly unable to deal with many of the complex and
ambiguous situations of life, is overwhelmed by conditioned stimuli in
daily life, and avoids daily life tasks as much as possible.

Phobia of Change and Healthy Risk-taking

In order to live a normal life, we must not only be stable and maintain
beneficial routines and habits, but also make healthy adjustments and accept inevitable changes. Change is, of course, the essential bedrock of
successful therapy and of healthy adaptation to life. But for survivors,
change often represents feared losses or pain, the dangerous unknown,
or a repetition of something terrible that has happened in the past. The
fear of change makes it especially challenging for survivors to overcome
their structural dissociation.

Change requires activation of the exploration system. But change and accompanying feelings of anxiety or discomfort may evoke the defensive system, which deactivates the tendency to explore and experiment.

> Gloria, a patient with DDNOS and BPD, complained that she could not eat healthily, clean her house, or manage her feelings. She wanted to do these things, but felt unable to make the necessary changes. When her therapist explored this issue with her, it became clear that Gloria was afraid that if she changed and got better she would decide to leave her marriage: something she did not want to do. She also was afraid if she got better, her therapist would leave her, and that somehow she did not deserve to get better anyway.

Certain reflexive core beliefs make change difficult or frightening. Survivors often believe that change means "things will be worse" or "I will be forced to do something against my will." And one patient angrily said to her therapist, "You are trying to make me change so I won't be myself anymore; you don't accept me as I am!"

Chronic trauma survivors often associate risk taking with failure. Thus they are typically afraid to take a healthy risk, fearing that it will result in humiliation, shame, and disaster, their common childhood experience. Paradoxically, many survivors take outrageously dangerous and impulsive risks. But these are not the calculated and reflective risks that are necessary for adaptive change. Instead, they involve lower level reflexive behaviors that do not include consideration of potentially negative consequences or danger. They may take drugs, drink heavily and drive, have unsafe sex, walk alone at night in a park, fail to show up at work, or engage in destructive relationships with people. But they are less likely to risk looking for a better job, going back to school for a better education, or engaging in more vulnerable and intimate connections with a partner, or simply learning something new, because they are afraid they will be inept or stupid and ultimately fail, and life will be worse than ever. The fear of failure, change, and risk creates a need to maintain the internal status quo (i.e., structural dissociation).

THE COSTS OF MAINTAINING, AND GAINS OF OVERCOMING STRUCTURAL DISSOCIATION

The integrated personality is a highly complex system, coordinated and cohesive. As a result, its many subsystems are interconnected. In terms of nonlinear dynamic systems theory (Edelman & Tononi, 2000; Putnam, 2005; the term *nonlinear* is discussed in Chapter 9 and below), dissociative parts are unduly closed and simple subsystems compared to the integrated personality. These subsystems do not work together in harmony, they are often mediated by only one action system or a limited constellation of action systems, and overall engage in unduly low action tendencies. The field of consciousness that is a part of these subsystems is usually retracted to the goals of particular action systems, and not to integration with other action systems. For example, most EPs only engage in a limited number of defensive actions, because they are mediated by one or more components of the defense system, hence only experience a small range of mental and behavioral states.

Even though dissociative parts may be unduly closed and simple, they may be somewhat adaptive when the survivor's mental level is low, or when there is ongoing maltreatment such that chronic defense enhances survival. Survivors as EP usually react to perceived threat automatically, stably, and instantly, because they are focused on one major goal of defense. Their low level actions are well-practiced or highly conditioned, and they are not troubled by ambivalence or conflict that can emerge when different action systems would be simultaneously activated. These features involve an economic expenditure of energy when there is real threat. However, EPs cannot adapt to situations that require evaluation of a wider range of stimuli and action alternatives, or highly volitional control of perception and motor action. For example, as discussed, they do not sufficiently evaluate the context in which a conditioned stimulus appears, implying that they also engage in defensive reactions in situations that are actually safe. This lack of presentification and the associated investment of energy and time in substitute actions implies a major waste of mental and physical energy, and a decrease of mental efficiency. This waste often involves an imbalance between mental energy and mental efficiency. Inefficient investment of energy eventually results in posttraumatic decline, which involves exhaustion and decompensation (Janet, 1928b; Titchener, 1986).

Therapists therefore aim to raise the mental efficiency of EPs and ANPs to help these parts attain higher level action tendencies (see Chapter 9). In terms of systems theory, therapists try to increase the complexity of these subsystems of the personality such that their autonomy decreases. Dissociative parts become more complex when they integrate more elements; for example, when they increase the complexity of their perception–motor action cycles at higher levels in terms of the hierarchy of action tendencies. Thus, when an EP has started to communicate more with another dissociative part, this EP's system now includes new elements (i.e., new actions). The complexity of a subsystem (i.e., a dissociative part) involves the number of elements of a (sub)system that are connected in a nonlinear fashion. The connections among these elements are nonlinear when change in one element of the system is disproportional to change in one or more other elements of the system. Because dissociative parts as subsystems of the personality are nonlinear, this development can cause a disproportionate change in the system as a whole. In this sense, the survivor as this part now makes more efficient use of his or her energy. The survivor's return on investment of time, effort, and energy has increased.

ANPs represent more complex and more open systems than EPs. High functioning patients have particularly open and complex subsystems of the personality. Many survivors have ANPs that can usually integrate a wide range of stimuli. Some ANPs can coordinate many action system(s) of daily life, and this integration allows them to perform well in in this respect. However, all ANPs are unduly closed to integrating trauma-related actions, which limits their complexity. This closure consumes energy because it involves engagement in ongoing mental avoidance and escape.

Increasing complexity of dissociative parts as subsystems of the personality implies increasing complexity of the personality as a whole. First, dissociative parts are not totally separated from each other, and second, increasing mental efficiency in a part usually involves increasing connectivity with other parts. Due to this increasing complexity, the survivor's actions become less automatic and more flexible. These higher level action tendencies allow him or her to adapt more to a changeable environment. The survivor gradually stops the ineffective expenditure of mental and physical energy on substitute actions, and enjoys the fruits of more efficient and effective actions. He or she increases mental energy and efficiency with every well-executed and well-completed adaptive action (Janet, 1919/1925).

However, the costs of this gain are ambivalence, conflict, and delay of rewards (see Chapter 9). For example, when individuals develop reflective beliefs, they will also experience ambivalence (e.g., "I have several choices. What is my best option in this situation?"). And when they engage in prolonged action tendencies, they must wait before they get rewarded. For example, a person must study hard and consistently to get good grades, but the real "payoff" to these actions may not be evident until the end of a semester. Similarly, the gains of integrating traumatic memories are profound, but may take a long time to materialize. Thus survivors need much therapeutic support in learning to tolerate ambivalence, competing personal needs and wishes, and delayed gratification in order to succeed in the higher level action tendencies.

SUMMARY

Survivors of chronic traumatization are characterized by phobias of action that maintain their structural dissociation. Classical, operant, and evaluative conditioning, generalization, lack of context evaluation, and presentification are key among the many factors that contribute to these phobias. Overcoming trauma-related phobias is essential to successful treatment. Because dissociative parts of the personality avoid so much, they function as unduly simple, overly closed systems, acting rigidly and reflexively regarding the trauma-related stimuli they fear and despise. Survivors waste much energy and time in these and related substitute actions, such as recurrent reexperiences of traumatizing events, eventually leading to exhaustion and decompensation for some. Their dissociative parts thus need to become more open, complex, and flexible, more reflective in their actions, and more open to cooperation and coordination with the personality as a whole. The therapist therefore assists survivors in raising and in developing more balance between their mental energy and efficiency, which enables them to deal more effectively with complex internal and external stimuli.

Treatment of Chronically Traumatized Patients

Introduction to Part III

For everything there is a season, and a time for everything under the sun.
—Ecclesiastes (3:1)

She [the night child] was the key and I knew that unless I could integrate the night child with the day child, my nightmare would continue.
—Marilyn Van Derbur (2003, p. 242)

I N THIS PART OF THE BOOK we describe treatment interventions from the standpoint of the theory of structural dissociation in combination with a psychology of action, with a special focus on trauma-related phobias. The resolution of each phobia requires that the patient's mental level be raised such that higher level adaptive actions can take place, especially integrative actions of synthesis and realization.

In simple PTSD which only includes a rudimentary EP that encompasses hardly more than the traumatic memory, a straightforward application of empirically validated treatment approaches usually suffices. For example, standard treatments include prolonged exposure, cognitive behavioral approaches (Foa, Keane, & Friedman, 2000; Resick & Schnicke, 1993; Follette, Ruzek, & Abueg, 1998; Rothbaum, Meadows, Resick, & Foy, 2000) and EMDR (Chemtob, Tolin, Van der Kolk, & Pitman, 2000; Gelinas, 2003; Power et al., 2002). Treatment for patients with this type of structural dissociation was formulated long ago by Myers following his observations of acutely traumatized World War I combat soldiers:

> The treatment to be recommended . . . consists in restoring the 'emotional' [part of the] personality deprived of its pathological, distracted, uncontrolled character, and in effecting its union with the 'apparently normal' [part of the] personality. (1940, pp. 68–9)

Myers observed that when this re-integration has taken place in therapy,

> it becomes immediately obvious that the 'apparently normal' [part of the]
> personality differed widely in physical appearance and behaviour, as well as
> mentally, from the completely normal personality thus at last obtained.
> Headaches and dreams disappear; the circulatory and digestive symptoms
> become normal; even the reflexes may change; and all hysterical [i.e., dis-
> sociative] symptoms are banished. (1940, p. 69)

Patients thus have become much more adaptive in daily life and have
been able to realize that their memories of the traumatic experience(s)
are a part of their life history, and are not happening now. Indeed, (re)in-
tegration of the personality *implies* increased adaptation to life.

However, these straightforward treatments often fail or are inadequate
in more chronically traumatized individuals. A phase-oriented treatment,
the standard of care for chronic traumatization (D. Brown, Scheflin, &
Hammond, 1998), is considered the most effective approach for these patients. A strong emphasis on skills building and the improvement of the
mental level in Phase 1 is essential prior to direct treatment of traumatic
memories. Phase-oriented treatment aims to combine the best of therapeutic techniques for improving daily living, for resolving traumatic memories, and helping the patient (re)integrate his or her personality. The
field is especially indebted to the pioneers of the contemporary treatment
of complex PTSD and dissociative disorders, notably Daniel Brown, Chris
Courtois, Catherine Fine, Erika Fromm, Judith Herman, Richard Kluft,
Richard Loewenstein, Erwin Parson, Laurie Pearlman, Frank Putnam, and
Colin Ross, among others. These clinicians made ground-breaking strides
in applying phase-oriented approaches to the most complex cases and
educating other therapists in those methods. Since the 1980s many variations on phase-oriented treatment have been developed for chronically
traumatized individuals (e.g., Brown & Fromm, 1986; Courtois, 1999,
2004; Gelinas, 2003; Herman, 1992b; Horevitz & Loewenstein, 1994; Huber, 1995; Kluft, 1999; McCann & Pearlman, 1990; Parson, 1984; Steele,
Van der Hart, & Nijenhuis, 1994; Van der Hart, 1991; Van der Hart, Van der
Kolk, & Boon, 1998; see Brown et al., 1998, for an excellent overview).
Each basically follows the original approach found in Pierre Janet's seminal work more than a century ago (Janet, 1898c; cf., Van der Hart, Brown,
& Van der Kolk, 1989). Janet distinguished the following treatment phases,
each with its own treatment objectives or goals: (1) stabilization and
symptom reduction; (2) treatment of traumatic memories; and (3) personality (re)integration and rehabilitation. This approach prevents premature confrontation with traumatic memories. Therapeutic approaches
that aim at the improvement of daily living skills (e.g., Gold, 2000; Linehan, 1993) can be seen as part of Phase 1 treatment.

Phase-oriented treatment may be applied in a simple, straightforward way in less complicated cases of secondary structural dissociation (Van der Hart et al., 1998). However, in most cases of secondary and tertiary structural dissociation, treatment is long-term and the phase-oriented model takes the form of a spiral (Courtois, 1999; Steele et al., 2005; Van der Hart et al., 1998). This implies that as needed, Phase 2 treatment will be periodically alternated with Phase 1; and later in the course of therapy, Phase 2 and even Phase 1 work will again be alternated with Phase 3 treatment. Some recent clinical approaches utilize Phase 1 treatment with repeated short incursions into Phase 2 (Briere & Scott, 2006; Ford & Russo, in press). In all cases, the therapist who uses a phase-oriented treatment approach understands, respects, and works with the constraints of the mental level of the patient and his or her dissociative parts of the personality.

CHAPTER 11

Assessment of the Traumatized Patient

All too commonly, neither patient nor therapist recognizes the link between the presenting problem and the history of chronic trauma.
—Judith Herman (1992b, p. 123)

THE THEORY OF STRUCTURAL dissociation, with its emphasis on a Janetian psychology of action, is a guide for systematic assessment of a traumatized individual's integrative mental and behavioral actions. The theory suggests that the core of traumatization and structural dissociation is a lack of integration of traumatic experiences and their consequences. A central goal of treatment is thus to help the patient engage in synthesis and realization of traumatic memories and in related integrative actions, including more adaptive action in current daily life. Assessment therefore needs to focus to a large degree on understanding why the patient does not engage successfully in these actions, and how those adaptive actions can be promoted.

Therapists need to understand the adaptive problems specific to a given patient, and how the patient attempts to solve them. Adaptive problems are related to low levels of mental efficiency and/or mental energy. Thus one focus of assessment is on the patient's mental level, and that of various parts of the personality. In this context, assessment also focuses on trauma-related conditioning effects, such as the patient's predominant phobias, which can eventually be overcome by raising the mental level. Such an assessment forms the basis for a systematic, phase-oriented treatment that is tailored to the unique needs of individual patients, but also takes into account their underlying commonalities, such as integrative deficiencies.

The initial assessment with survivors of chronic traumatization must be thorough and methodical, covering all domains of life and mental functioning (e.g., Briere, 1997, 2004; Chu, 1998a; Courtois, 1999; McCann & Pearlman, 1990). Assessment of trauma survivors has three stages: The first stage is a standard clinical assessment, which includes some questioning of dissociative symptoms. The second stage entails a more specific assessment for trauma-related symptoms and disorders, thus an assessment of the severity of structural dissociation. Both stages involve making an accurate diagnosis and gathering basic information for treatment planning. The third stage encompasses ongoing systematic analyses of the structure, functioning, and history of the patient and his or her dissociative personality. These three different but related analyses should help the therapist understand the purposes of the patient's adaptive and maladaptive actions, and the functions and goals of various parts of the personality. This assessment—essential for treatment planning and adjustment of initial treatment plans—is ongoing.

STAGE 1: STANDARD
CLINICAL ASSESSMENT

Standard clinical assessment includes a family history of possible psychiatric problems and any transgenerational patterns of abuse and neglect. Some questioning about dissociative symptoms and about the experience of potentially traumatizing events should be a regular part of initial interviews with *all* patients (Courtois, 2004; Loewenstein, 1991a). But these inquiries are only preliminary, giving an overview of what the patient has experienced. At this stage, questioning should not delve into details. It is not appropriate to evoke overwhelming emotion without the safety of a solid therapeutic relationship and knowledge that the patient can tolerate intensity. A history is not to be taken perfunctorily, but rather therapists inquire reflectively, guided by the patient's symptoms and more general presentation, with the goal of understanding the patient and of planning treatment. And of course, the therapist makes a thorough assessment of the patient's strengths and resources, as these will need to be relied upon during the course of therapy, and are a source of self-esteem and competence for the patient (Ogden, Minton, & Pain, 2006).

The therapist can only note what is observed or reported at a given time, depending on what the patient—usually presenting as an apparently normal part of the personality (ANP)—shows, and is willing and able to share. The patient may not initially be able to give all of the pertinent history due to lack of memory, the inability to realize the impact of certain events, a perpetrator's threats not to tell, or avoidance of painful feelings such as fear, shame, or guilt. The best the therapist can do is to integrate available information, which forms the basis for a further relationship with the patient, and will eventually lead to more information. In this way, assessment is ongoing.

Impact of Assessment on the Patient

The way in which the therapist gathers information about a patient is a therapeutic intervention in itself. The therapist must be highly attuned to the patient's subtle behavioral and physiological reactions during assessment, monitoring hypo- or hyperarousal (Ogden et al., 2006) and indicators of dissociative symptoms such as intruding voices. And as hypo- and hyperarousal involve problems in balancing mental efficiency and mental energy, the therapist begins to help the patient to find a better balance between them beginning in the assessment sessions (cf., Chapter 12). The therapist must be especially sensitive to careful pacing for traumatized individuals in taking their history and asking about dissociative symptoms (Courtois, 1999; Steinberg, 1995). Because phobic avoidance is a central issue for survivors, rapid fire questions or questions that are threatening in some way may be too intrusive and contribute to decompensation or to a patient deciding not to return to therapy. The therapist who recognizes and appropriately responds to the patient's experience of dissociation and profound alterations of consciousness contributes to the patient's sense of safety. The patient can then experience that therapy need not be retraumatizing, but rather is an opportunity to receive empathy and help for experiences that are confusing, frightening, or shameful.

Thus, the presentation of the therapist is crucial. A calm, congruent, and genuine approach is essential. The therapist needs to observe and understand the ways in which his or her style may impact a given patient. For example, a more introverted, quiet therapist can be perceived as withholding and silently critical, while a more vivacious therapist can be perceived as intrusive and domineering. The therapist who provides genuine and modulated responses to the patient's actions engages in higher level action tendencies. These therapeutic actions will help the patient who is typically under- or overregulated in some manner to better regulate his or her actions (improve mental efficiency). The therapist's communications should be very clear and precise, leaving as little room for ambiguity as possible. This often involves making explicit even what should seem obvious to the patient; for example, stating that the patient is not obliged to answer certain questions, even though the patient may be asked about what makes it difficult to answer.

The Presentation of the Patient
During Assessment

The therapist needs to be attentive not only to the content of what a patient says, but also to the manner in which it is said, and what seems to be left unsaid. General assessment includes observation of the patient's affective and physical responses to questions and to the therapist. It is essential for the therapist to tend to the patient's nonverbal communications (e.g., Ogden et al., 2006). For example, voice tone, volume, lack of eye contact or aggressive staring, unusual or stereotypical movements or physical positions such as bracing, lowering of the head, freezing, rocking, or sexualized positions are all useful information, and can lead to further exploration *when the patient is ready*. For example, unexpected and repeated shifts in tone and volume of voice, physical postures, movement patterns, and topics of conversation may indicate alternations between dissociative parts. When the therapist observes these shifts, he or she should take note of them, but not immediately conclude that structural dissociation is present. The therapist must suspend judgment, and wait to confirm or disconfirm this possibility until sufficient data has been gathered.

The patient's attachment style (e.g., avoidant, resistant, preoccupied, unresolved) also offers information about what is needed in treatment in terms of relational approaches. For example, assessment may proceed slowly and with difficulty because the survivor does not seem to trust the therapist. He or she may too anxious or resistant to provide information, remaining silent or giving only very brief answers. Some patients ask questions such as, "Why do you want to know this?" and respond, "This has already been asked a thousand times before; I'm wasting my time!" When these behaviors are recurrent, they may be indicative of insecure forms of attachment, including disorganized/disoriented attachment. The therapist thus realizes that there is a need to focus to some extent on phobias of attachment and attachment loss.

The patient's style of speaking also offers important details. Analysis of narrative discourse has been emphasized in the attachment literature in determining adult attachment styles (cf., Hesse, 1999, for an overview). However, the patient's speech is also informative about a variety of other issues including the capacity to verbalize feelings and thoughts, apparent or potential gaps in autobiographical narrative memory, and the subjective experience of dissociation. For example, use of many indirect pronouns so that sentences are confusing (e.g., it, they), sudden changes in or unusual syntax, use of the third person in reference to self, discontinuities and lapses in discourse, pervasive vagueness, abrupt subject change, and sudden changes in tone or cadence raise the possibility of structural dissociation (e.g., Loewenstein, 1991a).

Significant memory gaps in the patient's history and other memory problems raise suspicion about dissociative amnesia or chronic alterations in consciousness, as well as concomitant neurological problems that may be due to neglect and abuse.

The Experience of the Therapist
During Assessment

Many (chronic) trauma survivors have consulted several clinicians across time, each of whom may have assessed a different mental disorder. This variability can relate to the common plethora of symptoms, and to the changeability of prominent symptoms caused by alternations of dissociative parts that dominate consciousness. Also, trauma-related symptoms may be viewed differently by previous therapists and put within the context of different diagnoses, depending on their particular theoretical biases.

The assessment can be derailed by details, digressions, vagueness, and the induction of alterations in consciousness in the therapist. These relate to actions of dissociative parts that attempt to avoid traumatic memories and related stimuli (cf., Loewenstein, 1991a). Therapists have described attempts to obtain clear, succinct answers from a dissociative patient as being like "herding cats." It is not unusual for a therapist to feel spacey, sleepy, confused, or forgetful in an initial assessment of a traumatized patient. Therapists have described some of these disconcerting experiences: "Like taking a sleeping potion"; "being hypnotized"; "wandering around in a hall full of smoke and mirrors"; "having one foot outside of reality"; and "having my train of thought suddenly disappear." Therapists must find ways to train themselves to remain present and maintain a high mental level and focus of attention.

Therapists may also find themselves having particular affective responses to a patient, such as sadness, boredom, anxiety, irritation, disgust, frustration, or pity. These responses may be indicative not only of potential countertransference but of the patient's transference, relational style, and projective identifications (Chu, 1998a; Courtois, 1999; Kluft, 1994a; Loewenstein, 1991a).

The Patient's Prior Treatment History

Traumatized patients often come with prior treatment failures or incomplete treatments. Exploring these can lead to helpful information about obstacles to therapy that can then be targeted. Inquiries into treatment terminations are helpful; were they precipitous or planned; were they initiated by patient or therapist; and how were they experienced by the patient? Also, in determining treatment planning, it is helpful to explore the ways in which previous therapies and therapists were or were not helpful.

Prior treatment failures can be due to the patient's issues, therapist mistakes, or both. Thus the current therapist must be careful not to label previous therapists as incompetent or to assume the patient is untreatable. However, many survivors have been retraumatized by therapists who had inadequate understanding and skills to treat complex trauma-related problems, who have undue prejudice against dissociative disorders, or who have complicated countertransference responses. We believe that many of these treatment failures result from therapists finding it difficult to pace therapy adequately with traumatized patients, and not always considering the patient's trauma history, lack of mental skills, and structural dissociation as essential elements of planning a phase-oriented treatment.

Diagnoses

Diagnosis can help direct treatment by indicating the need for particular evidence-based interventions, including psychotropic medications (e.g., Foa, Keane, & Friedman, 2000; Freeman & Power, 2005; Nathan & Gorman, 2002). There are assessment instruments available for diagnosing ASD (Bryant & Harvey, 2000); PTSD (e.g., Blake et al., 1995; Brewin, 2005a; E. B. Carlson, 1997; Stamm, 1996; J. P. Wilson & Keane, 2004), and complex PTSD or disorders of extreme stress (Pelcovitz et al., 1997). Specific instruments for screening and diagnosing dissociative disorders are also available, and will be discussed in more detail below.

However, chronically traumatized patients often fit many diagnostic categories, which may be due to various dissociative parts having different prominent symptoms. For example, a survivor as ANP may seem to have depersonalization disorder, schizophrenia, or major depression, while one EP manifests symptoms of panic disorder, and another EP meets the criteria for attention deficit/hyperactivity disorder or eating disorder. Therapists can become easily confused about prioritizing diagnoses, whether to follow treatment protocols for a single diagnosis or whether to combine protocols to fit a number of diagnoses. Thus, they should be able to *integrate* a variety of guidelines to effectively treat the complex problems of each patient.

Referral for Medication or (Neuro)psychological Evaluation

If a patient has symptoms that may be amenable to psychotropic medication, he or she should be referred for an evaluation and possible treatment in conjunction with therapy. But first, the therapist needs to explore the patient's beliefs about and experiences with previous medications to determine if therapeutic work must be done regarding reluctance to take medication. Additionally, because chronically traumatized patients can be overmedicated by uninformed psychiatrists, it is essential that such patients see a psychiatrist who is familiar with the psychophysiological complexities of traumatization and who is willing to collaborate with the primary therapist.

If the patient's presentation is highly unusual, complex, or confusing, or if severe cognitive and memory disturbances are present, neuro(psycho)logical testing is indicated (Brand, Armstrong, & Loewenstein, 1996). The role of neurological deficits should never be overlooked in traumatized patients, who have sometimes suffered closed head injuries, malnutrition, extensive drug use, and other experiences that might contribute to brain insults.

Comprehensive psychological testing, including the administration of the Minnesota Multiphasic Personality Inventory-2 (MMPI-2), the Millon Clinical Multiaxial Inventory (MCMI-II), or the Symptoms Checklist (SCL-90) can assist the therapist in determining the overall mental level of the patient and may clarify the role of persistent social defenses, intrapsychic conflicts, and trauma-related phobias in a patient's difficulties (see Briere, 2004, for an overview). However, it should be noted that in highly dissociative patients, test results may be inconsistent, depending on which part(s) participate and whether parts inhibit honest answers.

In sum, suspicion of structural dissociation is raised, and remains nothing more than a suspicion, when the patient reports apparently dissociative symptoms; displays verbal and nonverbal phenomena that might be manifestations of structural dissociation; reports or alludes to a history of extremely stressful events; has a perplexing history of many different diagnoses and treatment failures; and has not just one, but a remarkable combination of these features.

STAGE 2: ASSESSMENT OF TRAUMA-RELATED SYMPTOMS AND DISORDERS

The next stage of assessment involves a more detailed analysis of the patient's symptoms and disorders as they related to traumatization. The first step is to take the patient's history of potentially traumatizing events.

Assessment of Trauma History

A general assessment may raise a high index of suspicion that structural dissociation may be present; for example, persistent reexperiences, lost time, disremembered behaviors, or Schneiderian first-ranked symptoms. If so, a more specific and elaborate assessment of trauma-related symptoms should begin. There are a number of excellent resources on the clinical assessment of traumatized individuals (e.g., S.N. Allen, 1994; Bartlett,

1996; Brand et al., 2006; Briere, 1997; Briere & Spinazzola, 2005; E. B. Carlson, 1997; Chu, 1998a; Courtois, 1999, 2004; Loewenstein, 1991a; McCann & Pearlman, 1990; Newman, Kaloupek, & Keane, 1996; Steinberg, 1995; J. P. Wilson & Keane, 2004).

We use the Traumatic Experiences Checklist (TEC), because this self-report instrument has good psychometric characteristics, is not too confrontational for most survivors, can be completed in approximately 20 minutes, and inquires about 29 types of potentially traumatizing events (Nijenhuis, Van der Hart, & Kruger, 2002). A number of other instruments are also available (cf., Carlson, 1997; Courtois, 1999; Ohan, Myers, & Collett, 2002; Stamm, 1996; J.P. Wilson & Keane, 2004), such as the Evaluation of Lifetime Stressors (Krinsley, Gallagher, Weathers, Kaloupek, & Vielhauer, 1997) and the Trauma Assessment for Adults (Resnick, 1996). The therapist should inquire within the limits of the patient's mental level about abuse, neglect, traumatic medical procedures, and related fears of abandonment and death, loss and traumatic grief, and severe, early attachment disruptions. If the patient has had such experiences, further assessment of the impact of those events should be ascertained over time.

Assessment of trauma history, even if stressful, is appreciated by most patients and rewarding to therapists (Walker, Newman, Koss, & Bernstein, 1997). However, it may open a door to memories and feelings that the patient prefers to avoid or that may cause a more or less serious decrease of mental efficiency, thus leading to lower level action tendencies (cf., Courtois, 1999). Therapists must anticipate that various dissociative parts of a traumatized individual may have quite different reactions to inquiries about past traumatization, and that only a small portion of those reactions may be evident during the session. A dissociative patient can have great difficulty in pacing him- or herself adequately because of structural dissociation and a serious lack of mental efficiency. For example, a patient as a depersonalized ANP may report detailed traumatic experiences in session and leave appearing calm and grounded, only to later self-harm or make a suicide attempt because other parts became overwhelmed with traumatic memories.

The same problems with unexpected responses can also occur during assessment for structural dissociation (discussed below). Dissociative patients may come to therapy having had the experience that talking about dissociative symptoms can provoke these symptoms. This experience can make them apprehensive, thus limit their mental efficiency, which compromises their ability to manage feelings and memories evoked by assessment of structural dissociation. They may be afraid or ashamed to acknowledge "weird" symptoms such as acting like a child, hearing voices, finding themselves huddled in a closet, or making strange movements. They may be reluctant to report symptoms that might label them as "crazy" or "bad." Thus, a patient may not initially report or admit a history of sexual or physical abuse, or experiences such as hearing voices, losing time, self-harm, sexual acting out, or substance abuse. Many patients with complex dissociative disorders will attempt to hide their dissociative parts in the initial phases of assessment and therapy (e.g., Kluft, 1987b). They may present as a single part that experiences symptoms of intrusion, but are unaware or deny that structural dissociation of their personality is the underlying problem. And some parts may be only vaguely aware, or even be completely unaware, of the traumatic past, because memory and experience are not cohesive in traumatized individuals.

Instruments that Assess Dissociative Symptoms

When there are indications of structural dissociation (i.e., dissociative symptoms), a next step is to administer self-report instruments that evaluate the severity of psychoform and somatoform dissociative symptoms or self-report instruments that screen for the presence of a dissociative disorder. These instruments measure symptoms of both structural dissociation and alterations in consciousness. For example, the Multidimensional Inventory of Dissociation (MID; Dell, 2002, 2006; Somer & Dell, 2005) is a 168-item self-report, multiscale measure of pathological dissociation with robust psychometric qualities. The Dissociative Experiences Scale (DES; Bernstein & Putnam, 1986; E. B. Carlson & Putnam, 1993) evaluates the severity of dissociative symptoms and pathological alterations in consciousness. A cutoff score of 30 on the DES has been suggested in the screening for DSM-IV dissociative disorders (E. B. Carlson et al., 1993). Van IJzendoorn and Schuengel (1996) presented an important meta-analysis of the DES, which includes an indication of average scores for different diagnostic categories. The DES-Taxon (DES-T; Waller, Carlson, & Putnam, 1993) includes eight items from the DES which may indicate structural dissociation more than the DES. The Somatoform Dissociation Questionnaire (SDQ-20/SDQ-5; Nijenhuis, Spinhoven, Van Dyck, van der Hart, & Vanderlinden, 1996, 1997, 1998a) assesses the severity of somatoform symptoms of structural dissociation. Average scores for a range of different mental disorders can be found in Nijenhuis (2004). The SDQ-5 is a screening instrument for DSM-IV dissociative disorders. The cutoff score is eight. DES and SDQ-5 scores at the respective cutoff scores accurately predict the presence of a DSM-IV dissociative disorder in approximately 30 to 45% of psychiatric outpatients.

The higher the scores on these instruments, the more likely it is that the patient has a DSM-IV dissociative disorder. However, structural dissociation sometimes occurs at scores below the cutoffs, which usually is due to an ANP's lack of awareness or denial of dissociative symptoms. Dissociative phenomena can be clinically evident in these cases, or only become apparent upon extended clinical observation.

The symptom clusters of the Structured Interview for Disorders of Extreme Stress (SIDES, Pelcovitz et al., 1997) may be understood as having dissociative underpinnings (see Chapter 6; Van der Hart, Nijenhuis, & Steele, 2005).

Systematic Interviewing
for Structural Dissociation

Detailed interviews, such as an adapted mental status exam (Loewenstein, 1991a), a structured interview such as the Structured Clinical Interview for Dissociative Disorders-Revised (SCID-D-R; Steinberg, 1995, 2000) or the Dissociative Disorder Interview Schedule (DDIS; C.A. Ross, 1989; Ross et al., 1989) are essential in the assessment of DSM-IV dissociative disorders. However, the therapist must remain aware that structural dissociation also occurs in a number of other disorders, including BPD, PTSD, and somatoform dissociative disorders (see Chapter 6).

In a paced and step-wise manner the patient should be asked about episodes of amnesia, fugue, depersonalization, derealization, identity confusion, identity alteration, Schneiderian symptoms (discussed in Chapters 5 and 6), and other subjective experiences that might indicate the presence of dissociation (International Society for the Study of Dissociation, 2005; Loewenstein, 1991; Ross, 1989; Steinberg, 1995). In addition, patients are asked about normal and pathological alterations in consciousness (Steele, Dorahy, Van der Hart, & Nijenhuis, in press). The patient is encouraged to give examples of potentially dissociative experiences. Such experiences should be clearly distinguished from severe alterations in consciousness or other phenomena that have a different underlying cause. For example, vague recall or gaps in memory may be due to pervasive alterations in consciousness, structural dissociation, or both.

Asking the patient as ANP about dissociative symptoms and potentially traumatizing events tends to reactivate emotional parts (EPs), so pacing is essential. Assessment may bring to light conflicts among various parts of the patient's personality. For example, the survivor as ANP may want to share information with the goal of getting help, but an EP internally forbids it, with the goal of staying safe by not telling. Other times, a "child" EP will want to share memories with the goal of receiving care and protection, but ANP avoids and suppresses that part, with a goal of avoiding attachment and the difficult feelings related to it. The therapist should take into account that such conflicts are common during interviewing, and look for signs of it in the patient, such as speech hesitation, thought insertion or withdrawal, going blank, abrupt change of subject, or loss of eye contact. While the therapist must be aware of these phenomena, and manage them when they occur in this second stage of assessment, it is usually best for the therapist to stay focused on interviewing the presenting dissociative part of the patient. An in-depth analysis of dissociative parts generally should be postponed to the third stage of assessment.

To the extent possible, the therapist determines which parts have major functions in daily life, and which ones are interfering with daily life, such as child, persecutory, or fight EPs. In highly complex cases, it is not unusual for it to take many months or years before the whole dissociative organization of the patient becomes known. Furthermore, this organization can change over time with or without the patient's awareness, indicating the need for ongoing assessment of structural dissociation.

The distinction between ANP and EP is important because a priority in treatment is to strengthen ANPs and reduce intrusion of EPs, while still acknowledging their existence. The essential knowledge about dissociative parts necessary for effective treatment includes their mental actions (e.g., perceptions, feelings, memories, fantasies) and behavioral actions, the action systems by which they are mediated, the conditioned stimuli that (re)activate them, and their level of mental functioning.

Probably the most difficult assessment is of those patients that present with parts that appear to have a mix of ANP and EP features. Such parts are generally dysfunctional and are motivated primarily out of fear. Their behavioral and social defenses and trauma-related phobias are pervasive. Internal and external safety becomes an immediate treatment goal with such patients, and understanding and empathizing with this intense need for safety may reduce treatment failure.

Sharing of the Diagnosis

Many patients already carry a feeling of stigma and being "different" or "crazy." Having psychiatric labels attached to their problems may be overwhelming or stigmatizing and even precipitate a retreat from therapy. Thus the results of assessment and diagnosis must be shared with the patient in a timely and respectful way, at a pace that the patient can tolerate. The therapist should be honest and straightforward about diagnosis and what is understood about the patient from an assessment, including strengths and deficits (Ogden et al., 2006). This is all done in a language that the patient can accept and to which he or she can relate.

The patient can only give full informed consent when the therapist helps him or her to accept and comprehend the disorder and the treatment plan. The therapist's educational and emotional support should be provided at a pace that matches the level of action tendencies the patient can reach. When the patient feels accepted, supported, and understood by the therapist, he or she will more inclined to embark on the demanding therapeutic journey. Shared information regarding the diagnosis and the basics of treatment should lead the therapist and patient to discuss:

(1) identified problems, and their possible basis in trauma-related structural dissociation; (2) the patient's strengths and weaknesses; (3) how patient and therapist can best work together as a "therapeutic team" to solve identified problems; and (4) how dissociative parts can work with each other and the therapist.

A few dissociative patients are at risk for decompensation when they receive a diagnosis, even when the diagnosis is presented appropriately. Their phobias of traumatic memories, dissociative parts, and trauma-derived mental actions tend to be so powerful, and their mental level so low, that they may be unable to tolerate conscious awareness that they have a trauma-related disorder. On the other hand, refusing to share information on diagnosis is not helpful to a patient who is trying to understand and make sense out of complex and disturbing symptoms. Despite his or her integrative limitations, the patient may find the strength, with adequate assistance from the therapist, to gradually realize the nature of the diagnosis.

STAGE 3: SYSTEMATIC ANALYSIS OF THE PERSONALITY STRUCTURE AND FUNCTIONING, AND HISTORY OF THE PATIENT

Assessment of the patient's dissociative parts and their actions is an ongoing therapeutic activity, particularly with patients who have complex levels of structural dissociation. The structural and dynamic organization among parts, and their respective functions and limitations should be assessed in a systematic fashion. To this end, the therapist engages in three kinds of continuing and interrelated analyses: structural, functional, and historical.

Analysis of the Structure of the Patient's Personality

Effective treatment requires an in-depth assessment of the structure of the patient's personality. Thus therapist and patient collaboratively explore the presence of dissociative parts and their core features, but only when the patient is up to it. Components of structural analysis include: (1) assessment of the degree of emancipation (actual or perceived separation and autonomy from the influence of other dissociative parts) and elaboration of parts; (2) assessment of the goals of various parts and the patient as a whole; (3) the action (sub)systems and modes that mediate various parts; (4) the general mental level of various parts and the patient as a whole; and (5) the action tendencies in which the patient can and cannot engage, and which actions are preferred by the patient.

Mental level. The patient's mental level depends on his or her general degree of *mental energy* and *mental efficiency*, and the dynamic relationship between them. The overall quality of the patient's actions must be assessed as a manifestation of his or her mental level: To what degree is the patient able to initiate, execute, and complete actions with intention and mindfulness? The lower the mental level, the more the patient (or particular dissociative part) will resort to substitute or maladaptive actions, and be more reflexive rather than reflective in thinking and behavior. The essential issue is for therapists to understand whether it is mental energy or mental efficiency that needs to be raised, or a combination of both, because treatment approaches differ (see Chapter 12). For example, Mary was extremely depressed and had trouble getting out of bed, and spent hours just sitting and staring at the wall. Her mental energy was too low, and the therapist made interventions to alleviate the depression, with medication and cognitive therapy. On the other hand, Joseph was hypomanic, unable to sleep, rambled in his thoughts, and drank too much. He had too much mental energy for his low degree of mental efficiency, and the therapist thus made interventions to raise his mental efficiency by stopping his drinking, getting him on medication, and encouraging him to keep a routine schedule. Many treatment failures may be rooted in an insufficient identification of problems related to these different dimensions of the mental level.

Chronically traumatized patients often have strong oscillations in the mental level, depending on specific areas of functioning. For example, a patient may excel at work, but is unable to function at home. Thus, the patient's mental level in specific situations is assessed, as well as the mental level of various ANPs and EPs.

Skills. Skills include the ability to engage in the right level of action in the hierarchy of action tendencies. As noted previously, many traumatized individuals never learned adequate mental, relational, and other life skills. Essential skills include capacities to (1) regulate action tendencies (affect and impulses), including coping with distress, self-soothing, and seeking appropriate comfort and support, and regulation of social emotions such as self-hatred, shame, and guilt; (2) tolerate aloneness; (3) verbalize instead of acting out; (4) be in the present (mindfulness and presentification); (5) have empathy toward oneself and others; (6) have social and intimate connection with others; (7) distinguish internal from external reality; for example, realizing that feeling anger is different from acting it out; internal reenactments of traumatic experiences are not occurring in reality; (8) accurately perceive context and current reality; distinguish the past and future from the present; and (9) accurately perceive and understand the motivations and intentions of others and of oneself (i.e., mentalization). The patient's general strengths and weaknesses in all these areas must be assessed, recognizing that some parts are likely to have more skills than others.

A structural analysis thus describes the different dissociative parts a survivor encompasses, as well as their core features and skills. This analysis is a necessary step toward understanding how these dissociative parts operate as a complex personality system, both generally and in specific situations.

Analysis of the Functioning of the Patient's Personality

Next, the functioning of the patient's personality system as a whole is assessed. The therapist explores how the patient generally attempts to realize his or her goals, how effective these efforts are, and how adaptive these goals may be. It is essential to determine in what areas the patient functions well (i.e., areas that are relatively uncompromised by traumatic experiences and skills deficits), and in what areas the survivor is dysfunctional (Ogden et al., 2006). It is essential to determine whether the patient is generally dysfunctional in daily life due to serious skills deficits, a low mental level, or severe internal conflicts between dissociative parts, or is only dysfunctional in particular areas of life.

The therapist assesses how well different action systems are developed, and how adaptive the patient (or dissociative part) is when each action system is activated. He or she explores what action systems are easily accessible and functional, and which are underactivated or overactivated and dysfunctional. For example, a patient may study too much (exploration system), but sleeps far too little (energy management), because studying provides external rewards and a safe haven from bodily feelings that reactivate traumatic memories and nightmares.

The therapist can thus determine the degree to which various action systems are coordinated, because this is an indication of the degree of (dis)integration. That is, it describes how various parts relate to each other. Do they generally cooperate or compete with each other? What is the degree of conflict among parts? What are their major conflicts? Do two or more parts perhaps agree on a certain goal (e.g., safety), but disagree on the way to realize it? What is their level of mutual cognitive and emotional awareness, empathy, antipathy, cooperation, and negotiation? What psychodynamics are involved? What general factors promote switching among parts? What substitute actions maintain structural dissociation?

The therapist also needs to understand how the patient (and various dissociative parts) functions in particular situations. He or she details the kind of action tendencies in which the survivor engages in specific, important situations (e.g., in a relationship, at work), and how adaptive these action tendencies are. The therapist examines particular situations in which the survivor engages in symptomatic actions, including pathological alterations in consciousness, experiences that are too high or too low on the hierarchy of degrees of reality; hypoarousal and hyperarousal; and other substitute mental and behavioral actions such as substance abuse, self-harm, or maladaptive fantasies and beliefs.

In this way, the therapist begins to understand how dissociative parts attempt to attain their respective goals in specific situations, and how adaptive they are in dealing with the situation, which is an indication of their mental level. The therapist can also learn the conditioned stimuli that evoke these reactions in a given situation, the goals various parts seek to attain, and the consequences of their (re)actions, such as positive or negative reinforcement, or punishment (detailed in Chapter 10). Such analyses should also focus on the *quality* of actions.

> Sandra, a patient with DDNOS, reported to her therapist that she had an unpleasant reaction when a coworker came from behind and unexpectedly patted Sandra on the back. Sandra found herself freezing, but did not understand why and felt foolish about her response, because consciously she did not feel afraid, and liked the touch. On closer questioning, it became clear that an EP found it quite frightening, evoking a fear of sexual abuse by a perpetrator who often approached her from behind.

Analysis of the Patient's History

The therapist needs to know not only the content of the patient's history, but how particular action tendencies arose over the course of the individual's development. Many of the patient's current actions are strongly influenced by his or her history.

> John, a patient with DDNOS, seeks out therapy, but is restless during sessions. The therapist observes an exhausted and demoralized ANP that hears an angry voice in his head telling him to leave and threatens to hurt him if he does not do so. Later in the therapy, it becomes clear that the angry part does not want to become attached or dependent on the therapist because this part fears getting hurt again. The internal conflict between ANP and the angry EP explain ANP's restlessness. The therapist learns that John as ANP has been able to cope with daily life for the most part, but has intrusions. ANP has become conditioned to avoid traumatic memories and associated EPs because this reduces John's fear of realizing these aspects of himself. However, John's ongoing mental avoidance as ANP took much effort and has exhausted his mental energy. The more exhausted John as ANP became, the more this part was intruded upon by EPs through flashbacks and internal voices. Eventually, John as ANP became unable to continue with normal daily life because of recurrent intrusions, and exhaustion. He was unable to work effectively, leading to a significant loss of material, social, and emotional rewards. These losses entailed a major frustration, and significantly reduced John's mental efficiency. The therapist also learns that John was triggered in specific situations. At work, his boss reminded him of his abuser and served as a conditioned stimulus that evoked a terrified EP. When John was home alone he tended to hear a critical, angry voice telling him to hurt

himself. This was a reaction to feeling alone and overwhelmed when John
as ANP no longer had the stimulation of the day to distract him. The therapist could thus target interventions toward these two specific and problematic situations.

This kind of detailed analysis suggests several therapeutic measures.
For example, it indicates that John as ANP is initially best helped to avoid
intrusions more effectively, so that his mental level is raised. It also shows
that John's mental level is too low to accomplish integrative actions, such
as acknowledging the existence of EPs or communicating with them, let
alone integrating traumatic memories. This analysis indicates that some
EPs need urgent help to feel safer, which might reduce substitute actions,
and others need attachment-related interventions to deal with fears and
resistance around dependency and attachment.

Analysis of Trauma-Related Phobias

Phobias are a major focus of treatment. The therapist can begin during
assessment to gently inquire about what the patient is afraid of or concerned about. For example, what does the patient as ANP fear will happen if he or she feels a particular feeling or has a certain thought, allows
a dissociative part to be acknowledged, or shares particular information
with the therapist? If the patient becomes attached to someone, what does
he or she (or a particular dissociative part) worry about? Gradually it becomes clearer to therapist and patient what intolerable feelings, maladaptive beliefs, and effects of (classical, operant, and evaluative) conditioning
are at work; which skills need to be gained; and how avoidance strategies
regarding these phobias can be overcome within the patient's mental
level.

This assessment will often suggest that ongoing nonrealization of trauma-
related phobias contribute to the survivor's difficulties in engaging in successful therapy. "Resistances" in therapy can be understood as the maladaptive avoidance and escape strategies of a traumatized patient. These
strategies include not only physical defense in some EPs, but prominent
social defenses and trauma-related phobias in virtually all parts, since relationships, abandonment, rejection, and internal experiences may be
threatening and overwhelming.

To the extent possible early in therapy, the therapist should attempt to
understand which phobias are present in various dissociative parts of the
personality. This understanding will guide treatment to a large extent.
For example, one patient as EP repeatedly said, "I love dogs. I want to be
with my dog." This fixation on dogs was an extreme retraction of her field
of consciousness to moments in which she felt safe and loved by her dog

as a child in a highly disturbed home. Yet the focus on the dog also helped her avoid painful memories of rejection and abandonment. It prevented her from attaching to the therapist in the present moment and in realizing her generalized fear of attachment and extreme avoidance of people.

When a survivor cannot avoid phobic stimuli, vehement emotions may be activated. The therapist determines when it is likely that a patient will regress to these substitute actions (e.g., in the face of abandonment or rejection, loneliness, frustration, loss). The therapist should distinguish between vehement emotions and *intense adaptive feelings*: those feelings that are experienced within an adequate mental level, are reflectively expressed in interpersonally appropriate ways, help the patient have a better life, and give him or her enduring rather than temporary relief (cf., McCoullough et al., 2003). Adaptive feelings, even when intense, often involve self-reflection about what we are experiencing and why, include relatively accurate perceptions and predictions based on the present, and involve much more control over reflexive reactions.

Analysis of the Patient's Social Environment

The patient's social milieu should be thoroughly assessed because it has a major impact on his or her functioning. A psychosocial history is taken early as part of a general assessment, including the functioning of the family or other setting in which the patient was raised, what the patient experienced at school and with peers, the patient's adolescent and early adult romantic relationships, the patient's current support system, and the clinical services in which the patient has previously been involved. A further analysis formulates how the patient is affected by and affects his or her current social milieu. It is crucial to know for treatment planning how significant others respond to the patient's symptoms and behaviors. For example, how supportive, disqualifying, or neglectful are they? Do they intentionally or inadvertently reinforce the patient's symptomatic actions? Do they pose a threat to the patient's safety? Could they have a motive to interfere with the changes that treatment will bring? Are there any other professionals working with the patient, how do they relate to the patient, and what is their role in his or her treatment? If the patient gives informed consent, it can be helpful to invite the patient's partner or other support person for a session with the survivor and observe how he or she interacts with close others. Solid treatment plans incorporate the helpful use of the patient's support system in treatment, if possible. Patients must profoundly reshape their social environment when significant others are abusive or emotionally unavailable. This change is a first concern of treatment in many cases, and typically is ongoing.

The therapist explores how the patient relates to his or her children. In cases of suspected or evident abuse or neglect, the children should be assessed directly (Braun, 1984; Coons, 1984; Silberg, 1996). The treatment plan incorporates interventions with respect to the patient's children when there is a need.

PROGNOSTIC FACTORS AND
TREATMENT TRAJECTORY

One goal of assessment is to determine a general prognosis and treatment course (Kluft, 1993a, 1993b). However, sometimes the patient's capacity to change does not become clear until well into therapy, because it depends upon raising the mental level, which can be a difficult and prolonged endeavor. There are basic criteria the patient must meet for outpatient therapy to be possible, including experienced safety in the session, the ability to attend sessions regularly and pay the fee, a minimal capacity to engage in a relationship with the therapist, and absence of serious psychopathy that would indicate inpatient treatment. It is nearly impossible to engage in effective treatment with patients who continue to live with or are significantly entangled with perpetrators or an abusive partner, but often the patient's relationships are far from sound and are a target of therapeutic intervention.

The clinical literature on treatment of complex dissociative disorders distinguishes the prognosis of three subgroups of patients (Boon, 1997; Chu, 1998a; Horevitz & Loewenstein, 1994; Kluft, 1994b, 1997, 1999; Van der Hart, Van der Kolk, & Boon, 1998). Of course, patients may move from one category to another over the course of therapy, depending on the success of treatment. The first subgroup consists of high functioning patients with secondary or tertiary dissociation. Such patients have a very functional ANP(s) with a considerably high mental level, internal cooperation and empathy, and various social, educational, and professional assets. There is little self-destructive behavior, and existing comorbid disorders (e.g., depression) respond well to treatment. At least the major dissociative parts that function in daily life have a modicum of emotional and relational skills, and social defenses and trauma-related phobias defenses are available for modification. Treatment is usually faster and proceeds in a rather straightforward manner.

The second subgroup consists of more complicated cases with less functional ANPs or more intrusion of EPs into daily life matters. The mental level is lower in general than in the high functioning group. Axis II issues, especially borderline and avoidant personality disorders, are common, along with other serious comorbid conditions, such as affective disorders, eating disorders, and substance abuse disorders. These patients engage in significant social defenses and trauma-related phobias as a matter of course, and have poor emotional and relational skills. They also have difficulty regulating a variety of action systems, such as, energy management, sexual activities, and care giving. Treatment is more difficult and prolonged, often accompanied by crises and psychiatric admissions. Phobic reactions to trauma-related stimuli are generally more entrenched and resistant to change.

The third subgroup is much more refractory to treatment, at times manifesting persistent negative therapeutic reactions and extreme difficulty in managing daily life. Social defenses and trauma-related phobias are deeply ingrained, ego syntonic, and available for modification only with great difficulty and effort. Such patients exhibit the lowest mental level, resulting in chronic vehement emotion, impulsivity, and persistently low level action tendencies. They tend to have either unmanageable dependency or near complete lack of attachment to the therapist (cf., Steele, Van der Hart, & Nijenhuis, 2001). There are uncontrolled alternations between ANPs and EPs, causing rapid and easy switching. ANPs and EPs tend to be sadomasochistic, both among themselves and in external relationships. These patients are usually characterized by persistent pathological alterations in consciousness. They often manifest severe, chronic, and intractable self-destructive behavior that are substitutes for higher quality adaptive actions, and more often have characteristics of psychotic disorders, refractory affective disorders, and severe personality disorders. This subgroup has the least favorable prognosis: Often, treatment needs to be limited to Phase 1 interventions (Boon, 1997; Van der Hart & Boon, 1997).

SUMMARY

Traumatized patients are assessed in three stages. A standard clinical assessment is a first step. In a second stage, therapists assess trauma-related symptoms and disorders, as well as a history of potentially traumatizing events such as abuse, neglect and attachment loss. Dissociative symptoms are assessed with a number of self-report instruments, but require a systematic clinical interview to diagnose a dissociative disorder. A third stage involves ongoing systematic assessment of the dissociative structure of the patient's personality, the ways in which his or her personality functions, and how this structure and functioning evolved over time. In this collaborative effort of therapist and patient, the theory of structural dissociation with its emphasis on a psychology of action is a vital guide. The patient's mental and behavioral actions can be understood clearly and targeted for specific treatment interventions by using this theory.

CHAPTER 12

Promoting Adaptive Action

General Treatment Principles

*Psychotherapy will gradually become more and more a good ad-
ministration of the energies of the mind.*
                                        —Pierre Janet (1937, p. 103)

*One must live in the present, and it is not always useful to begin the
past all over in order to live in the present.*
                                        —Pierre Janet (1937, p. 102)

IN THIS CHAPTER WE BASE phase-oriented treatment principles on the theory
of structural dissociation and a Janetian psychology of action. Interventions from many theoretical orientations can be incorporated into this
model by understanding how each helps the patient develop more adaptive mental and behavioral actions. Adaptive actions are based on an adequate mental level (i.e., sufficient mental energy and efficiency and an optimal balance between the two). However, survivors have an insufficient
mental level to integrate their traumatic history, and often also a level that
makes it difficult to function well in daily life. Thus, treatment principles
can be understood as promoting a "mental economy" (Janet, 1919/1925,
1928b, 1932b) in terms of the degree of and balance between mental energy and efficiency required for adaptive actions. In the same way a balanced budget is desirable for financial stability and security, we must work
with our available "psychological" budget to achieve adaptation in daily
life (cf., Ellenberger, 1970; Janet, 1919/1925; L. Schwartz, 1951). Mental
energy must be produced, conserved, and spent wisely.

Each of the three phases of therapy emphasizes a specific set of economic principles. During the first treatment phase, *stabilization and symptom reduction*, increasing mental energy may be an initial goal that lays the groundwork for a second major goal, that of improving mental efficiency. In Phase 2, *treatment of traumatic memories*, mental energy and efficiency must be sustained and developed further for the patient to take major steps toward resolution of his or her traumatic past and attain realization. In Phase 3, *Personality integration and rehabilitation*, the emphasis of therapy is on raising the mental level to a degree at which the patient has success in major areas of normal life.

GENERAL TREATMENT PRINCIPLES
IN TERMS OF MENTAL ECONOMY

Conceptualizing treatment in terms of a balanced mental economy can help the therapist assist patients in coping more adequately with daily life and in overcoming their traumatic past at a pace that is uniquely tailored to their capacities and needs. Some chronically traumatized individuals have sufficient mental energy, but experience difficulty in maintaining adequate mental efficiency: Their actions, at least in some important domains, tend to be maladaptive. Those who are in more advanced stages of posttraumatic decline tend to have even more severe adaptive problems. They have both insufficient mental energy *and* mental efficiency so that they are in a chronic state of exhaustion and have difficulty functioning in daily life. Treatment will vary according to the patient's level of mental energy and quality of mental efficiency, and the balance between them. The therapist must accurately assess and then accept the survivor's current mental economy. If the therapist overestimates the mental level of the patient, he or she may be asked to engage in mental and behavioral actions that are too difficult, and thus may become discouraged and overwhelmed. If the therapist underestimates the patient's mental level, he or she may refrain from asking the patient to engage in more difficult actions that could result in further integration. For example, the therapist may join with ANP's avoidance of traumatic memories.

As with finances, a mental economy includes four simple principles based on the dynamic interplay between mental energy and mental efficiency: (1) *increase income* (of mental and physical energy); (2) *decrease or eliminate unnecessary expenditures* (of mental energy); (3) *reduce and eliminate debts*, that is, complete major unfinished actions (emotional, historical, relational, daily life tasks, etc.) that drain mental energy and inhibit the development of higher mental efficiency; and (4) *manage available income (energy) wisely* by an increase in mental efficiency; that is, invest in/develop more adaptive actions.

Developing a Secure Therapeutic Relationship
and Treatment Frame

A core problem for survivors is that they often perceive attachment as a *threat*, and thus avoid it, but are also unduly threatened by perceived attachment loss. They are haunted by expectations of betrayal and loss because that has been their previous experience, and also because their perception–motor action cycles remain strongly influenced by the defense system, and thus they are unduly focused on threat cues in relationships. Subsequent relational approach-avoidance, which will be discussed extensively in Chapter 13, forms the basic milieu in which psychotherapy must be conducted (Steele, Van der Hart, & Nijenhuis, 2001).

A secure therapeutic relationship gradually improves the patient's mental efficiency—we all function at our best within a secure attachment that provides psychophysiological regulation (Bowlby, 1969/1982; Schore, 2003a, 2003b). Secure attachment will allow the patient to test both maladaptive and adaptive "if–then" rules about relationships; for example, "If I get mad, then she will leave me"; "If I am sad then she does not make fun of me and she really listens to me." And gradually, the patient learns to engage in adaptive mental and behavioral actions in interpersonal relationships. Secure attachment is a working model that the patient develops only from long experience, and thus is a work in progress during much of therapy. A securely attached individual enjoys the advantages of relational regulation, which improves mental efficiency. And secure attachment with a safe other is also a manifestation of higher mental efficiency to engage in accurate rather than false relational predictions.

Phase-oriented treatment is successful when therapist and patient collaborate from the first session to develop a secure therapeutic relationship and basic treatment frame that will support the therapy. The cultivation of a secure therapeutic relationship and therapy frame are the sine qua non of effective psychotherapy with chronically traumatized individuals (cf., Cloitre). A fundamental aspect of establishing secure attachment with survivors is *empathic attunement*, a term derived from self psychology (Kohut, 1971; Rowe & Mac Isaac, 1991). It involves the therapist's consistent empathy with the patient's experiences of him- or herself and others, the therapist's awareness of and adaptive responses toward the patient's dissociative parts, and the therapist's ability to offer the possibility of secure attachment (cf., J.P. Wilson & Thomas, 2004). Empathic attunement should be directed toward goals that decrease the patient's need for defense—including attachment cry—while supporting activation of other action systems such as attachment, sociability, and exploration (Cassidy, 1999; McCluskey, Hooper, & Miller, 1999). Effective empathic attunement can only emerge when the therapist is present and genuinely authentic, meaning he or she must engage in core (in the moment) and extended (over time) presentification with the patient. However, although the therapist's empathic attunement provides a social environment in which a survivor can learn to develop secure attachment, it is not sufficient. Secure attachment also requires clear and consistent boundaries and limits (i.e., a therapeutic frame).

The therapy frame. The therapy frame is a set of relational guidelines and beliefs that define the role and degree of involvement of therapist and patient in treatment: It provides a structure for expectations about the relationship (R. S. Epstein, 1994). The frame includes the stable relational boundaries, limits, and rules of therapy that are flexible within limits, and that thus support the establishment of secure attachment. These boundaries, such as how often the patient is seen and the amount of extrasession contact that occurs, help provide an optimal balance between relational closeness and distance between therapist and patient. The patient is neither maladaptively dependent nor feels unsupported, while the therapist is neither engaged in maladaptive caretaking nor feels defensive about preserving his or her personal space and time. This ideal balance serves to improve the mental level (both energy and efficiency) of patient and therapist. Boundaries protect patient and therapist from becoming too overwhelmed by the demands of such difficult therapy, which can result in lowered mental energy and insufficient mental efficiency. For example, if the patient begins making daily crisis phone calls to the therapist for contact and the therapist is unable to address attachment cry issues effectively in session and limit the phone calls, the patient will continue to escalate, while the therapist will become ever more resentful and overwhelmed. The therapy frame defines how therapist and patient can form a therapeutic team in which their respective roles and expectations are clearly delineated (e.g., Chu, 1998a; Courtois, 1999; Dalenberg, 2000; Pearlman & Saakvitne, 1995). It is the direct responsibility of the therapist to define and maintain the therapy frame in a way that is optimal for both parties. However, it does include some negotiation (Dalenberg, 2000), and certainly includes informing the patient about the frame and its purposes. It must be established at the outset and carefully monitored and maintained over the course of treatment.

There is perhaps nothing more threatening for chronically traumatized patients than inconsistency, unpredictability, and uncertainty. Consistent and empathic efforts to help the patient understand the guidelines of therapy and why they are important and helpful, and sustained efforts to maintain a healthy therapeutic relationship provide security, support, adaptive limits, and thus safety. To this end, the therapist should explain empathically why, for example, sessions begin and end on time, why phone calls are limited, and why a personal relationship would not adaptive, no matter how much it is yearned for. Although many have attempted to delineate "rules" for the therapy frame (i.e., "do's and don'ts") we find it helpful, along with others, to think of more flexible guidelines that inform therapy (Borys, 1994; Dalenberg, 2000; Kroll, 2001; Lazarus, 1994; Simon, 2001). For example, many therapists follow a rule of never touching a patient. But there may be times when nonsexual touch is appropriate and effective. Above all, the therapy frame should help minimize activation of physical, social, and interoceptive defenses in patient and therapist, and activate action systems and action tendencies that are geared to supporting the patient in making adaptive changes.

Therapists are advised to check their professional society's guidelines or ethical code for specific recommendations related to establishing and maintaining a therapy frame. In addition, there are a number of publications that discuss in detail the parameters of the frame (e.g., Bridges, 1999; Chu, 1998a; Courtois, 1999; Dalenberg, 2000; R. S. Epstein, 1994; Gabbard & Lester, 1995; Kluft, 1993a, 1993b; Pearlman & Saakvitne, 1995).

INCREASING MENTAL ENERGY

We must have money in the bank before we can spend it. In the same way, we need mental energy that is available and can be mobilized when we want to use it (Ellenberger, 1970). Some mental "debts" and unnecessary expenditures should be addressed immediately in therapy, while others require more mental efficiency than the patient will have available, so must be postponed until later in therapy. *An early goal is for the therapist and patient to assess accurately the therapeutically desirable actions that are within the patient's reach at the time, and focus on accomplishing those actions first*. It is essential that the patient be challenged sufficiently to make progress, but not be prematurely faced with actions that require more mental resources than are available to him or her in the moment. In this way the patient's (often limited) mental energy can be conserved for achievable actions. For example, the patient is encouraged to learn to cope with the emotions and goals of everyday life first before dealing with the difficult emotions related to traumatic memories, because the latter generally requires much more mental energy and efficiency.

Increasing Income

Many patients drain mental (and physical) energy by excessive work, busyness, or compulsive caring for others. For instance, dissociative patients often focus at work for long stretches of time without any break. This is due to serious retraction of the field of consciousness, and to the tendency of dissociative parts to restrict attention only to the action (sub)system or mode by which they are mediated, preventing them from integrating other needs outside their limited domain. The ensuing stress and low mental energy may allow for the reactivation of traumatic memories because the survivor does not have sufficient energy to continue to avoid them. The major therapeutic target in this case would not be treatment of intrusive traumatic memories. Rather, in order to increase income (mental energy), the aim would be to reduce the patient's level of stress and exhaustion, which precipitate flashbacks.

In Phase 1 the emphasis should be place on fostering an increase of mental (and physical) energy by helping patients learn to use their energy management action system more adaptively. They must practice regular self-care through adequate rest and recreation, sleep hygiene, exercise, good nutrition and a healthy diet, disease prevention, stress reduction, and relaxation training. Patients should become more aware of the need for breaks during the day, regular time off each week, and some type of vacation. These may seem like elementary issues, but they are often overlooked by therapists, and can be problematic in the lives of many traumatized individuals, who often need specific help with the most basic self-care.

Decreasing Expenditures

Treatment of insufficient mental energy may involve the need for patients to eliminate unnecessary use of energy and to correct problems that are chronic drains on energy. Physical conditions that affect energy must be dealt with early in therapy if possible. Persistent and serious medical conditions, and their impact on mental energy in survivors of chronic traumatization should not be underestimated (cf., Felitti et al., 1998). Other drains on energy include lack of physical or emotional safety, unnecessary work, worry, or obsessions, "high maintenance" relationships, chaotic lifestyles, and chronic hyper- or hypoarousal. Some of these may not be ameliorated early in therapy due to the patient's lack of mental efficiency. A major area of energetic expenditure is the patient's ongoing engagement in phobic mental and behavioral avoidance (i.e., trauma-related phobias). When this avoidance can be decreased, that mental energy then comes available for higher level actions provided mental efficiency is also improved and the patient is no longer so afraid of intrusions; otherwise the extra mental energy may be used unwisely.

Establishing safety. First and foremost, therapy begins with the establishment not only of safety within the therapeutic relationship, but also safety in the life of the patient, if indicated (Herman, 1992b). However, survivors often perceive threat when they are actually safe (e.g., in the relationship with the therapist), or do not synthesize or personify stimuli that would indicate they may *not* be safe in other situations. Thus, much work must be done to help patients assess and realize whether they are actually safe or not—and if not, what actions need to be taken. Indeed, when they feel unsafe they will invest much time and effort in unnecessary defensive actions.

Therapy demands a degree of mental efficiency that includes reflective thinking. This kind of thinking is impossible when the patient is not safe, or does not perceive physical, emotional, or relational safety issues. Relational or emotional threats that do not include physical violence may be less obvious to the therapist than physical threats, but are no less of an impediment to the patient, such as an emotionally abusive partner or family of origin, or exploitive friends.

Simplifying daily life. The therapist should help those patients who do too much to simplify their lives. A therapeutic goal is *to reduce the energy and time spent on, and the number of nonessential daily life tasks*. A thorough assessment of all the daily life tasks in which patients are involved often indicates that they have chronically overburdened themselves. For example, the patient may spend inordinate time and energy on cleaning or constantly doing things for others. These patterns can be due to a number of problems: avoidance strategies, limited conscious awareness of and cooperation between parts that are involved in daily life, an inability to problem solve or prioritize, difficulties with time management, or lack of assertiveness in setting limits. In obsessive patients it may be related to trauma-related beliefs about achieving perfection, or about the need to get everything done so there will be no punishment.

Some survivors are overly focused on one area of life to the exclusion of others. They experience stress because, for example, they work too much or play video games constantly, and become too isolated, and do not keep up with other essential activities of daily life. Sometimes doing too much is based on phobias of feelings, wishes, or memories. Frenetic activity then becomes a coping strategy, as Marilyn Van Derbur (2004) testified, "Although I had no understanding of it at the time, that was my *survival mechanism*, staying so busy there was no time to have unthinkable memories surface" (p. 45).

Setting limits on demanding relationships. Survivors often surround themselves with difficult people who are insecurely attached, affectively labile, argumentative, guilt inducing, and exacting. These relationships are unusually demanding because they not only require excessive activation of sociability, attachment, and caretaking, but they also trigger the patient's defense action system (e.g., fear of abandonment and rejection, hypervigilance when others are unpredictable). In addition, many patients themselves behave in the same difficult ways and evoke defensive reactions in other people, then feel attacked and rejected. This leads to endless cycles of relational conflict and entanglements that drain everyone's energy. A therapeutic goal is for the patient to *set limits on unreasonably demanding relationships.* Such limits will save mental energy. However, changing the way patients respond to such people and their demands often involves more mental efficiency and assertiveness than they can muster, and thus also involves therapeutic principles that improve mental efficiency. In fact, this is a therapeutic task that may need to continue over time. But the first step is to help patients become consciously aware of inappropriate demands and of their own submerged feelings of resentment and guilt. Then in a stepwise manner, patients can be helped first to *reduce* the pressure they feel in conflicted relationships, and eventually to *resolve* those relationships.

Paying Off "Debts"

The completion of unfinished actions can be understood as "paying off debts." Unfinished major actions ("unfinished business") drains mental energy and lowers the mental level (Janet, 1919/1925; L. Schwartz, 1951). Unresolved experiences tend to haunt us until they can be finished (cf., Chapter 9). The lives of survivors of chronic traumatization are usually replete with both major and minor unfinished actions. These include unsuccessful transitions in the life cycle and unresolved past conflicts involving painful encounters with mental health agencies, unfinished projects, school, relationships, and, last but not least, traumatic memories.

Incomplete mental and behavioral actions can only be finished when the patient has enough mental energy and efficiency to do so. For example, several years of delinquent taxes may be too much for a patient to tackle at first, but getting the dishes done and paying overdue bills from the past month might be achievable. In terms of emotional debts, resolving less difficult issues such as dissatisfaction with the plumber's inadequate repair of the bathroom is much easier and requires less mental efficiency than resolving major issues related to a partner who is occasionally emotionally abusive. Yet one small step toward assertiveness leads to more over time. Resolving debts should involve complete resolution, but containment is often a more realistic *initial* goal than complete resolution. In general, patients should grasp the concept that completing unfinished actions is an ongoing part of life, including therapy.

IMPROVING MENTAL EFFICIENCY

Even when trauma survivors have sufficient mental (and physical) energy, they often lack mental efficiency. In general, the principle of improving mental efficiency involves patients learning to master increasingly complex mental and behavioral actions that support adaptive living, including the ability to prioritize and adjust their goals when needed, to consider the short- and long-term costs and benefits of (major) actions, and to take into consideration their needs as a whole person. This is particularly difficult for dissociative patients, because various parts may have limited or no awareness of the needs of other parts. They have not integrated these needs, or may be in direct conflict with other parts and their goals.

Excess mental energy occurs when there is insufficient mental efficiency to channel it adaptively for the tasks at hand; it results in agitation, anxiety, and other substitute actions. In such cases, the extra physical rest prescribed for those with low mental *energy* is usually contraindicated. Instead, healthy mental and physical activity is a treatment of choice.

Therapeutic Stimulation

Therapeutic stimulation involves encouraging the patient to execute more complex and demanding actions as an improvement in mental efficiency allows (Janet, 1919/1925). Stimulation may be emotional, cognitive, or behavioral, and usually involves evoking a patient's curiosity and desire to learn and change; that is, it may activate the exploration action system. The patient must already have sufficient (latent) mental *energy* and have the necessary mental efficiency within reach. Treatment techniques range from psychoeducation to encouraging the patient to engage in and complete adaptive challenges.

The therapist should help the patient take advantage of opportunities to engage in activities that he or she will find greatly rewarding and enjoyable. Such actions improve mental efficiency because the patient spends energy on favorable mental and social investments rather than poor ones, in the process of learning how to gain a higher return on investment. He or she practices emotional, cognitive, motor, and social skills along the way that increase personal capital. This improved mental efficiency may generalize in a gradual fashion to support an increase in higher level actions in other domains of life, across action systems.

Psychoeducation

Psychoeducation is a very important principle in raising the patient's mental efficiency: It involves sharing essential information of which the patient is unaware or has not fully understood. Psychoeducation improves mental efficiency when the patient can listen, begin to reflect more, and postpone (suspend; cf., Chapter 9) immediate (re)actions. Inviting patients to pause and reflect stimulates them to engage in more advanced action tendencies. In fact, the very act of thinking about one's mental actions is metacognition, which is a higher level action in itself.

The therapist makes a functional analysis of the patient's current mental level and existing fears and phobias before psychoeducation can begin (Chapter 11). In general the guidelines for effective psychoeducation are to: (1) provide information according to what the patient can synthesize and realize at a given time; (2) repeat new information frequently because learning often requires repetition; and (3) never assume the patient has completely understood the message. Dissociative patients are well known for having much difficulty in integrating information that challenges their worldview and creates cognitive dissonance or evokes painful feelings. They may distort the information due to inaccurate perceptions or reflexive beliefs; or particular parts may block out information. For this reason, it is often helpful to write down or audiotape essential information for patients to take home, if they find it helpful to do so. Sometimes it is useful to prescribe additional reading or other homework assignments. Above all, the patient must practice: Mastery takes place through repetition.

Psychoeducation is an ongoing therapeutic action which facilitates specific treatment goals in various treatment phases. Early in therapy it is generally helpful for the therapist to explain the nature of traumatization and structural dissociation, paced according to what the patient can integrate. The therapist also assists the patient to understand the treatment frame, phase-oriented treatment, the data from the assessment regarding the patient's diagnoses and related problems, and the importance of the therapeutic relationship. A treatment contract and therapeutic goals should be shared, including ways in which patients might best work toward them. Education about basic life skills, such as proper nutrition, sleep hygiene, exercise, and boundaries can be invaluable.

Patients may need psychoeducation about balancing life activities, and thus their action systems. The therapist should help them think through their goals by suspending immediate actions, and thus engage more in the action of presentification in the moment and over time. Patients also need information and support on how to relax the defensive action tendencies of various parts toward each other and to promote internal empathy and self-care among all parts (i.e., activate caregiving and sociability internally).

Exploring "Resistance"

Resistance can be defined as the patient's attempt to protect his or her vulnerability (Messer, 2002; Rowe, 1996; Stark, 1994), and to maintain the status quo, including structural dissociation of the personality, in order to prevent feared destabilization. It includes "all those behaviors in the therapeutic system which interact to prevent the therapeutic system from achieving the [patient's] goals for therapy" (C.M. Anderson & Stewart, 1983, p. 24). The therapist also may engage in *counterresistance* to protect him- or herself from feared destabilization by colluding to prevent adaptive change in therapy (Strean, 1993). For example, a therapist highly invested in being needed, who has a hyperactivated caretaking action system, may unconsciously act in ways that prevent a patient from becoming more independent.

Dissociative patients tend to have a bad reputation for being "resistant" and "not ready to be in treatment." They have been described as having disruptive resistances ranging from severe lack of trust issues and boundary violations to extreme avoidance of dealing with traumatic memories (Chu, 1988a, 1988b). Some "resistance" in these patients, however, involves understandable reactions to mistakes and misattunements by therapists who fail to appreciate the nature of traumatization, its implications for the therapeutic relationship, and use inappropriate treatment interventions. Even seasoned therapists can evoke such "resistances" when they inadvertently overwhelm the patient in some way, demand adaptive actions not yet achievable, or create attachment disruptions (Hahn, 2004; Messer, 2002; Rowe, 1996).

Resistance is inevitable and ubiquitous, and once the therapist grasps what is behind it, it is often very understandable. It is often not the resistance itself, but the way in which the therapist responds to resistance that makes a difference for better or worse in treatment. Many psychological theories and treatment approaches focus on working with resistances (e.g., C. M. Anderson & Stewart, 1983; Blum, 1986; A. Ellis, 1962; Horner, 2005; Leahy, 2001; McCullough et al., 2003; Messer, 2002; Stark, 1994). Most promote the idea that *one of the most essential interventions is the therapist's empathic understanding of and working with the patient's resistances rather than directly opposing them.*

Resistance involves the patient's defensive actions to *avoid* something that is feared, and is often due to their avoidance of integrating some dreaded aspect of experience, such as feelings, memories, or relational conflicts. In fact, we can understand resistance in terms of the various trauma-related phobias. For example, patients resist attaching to the therapist (phobia of attachment), owning their feelings (phobia of trauma-derived mental actions), or accepting dissociative parts (phobia of dissociative parts), because they fear these actions will result in negative consequences. Thus the patient continues to act according to maladaptive "if–then" rules: "You will hurt or leave me"; "I won't be able to stand what I feel"; "People won't like me if I am angry"; "That part is bad, and if I accept it, then I will be bad." Yet, overcoming these phobias and engaging in full integration (synthesis, personification, and presentification) results in positive rather than negative change; something the patient cannot yet realize. It is thus essential for the therapist to inquire about what the patient is concerned about or fears when working with particular resistances (e.g., McCann & Pearlman, 1990).

Resistance serves a function of keeping certain perception–motor action cycles closed to input from the external and internal world that the patient (or the dissociative part) regards as a threat. The fear is that the feedback (e.g., being aware of feelings, taking care of oneself, listening to other parts) would disrupt a steady, albeit rigid state of the patient's personality, and create instability. However, therapeutic goals involve change. And change only occurs when maladaptive perception–motor action cycles are destabilized and the patient is able to reorganize them more adaptively. But resistance often takes less mental efficiency, and sometimes less energy than does coping with the destabilization of fixed mental and behavioral actions and adaptive reorganization. In other words, resistance usually involves mental and behavioral substitute actions.

Therapists are best able to help their patients resolve resistances when they are open to hearing about their own mistakes and inevitable normal misattunements, and understand the fear and pain that underlie the patients' resistances. To this end, therapists are most effective when they avoid an authoritarian stance, are open to negotiation, have empathy for patients' stuckness, value a variety of approaches to solving problems, avoid persuasion or criticism, educate only with permission, accept the patient's freedom of choice, are not overly invested in change, and realize that change may be very slow and cannot be imposed. Therapists must avoid having their own defensive system activated with the patient, and instead, utilize powerful combinations of attachment, sociability, exploration, and play to engage with patients.

Skills Development

Survivors of chronic childhood traumatization generally have serious skills deficiencies in various areas of life, mostly because these skills were not modeled by caretakers early in life. Instead they may have learned maladaptive coping strategies through modeling and subsequent imitation that are low-level action tendencies, or by trying to cope on their own without adequate relational support. Because survivors are so often influenced by the defense system, their ability to learn in social situations is impeded. The literature has focused primarily on skills related to affect and impulse dysregulation and relationships (e.g., J.G. Allen, 2001; Chu, 1998a; Courtois, 1999; Gold, 2000; Linehan, 1993; McCann & Pearlman, 1990; Van der Kolk, Pelcovitz et al., 1996). These basic mental skills, as well as many others, are essential for survivors to learn and practice until they are mastered. They play an important role in developing and maintaining a high mental level, with an optimal balance between mental energy and efficiency. In large measure, these skills support our capacity to adequately integrate our experiences so that we can move through the vagaries of both internal and external life with some degree of balance and equanimity.

Structural dissociation is a major impediment to learning skills unless the therapist is attuned to the fact that not all parts learn skills simultaneously or can master them equally well. Lack of sufficient integration among action systems impedes adaptive regulatory functions that stabilize mental and behavioral actions. For example, the regulatory skills of the survivor as ANP may not be able to influence a highly emotive EP. At times, all parts will be in need of a specific skill, such as affect regulation. When at least one part has a skill, every effort should be made by the therapist to encourage that part to share the skill internally with other parts rather than relying on the therapist to teach it. Essential skills unique to working with dissociative patients include learning internal communication, cooperation, transfer of learning, and negotiation prior to complete integration (see Chapter 15). These skills involve the ability to relate to one's dissociative parts, thus to oneself in an adaptive way. In terms of the hierarchy of action tendencies, they involve presymbolic and symbolic sociopersonal action tendencies.

Many skills are learned primarily through cognitive behavioral techniques (J. G. Allen, 2001; Chu, 1998a; Janet, 1919/1925), and should be assessed and taught in early in therapy. They often involve an initial improvement in the patient's mental efficiency. Skills are first learned cognitively, then practiced behaviorally in small steps. Ideally, each step is practiced by parts until it has been reasonably mastered: Simple steps provide the foundation for more complex and difficult steps (cf., Ellenberger, 1970; Janet, 1919/1925). These practical skills gradually become integrated into a much more adaptive way of living, as components of a course of higher level action that is developed throughout therapy. With each success generated by new skills, the patient's balance between mental energy and efficiency is improved.

The learning of mental skills involves a certain amount of adequate synthesis, personification, and presentification, and coordination of action systems in ways that survivors may not have previously been able to achieve. For example, social skills promote activation of sociability and other daily life action systems instead of the use of defense. These shall involve higher level and more complex action tendencies. Social skills are not only useful for dealing with other people; they are essential for parts to interact with each other internally. Most skills thus require an increasing ability to coordinate and control which action systems are operative in a given situation; thus, parts must learn to negotiate and cooperate to a greater degree. This involves a capacity of each part to adequately synthesize (evaluate) the context as well as the content of a stimulus or situation, to personify the situation, and to experience it as real and act accordingly. Many skills involve complex integration of action systems; higher action tendencies for each part of the personality. For example, assertiveness skills include highly evolved defense strategies that are combined with sociability. Relaxation training can include energy management and at times, sociability, along with deactivation of defense action tendencies such as hypervigilance. Development of healthy personal boundaries can include energy management, caretaking, sociability, an evolved defense action system, and agreement among parts about boundaries. Parenting skills include activation of caretaking and all other action systems of daily life, with minimized defense or reactivation of child parts. Skills involve all levels of action tendencies. Lower and intermediate levels of action tendencies must be learned before higher level ones. For example, the patient must learn to wait, and not immediately act, before being able to reflect on why he or she is engaging in a maladaptive action. The patient learns to tolerate and modulate the emotions of everyday life before dealing with the emotions related to traumatization. Traumatized patients often find it difficult to be present in the moment, and must learn this before they can be present over extended periods of time. They reflexively respond to conditioned stimuli in relationships, and must learn that the presence of a conditioned stimulus does not always signal that they will be traumatized again. Only then can they learn the relational skills that support secure attachment.

The mastery of some skills enhances the learning of others. For example, learning to empathize, communicate, cooperate, and negotiate with dissociative parts often leads to learning better affect regulation, time management, and relational skills. We have listed major skills in Table 12.1, as space limitations prevent further discussion. Therapists are encouraged to be proficient in helping patients learn these skills.

Transforming Substitute Actions into Adaptive Actions

When some kind of action is necessary in response to a situation, and adaptive action is still out of reach because of inadequate mental efficiency or too little energy, survivors tend to resort to *substitute actions*, which are by definition lower order actions. Certain dissociative parts, such as EPs fixed in defense or attachment cry, tend to engage in substitute actions the majority of the time, while other parts may have a wider range of adaptive actions available to them. We distinguish two categories of substitute actions: One type lacks a specific goal, and the other type is meant to achieve a goal, but does so in a maladaptive way.

TABLE 12.1
Skills

Psychophysiological regulation (management of hyper- and hypoarousal)

Capacity to regulate, tolerate, and manage affects, impulses, and other mental actions
> Regulation of self-conscious or social emotions such as self-hatred, shame, guilt
> Regulation of intense emotion: rage, anger, yearning, sadness, grief, loneliness
> Distress tolerance
> Containment of affect
> Self-soothing and seeking appropriate comfort and support from others
> Tolerance of aloneness
> Relaxation skills
> Stress management skills
> Energy management (balance of work, rest, recreation)

Capacity to symbolize experience
> Development of a vocabulary for internal and relational experience

Relational skills
> Mentalization (accurate perception and understanding of the motivations and intentions of others and of oneself; development of metacognition)
> Capacity for empathy, cooperation, and negotiation with self and others
> Assertiveness skills
> Social skills
> Setting and maintaining healthy personal boundaries
> Parenting skills

Capacity to accurately perceive reality
> Distinguish the present from the past and future
> Distinguish internal (interoceptive) from external (exteroceptive) reality
> Capacity to be present (presentification; mindfulness)

Time management skills (dependent upon presentification)

Organizational skills (help organize perception–motor action cycles)

(continued)

TABLE 12.1
(Continued)

Attentional skills
    Maintaining concentration and focus within and between different action tendencies/systems
    Regulating alterations in field and level of consciousness

Problem-solving skills
    Capacity to prioritize (requires conscious awareness of different priorities, as well as integration among action systems)
    Ability to consider short- and long-term costs and benefits of actions (requires core and extended presentification)
    Ability to consider needs as a whole person (implies integration of all action systems)

Diversions. The first type of substitute actions involve the lowest levels of actions: disorganized movements that ensue when the individual lacks all mental efficiency to use available mental energy for goal-directed action (cf., Chapter 9). Janet called them *dérivations*, which in his native French meant that mental energy was *diverted* away from a proper course of adaptive action (Janet, 1909a; 1919/1925). The most serious form of diversions, found in only some survivors, are pseudoseizures (Bowman & Markand, 1996; Janet, 1928b; Kuyk, 1999).[1] More common diversions include generalized agitation with motor, emotional, and cognitive elements (Janet, 1903, 1909b; Chapter 9). Serious agitation includes such behaviors as screaming, flinging one's body around, throwing objects, or head banging. Less serious agitation includes jiggling legs, rocking, shaking, shuddering, fidgeting, pacing, and tics (cf., Janet 1919/1925, 1928b). These substitutes are often described in the current literature as manifestations of affect dysregulation (in the form of undercontrol). Indeed, sometimes there *is* a purpose to disorganized movements; for example, when the patient engages in these behaviors as an (unconscious) avoidance of feared higher order mental and behavioral actions.

Treatment consists of gradually moving the patient from this very low level of action tendencies to ever higher ones. First the therapist can gently

---

1. Pseudoseizure is "a paroxysmal involuntary behavior pattern mimicking epileptic events, characterized by a sudden and time-limited disturbance in controlling motor, sensory, autonomic, cognitive, emotional and/or behavioral functions and is mediated by psychological factors" (Kuyk, 1999, p. 9).

but firmly interrupt such actions, and establish contact with the patient by using simple language and eye contact, and if appropriate, judicious physical touch that helps the patient become more present (Hunter & Struve, 1998). These interventions stimulate presymbolic sociopersonal action tendencies that can help the patient regulate his or her actions more adequately (Nijenhuis & Den Boer, in press; Porges, 2001; Schore, 2003b). Although these are also lower-level action tendencies, they are still higher than basic reflexes or presymbolic regulatory action tendencies, and the patient may need to be brought in a stepwise fashion to higher tendencies. Therapists also help patients reorient to their surroundings; that is, engage in context evaluation and some limited degree of personification and presentification. They may employ techniques to regain psychophysiological regulation, often first through social engagement. Thus, presymbolic sociopersonal action tendencies need to be reactivated immediately if possible. Then patient and therapist can engage gradually in higher action tendencies of systematic exploration and reflection to discover what precipitated the diversion and whether particular parts were evoked. Finally, the therapist can help the patient develop higher degrees of presentification. To this end, he or she stimulates the survivor to increase more realistic predictions about the near and distant future, to carefully evaluate past actions and situations, and to adapt his or her actions accordingly.

Goal-directed substitute actions. The second category of substitute actions are those which *do* have specific goals, but either the goals are not adaptive in the present moment, or the actions used to attain the goal are not ideal. The first step is for therapist and patient to understand the goal or function of the behavior, and whether the goal itself is adaptive. For example, Millie wanted to punish herself, which on the surface seemed to be a maladaptive goal. But actually she believed if she punished herself (both physically and emotionally), she might be able to correct what was wrong with her (an adaptive goal if something was indeed wrong). This then requires therapist and patient to explore the various (usually reflexive) beliefs of dissociative parts about what is wrong or bad about themselves or other parts; what are the most effective ways to help a person correct his or her "faults"; and ways in which empathy toward all parts can be a powerful adaptive mental action. Of course, using this sort of logic does not quickly alleviate self-punishment. Rather, it is a point of departure for challenging reflexive beliefs and habituated behaviors that may be contained in specific parts of the personality and directed toward other parts. And it is a way for the therapist to empathically understand the underlying needs of a patient who is self-destructive.

Various parts of the personality may also engage in actions derived from action systems that are inappropriate to the situation. For example, a part may reflexively engage in freezing (a subsystem of the action system of defense) when banter among friends is perceived as an emotional attack. Such (re)actions substitute for more complex and integrated social interactions.

Overcoming phobias. Trauma-related phobias are the most pervasive form of substitute actions in survivors. Overcoming these phobias involves helping patients to transform these substitutes into adaptive actions. The cost in energy involved in maintaining these phobias cannot be underestimated by the therapist: Trauma-related phobias are a major obstacle to improving mental efficiency and consume much mental energy. Patients are often convinced that the actions—particularly mental actions—needed to overcome these phobias are beyond their reach, and are afraid to even approach the the phobic stimuli. Thus the therapist helps the patient to sufficiently improve mental efficiency to begin an approach of graduated exposure or systematic desensitization. And each successful step in overcoming the phobias also improves mental efficiency.

The treatment for overcoming phobias of the inner world is not much different from that of external phobias such as spiders or heights. It consists first of exploring and understanding the patient's defenses as avoidance and escape measures. Resistances to particular mental contents, or rather, the mental actions that generate these contents, can then be approached empathically and at least some fears related to mental actions can be resolved with psychoeducation, skills building, and experiential practice. The patient is gradually exposed to the conditioned stimuli (feelings, body sensations, etc.), and he or she must engage in the mental actions of synthesis and realization (e.g., learning that "this sensation in my stomach does not mean I am in danger"), while preventing maladaptive responses such as panic. The survivor's mental efficiency (and sometimes mental energy) level must first be increased to raise the probability that he or she is able to engage in integrative actions during the exposure, rather than in avoidant and other substitute actions. The successful integrative action during the exposure improves mental efficiency. The survivor must integrate the fact that conditioned stimuli do not refer to or signal the feared outcome (the unconditioned stimuli) in the present context. It is a waste of energy for the patient to believe, for example, that an angry face always precedes physical abuse: It does not in the majority of contexts.

The first step is to help patients realize their phobias. Conditioned avoidance becomes very automatic when it is often practiced, reducing the need for conscious awareness. Thus many survivors are so practiced in avoidance that they are not consciously aware of what they are avoiding or why. These automatic actions have become simple reflexes, which are the lowest level of action tendencies, requiring little mental energy and efficiency. Survivors must first confront the fact that they *have* a phobia before they can begin to confront the feared objects or experiences related to the phobia. The second step is to assess trauma-derived phobias and rank their degree of severity. For example, if a patient cannot even speak about anger or shame without abruptly changing the subject, completely spacing out, or switching, the phobia of trauma-related mental actions is likely severe and must be approached slowly. (Here the phobia relates to engaging in mental actions that generate certain feelings.) Therapists often overestimate a patient's capacity to engage successfully in the integrative mental actions required to feel an emotion, understand it, and complete it. The third step is to help the patient (i.e., all dissociative parts) verbalize to the degree possible what she or he fears about approaching objects or experiences related to the phobia. Such verbalization is a narrative account that involves linguistic, hence symbolic representation of an experience rather than the literal experience itself. A narrative solidifies increasing realization of what is feared and how it can be approached safely. Gradually, the patient will have developed sufficient mental efficiency to be able to talk about what she or he fears will happen, which provides a safe entrée to resolving the phobia. Putting these fears in words is a higher action tendency than merely expressing them in nonverbal forms. Each time the patient can experience that feelings of panic and terror are not dangerous, mental efficiency is raised a bit more because she or he has developed the skill of experiencing emotion without resorting to substitute actions. The adaptive experiencing of emotion is a major goal of acceptance and commitment therapy (ACT; Hayes, Luoma, Bond, Masuda, & Lillis, 2006), a recent trend in behavior therapy which focuses on exposure of the patient to mental actions (emotions, in this case) and prevention of mental avoidance (substitute actions). These principles are central to the psychology of action described in this book.

Although steps to overcome the various phobias can be taken throughout therapy, each treatment phase can be described in terms of overcoming specific phobias. Thus, Phase 1, *symptom reduction and stabilization*, is dedicated to overcoming the phobias of attachment and attachment loss with the therapist, dissociative parts of the personality, and other trauma-derived mental actions. Gradual resolution of these phobias should improve the patient's mental efficiency (and increase his or her mental energy) to such a degree that in Phase 2, *treatment of traumatic memories*, a start can be made to overcoming phobias related to insecure attachment to the perpetrator(s) and traumatic memory. Phase 3, *personality integration and rehabilitation*, is dedicated to overcoming the phobias of normal life, healthy risk-taking and change, and intimacy. We discuss these various trauma-related phobias and their treatment in more detail in succeeding chapters.

Completing Adaptive Actions

A fundamental treatment principle is for survivors to learn to successfully complete both minor and major adaptive actions. Completing an adaptive action commonly generates positive personal, social, and sometimes material rewards, and thus proffers income. It brings a personal sense of mastery and pride, as well as social praise, and it often satisfies the goal(s) of an action tendency or, more generally, an action system. These effects tend to improve mental efficiency. For example, the successful integration of one traumatic memory will teach the patient the required skills, and will instill or strengthen the reflective belief that he or she will be able to integrate other, perhaps even more painful traumatic memories. As Janet noted, "The completed and terminated act heightens psychological tension [mental efficiency] of the individual, while an incomplete and unachieved act lowers it" (cited in Ellenberger, 1970, p. 383). Completing adaptive actions also puts to rest investment of mental energy in a particular action tendency, and it relieves mental "debts."

Survivors often not only have to learn to complete the mundane tasks and responsibilities of daily life on a regular basis, but must learn to engage in and complete difficult actions. They must be able to start and complete a conversation with a partner about a painful subject without spacing out or becoming distracted, finish a thought, tolerate and resolve conflicted feelings, and stay focused at work. Dissociate parts fixated in defense actions must learn to overcome conditioned responses such as freezing or flight, and become reflective, consciously thinking about what is happening, becoming aware of the current context, as well as other options available to them. This includes learning to suspend impulses to engage in immediate behavioral action, to engage in social contact, to symbolize their experiences, first in nonverbal and then in ever higher (i.e., more abstract) levels of language, rather than engage in reenactments of traumatic experience.

Patients must be able to engage successfully in all the phases of action with both mental and behavioral action tendencies: latency, planning, initiation, execution, and completion. Many actions are complex, including different component actions, each of which must be initiated, executed, and completed. For example, working well with others implies a multitude of mental and behavioral actions: cooperation, reflection, mentalization, analysis of problems, and integration of social and work skills. The capacity to engage in these actions depends to a large degree on being able to engage in the actions of personification and presentification. Behaviorally, acting in a hesitant, half-hearted, disinterested, or depersonalized way may lead to the completion of the motor component of the action, but not to a subjective sense of completion, and may even lead to deterioration of mental efficiency (Janet, 1903). For example, sexually abused patients who compulsively wash their bodies because they are "dirty" find no relief in the action when they have not personified their body or the sexual abuse. To make it a subjectively high-quality action, strong motivation, a relatively energetic and personified execution of an action, as well as realization of the motivation are essential.

Completing actions to resolve debts. Completing unfinished actions requires a certain degree of mental efficiency that patients often do not have early in therapy. But as they gradually improve their mental efficiency, these incomplete actions can be finished. There are three main types of unfinished actions (or "debts," in Janet's language) that must be addressed in a gradual manner, beginning with the most simple and ending with the most complex: (1) debts in current daily life; (2) debts from the past that are not necessarily trauma-related; and (3) trauma-related debts. The first goal is to complete actions in order to *resolve debts (complete unfinished actions) involving basic daily life tasks*. The more patients can be helped to complete daily life tasks well, to set realistic schedules for finishing, and to integrate action systems more effectively, the more mental energy (previously unavailable) they will have for more complex and emotional tasks, and the more their mental efficiency will automatically improve. Success in completing these tasks may also involve learning time management and organizational skills, and how to set priorities and goals. Patients must also be helped to learn to deal with the mental actions that pertain to everyday life, such as feelings, thoughts, and wishes.

The second therapeutic goal is to complete actions in order to *resolve unfinished emotional and relational actions from the past*. Unfinished issues from the past might include previously unsuccessful or incomplete transitions in the life cycle, and unresolved past relationships.

The third and perhaps most difficult goal is to complete actions in order to *resolve traumatic memories*, a special and extremely costly form of incomplete actions: "Such patients . . . are continuing the action, or rather the attempt at action, which began when the thing happened; and they exhaust themselves in these everlasting recommencements" (Janet, 1919/1925, p. 663). Resolution of traumatic memories can be a long and arduous task, requiring many small and repetitious steps. It requires the execution of the complex actions of integration in the forms of synthesis and realization, including personification and presentification.

FOSTERING REALIZATION

Incomplete major actions highlight the core problem of *nonrealization* for survivors, not only of their traumatic pasts but of many more aspects of their lives. Thus, a constant therapeutic principle is to promote the well-initiated, executed, and completed actions of synthesis and realization among all parts of the personality, so that the survivor as a whole learns to perceive reality as adaptively as possible and respond to it by completing essential mental and behavioral actions. Ideally, every intervention is toward the end of heightening mental level and increasing realization. The therapist helps the patient become more present in the moment and across time, more attentive, better able to set realistic goals, and take responsibility for his or her actions—all components of personification and presentification. The agency of the patient as a whole is thus emphasized and supported.

Survivors are encouraged to move gradually from lower action tendencies to higher ones with stepwise interventions. As described in Chapter 9, each level of action tendencies has its own degree of personification and presentification, each level building on the ones before, until integration can be achieved. The therapist must often hold full realization for a patient for a long time, but always supports ongoing steps toward realization. For example, the therapist can often remark to the patient that even though one part may have amnesia for what another part does, both parts remain aspects of a single person: "Even though it may not seem so to you, that is actually a part of you. Can we find ways to understand that part of yourself a bit better?" The therapist can encourage the patient to reflect more and consciously experiment, beginning with asking if–then questions: "If you were to remember, then what do you imagine would happen? If you did express your anger toward me, then what do you imagine my response would be?" Such questions open the door for testing whether catastrophic expectations will be real or not. The survivor's realization of his or her fears that inhibit adaptive actions are already a major step toward integration.

SUMMARY

This chapter focuses on general treatment principles geared toward promoting adaptive, integrative actions in survivors and among all parts of the personality. Each principle is designed to support gradual progression from lower order mental and behavioral actions to higher order ones. The first major principle is to establish a therapeutic relationship and a stable yet flexible therapeutic frame that serves to minimize activation of defenses and maximize higher order adaptive actions in both therapist and patient. Once a clear frame has been established, the therapist and patient focus on the major task of building the patient's mental level; that is, sufficient and balanced mental energy and mental efficiency. This is achieved by following principles of a mental economy: increasing mental energy, decreasing unnecessary expenditures of mental energy, and paying off mental "debts" (i.e., unfinished actions). Achieving adequate mental energy may lead to the establishment of higher and more sustained levels of mental efficiency, allowing for ever more adaptive and complex actions. But increased mental efficiency also results in less wasted energy, and even in an increase in mental energy. Eventually, the patient is encouraged to engage in and complete major adaptive actions, including realization, as a matter of course in daily life. This involves high levels of personification and presentification, and the ability of all parts of the personality to accurately perceive and place accounts of reality along a continuum of degree of reality.

CHAPTER 13

Phase 1 Treatment and Beyond

*Overcoming the Phobia of Attachment
and Attachment Loss with the Therapist*

> *Contact itself is the feared element because it brings a promise of
> love, safety, and comfort that cannot be fulfilled and that reminds
> [the patient] of the abrupt breaches of infancy.*
> —Lawrence E. Hedges (1997, p. 114)

SOME OF THE FIRST AND MOST difficult issues that arise in therapy with chronically traumatized individuals are their painful and tenacious problems with social contact and attachment. Thus, even in initial sessions many survivors are fearful and avoidant of the most basic contact with the therapist, before any attachment has had time to develop. They may fear the mere experience of being in contact with the therapist in part because it signals the approach of their haunted inner world that is the purvue of therapy. This initial *phobia of contact with the therapist* is the first obstacle to overcome in treatment, and is a harbinger of other painful struggles later in therapy with attachment and mental contents. Many patients have persistently low mental levels that increase the likelihood that they will engage in maladaptive substitute actions that will interfere with genuine contact and eventual secure attachment, not only in daily life but also in therapy. The most pernicious of these actions involve the *phobia of attachment and of attachment loss*: The fear of being close to and of losing another human being, or of being engulfed by another and losing all autonomy and control; of being ridiculed, rejected, or abandoned in the face of intolerably strong needs for support, acceptance, and reassurance. Attachment also evokes trauma-related stimuli such as feelings, unfulfilled wishes and needs, and memories, all of which survivors have tried to avoid. The costs of these and other trauma-related phobias are enormously difficult for survivors to maintain (cf., Chapter 10), and result in ongoing low mental levels that prevent adaptive functioning in daily life.

Attachment phobias are manifested intensely in the therapeutic relationship. They are the core of transference phenomena, involve reenactments of old attachment patterns, and their resolution is essential for successful treatment outcomes. They occur throughout therapy, in virtually every session, and generally are slow and difficult to resolve. Every interaction, every intervention will be influenced directly or indirectly by the manifestations of and the solutions to these phobias of attachment.

THE ROLE OF ATTACHMENT IN TREATMENT

Secure attachment supports integration of our personality so that we can be adaptive to the maximum of our potential: It predisposes us "toward more differentiated, coherent, and flexible functioning" (Slade, 1999, p. 584). In other words, secure attachment raises our mental level and supports our functioning at the highest levels of action tendencies. Secure attachment inhibits undue activation of defense, and supports full development of the other action systems of daily life (cf., Chapter 3; Nijenhuis & Den Boer, in press). Yet attachment is not without the risk of hurt and loss even under the best of human circumstances. For those fortunate to have secure attachments, relational pain and loss can be met adaptively because the individual knows the natural rhythm of healthy relationships: *Attunement, disruption, repair.* Healthy individuals synthesize secure attachments in such a way that they eventually become permanent internalized mental representations (also known as *internal working models* or *object relations*) that can always be drawn upon for support, regardless of whether the attachment figure is actually available or not.

But attachment for chronically traumatized individuals has been insecure at best, and often is an essential part of trauma. Survivors synthesize malevolent internal mental representations of attachment figures and self that can be understood as dissociative parts of the personality (e.g., Blizard, 2001, 2003; Howell, 2005; Liotti, 1995; Chapter 3), leaving them with little or no capacity for internal soothing, support, or reassurance, and lowering their mental level. Survivors, or specific dissociative parts thus often operate at middle and lower levels of action tendencies in the realm of attachment, which also affects their function in other domains. They may be unable to adequately synthesize and realize current relational cues from the therapist, misreading them as danger signals, so that their defenses are evoked, even while they desperately cling to the therapist. They are unable to mentalize and have fixed beliefs about the therapist's perceived hurtful or neglectful intentions. They are thus unable to predict accurately much of what happens in healthy relationships.

In terms of learning theory, they have maladaptive conscious and unconscious if–then reflexive beliefs: "*If* she really knew me, *then* she would despise me"; "*If* I get close, *then* I will be controlled." From the standpoint of classical conditioning, many patients have never associated attachment with an internal state of felt security, the goal of secure attachment (Cassidy, 1999). Instead it signals or is a reminder of physical or emotional pain. Negative evaluative conditioning involving shame and fear hampers an initial positive connection: "I am inherently disgusting and weak, and this therapist is inherently useless or dangerous."

Survivors have trouble engaging in adequate context evaluation of the therapy situation. Instead, the most intense negative feelings of which humans are capable can be evoked: Shame, guilt, rage, jealousy, revenge, abandonment panic, terror, unfulfilled yearnings for love and care, and grief. Other, more positive feelings can also be triggered, such as intense love, sexual feelings, tenderness, excitement, or joy. Patients can be avoidant of these feelings as well, and some of these emotions can serve as avoidance strategies for more painful affects.

The phobias of attachment and of attachment loss are two sides of one coin based on fears that attachment will be painful in some fashion. But these two phobias evoke different action systems, and thus often activate different parts of the personality. In the phobia of attachment, parts are typically focused on defenses that dismiss and avoid attachment and related mental contents: "You are paid to like me so it doesn't count"; "I don't feel anything when I am with you." In the phobia of attachment loss, parts are fixed in attachment cry or fight defenses that serve to avoid loss of attachment and related mental contents: "Please don't leave me; I can't live without you"; "If you leave me, I'll make you sorry." These conflicting phobias are the essence of disorganized/disoriented attachment (see Chapter 3; Liotti, 1999a, 1999b; Main & Solomon, 1986).

Yet, in spite of these intense phobias the therapeutic relationship is the matrix out of which all of therapy develops, and the resolution of other phobias and problems for survivors often depends upon its quality. A secure therapeutic relationship with survivors is essential for successful treatment (Alexander & Anderson, 1994; Kinsler, 1992; Laub & Auerhahn, 1989; Olio, & Cornell, 1993; Steele & Van der Hart, 2004; Steele et al., 2001). However, although necessary, it is typically not achievable early in therapy (e.g., Kluft, 1993a). Rather, it is a work in progress that is, in itself, a major focus of therapy.

Change in therapy flows from relational interaction. A major goal of therapy is for therapist and patient to find and maintain an optimal balance between relational closeness and distance because this will promote higher and more stable mental levels in both individuals. This balance is dynamic, needing subtle adjustments for different patients (and therapists), for various phases of treatment, and between various parts of the patient's personality and the therapist. At times a more objective stance by the therapist is needed, at others a warmer attitude (Janet, 1919/1925; Steele & Van der Hart, 2004b).

ATTACHMENT PHOBIAS THROUGHOUT PHASES OF TREATMENT

The phobias of attachment and attachment loss are difficult to overcome for those survivors whose experiences included long term relational trauma. Thus, attachment issues generally manifest over all three phases of treatment. In early Phase 1, *symptom reduction and stabilization*, the patient or presenting dissociative parts typically may exhibit varying levels of avoidance. Attempts by the therapist to connect may be rebuffed and may evoke serious approach/avoidance conflicts that may not be evident to the therapist at first. Some parts may reveal more information than other parts are comfortable with, and may attempt to experiment with the trustworthiness of the therapist by engaging in "testing" behaviors early in treatment rather than discussing the issue directly.

As the therapeutic relationship develops over time, the conflict between the fear of and need for attachment may intensify. In the first phase of treatment, the therapist must be alert to signs of this dilemma within the patient and between parts of the personality. The therapist must guide the relationship according to the mental efficiency of the patient and of various parts of the personality, particularly those most active in treatment at the time.

In Phase 2, *treatment of traumatic memories*, the patient has gained a sufficient mental level to consciously synthesize and realize traumatic memories. The patient may reenact traumatic relationships before he or she can fully realize them, and this will be played out with the therapist. Various parts of the personality have fixed perception–motor action cycles through which they repeat rigid attachment paradigms from the unintegrated past. Thus, the therapist will alternately be placed by the patient in the role of the neglectful parent, the sadistic abuser, the idealized rescuer, and the seducer (Courtois, 1999; J.M. Davies & Frawley, 1994). Second, reflexive beliefs about being bad, shameful, or dirty that are related to abuse and neglect, may intensify the patient's fears that the therapist will reject, criticize, or abandon him or her. Finally, the patient already has a phobia of mental actions and of traumatic memories, and will experience desperate yearning and clinging to the therapist in at least some parts of the personality, hoping to be rescued from overwhelming affects and conflicts. Much work in Phase 2 is directed toward the resolution of attachment phobias as they relate to traumatic memories.

In the third phase of treatment, *personality integration and rehabilitation*, attachment issues continue but less intensely. A degree of secure attachment with the therapist now supports the patient in more exploration and risk taking in normal daily life, and in intimate relationships with others. The fear of abandonment may reemerge with the possibility of termination, and this must be explored and resolved.

PHOBIA OF INITIAL CONTACT
WITH THE THERAPIST

Long before attachment develops, the very action of being in contact with the therapist during initial sessions can evoke disturbing sensations and affects, various dissociative parts, and traumatic memories. In other words, initial contact with the therapist can activate not only phobias of attachment, but also of trauma-derived mental actions, dissociative parts, traumatic memories, and change. In fact, the act of engaging in attachment implies the mental actions of emotions and bodily sensations, of which survivors are so often phobic. Even though survivors come for help with specific problems, they sometimes sense or hear internal cautions or threats not to talk or engage with the therapist, and are inhibited by shame, guilt, fear, or an inability to put their experiences to words. They may fear breakdown of what they experience as a tenuous hold on functioning (Parson, 1998). They may also come with inaccurate beliefs about what therapy entails, particularly trauma therapy.

The therapist should make initial attempts to alleviate unspoken fears by noting that many people find it difficult to talk about themselves at first, that the patient is welcome to share at his or her pace, that therapy should not be overwhelming, that therapy is a collaborative effort. Ample opportunity for the patient to ask questions should be provided. The patient is encouraged to be aware of the present moment and to synthesize consciously and realize his or her current experiences in the sessions as much as possible. This includes awareness of attachment issues and conflicts. The therapist can communicate verbally and nonverbally that he or she will ensure clear boundaries and explain them, will be empathically attuned to relational and other phobias and problems, and understands that trust is a long process, not to be expected early in treatment. Discussion of dissociative parts is often too frightening in the beginning, but the therapist can already begin to address undue divisions and the activation of different action systems by saying something like this:

> As a whole person, you might have quite mixed feelings about being in therapy and sharing some things about yourself. It's not so unusual for a part of ourselves to want to share in order to get help and not feel so alone, while

another part would rather keep it to ourselves. I am confident that we will find ways at your own pace to listen to, respect, and begin to understand all aspects of you. And should you ever feel as though there is a kind of tug of war inside, it would be helpful if you could share that with me in your own way and your own time so we can find ways to understand and resolve it.

The therapist aims as much as possible to activate the patient's attachment system rather than the defense system, at levels that the patient can synthesize and realize. This can be supported by the therapist's attenuated affects and language, mirroring the patient in modulated fashion. Attachment work is done in systematic and hierarchical steps, based on the therapist's careful judgment, and on the patient's verbal and nonverbal feedback. This does not mean the therapist appeases the patient, but implies empathic attunement and patience, knowing that therapeutic change takes time.

ATTACHMENT AND THE THERAPIST

Attachment issues must be attended to consistently in every interaction with the patient, no matter how seemingly innocuous. In order to help the patient overcome the phobia of attachment and attachment loss, the therapist must realize the role of various dissociative parts in maintaining these phobias, and work to diminish their need to engage in substitute and defensive actions that serve to avoid attachment or abandonment in normal interactions. The therapist must maintain a high mental level to respond with high order action tendencies to reactions of the patient, because the most intense emotions can arise in regards to attachment and its loss, not only in the patient, but also in the therapist. There is nothing more powerful than the patient's attachment issues that challenge the therapist's mental level and pull for his or her engagement in substitute actions that are not therapeutic. It is the patient's phobia of attachment and abandonment, and his or her intense needs and yearnings that often evoke either excessive caretaking or defense in a therapist, leading to one of the two countertransference poles of enmeshment or distancing (Steele et al., 2001; J. P. Wilson & Lindy, 1994; J. P. Wilson & Thomas, 2004).

The therapist must fully realize that the patient is often reenacting traumatic attachment patterns not only with the therapist and significant others, but more importantly, internally among dissociative parts, each of which contributes to the maintenance of the reenactment rather than to its resolution (cf., Blizard, 2001, 2003). Unless the therapist helps the patient address and resolve these maladaptive internal relationships among dissociative parts, the phobia of attachment and attachment loss will not be resolved.

When the therapist's mental level is lowered in response to the on-slaught of the patient's needs, demands, and maladaptive actions, he or she is less able to symbolize and thus less able to realize that the patient's attachment behaviors are reenactments and defensive actions to be ad-dressed therapeutically. Also, the patient may project his or her disowned feelings and experiences onto the therapist, who should experience them without acting on them. But when the therapist's mental level is low, he or she can become overwhelmed by powerful affects (e.g., guilt, love, pity, rage, shame) and act on those feelings rather than on what the patient re-ally needs, which is a stable, consistent attachment figure that predictably helps the patient integrate conflicted parts of him or herself. The thera-pist then attempts to avoid or resolve his or her own intense feelings through substitute actions rather than remaining focused on the patient's actual, rather than perceived needs.

Whether through projective identification, genuine frustration, or unre-solved personal issues, the therapist may engage in defensive actions— becoming angry and shamed, and lashing out or distancing him- or herself from the patient; making cold interpretations about the patient's "pathol-ogy"; becoming passive aggressive; or engaging in outright aggression. The therapist who is guilt ridden and too sad (unable to tolerate the patient's pain), may engage in too much caretaking and violate therapeutic bound-aries. It is the therapist's ability to avoid unnecessary reenactments and to realize ones that have occurred that will support the ongoing realization of the patient and his or her ability to create a symbolic narrative rather than continue to engage in substitute actions in relationships.

PHOBIA OF ATTACHMENT AND ATTACHMENT LOSS WITH THE THERAPIST

The part of the patient that functions in daily life (ANP) is the part of sur-vivors that initially interacts directly with the therapist in most cases, re-gardless of the diagnostic category. Some survivors as ANP are avoidant of attachment, while others are not. But regardless of the attachment style of ANP, other parts may experience the therapist as a potential caretaker and will strive to prevent attachment loss, while defensive parts will fear and avoid the therapist. Thus begins the approach–avoidance struggle in the therapeutic relationship so common for survivors. *It is crucial that the therapist seeks a degree of optimal relational closeness and distance so the patient's approach–avoidance conflict is contained within his or her tolerance level (i.e., the current mental level).* Thus, the therapist should always hold in mind the need for balance in interventions such that neither the phobia of attachment nor of attachment loss is intention-ally evoked too strongly.

Initial interventions are directed primarily toward the survivor's functioning in daily life (i.e., toward ANPs). Within a skills-building approach, the first interventions involve psychoeducation about the therapeutic relationship, attachment, dependency, and autonomy (cf. Chapter 12). It may be helpful to talk "through" ANP to EPs beginning in the early phase of treatment. A common error is to assume that the experience of ANP in therapy is the patient's entire experience. Thus the therapist should phrase words in such a way that all parts can feel heard and understood.

Empathic attunement is essential to prevent and resolve therapeutic impasses. This is not only a necessary response to the survivor's suffering as a result of trauma, but also a response to any perceived attachment disruptions between therapist and patient. The therapist empathizes with the patient's *experience* of the disruption without being defensive, regardless of whether the patient is misperceiving the reality of what happened. The relational repair is in the attunement to the patient's experience, and in relating it to possible historical origins, not in "fixing" or defending what happened. Only *after* this repair has been achieved can the therapist help the patient correct any inaccurate beliefs or perceptions.

The consistency and predictability of the therapist are essential in reducing the phobia of attachment and attachment loss, and also in supporting the patient's growing mental efficiency. Although constant availability is neither possible nor helpful, *predictable availability* is highly recommended (Gunderson, 1996). The patient should have a clear understanding of the extent and limitations of outside contacts such as crisis telephone calls with the therapist, and have access to crisis support in the event of the therapist's absence.

Overcoming the Phobia of Attachment

Survivors, or dissociative parts who are phobic of attachment tend to maximize actions that prevent or disrupt relationships. They inhibit affects related to attachment and its disruption (Slade, 1999). They have learned to associate attachment with physical or emotional pain, harsh rejection or criticism, unfulfilled needs, and traumatic memories. They may find dependency repulsive and "childish," and are particularly avoidant of EPs that have attachment needs, especially ones that experience themselves as needy children or infants. In particular, EPs that are modeled on the abuser despise and are ashamed of these parts, and punish them relentlessly in a reenactment of traumatic attachment patterns. Some parts are so avoidant of attachment and fixed in other action systems that they completely deny any feelings or need for connection: "I only work; relationships are a waste of valuable time." Table 13.1 lists some basic interventions to overcome the phobia of attachment.

TABLE 13.1

Interventions to Overcome the Phobia of Attachment

- Do not overly encourage attachment, but rather stay predictably (not constantly) available
- It is essential to remain consistent and predictable, as attachment phobic patients may not appear to have negative reactions to the therapist's lateness or inconsistencies. This may encourage the therapist to be lax, which further promotes phobia of attachment
- Gently approach talking about the therapeutic relationship with all parts
- Recognize and challenge reflexive beliefs about attachment (e.g., "Everyone is out to get something"; "Getting close always hurts"; "Dependency is for babies").
- Recognize negative evaluative conditioning that makes the patient fear rejection or criticism: ("I am bad and worthless"; "I am shameful"; "I am a slut").
- Initially engage avoidant parts within the range of their action systems (e.g., work) and gradually support their awareness of and engagement with other parts that are more amenable to attachment
- Explore the patient's difficulties with attachment related affects: love, hate, shame, etc.
- Avoid expressions of caring that are too intense with abandonment phobic parts, as this can evoke attachment phobic parts to engage in defense
- Gradually help the patient as a whole discuss fears of attachment (rejection, feelings of need, etc.)
- Do not offer extra contact or transitional objects unless the patient asks, but let the patient know these are available if requested and helpful
- Talk about perceived advantages of minimal attachment (empathize with the resistance), and gradually lead in to the difficulties (e.g., loneliness, lack of support).

In the following vignette involving a patient and his therapist, the phobia of attachment predominates, but it becomes obvious that the phobia of attachment loss is also at play. Ray, a patient with complex PTSD who rarely phoned the therapist, made a legitimate urgent call between sessions, but the therapist was unable to return it for some hours. In session Ray apologized profusely for calling while also appearing angry. He experienced that the therapist was angry with him. Ray was encouraged to share his feelings with the therapist, who then helped him explore further his attachment issues:

Therapist: So, you feel hurt and angry that I didn't return your call right away because you believed I was mad at you. I'm very sorry if I gave you that impression and would like to talk with you about it [*Empathic attunement and repair; encourages presentification by staying in the here and now; avoids engaging in defensive explanations, but instead promotes attachment and exploration*].

Ray: Yeah, well, it's no big deal [*avoids feelings and attachment*]. It's just that I know you hate it when I call you, so you must have been mad [*reflexive belief; traumatic reenactment; inability to mentalize; projection*]).

Therapist: What leads you to believe that? [*gradual approach to reflexive belief; attempts to understand maladaptive perception–motor action cycles*].

Ray: Well, you sounded grumpy [*synthesis of perceptions from a defensive perspective*].

Therapist: I am aware that I was tired when I returned your call. I wonder if that contributed to me sounding "grumpy?" [*validation that patient did in fact notice something different*]. I wasn't aware of feeling so, but I can see how you might have heard something in my voice that was disconcerting and that evoked a painful experience for you [*empathic attunement*]. Then you felt angry and hurt and wanted to withdraw [*acknowledges the complete perception–motor cycle which supports realization; recognizes the patient's current experience*].

Ray: Yeah. Maybe. But I'm just such a sniveling brat, always whining [*reflexive beliefs and negative evaluative conditioning*]. Everybody hates that [*undue generalization*]. I feel ashamed that I even called [*shame reinforces avoidance of need for contact and inhibits other affect; indicates phobia of mental actions, i.e., needs and wishes for care*].

Therapist: Those are harsh words about yourself. Perhaps we might be able to see what is under those beliefs [*engages the patient on a higher, more reflective level of action by activation of the exploration action system; recognizes the interplay between phobia of attachment and attachment loss*]. I wonder if you have heard those words before? [*encourages synthesis and realization between the past and the present*].

Ray: Yeah, my father used to say that about all of us, and sometimes I hear it in my head almost likes he's here [*engages in some degree of realization; hints at the possibility of a persectory dissociative part of the personality that is engaged in defense*].

Therapist: So your father wasn't able to understand that you must have needed something and were trying really hard to ask for help with it. It's so painful and overwhelming for a child when a parent does not recognize his legitimate needs and punishes him for having them [*empathic attunement and initial steps toward helping the patient mentalize that the father had his own limitations that were not the fault of the child; provides psychoeducation that needs are normal and acceptable*].

Ray: Yeah. I think it must have been pretty bad [*language indicates lack of personification*].

Therapist: Perhaps what you felt with me about the phone call is a small taste of what it might have been like then? [*encourages more realization, including personification, and links (binds) the present with the past in the patient's experience*].

Ray: Yes! (crying). But all I hear inside is that I'm just a crybaby! [*activation of dissociative part engaged in defense against painful affects and connection with the therapist*].

Therapist: Well, I can imagine that part of you inside doesn't yet fully understand and is trying to keep you safe because it wasn't very safe for you to have needs or cry as a child [*enhancement of presentification*]. Perhaps that part is angry and rejecting, just as you experienced I was. I hope that part is listening now, because you and I can certainly understand that it is natural for all of us to reach out when we are scared or in pain. Even though it wasn't safe for you as a child, it can be safe now [*acknowledges and engages with the dissociative part indirectly by "talking through"; encourages more reflection; hints at the projection that must be realized by the patient eventually; understands that dissociative parts operate at different levels of action tendencies and from different perspectives based on their respective action systems (defense vs. attachment); offers psychoeducation that counters maladaptive defense and activates attachment; supports differentiation between then and now; i.e., an accurate account of current reality and accurate context evaluation; encourages interaction among parts, which promotes more adaptive synthesis and realization for the patient as a whole*].

> *Ray*:   I still feel miserable, but better in a strange way. You kind of get it (smiling a little). [*Patient's mental level is raised: He can tolerate his feelings, is present, and connected with the therapist. Repair has been successful.*]
>
> *Therapist*:   Well, you really *are* suffering, and it helps to share and understand that suffering. It's sad that you learned to be so fearful of reaching out to others. Yet you are taking the risk to share with me right now. What is that like? [*continues to reinforce presentification and foster secure attachment*].
>
> *Ray*:   OK so far. It feels kind of good, like you understand, you know? Hey, I think *I'm* getting it, too [*increasing realization, including personification; mental level has been raised*].

Overcoming the Phobia of Attachment Loss

Survivors, or dissociative parts who are phobic of being abandoned attempt to maximize actions that pull for attachment and also for dependency. Because attachment cry involves panic, they will exhibit an excessive focus on internal distress states, with frantic pursuit of relief, and tend toward enmeshed and intense relationships (Slade, 1999). They are preoccupied with the literal availability of the therapist, being greatly upset by planned or unplanned absences. They are attuned to every nuance of the therapist's actions, often misperceiving them as rejecting or critical or a sign of imminent abandonment. In other words, they have reflexive predictions that the therapist will indeed leave them, and persecutory or protector EPs may give internal threats about being abandoned, which only serves to heighten their desperation. Attempts to enlist care, support, and reassurance from the therapist are ongoing and sometimes relentless, and may include many substitute actions, such as self-harm, urgent phone calls, or requests for ever more contact.

So long as traumatic attachment patterns continue to be reenacted by dissociative parts, no amount of contact with the therapist will suffice, and interventions to calm and reassure attachment cry parts will only be temporarily effective. *When a patient begins manifesting intense phobia of attachment loss, the therapist must immediately work not only with those parts fearful of rejection and abandonment, but also with those parts that eschew attachment and seek to interfere internally with the therapeutic relationship.* Thus, the patient is supported in developing an adaptive dependency that has a specific goal of *felt security* rather than constant availability of the therapist (Steele et al., 2001). Certain therapeutic limits and boundaries are necessary to prevent maladaptive dependency that unduly focus on attachment cry EPs at the expense of functioning in daily life (Steele et al., 2001). The patient must learn not only to rely on the therapist, but to depend on more functional parts of him- or herself. Thus ANPs and more adaptive EPs are strongly encouraged to respond empathically to needy EPs: That work does not belong to the therapist alone. Again, the internal reenactment of traumatic relationships must be resolved among dissociative parts, which takes the active involvement of all parts of the personality.

Maladaptive dependency needs can be overwhelming and evoke ever more frantic efforts at relief, resulting in a spiraling cycle of dependency, desperation, and helplessness. This spiral leads the patient to engage in substitute actions that are low in the hierarchy of action tendencies, such as self-harm or serious boundary violations directed toward the therapist or significant others. In these cases, the more the therapist encourages dependency and allows the substitute actions to continue, the more the patient becomes regressively dependent. Thus the therapist must find a balance between accepting dependency needs and yearnings and meeting what is necessary for secure attachment, and helping the patient contain those needs within the tolerance of both patient *and* therapist (i.e., within their mental level). *It is essential to ensure that the patient as a whole is exposed to small, graduated degrees of affect along with the therapeutic relationship*. Affect regulation is a major key to successfully overcoming the phobia of attachment loss, as shame, rage, and panic are often driving the phobia. The therapist often makes the mistake of deepening the attachment without simultaneously increasing the patient's affect regulation skills. The patient must have some small degree of realization that the therapist cannot possibly meet all his or her attachment needs. Table 13.2 lists some basic interventions to overcome the phobia of attachment loss within the tolerance of the patient.

In the following vignette about overcoming the phobia of attachment loss, Rita, a patient with DID, struggles with her fears of abandonment after sharing something shameful with the therapist.

> *Rita*: (switching to childlike EP) You gonna leave me? I know I'm so bad! [*For the patient, sharing something shameful is a conditioned stimulus for rejection that manifests in reflexive belief. The conditioned stimulus reactivates abandonment panic. In other words, the patient's perception–motor action cycle includes the prediction that telling something shameful will cause abandonment.*]
>
> *Therapist*: What just happened with that other part of you? [*Before addressing the panic, the therapist helps the patient focus on switching as a response to the panic.*]
>
> *Rita*: Dunno. You want me to go away cause I be bad? (crying, mumbling) [*Increasingly "young" behavior has a goal of en-*

TABLE 13.2

Interventions to Overcome the Phobia of Attachment Loss

- Predictable rather than constant availability is the key to secure attachment
- Begin and end sessions on time, and have the same appointment time each week
- Extra contact and sessions should be given with careful consideration to what the patient as a whole needs and can tolerate. More is not necessarily better, but neither is less
- Discuss the limitations of consistency and predictability, meaning limits on availability and the fact that therapists make human mistakes
- Explain your typical patterns of being in and out of the office
- Put up a notice board that lists planned absences well in advance
- Provide a backup therapist for absences, if needed
- Describe what will happen if you or the patient is late or misses a session
- Discuss patient's fears of being abandoned without offering unrealistic reassurance, e.g., do *not* promise to "always be there," or "never leave"
- Do promise that if you should need to leave your practice for an unforseen reason, you would give as much notice as possible and help the patient find a new therapist
- Recognize the role of persecutor and protector parts in maintaining an internal environment of rejection and criticism, "You're such a crybaby, no wonder that stupid therapist hates you!" (negative evaluative conditioning)
- Do not pretend, assume, or believe that you can "make up" for the attachment losses the patient has suffered
- Comfort can be helpful, but is not an end in itself, and does not mitigate severe loss; comfort should have a goal of raising the patient's mental level and ability to engage in more adaptive behaviors
- Sitting with hopelessness and despair is a very necessary part of the process.
- The therapist must tolerate, and help patients tolerate what they believe they cannot tolerate, although at their own pace ("If I show my deepest pain, you will run")
- Explore, challenge, and test reflexive beliefs regarding dependency, autonomy, and independency
- Clear guidelines for emergency calls should be discussed and set
- Return phone calls predictably without reinforcing calls as a way to have contact
- Phone calls should be limited in scope to grounding, orienting, safety, and helping parts to engage adaptively with each other in the crisis

(continued)

TABLE 13.2
(Continued)

- Extra phone calls should be time-limited, to be used for occasional crisis, not as regular and ongoing support, because in the majority of patients that will evoke uncontained dependency
- Content of urgent phone calls as well as session content should be processed to determine if attachment issues were an underlying source. If so, this should be discussed during the session while the patient is in direct contact with the therapist
- Help patients learn to symbolize, preferably verbalize, feelings rather than act them out
- Maintain therapeutic boundaries
- Be aware that various parts will have different needs and fixed perception–motor action cycles regarding attachment (loss) issues, and communicate this awareness with the patient in such a way that synthesis and realization are enhanced.

> *listing greater caretaking behaviors from the therapist, i.e., a hope for stress reduction—negative reinforcement—through acceptance and consolation by the therapist. This "young" behavior can serve as a substitute comfort which can prevent resolution of inner conflict. The lapse into "young" language indicates a drop to lower levels of action tendencies; the patient also invites the therapist to reassure her that she is not bad, avoiding realization of her own internal negative evaluative conditioning.*]

Therapist: I wonder if that part can be with you now, along with as many other parts as possible? Then you can all have a sense of being here so we can talk about this very important topic. You don't want me to leave, but as long as parts of you are not very present for this conversation you may continue to have a sense that I am not really here for you [*Encourages internal communication and cooperation, which will raise the mental level and a greater level of personification and presentification; focuses first on resolving avoidance of other parts prior to helping the patient begin to resolve her fear of abandonment and sense of being bad.*].

Rita: But don't you like me? [*continues to avoid dealing with other parts, and continues to pull for the therapist to reassure her, externalizing the conflict*]

Therapist: I like all of you, as a whole person. That's why it's important that all parts be here, if they can, because I am concerned that perhaps you don't like yourself, that you believe I would leave you because *you* believe you are bad inside. Does that fit? [*responds genuinely, but keeps the focus on the patient's reflexive evaluation of herself*]

Rita: Yeah, it sure does. Will you promise not to leave me? I'll be good, I promise! [*Again avoids the internal conflict. She is fixed in a conditioned attachment cry and submissive behaviors.*]

Therapist: It's completely understandable that you don't want me to leave, and I have no plans to do so, nor should you feel you have to please me to keep me here. We have an agreement to work together that we both honor. My comings and goings have nothing to do with how I feel about you. Would it be all right if we found out more about that fear you have of me leaving because you are bad?

Rita: Yeah, we mostly believe we are very bad and we told you something so bad so that now you will hate us. Everybody leaves me [*overgeneralization*]. They make fun of me 'cause I am so bad. That's just who I am. [*reveals reflexive beliefs; very limited personification and presentification; shame*]

Therapist: Those are painful experiences. And what is your experience with me now? [*empathic attunement; encourages presentification; activates exploration and attachment by reducing the attachment cry defense (not by rescuing, but by modulation), i.e., higher level action tendencies*]

Rita: It's OK, I guess. I'm not so afraid. It's more quiet inside.

Therapist: Good. Is it all right then that we continue to talk about this with all parts present and with us connected like this? [*encourages internal communication and cooperation; ensures work is within the patient's integrative capacity; returns to the patient's struggle*].

SUMMARY

The phobias of attachment and attachment loss are pervasive in survivors of chronic traumatization and manifest in the therapy relationship through all phases of treatment. Overcoming these phobias is essential for further therapeutic gains, as attachment is the matrix in which all therapy takes place. The patient is supported to develop a secure attachment with the therapist through predictable rather than constant availability.

This attachment supports ongoing synthesis and realization (integration), and thus, it raises the mental level. However, the patient and therapist will find attachment very difficult because of the patient's learned asssoci-ations between attachment and (emotional and physical) pain, and due to fixed perception–motor action cycles related to attachment. Survivors, or dissociative parts who are phobic of attachment, engage in actions that prevent or disrupt relationships, while those that are phobic of attach-ment *loss* engage in actions to prevent rejection or abandonment. The phobias of attachment and of attachment loss are inextricably inter-twined, with one affecting the other. However, these respective phobias can each evoke different action systems and affects as they involve differ-ent parts of the personality. Thus, the therapist must be highly attuned to recognizing and working with dissociative parts. Patients generally have an initial phobia of contact with the therapist, which can be understood as avoidance of not only attachment, but of mental actions, particularly traumatic memories. A lowering of the therapist's mental level in response to the patient's intensity will result in enmeshing or distancing counter-transference (i.e., lower order substitute actions). The therapist must bal-ance interventions such that neither the phobia of attachment nor of at-tachment loss is intentionally evoked too strongly for various parts of the personality. Specific interventions designed to assist the patient in over-coming these relational phobias were discussed. The phobias of attach-ment and attachment loss are intimately connected to other phobias of mental actions, of dissociative parts, of traumatic memories, and of change.

CHAPTER 14

Phase 1 Treatment and Beyond

Overcoming the Phobia of Trauma-Derived Mental Actions

I was unable to explain to anybody why I was so tied up, walled off and out of touch with my feelings. . . . To be in touch with my feelings would have meant opening Pandora's box.
—Marilyn Van Derbur (2004, p. 98)

MENTAL ACTIONS, WHAT WE FEEL, think, wish, need, sense, play an essential role in adaptive functioning, and thus in supporting our highest mental level. Whether or not we will be guided adaptively by our mental actions is predicated upon our capacity to perceive them accurately, to own (personify) them, and to give them a proper place in reality by understanding that they are internal experiences that may not necessarily call for behavioral action. Fear can help us stay safe, and love can keep us connected even when there is conflict in a relationship. Wishes encourage us to choose the goals on which we focus our energy. Thoughts assign meaning and understanding, which help us adapt to life more effectively. Body sensations help us recognize our emotions, signal whether we are sick or well, help determine how we move and act, and are related to our body image for better or worse. When survivors persistently avoid or strongly inhibit any of these mental actions, they eliminate an essential source of information that could help them integrate and live their lives more effectively and with greater meaning. As we noted before, survivors do so especially with regard to the mental actions they have associated with traumatic memories. Hence, we say that they have a *phobia of trauma-derived mental actions*.

The failure to synthesize and realize trauma-derived mental actions is a major factor in maintaining structural dissociation and in preventing presentification. A central focus of therapy is for survivors to overcome their phobias of inner trauma-derived feelings, thoughts, wishes, fantasies, needs, sensations, and memories. In fact, psychodynamic conflicts and cognitive distortions can be understood in terms of these phobias (cf., McCullough et al., 2003). Patients develop a range of physical, social, and mental actions to avoid or escape certain trauma-related mental actions, and have substitute beliefs that perpetuate this avoidance (e.g., "Feelings are bad"; "My body is disgusting"; "I'll never stop feeling despair if I start to cry").

Mental actions are not completely separate from each other, but are inextricably linked together in perception–motor action cycles that are geared toward particular goals and action tendencies. Therefore, the therapist should be aware that what has been called a *phobia of affect* (McCullough, 1991; McCoullough et al., 2003) also involves avoidance and inhibition of related trauma-derived mental actions. Our emphasis on the phobia of affect in this chapter is based upon the fact that other mental actions such as perceptions, goals, evaluations, cognitions, and physical sensations are inherent in our emotions, at least to some degree. This phobia of mental actions has also been called *experiential avoidance* (Hayes, Wilson, Gifford, Folette, & Strohsahl, 1996, p. 1154). The phobia of mental actions is, or course, also directly related to the phobia of trauma-derived behavioral actions (also discussed in Chapter 10), which is the focus of many manuals on the treatment of phobias and thus receives less attention here.

The phobia of trauma-derived mental actions is a generalized form of the specific phobias of traumatic memories and dissociative parts. It is essential for the therapist to be aware of the potential for conflicted mental actions within different parts of the personality to create serious internal distress and ambivalent behavior for the survivor. Treatment begins with the therapist making a systematic analysis of the patient's mental actions that are tolerated or avoided; of the defenses various parts engage in to avoid realization of certain mental actions; factors that maintain the phobia of mental actions such as maladaptive beliefs and affect dysregulation; and the reasons the patient has become phobic of mental actions.

WORKING WITH TRAUMA-DERIVED MENTAL ACTIONS THROUGHOUT PHASES OF TREATMENT

The phobia of trauma-derived mental actions is primarily addressed in the first phase of treatment because it is the sine qua non necessary to address dissociative parts and traumatic memories. A common mistake is for the therapist to attempt to proceed with painful work involved in the treatment of traumatic memories (Phase 2) before the patient has learned to understand, regulate, and tolerate strong emotions and other mental actions (cf., Wald & Taylor, 2005). Two major interventions are simultaneously employed from early in treatment to help the patient overcome the phobia of trauma-derived mental actions. The first is use of the therapeutic relationship as a regulating factor (D. Brown, Scheflin, & Hammond, 1998), and the second is the patient's development of regulatory skills, which can be taught by the therapist or in skills training groups (see below). *Prior to beginning the second phase of treatment, the patient and at least major dissociative parts should be able to regulate and tolerate most trauma-derived mental actions.*

Phase 2 treatment, which focuses on the synthesis and realization of traumatic memories, requires the patient to withstand a degree of emotional intensity, although intensity should always be modulated within the patient's mental level if possible. The realization of traumatic experiences involves painful feelings, sensations, and cognitions, and integration can only occur if the patient and his or her various dissociative parts are not avoiding trauma-derived mental actions (see Chapter 15).

In the final phase of treatment, *rehabilitation and integration*, the emphasis is on helping patients learn to act in the world with maximal effectiveness. However, although many trauma-derived mental actions have become resolved, some remain for Phase 3; for example, the phobia of intimacy. In this phase, survivors learn how to live life with both positive and negative feelings, thoughts, and wishes; to tolerate conflict and ambivalence in life and relationships; to rely upon their mental actions as informative guides rather than as rigid dictators; and to experience their own inner worlds as natural and normal.

ANALYSIS OF THE PHOBIA OF
TRAUMA-DERIVED ACTIONS

It is useful for the therapist to engage in an analysis of the structure and functioning of the patient's personality as whole, and, more specifically, an analysis of the phobia of trauma-derived actions, to determine where resistances, defenses, and capacities to tolerate trauma-derived mental actions lie, and how various parts interact (or not) in relation to particular mental actions. Then parts that have higher mental levels can be further strengthened and encouraged to interact with and support parts that have lower mental energy and efficiency with regards to particular mental actions. For example, analysis of the structure and the functioning of the personality can reveal an ANP that has a relatively high mental level that can be enlisted to help an overwhelmed childlike EP through internal soothing and reassurance and information about the safe present. Dissociative parts that have lower mental levels can be supported temporarily with interventions of containment until their mental efficiency can be increased gradually.

As part of an analysis of the functioning of the patient's personality, the therapist should determine which dissociative parts of the personality are phobic of each other due to avoidance of particular trauma-derived mental actions that are experienced as shameful, disgusting, or fearful. Various dissociative parts are afraid to realize mental actions that belong to other dissociative parts, and have been conditioned to avoid them. Parts may avoid some feelings and sensations (e.g., anger and sexual arousal), but not others (e.g., sadness and physical pain). Some may avoid all feelings (e.g., emotionally numb or intellectualized observer parts) or sensations (e.g., parts that have no physical feeling or claim to be dead).

The therapist can miss the fact that the patient has dissociated trauma-derived mental actions that need attention if he or she takes the patient's statements about a potentially conflicted issue as without ambivalence. Strong conflicts can be present without the awareness of the part of the patient that presents to the therapist. For example, Deborah, a patient with DDNOS, denied suicidal ideation as ANP. But the therapist also accessed a part of her that was not only severely despairing, but had a plan for suicide in which she would drown herself in her bath.

Substitute Beliefs and Maladaptive Cognitions

A functional analysis of the patient's personality will also reveal particular substitute beliefs and cognitions that maintain resistances to trauma-derived mental actions. Patients have learned by association that having feelings or other mental actions is something harmful. For instance, patients learn to be phobic of mental actions because they never had sufficient social support to improve mental efficiency enough to explore, express, and regulate their overwhelming inner experiences. Some survivors had the experience of being punished or physically hurt if they expressed particular feelings as children. They thus learn, "*If* I express my feelings, *then* I will be hit," and subsequently engage in physical defense strategies when particular feelings emerge that have become a conditioned stimulus for physical abuse. A survivor might involuntarily cringe and expect the therapist to lash out and literally hit when he or she feels needy, or a fight part might threaten a therapist who is perceived as evoking painful feelings. A survivor also learns to be ashamed of particular inner experiences because he or she has been rejected or ridiculed by others for expressing them (Gilbert, 2000): "*If* I cry, *then* people will laugh at me and call me a crybaby." Thus they avoid certain mental actions that are conditioned stimuli for rejection in order to maintain attachments and social positions. Patients fixed in lower levels of action tendencies may have maladaptive beliefs that are very simplistic and literal: "If I feel angry, then I am just like my sadistic father who was angry." A goal of therapy would be to help such a patient reach a higher mental level that allows a different belief: "I can be angry constructively, and I am a different person from my father in my feelings and behavior." Early treatment focuses on identifying these reflexive beliefs that may have been adaptive at one time, but are now not useful to the patient. The therapist can then challenge these beliefs by encouraging the patient to gradually experiment to test these beliefs in session, and later, outside session.

Inhibition and Activation of Trauma-Derived Mental Actions

As part of a functional analysis of the personality, the therapist can determine which dissociative parts inhibit trauma-derived mental actions, and how, and which parts are fixed in vehement emotions. The phobia of trauma-derived mental actions may be expressed along a spectrum of avoidance. Some dissociative parts strongly *inhibit* affect: Many ANPs inhibit their mental contents at least to some degree. They are numb, depersonalized, and avoidant of conflicted, painful, or very pleasurable feelings and sensations. They tend to avoid intensity and conflict in relationships in order to limit activation of strong feelings.

However, for many patients or particular dissociative parts the problem is that the experience of certain mental actions is too intense. This is commonly seen in EPs. At first glance, survivors who feel intensely do not appear to be phobic of affects, but rather overly focused on and affected by them. But in fact, they are phobic of *adaptive* feelings and chronically experience chaotic, vehement emotions that are beyond their mental level to integrate and which can serve as defenses against adaptive feelings. Some parts tend to be fixed in vehement emotions such as rage, terror, or panic, and are easily activated to an extreme degree in response to the vicissitudes of daily life.

Survivors or various dissociative parts can be distressed easily and their emotional turmoil creates frequent disruptions in their lives and in therapy. Although expression of adaptive feelings is helpful, the expression of vehement emotivity is actually harmful, because it is overwhelming to the patient and is a manifestation of a severe imbalance between mental energy and efficiency (i.e., too much mental energy and insufficient mental efficiency). Thus, catharsis is contraindicated for vehement emotions.

Whether the patient (or dissociative part) is inhibiting affect in general or experiencing overwhelming emotivity, the treatment is to increase the mental level and have sufficient balance between mental energy and efficiency so that he or she can be gradually exposed to adaptive feelings, which can be synthesized and realized. For those with vehement emotion, early interventions include physiological regulation, such as grounding and breathing exercises, and cognitive techniques that support reflective awareness of and thinking about inner experiences (i.e., development of a theory of mind).

Avoidance of Positive Mental Actions

Analysis of the phobia of trauma-derived mental actions is not only focused on how and why the patient avoids both negative and positive mental actions. Some mental actions are pleasantly intense, such as joy, sexual feelings, or excitement, and certain fantasies and beliefs. These experiences normally activate adaptive feelings. However, many chronically traumatized individuals have substitute beliefs about not deserving to feel good or have good things happen, or have experienced that something bad always follows something good. They have become strongly sensitized to feelings and sensations, and tend to react more strongly to them than the average person. They find the line blurred between pleasurable excitement and traumatic hyperarousal, and also may associate guilt or shame with pleasure (Migdow, 2003; Ogden, Minton, & Pain, 2006).

The Patient's Experience of Trauma-Derived Mental Actions

Finally, analysis of trauma-derived mental actions helps therapist and patient understand the patient's *experience* of mental actions because this helps both of them to know whether emotion is adaptive or is too intense or insufficient for the patient's current mental level. Both patient and therapist may mistake vehement emotion for adaptive feeling if the patient's experience is not thoroughly explored. The therapist might ask, "What is it like for you when you feel angry?" "What do you experience in your body right now?" "How do other parts experience this anger?" "What are you thinking as you feel this anger?" If the patient is unable to focus on his or her internal experience and verbalize it, or describes it as overwhelming (e.g., "a tornado"; "a monster tearing at me to get out and kill"), he or she is likely to be experiencing overwhelming emotion and should be helped to decrease it. The therapist should thus be aware that the patient's expression of intense emotion (catharsis) may not necessarily be therapeutic.

TECHNIQUES FOR OVERCOMING THE PHOBIA OF TRAUMA-DERIVED MENTAL ACTIONS

Although analysis is ongoing, once the therapist has general overview of the patient's defenses and dissociative parts, work can begin on overcoming the phobia of trauma-derived mental actions. Psychoeducation and skills building are central to the resolution of this phobia. The therapist must have a thorough understanding of the differences between vehement emotion and adaptive feeling, so the former can be transformed into the latter. The therapist should also be alert to hidden mental actions of which the patient is ashamed, such as particular feelings, beliefs, or fantasies.

Psychoeducation and Skills Training

Psychoeducation regarding the function of trauma-derived mental actions and their degree of reality must be constantly reinforced. The patient should understand that his or her feelings, thoughts, or wishes are designed to help with functioning in the world, and have an impact on behavior and relationships. Many patients cannot tell the difference between feeling and behavior. For example, if they feel angry, they fear they will act in uncontrollable rage, thereby increasing aversion to angry feelings, wishes, and fantasies (see Chapter 8). The therapist must reinforce that mental actions do not necessarily end with behavioral actions, and help the patient understand by providing examples from the patient's life. Then patients begin more reflective thinking in lieu of impulsive action. More particularly, the therapist should help the patient develop a theory of mind (Fonagy, 1997) by constantly drawing the patient's attention to his or her inner experience in the moment, labeling it, and encouraging the patient to observe and understand it. Role play with the therapist is a particularly effective tool for some patients to learn how to behave differently and be aware of their inner experience, so long as all dissociative parts are aware that role play is not actual reality.

It cannot be emphasized enough that chronically traumatized individuals need specific training in regulatory and relational skills that will raise their mental level to better support management of mental actions, particularly emotions. There are many structured skills models available (Cloitre, Koenen, Cohen, & Han, 2002; Donovan, Padin-Rivera, & Kowaliw, 2001; Fallot & Harris, 2002; Ford & Russo, in press; Fosha, 2000, 2001; Linehan, 1993; Najavits, 2002; Rosenberg et al., 2001; Spiegel, Classen, Thurston, & Butler, 2004). The patient must practice these skills regularly in session and out, first with the minor feelings encountered in everyday life such as irritation, frustration, and dislike, and only later with more intense affects such as rage and shame.

Use of Symbolism

The use of metaphors and similes can help the patient begin to recognize, verbalize, and regulate mental contents, but many patients are not operating at a sufficiently high level of action tendencies to use symbolic language, and will explain their experience more concretely. For example, one patient might describe a physical sensation in the stomach as, "like a churning cauldron," indicating the ability to symbolize. Another may describe the sensation as, "that is where my mother [her abuser] lives," indicating a lack of symbolic ability and operation at a much lower level of action tendencies. When the patient is able, the therapist can continue metaphors toward more realization and a broader theory of mind by asking questions—using the patient's language—such as, "What is churning in the cauldron?" "What keeps the cauldron churning?" "Is there something that could calm the churning?" "If the churning could speak, what would it say?" The therapist could also employ guided imagery in such cases (Van der Hart, 1985; Witztum, Van der Hart, & Friedman, 1988). The therapist should be careful to avoid symbolism with patients who cannot yet use it. Instead they may be offered reality testing and clarification of what they mean: "Does your real mother actually live in your stomach?"

Focusing on Physical Sensations

Physical sensations and movements are a rich source of information about mental actions and patients' fears about their own thoughts and feelings (Ogden et al., 2006). The therapist and patient's awareness of mental actions can be facilitated partially through sensorimotor aspects of experience. Physical sensations and movements accompany feelings and thoughts: They are an inherent part of perception–motor action cycles beginning with the lowest levels of action tendencies. For example, a scared patient might feel her heart beat rapidly and have a dry mouth, hold her body rigidly, and scan the room with her eyes. The patient's attention can be drawn to his or her physical experience in the moment, notice where avoidance or inhibition tends to occur, and where activation is possible. The therapist can use his or her own observations of the patient's sensorimotor experience to guide the patient into more adaptive tolerance and regulation of mental actions (Ogden et al., 2006). For example, Rosemary, a patient with complex PTSD presented as an ANP that was phobic of anger, and the session content was focused on something that happened to Rosemary that would normally provoke anger.

Therapist: I notice your breathing is faster than it was just a moment ago. Are you aware of that?

Rosemary: I wasn't, but now I am.

Therapist: Just notice that and see what happens. [*Encourages presentification; does not yet direct the patient to make meaning of the experience, but rather only to observe. This builds tolerance of the sensations and related affects.*]

Rosemary: I feel I want to run away. [*defensive avoidance in the form of flight*]

Therapist: What is that feeling of wanting to run away like in your body right now? [*stays with the patient's experience of the mental actions without moving toward more cognition*]

Rosemary: My legs are shaky. I'm tense all over, like I could just jump up and go.

Therapist: Would it be all right to allow those sensations to continue for a moment without interrupting them? [*continues to support tolerance of mental actions without behavioral action; encourages completion of the sensations*]

Rosemary: Yeah, I guess so.

Therapist: And what do you notice?

Rosemary: I imagine running really fast, away from something.

Therapist: Running away fast from what?

Rosemary: Umm, feeling angry I think. When my legs stop shaking I feel kind of angry, like I could yell, "Get away from me!!" [*patient engages in adaptive feeling after completing the avoidant action of shaking in her legs that accompanies defensive flight*]

Extensive interventions regarding sensorimotor experiences with trauma survivors are delineated elsewhere (Ogden et al., 2006).

Working with a Phobia of Affect

One of the most essential interventions in treating the phobia of trauma-derived mental actions is to help the patient or dissociative parts stop persistent vehement emotivity and instead to experience adaptive feelings. Vehement emotions are not intense feelings, but are lower-order substitute actions that maintain the phobia of mental actions. They are overwhelming, reflexive, automatic, and often without language. They typically involve inaccurate perceptions of the present and catastrophic predictions of the future. There is no reflection by the patient on what he or she is experiencing; no theory of mind. Vehement emotions make a situation worse instead of better. On the other hand, adaptive feelings, even when intense, involve self-reflection by the patient about what he or she is experiencing and why; include relatively accurate perceptions and predictions based on the present; and involve much more control over immediate reactions. Adaptive feelings support relatively accurate narrative accounts of both internal and external experience.

There are several major affects that may spiral into vehement emotivity, which inhibits adaptive feelings in trauma survivors: shame, disgust, guilt, fear, panic, rage, and persistent emotional suffering based on hope-lessness and helplessness. *The first step in transforming vehement emotions into adaptive feelings is to interrupt the emotivity and not encourage its expression, which involves increasing mental efficiency* (cf. Chapter 12). Another early step is to refer the patient for psychotropic medications that will help to regulate the patient's physiology. In therapy, the therapist encourages the patient to slow down, to breathe, to be aware of his or her surroundings, to stay in relational contact. The patient is supported in sharing catastrophic predictions of what will happen, and is directed time and again toward his or her inner experience in the moment: "What are you experiencing right now?" Thus the therapist supports a higher mental level and higher action tendencies involving the ability to use language, and encourages presentification as much as possible. As the patient describes his or her inner experience, neither therapist nor patient should shift prematurely to cognitive interpretations. The patient should be taught to "savor" and reflect on current experience. Meaning making is effective only after the patient has learned to tolerate the experiences (e.g., feeling fear or anger, thinking about a problematic relationship, remembering horrible events) that their mental actions generate.

Survivors can be triggered easily into emotivity, and at times this takes the therapist by surprise. For example, a patient may become enraged at a seemingly innocuous statement by the therapist, who then has an inadequate and defensive reaction that is not therapeutic. In these cases it is essential to return to the issue in the next session when the patient and therapist may have higher mental levels, and ask what the patient would find helpful from the therapist the next time. This offers reattunement and repair to the relationship and provides a new prediction about what will happen if the patient becomes angry with the therapist. The therapist can also ask the patient to try something different the next time: "Let's talk about finding a way for you to let me know you are angry that doesn't involve shouting." In this way, a new script of perceptions, evaluations, and predictions can guide the behavior of the therapist and the patient.

Shame. Shame is an integral part of traumatization (Leskela, Dieperink, & Thuras, 2002) and is strongly related to dissociation (Irwin, 1998). The patient typically has few words to describe shame; it often produces reactive and automatic withdrawal, freezing, submissive behaviors, maladaptive actions related to self-hatred, and sometimes vigorous fight responses. Therapists often fail to attend actively to shame's prominent role in maintaining maladaptive actions. Virtually every publication on treatment of childhood abuse addresses the need to work with shame in the survivor as part of posttrauma therapy, yet little has been published about how to do so.

From the outset of therapy with trauma survivors, the therapist should be aware that shame is likely operating, even though the patient does not verbalize it. Often it emerges in the patient's projection of rejection onto the therapist, and his or her reactions to perceived rejection. Internal voices of dissociative parts may remind the patient of how shameful he or she is. The therapist should understand these internal messages are often immune to cognitive therapy alone and need to be countered with experiences in the therapeutic relationship and by dealing directly not only with shamed dissociative parts, but with shaming parts (i.e., protectors and persecutors). Internal empathy is encouraged among parts for each other and their respective mental and behavioral actions.

The therapist should not wait for shame to emerge in a verbal form, but learn where to expect it and be proactive in preventing it. For example, with sexually abused patients shame often is prominent if there was any kind of sexual arousal. Dissociative parts that might have engaged in sexual behavior are disowned by other parts with disgust and shame. Thus the therapist educates the patient early on that it is not uncommon for victims to feel sexual arousal during abuse and this is a normal and even unavoidable physiological process, just as when one automatically salivates when candy is put in one's mouth.

Shame is often not related to specific events or behaviors, but is more pervasive: "I am ashamed of existing"; "I am ashamed of who I am." This type of shame is slower to resolve, and requires persistent relational repair right up through the end of Phase 3 treatment. The therapist should not strongly negate the patient's experience of shame, but empathize and help the patient to verbalize and explore shame. The physical experience of shame often includes a sense of internal collapse, inhibition, shrinking, and hiding—sensations that are phenomenologically similar to those of freezing and submission. It is helpful for the therapist to help the patient become more aware of those sensations and shift them to more confident, self-revealing actions. The patient is often reluctant to reveal aspects of him- or herself out of fear of rejection. The therapist can help the patient with predictions by asking, "If you shared with me something that you were ashamed about, what do you imagine would happen?" "What do you imagine that would be like for you?"

Fear. Fear is similarly a common problem for survivors that often inhibits particular mental actions (e.g., sexual feelings, love, anger) and maintains the aversion many parts have for each other. It is a central factor in the maintenance of dissociation (see Chapter 10). In some cases, fear may be activating, such as producing a tendency to flee or fight. But in many cases with survivors, the fear is overly strong and hyperactivates behaviors and feelings that are inappropriate to the context. The treatment of fear, whether it activates inappropriate responses or inhibits adaptive ones is the same: Gradual exposure to the avoided adaptive mental actions, with regulation of anxiety, and prevention of avoidant mental actions.

Other vehement emotions. Although shame and fear are central to the development and maintenance of dissociation, other emotions may be vehement, such as guilt, rage, panic, confusion, pathological grieving, and manic excitement or joy. Again, treatment consists of slowing down the physiological hyperarousal of the patient, to ground him or her in the present, to encourage reflective thinking through, to prevent maladaptive behavioral actions, and to encourage presentification.

The following vignette illustrates interventions for a phobia of the mental action of sadness that is related to a phobia of one part for another. Betty is a patient with DID in the late stages of Phase 1 treatment, and she and her therapist are discussing something sad that happened in her life.

> *Betty*: I might start crying and never stop. It's scary. [*time distortion; misunderstanding of how feelings are part of complete cycles*]
>
> *Therapist*: That *would* be scary. Have you had that happen before? [*empathic attunement to the resistance; challenges patient's real experience*]
>
> *Betty*: No, not exactly. That's because I don't feel it. But that little kid inside cries all the time. [*attributes sadness to dissociative part; avoidance of adaptive feeling through numbness*]
>
> *Therapist*: Perhaps that young part of you that cries all the time because she never gets any relief, never gets to finish what she is feeling because she is stuck. [*empathic attunement with both ANP and EP; subtly reinforces greater personification by using language, i.e., "that part of you"; reinforces success in the past with dissociative parts; psychoeducation about the need to complete actions*]
>
> *Betty*: I guess so. I just know I don't like her and can't stand the crying. [*negative evaluative conditioning*]
>
> *Therapist*: What about it is hard to stand? [*assists patient to engage in reflection rather than automatic reaction*]
>
> *Betty*: I'm ashamed of such a crybaby and I don't like to feel sad. Well, I just won't go there. I'm an adult [*negative evaluative conditioning; shame as a defensive inhibitor of crying and feeling sad; cognitive overgeneralization: children cry; adults do not cry*]
>
> *Therapist*: Yes. Absolutely you are. But adults have feelings and needs, too. But adults who were fortunate to have good role mod-

els have learned to manage those feelings differently from children and to get their needs met in ways that are appropriate and effective. But since your parents didn't know a lot about how to deal with feelings, except to yell at you or forbid you to cry, you learned to cope with them by avoiding them and being afraid or ashamed of those feeings [*empathic attunement with defense; psychoeducation; offers the possibility of change*]

Betty: Yeah. I just think of feelings as bad. It just wasn't very safe to have them: I'd get hit everytime I cried. [*negative evaluative conditioning of feelings; operant conditioning: She was punished for having feelings; mental level is insufficient to support adaptive feelings*]

Therapist: Yes! It wasn't safe then, and there was a lot to feel bad about. Does it still feel that way to you? [*empathic attunement; encourages presentification by drawing patient's attention to here and now; begins to help patient differentiate the past from the present*]

Betty: Yeah. It does. Even though I know in my head that things are OK now. It doesn't *feel* that way. Those feelings pull me down, make me depressed, anxious. Then I don't want to do anything, go anywhere. [*lack of realization; conditioned response; reveals vehement emotivity drains her mental energy*]

Therapist: Well, it's important that we don't do things here that cause you to be unable to function. What is your experience right now, so we can make sure we are not doing something that is too much? If you were to put you level of distress on a scale of 1 to 10, where would it be right now? [*again reinforces pacing; encourages presentification by calling attention to current experience; offers intervention (subjective units of distress), that helps patient be reflective rather than reactive, thus raising the mental level*]

Betty: I'm OK. I guess about a 3. But I hear that crying inside, like it's far away. I guess that part of me is a 15 all the time. It makes me kind of sick. I just want to get out of here, talk about something else, sing a song loud in my head to make it go away. [*demonstrates that ANP and EP may have quite discrepant experiences; EP lacks presentification and realization; ANP wants to engage in avoidance and escape, but is able to verbalize rather than act, indicating a heightening of her mental level*]

Therapist: Well, one way to help you is to help that part feel less sad all the time and more calm, to know she could get help if she needed it. I bet we could do that. But I'm aware that you feel a lot of shame and fear in response to that part of you. I would guess that feeling ashamed and afraid is also painful, isn't it? [*stays with the patient's goal of "avoiding" sadness, but reframes it adaptively; empathic attunement; encourages reflection on the costs of maladaptive mental actions; shame and fear are inhibitory affects*]

Betty: Yeah. Gets to be too much sometimes. Then I just shut down and don't feel anything. I'm damned if I do, and damned if I don't, I guess. [*numbing is another maladaptive coping strategy*]

Therapist: Well, let's see if we can find a way out of that double bind. Let's notice together your inner experience as we are talking together now. Take some deep breaths and focus on what is happening inside right now, and stay in contact with me at the same time. [*empathic attunement with substitute belief paired with psychoeducation; understands that the patient does not have the mental level to experience painful feelings yet; encourages presentification; gives patient the opportunity to have inner experiences within a secure attachment.*]

Working with a phobia of thoughts. Survivors not only have many maladaptive cognitions and beliefs, but are sometimes afraid of their own thoughts, and attempt to avoid them. Generally this occurs because they assign too much reality to them, and subsequently fear they will act on what they think. Psychoeducation in this case, along with experimentation is helpful. Some patients complain of hearing "loud thoughts" or voices of which they are afraid. These, of course, are dissociative parts that internally verbalize thoughts. Treatment consists of helping patients accept the dissociative parts and their respective thoughts, and helps them realize that these are ultimately the patient's own thoughts.

Working with a phobia of needs. Patients are often severely afraid or ashamed of their yearning and human needs for contact and love, because these wishes and needs were never met adequately for them, and thus are disowned to prevent disappointment and feelings of rejection. Often some of the most difficult work in therapy is helping patients recognize, accept, and personify their own needs and learn to get them met appropriately. Treatment consists of psychoeducation about the basic needs of all humans (to rest, play, work, love and be loved, to receive care and support when appropriate, etc.) and gradual exposure of various parts of each other's needs.

Working with a phobia of wishes and fantasies. Like needs, wishes and fantasies are often shameful or fearful for traumatized individuals. Patients are generally reluctant to share what they wish for and fantasize about. Some patients have mistaken beliefs that if they wish or fantasize something bad (e.g., "I wish my mother was dead!"), it will come true, indicating they are operating at a very low level of action tendencies, and are very concrete without the ability to symbolize. They must be helped to realize that wishes and fantasies are internal experiences that other people do not know about, and which cannot affect other people. Wishes for care and love, for a better life or childhood, are particularly shameful for many survivors (or dissociative parts), and must be elicited with respect and empathy by the therapist. The therapist must take care in helping the patient express wishes that he or she does not give the impression that those wishes can always be fulfilled. Such wishes have often become associated with early childhood biological *needs* for survival (Steele, van der Hart, & Nijenhuis, 2001), and are thus overwhelming if unmet. Patients need to learn that all humans have such wishes and they represent important goals (e.g., receiving care), but they must also learn that there are adaptive ways to meet those goals.

Fantasies may be easily confused with reality, and patients may base their behavioral actions (or inaction) on those fantasies.

> Mary, a patient with DID, had a fantasy of having a wonderful family. She acted out that fantasy by working as a nanny for other people's children and had no real home and virtually no life of her own. But the fantasy was also a reenactment of her actual family of origin: "If you are in a family, you are not allowed to have your own life and you must have a miserable life. You must not have needs of your own." The therapist helped the patient gradually (over some years) realize that her enactment of the fantasy as reality and as a replay of her history had to become more symbolic (i.e., verbalized instead of acted upon). The patient's mental level was very gradually raised, and she was helped to realize the present and the past.

Working with a phobia of one's body. Chronically traumatized individuals typically have some degree of phobic response related to their own bodies, particularly due to shame and disgust. This is particularly true of those whose bodies have been assaulted, especially sexually (Andrew, 2002; Armsworth, Stronk, & Carlson, 1999; Goodwin & Attias, 1999). Body shame involves "negative experiences of both appearance and functions of the body, which can involve various sensory modalities," such as taste, smell, sounds, and sights (Gilbert, 2002, p. 3).

TABLE 14.1

Interventions for Overcoming the Phobia of Trauma-Derived
Mental Actions

- Ascertain the patient's current mental level so therapy can be paced within his or her integrative capacity
- Provide psychoeducation regarding mental actions (e.g., feelings are information; feeling and fantasies are different from behaviors; people cannot read minds)
- Offer training in specific skills such as affect recognition and regulation (cf., Chapter 12; Linehan, 1993)
- Hypnotic techniques to contain and titrate affect and sensations may be useful if the therapist has adequate training in hypnosis with trauma patients (cf., Cardeña, 2000; Hammond, 1990; Kluft, 1989, 1992; Peterson, 1996)
- Modified EMDR techniques in combination with hypnotic techniques may be helpful with survivors of chronic traumatization, if the therapist has adequate training in EMDR (Fine & Berkowitz, 2001; Gelinas, 2003; Phillips, 2001; Twombly, 2000)
- Teach the patient to ask, "What are my feelings, sensations, wishes, needs telling me?" (McCullough et al. 2003). This engages the patient in developing a theory of mind (Fonagy, Gergely, Jurist, & Target, 2002)
- Repeatedly call attention to the patient's inner experience so that it becomes less reflexive over time (Grigsby & Stevens, 2000), thereby developing a theory of mind
- Assist the patient in raising his or her level of action tendencies to the point where verbalization of mental actions is possible, instead of acting out or avoidance (substitute actions)
- Encourage use of symbolism (metaphors, similes, rituals) to describe inner experiences, if and when the patient is able
- Encourage the patient to develop empathy and understanding for his or her needs, wishes, and feelings
- Reframe resistance and maladaptive behaviors as ineffective ways to stay safe or get needs and goals met
- Reframe internal critical voices/thoughts as ways to avoid mental actions and social rejection of those actions
- Provide a secure attachment with empathic attunement and consistent boundaries, which is a physical and mental regulator for the patient
- Identify which mental actions are tolerated and which not, and by which parts. Do not overlook fantasies and wishes as a source of phobic responses
- Identify substitute actions, such as vehement emotions, avoidance and escape strategies, that prevent adaptive mental actions

(*continued*)

TABLE 14.1
(Continued)

- Identify resistances to mental actions and related social defenses and trauma-derived phobias
- Identify inhibitory affects such as fear, shame, disgust that prevent adaptive feelings
- Encourage the patient to become more aware of avoidance strategies without acting on them: switching, numbing, inhibitory affects such as shame or fear
- Encourage the patient to be aware of how a particular mental action (e.g., engaging in a particular thought) inhibits or activates certain behavioral actions. This intervention assists patients in better linking of their mental and behavioral actions
- Identify activating affects such as excitement or joy to which the patient has a phobic response
- Encourage the patient to experience positive mental actions without avoidance, and distinguish them from traumatic hyperarousal
- Identify adaptive feelings, such as sadness or anger that need to be synthesized and realized
- Encourage expression of adaptive feelings
- For patients or parts fixed in vehement emotions, use grounding, breathing techniques, and a cognitive focus to improve reflective thinking
- Avoid emotional expressive work (catharsis) with patients who experience chronic vehement emotions such as rage (because they cannot yet experience adaptive feeling)
- Support core presentification (i.e., being present), which includes mindfulness, so the patient's mental actions in the moment can be explored and experienced safely
- Model awareness and verbal sharing of mental actions by the therapist
- Gradually expose specific parts of the personality to previously avoided aversive mental actions, beginning primarily with ANP(s)
- Begin graduated exposure with minor, everyday affects, and in stepwise fashion move to major (core) affects as the patient's mental level allows
- Encourage the patient to feel adaptive emotions for very short periods of time and explore their *experience* of the affect (e.g., "What is it like for you to feel sad right now?")
- Promote internal empathy, cooperation, and negotiation so that various parts will not avoid the mental actions of other parts, and they can be experienced and expressed adaptively

---

This phobia is based on substitute beliefs: "My body is disgusting"; "My body sounds and smells are horrible." A common belief is that one's body is dirty or disgusting. The disgust or shame may involve one's appearance (e.g., "I am too fat"; "I am ugly"); body function and one's sensory experience (e.g., "I can't stand the feel and smell of sweat"; "I have panic when I feel sexually aroused"; "I can't stand if someone hears me going to the bathroom"); or specific body parts (e.g., "Penises make me sick"; "I hate my breasts"; "My hands look just like my mother's: I want to cut them off").

Such phobias may include specific maladaptive behavioral actions that depend on whether the patient becomes inhibited or activated by the phobia. If the patient (or dissociative part) is inhibited, he or she will avoid whatever about the body is shameful or frightening. Perhaps this results in being unwilling to undress in a locker room, or not looking in the mirror at oneself, or avoiding bathing or touching one's body. If the patient becomes activated, he or she may engage in behaviors such as excessive bathing and attention to hygiene, obsessive thoughts about body smells or sounds, or may hurt parts of the body or even try to get rid of them by cutting them off. Eating disorders are strongly correlated with body shame (Burney & Irwin, 2000).

There are countless interventions to deal with the phobias of trauma-derived mental actions. Below we provide a list of essential interventions (Table 14.1).

SUMMARY

Mental actions—perceptions, thoughts, feelings, wishes, needs, fantasies, and body sensations—are essential to adaptive functioning. They precede and accompany behavior, and are ultimate guides of our behavioral actions. However, survivors have often become phobic regarding various mental actions because they signal or refer to unresolved traumatic experiences—hence, they are called trauma-derived mental actions. And evaluative conditioning has led patients to experience certain trauma-derived mental actions as fearful, shameful, or disgusting. Thus survivors are often afraid of their own feelings and thoughts, and the sensations that accompany them. The therapist should assess which mental actions are difficult for the survivor to tolerate, which are inhibited, and which easily overwhelm the patient when they are activated. The therapist can also determine the mental actions that each dissociative part of the personality might specifically avoid and fear. It is important to realize that survivors not only avoid and fear negative affects and sensations, but also positive ones. The therapist and patient can begin to explore maladaptive if–then rules that the patient has applied to mental actions: "If I feel sad, then I will never stop crying." The therapist carefully explores the patient's *experience* of mental actions (e.g., what the patient experiences when he or she feels angry, such as particular sensations, hearing internal voices, having negative thoughts or beliefs). When working with a phobia of affect, the therapist must make a clear distinction between vehement, overwhelming emotions that are maladaptive substitutes, and intense emotions that may be adaptive. The patient may not only experience a phobia of affect, but also a phobia of thoughts, needs, wishes, fantasies, and a phobia of body sensations and the body. Numerous techniques are described to overcome these phobias of trauma-derived mental actions.

CHAPTER 15

Phase 1 Treatment and Beyond

Overcoming the Phobia of Dissociative Parts

No matter how many times I had gone to talk therapy, I [ANP] couldn't find a way to connect with the night child [EP] I had abandoned. I just hated her. I had no compassion for her at all. I was finally understanding that I would be stuck in the muck of dysfunction until I could find a way to stop judging her so unmercifully.
—Marilyn Van Derbur (2004, p. 281)

T HE PHOBIA OF DISSOCIATIVE parts requires particular interventions in addition to those described in the previous chapters. Overcoming this phobia is a major therapeutic avenue toward increasing the patient's capacity for adaptive action and integration. This involves the development of internal empathy and more cooperation among parts of the personality, and more realization that each part belongs to a single *I* (i.e., personification).

Various stimuli activate certain dissociative parts, leaving survivors at the mercy of abrupt and maladaptive changes in their basic emotions, goals, and behaviors; that is, in problematic perception–motor action cycles. Much of the dissociative patient's mental energy is thus tied up in phobic avoidance and inner conflicts among parts, contributing to an overall lower mental level.

Overcoming the phobia of dissociative parts requires high level mental actions, not only in the patient, but also in the therapist. All interventions are directed toward helping the patient engage in actions that promote synthesis and realization within the personality as a whole. The therapist understands that interventions directed toward any individual part also have systemic consequences. Interventions for overcoming the phobia of dissociative parts can be understood not only from a learning theory perspective of gradual exposure and successive approximation, but also from a dynamic systems perspective in which the therapist is concerned with systemic actions that effect adaptive change (Benyakar, Kutz, Dasberg, & Stern, 1989; Edelman & Tononi, 2000). That is, the therapist promotes adaptive mental and behavioral actions in and between all parts of the personality to support the patient in functioning as a whole person.

FUNCTIONAL ANALYSIS OF THE PHOBIA
OF DISSOCIATIVE PARTS

The therapist should have already made an initial functional analysis of the patient's personality system and its various subsystems (dissociative parts; see Chapter 11). Appropriate selection of interventions requires ongoing functional analysis of the dynamic relationships among dissociative parts within the individual as a whole, of what activates or inhibits dissociative parts, and what will support action systems in becoming more cohesive and coordinated. The DID literature sometimes describes this as "mapping" the personality system of the patient (Fine, 1999; Kluft, 1999; Sachs & Peterson, 1996), and it can also be employed with secondary structural dissociation.

The empathic and open-ended questions asked of the patient in this analysis are an ongoing intervention in themselves because they foster the patient's capacity to engage in reflective actions such as metacognition (awareness of one's own thoughts, perceptions, feelings, defenses, etc.). The therapist inquires in a way that demonstrates he or she is neither fascinated with nor resistant to the idea of parts of the personality, but is empathically attuned to the patient's experiences and beliefs. The therapist thus models a stance for the patient that is respectful of and even-handed with all parts. Any tendency to retract the therapist's field of consciousness to work with one part in favor of another (e.g., cognitive vs. emotive parts, "child" vs. persecutory parts), or ignore the fact that other parts exist should be strongly avoided (Kluft, 1993b, 1999). This modeling encourages all dissociative parts of the patient to become more consciously aware of each other and their respective goals, and of how the patient's parts operate as a whole system.

Prior to exposing dissociative parts to each other, the therapist inquires about why parts may be phobic of each other, realizing that a powerful intervention is joining with the patient's resistances. Conditioned avoidance actions and resistances should be thoroughly explored. For example, the therapist can ask, "What is the worst thing you are afraid of if you get to know that angry part of yourself?" Then the therapist can work gradually with the patient's maladaptive predictions. "You are afraid that part might tear up the room. Has that ever happened before? Do you suppose you could check with that part and see if that is so?" Thus the patient is gently encouraged to be more reflective and engage in experimental actions. In this way unfinished actions can be completed (in this case, of being adaptively angry).

A functional analysis dictates the timing and order of interventions. For example, it is useful to understand which parts can be labeled as ANP (those that function in daily life), and which are EPs (those that are fixed in trauma-related actions). Then the therapist can focus on strengthening ANP(s) prior to work with EPs, and on helping them simplify life and build safety in order to improve mental energy. And when the therapist can assess that the patient as ANP does not have the mental efficiency to approach EPs, then they can begin with interventions that raise the mental level of ANP rather than trying to expose ANP to EP prematurely. By assessing the level of action tendencies of a part, the therapist can gear interventions to fit within the mental level; for example, finding nonverbal methods—a lower level action tendency—to help a part communicate if it currently functions below the capacity for language. When the therapist assesses that some parts are less phobic than others, gradual exposure can thus begin with less phobic parts, giving the patient a greater likelihood of success with exposure, thus raising his or her mental level to continue with further exposure.

Systemic interventions geared toward all parts of the personality are preferable when possible. The therapist realizes that all interventions with specific parts have systemic implications for better or worse. Assessment may also guide the therapist as to when to address the relationships between parts. Neither the therapist nor the patient is aware of the whole personality system, of all conflicts and resistances, which only unfold over time and with trust and increasing awareness. Thus, analysis of the patient's personality functioning is ongoing and collaborative.

Some parts will be more closed to each other than others, but it is wise to assume that there is some degree of conscious and unconscious connectivity among parts. Although neither the therapist nor the patient may necessarily be aware of these connections, such associations may allow parts to change even when they are relatively closed systems. For example, when a few major parts begin to feel safe with the therapist, this may generalize to other parts. On the other hand, relatively closed parts may attempt to diminish or sabotage changes in other parts (e.g., one part hurts another internally or with actual self-harm). When parts of the patient are resistant, the therapist should assume that there is good motivation to avoid changes, and this should be explored empathically. Above all, the therapist should not get into a power struggle with the patient, as this promotes lower level reflexive actions by both therapist and patient.

WORKING WITH DIFFERENT LEVELS
OF STRUCTURAL DISSOCIATION

The complexity of structural dissociation in a patient will determine the types of systemic interventions aimed at overcoming the phobia of dissociative parts.

Primary Structural Dissociation

A number of survivors of chronic child abuse and neglect present with a type of primary structural dissociation in the form of one ANP that is the adult and "main shareholder" of the personality (S. Fraser, 1987) and one elaborated "child" EP that holds all the traumatic memories of abuse and neglect. The patient as ANP typically has strongly developed, conditioned fear, disgust, and avoidance patterns toward the EP. Although patients with simple PTSD respond well to standardized treatments (cognitive–behavioral therapy, prolonged exposure EMDR), those with this more elaborated type may not. Overcoming the phobia of this type of EP—such as the "night child" described by Van Derbur (2004)—is more of a challenge because ANP is extremely avoidant of EP, which contains years of traumatic history rather than a single event. That is, this type of EP often has a wider array of fixed perception–motor action cycles than an EP in simple PTSD.

The first task is to support and improve the functioning of the survivor as ANP in daily life. The two parts of the personality are first introduced to each other and then helped to become empathic toward one another and to cooperate in accomplishing actions that will benefit the person as a whole, such as completion of daily tasks and mental actions necesssary to modulate and tolerate mental actions. At this point in treatment cooperation should focus on daily life activities and not on traumatic memories. This will directly improve normal daily functioning and provide increased mental efficiency to eventually deal with EPs.

Survivors often have an unrealistic view of being an adult; for example, they may believe that adults must never cry, always know how to solve problems, and do not make mistakes. Such substitute beliefs are often based on what they learned in a dysfunctional family. They are unable to realize what it means to be a human, fallible adult. These reflexive beliefs contribute to ongoing avoidance of any perceived "weakness," or "neediness" in EP. Psychoeducation and modeling by the therapist are of help in this situation.

The second task involves paced modification of ANP's conditioned negative evaluation of EP by helping the patient understand the needs and goals of EP (e.g., to be safe, comforted, to receive empathic attunement), and to realize EP has played an important role in helping the patient as whole function in daily life. As Marilyn Van Derbur (2004) observed:

> My night child [EP] kept her part of the deal. She had "taken it" [i.e, the recurrent sexual abuse and related traumatic memories] until I [ANP] was strong and secure enough to come back and rescue her. Now, instead of gratitude for her sacrificing herself, I loathed, despised and blamed her. (p. 191)

The therapist empathizes with the burden of ANP in needing to cope not only with external stress, but with the intrusions of and inner conflicts with EP. The therapist gradually guides the survivor as ANP to develop a more positive, empathic relationship with the "inner child" EP, which includes imitation of being a good parent to a literal child. The therapist might pose the question, "If this were a literal child, what would you do?" Then he or she can help the patient find a way to translate that knowledge into adaptive actions in regard to EP. The patient might engage in imaginative actions ("I can imagine holding her and telling her she is safe now"), or find more literal ways ("I can reassure her that she has enough to eat and provide myself with healthy food"). The therapist does not need to invite EP to be in executive control in the session, unless it is to promote further exposure of ANP to EP or specifically to orient that part to the present; for example, ANP might imagine sitting on the sofa having a conversation with EP. The point is that the therapist should avoid the pitfall of becoming a "babysitter" who is supposed to comfort or help EP, while ANP continues to avoid EP.

Secondary Structural Dissociation

Much of what was described above as essential for working with a single elaborated EP also applies to the treatment of patients with secondary structural dissociation (i.e., with one ANP and two or more EPs). ANP, which comprises the vast majority of the patient's functioning and action systems in primary and secondary structural dissociation, may need to learn skills not only to function in daily life, but also to approach and contain distressed emotional parts (EPs). Patients as ANP often have low mental energy due to depression, working too much, or other factors, and one of the first goals of therapy is to raise their mental energy and efficiency.

Although survivors may have chaotic presentations of their dissociative parts, there is typically a specific order in working with parts that the therapist and patient will find helpful. In Phase 1, the therapist generally should begin work first with those parts that function in daily life (i.e., ANPs). Such work with ANPs prior to intensive work with EPs ensures that stability can be maintained and improved.

However, it is also crucial at some point in Phase 1 to begin to gradually expose parts to each other, with the understanding that survivors as ANP must be actively and empathically involved with other dissociative parts. In Phase 1, the therapist generally should not wait for the emergence of parts, but assess their presence, functions, strengths, and limitations as soon as the patient's mental level allows this type of inquiry. Taking a passive stance in waiting for parts to emerge overtly may make treatment more prolonged than necessary (Kluft, 1999). If ANP remains too phobic of EPs, the therapist may need to approach these EPs more individually by initiating contact for the purposes of grounding and safety, and thus serve as a role model for ANPs in their interactions with EP.

But it may be difficult to determine the presence of dissociative parts: Patients with secondary structural dissociation often have EPs with little elaboration, sometimes without many identifying characteristics such as age or name. These parts manifest primarily in reexperiences of trauma and in symptoms that are refractory to standard psychotherapeutic interventions (e.g., physical pain, panic, bouts of loneliness). As ANP, such patients may have excellent insight, but are unable to effect changes because their symptoms emanate from EPs that do not gain executive control, but that nevertheless influence the patient's actions as ANP.

A gradual, paced inquiry should be made in which the therapist avoids undue suggestion about the possible existence of dissociative parts. When a patient with a trauma-related disorder has a symptom that the therapist suspects is an action of a dissociative part, the symptom itself can be used to connect with the part, and the issue or concern can be addressed directly (Kluft, 1999). For example, if the patient is suddenly suicidal, the therapist can ask, "Would it be an idea to see if there might be a specific part of you that is feeling suicidal right now? And if so, perhaps that part could let you know why suicide seems like the best option?" Or if a patient has a sudden headache, the therapist could ask, "If the pain had words, what would it say?" or "If the pain could express itself in another way, how would it do that?" or "Perhaps a part of you knows something more about this pain. If so, we could invite this part to raise a finger as a sign to you and me."

In addition to exposing parts to one another, the therapist may need to intervene to decrease or at least contain the emotivity of certain EPs by working with them individually, serving as a model for how parts should interact with and understand each other (Kluft, 1999; Ross, 1997; Van der Hart, Van der Kolk, & Boon, 1998). The therapist works to orient and ground these parts as the initial small steps on the long road to helping them become more presentified. Parts that have some grounding in the present and are connected to some degree with the therapist are better able to tolerate work with traumatic memories. The therapist may use a metaphor such as mountain climbing: One does not just go out and climb the mountain. One needs first to develop skills and make appropriate preparations.

Tertiary Structural Dissociation

When dissociative parts have developed obvious emancipation and elaboration, as is often encountered in the form of several ANPs in DID, the therapist should ensure that parts become less separate, and must work within the patient's reflexive *belief* of being separate entities.

Patients with tertiary structural dissociation have the most complex personality systems, which nevertheless may vary widely in their complexity. Even though a few parts may be quite emancipated and active in daily life, many dissociative parts in DID patients never gain executive control, but work primarily through "passive influence" (Kluft, 1999). Some of these parts are not at all elaborate, while some have intricate lives within a rich internal fantasy life.

A first step in working with tertiary structural dissociation (DID) is to foster communication, empathy, and cooperation among ANPs as this will improve the patient's daily life. The therapist works to reduce the conditioned avoidance of ANPs for each other, beginning with the least fearful and avoidant ANPs.

Marieke (DID) entered treatment as an ANP that avoided accepting her disorder, refused to interact with other dissociative parts, and avoided integrating traumatic memories by focusing on her studies and work during the day, and by drinking wine and smoking marihuana at night. Another ANP called "The Caring Woman" took care of several EPs that held memories of severe childhood sexual and emotional abuse. Marieke's avoidance strategies had exhausted her mental energy, and "The Caring Woman" was exhausted from trying to engage Marieke in caring for fearful child EPs. This left the patient as a whole in a miserable, depressed condition with a low mental level. The therapist explained to Marieke that her avoidance had helped her to succeed in her studies and work despite her difficulties, but that this avoidance now blocked progress and depleted her energy resources. Although Marieke cognitively appreciated this explanation, she continued to resist interaction with the "The Caring Woman." When she made feeble attempts to do so, she complained of a severe headache, which the therapist interpreted as a probable effect of her mental effort to deny the other ANP. The therapist instructed Marieke to create a safe imaginary place where she would meet "The Caring Woman" in a stepwise manner. He suggested that Marieke would first see how "The Caring Woman" looked. To

*that end, he instructed "The Caring Woman" to enter the room and to
remain silent. Once Marieke had become accustomed to looking at the
other ANP, the therapist asked "The Caring Woman" to talk with Marieke
in a supportive way. When Marieke could tolerate this degree of exposure and could abstain from her urge to mentally avoid, he invited both
parts to discuss some relatively uncomplicated issues of daily life. One
of these issues involved "The Caring Woman's" confirmation that
Marieke's headaches were due to her intense resistance to accept the existence of other dissociative parts and her efforts to evade these parts. As
a next step, the therapist instructed both ANPs to have daily meetings to
resolve minor problems of daily life. Marieke also received the assign-
ment of writing a report on the results of each internal gathering and to
bring these reports to the treatment sessions. In this way, Marieke slowly
overcame her phobia of "The Caring Woman," but initially needed
weekly sessions with the therapist to refrain from relapsing back into
avoidance.*

Various ANPs and EPs may have a strong investment in the belief that
they are separate persons. This substitute belief must be met with gentle
but consistent challenges by the therapist. If parts insist on being called
by another name, the therapist may do so, but also should regularly refer
to such parts as aspects of a whole person. Dissociative parts can be asked
to notice stimuli that are inconsistent with their sense of self. For example, "child" parts can be asked to notice how tall they are; "adolescent"
parts that are sexually acting out can be asked to notice they have children and are married. Other parts are also asked to share information
with these parts internally (e.g., "you are grown up and live in your own
home"). The therapist thus helps emancipated and elaborated parts engage in integration that differentiates the past from the present, and internal experiences from external ones; for example, "I am not the same
as when I was a child; I am now different, and I now live in a different
place"; "Different parts of me think they have their own body, but they
have now become more aware that we share one body."

At the same time the therapist helps the patient reduce a sense of separateness, he or she also realizes that various parts operate at quite different levels of action tendencies, and plans interventions accordingly. Some
EPs are only able to engage in lower level action tendencies. Thus they
have difficulty with impulse control, with understanding complex and
conflicting human behavior, and may have limited capacity for language
and symbolism. For example, a "young child" part may be unable to understand words which the patient as ANP can comprehend. The therapist
may then adjust his or her vocabulary, while still addressing the patient
respectfully as an adult. Other EPs may even be largely nonverbal, or only
possess presymbolic regulatory abilities.

TREATMENT INTERVENTIONS FOR
OVERCOMING THE PHOBIA
OF DISSOCIATIVE PARTS

The therapist should always think of the patient systemically, realizing all interventions are geared to reach as many parts as possible and influence their relationships with each other. Thus the therapist's actions are guided by a persistent and empathic curiosity about why one part avoids another, and how they could be encouraged to interact more adaptively. This work may be done at different levels within the personality system, depending on the patient's needs and the mental level of various parts.

First and foremost, the therapist makes interventions at the level of the entire personality. For example, the therapist should often comment to the patient that all parts belong to one person, and that all parts must learn, in their own time, to find ways to communicate, understand each other, and work together in harmony. Initial systemic interventions include talking "through" the survivor as ANP to all parts, and inviting all parts to become more aware of their tolerance of therapeutic work, to participate reflectively in regulating the pace of therapy. For example, the therapist may speak to all parts and say something like this:

> No matter which part is "out" in therapy, would all parts be willing to watch and listen to see if therapy might be something that could be helpful? Could each part agree to let yourself as a whole person know if something seems too overwhelming? And could parts agree to do that with words, or with an innocuous but unmistakable signal, instead of scaring or hurting other parts? I could imagine some parts of you might feel urgent about wanting to be heard and helped, while other parts may have equally strong urges to avoid dealing with overwhelming issues and do not believe I can possibly help. We must respect the needs of *all* parts of you: Both the most reluctant and the most urgent parts of you hold essential information about your need and readiness to deal with difficult issues. It is vital that we not favor one position over another, but take all into careful consideration to find the balance that is right for you. With such statements, the therapist models adaptive ways to deal with dissociative parts, helps the patient as a whole to participate in and be more consciously aware of his or her regulatory needs, provides initial ways for parts to communicate without resorting to self-harm or internal threats, helps the patient understand that each part has important functions and meaning, and reassures all parts that they will be considered in therapy rather than ignored.

Second, the therapist uses interventions geared toward facilitating empathic interactions among two or more dissociative parts within the larger personality system. This typically involves exposure of parts to each other with specific goals in mind: to explore resistances, to develop empathy, to carry out daily living tasks more effectively, to share skills or knowledge.

Third, the therapist may work with individual parts with the goal of raising their mental efficiency and preparing them for exposure to other parts. Usually intervention at this level of the personality system is reserved for parts that have the lowest mental levels and are most phobic of other parts, or for observing parts that can share with the therapist what is happening systemically when the patient is not yet ready to do so. It is a common mistake to underestimate the degree of avoidance of ANP toward EP and visa versa. Consequently the therapist ends up trying to work with dissociative parts individually as though they are not part and parcel of a system, often leading to therapeutic impasses and maladaptive dependency (Steele et al., 2001). Many interventions can be used with all three modes of working with the personality system.

Below we discuss a few major therapeutic principles and techniques based on a Janetian psychology of action, followed by an abbreviated list of related interventions and the principles behind them.

Psychoeducation about Dissociative Parts

Psychoeducation aims at improving the patient's mental efficiency. Psychoeducation about dissociative parts can be relieving to a frightened or ashamed patient, at least to a degree. It is generally very helpful for patients to reach a gradual understanding of the action systems and motives that guide various parts, even though they may try to reach goals in maladaptive ways. To this end, the therapist expresses empathy and understanding toward all parts, and toward their goals and related actions.

However, psychoeducation, as well as any other intervention, may also evoke the phobia of dissociative parts to some degree, at least in ANP. The therapist then switches strategies to focus on exploring the resistance and on fostering more reflective actions: "What do you suppose makes you so afraid or avoidant when we begin to discuss other parts of you?" In other words, reflexive beliefs about and avoidant reactions to the conditioned fear, hate, or disgust of other parts are gently and gradually transformed into reflective beliefs, realization of their importance, and related mental actions.

Reframing with Positive Labeling

The essence of positive labeling is to emphasize the potentially adaptive goals underlying maladaptive actions. Because parts often have been conditioned to find each other highly repugnant, fearful, or shameful, the therapist can help by reframing their maladaptive actions with positively labeling (Haley, 1963). That is, the therapist reframes these parts as having value for the individual (e.g.,"I hurt my body because self-harm keeps emotional pain manageable"; "I have sex to avoid unbearable loneliness") (Boon & Van der Hart, 2003). And the therapist maintains a reflective belief that the goals of various parts are or might have been adaptive at some point in the past, even when the positive goal is obscured by maladaptive behavior and beliefs.

Interventions with Specific Types of Parts

Interventions directed to individual parts are usually designed to regulate, orient to the present, work with specific resistances and defenses, and help specific parts engage in higher level action tendencies. This usually involves improving the mental efficiency of a part, exposing the part to avoided stimuli, challenging maladaptive, reflexive core beliefs, regulating affect and impulses, and building relational safety in the patient's life, with the therapist, and with dissociative parts internally.

Caution is needed when the therapist is working with an individual part and is given information that this part does not want other parts to know. This places the therapist in a bind of holding information that belongs to the patient. In general, the therapist should not withhold information, and should request that parts share the information themselves in their own time, perhaps with the help of the therapist. This is particularly true if the information involves safety; for example, when a part is acting out in a dangerous way.

However, there may be times when the therapist does withhold information for a later time, when the patient's mental level will allow it to be successfully communicated. For instance, an observer EP of a DID patient informed the therapist that there was a particularly difficult traumatic memory of which ANP was not aware, and that ANP was not yet ready to handle it. The patient was in no danger, and the memory was not reactivated, so the therapist did not share the information with ANP, but asked EP how all parts might prepare for this memory and how they would know when ANP was ready.

Although many types of dissociative parts exist (see Chapter 4), we focus on EPs that tend to be the most common and problematic for the therapist: persecutor, fight, and child parts. In addition we comment on working with observer and caretaking parts that may be of some assistance in therapy.

Working with persecutory parts of the personality. Persecutory parts, those EPs that have identified with the perpetrator(s), are almost invariably present in chronically traumatized individuals. However, whether or not the therapist should attempt to work directly with these parts in Phase 1 depends upon the degree to which these EPs affect the personality system as a whole early in therapy. The more these parts in-

terfere with therapy, the more pressing the need for the therapist to intervene early if possible by acknowledging and respectfully addressing
them. All parts of the patient should be educated early in therapy as to
the function of persecutory parts within his or her personality system: At
one time they served a necessary protective function during traumatization that was meant to ensure the survival of the individual. The therapist
must constantly explain to other parts the protective functions of these
parts of the personality in order to foster cooperation and empathy; that
is, engage in positive reframing.

The therapist is often overly focused on the actions of persecutor EPs
as problematic in the personality system. But therapist must also realize
the other side of the coin: These parts are defending against the most intolerable aspects of traumatic memories by believing they became the per-
petrator(s), and are the most disavowed and disowned parts of the personality, but they are trying to protect the patient (L. Goodman & Peters,
1995; Ross, 1997). As Ross states,

> Too often these [persecutor EPs] have been rejected, devalued, and
> hurt by the [ANP] and the referring therapist. . . . They have been
> defined as the problem, and usually the [ANP] regards [these parts]
> as the cause of her problems. From a systems perspective, the per-
> secutor [parts] are like the identified patient in a family system. The
> behavior of the bad [parts] is not the problem: It is the solution to a
> problem. The therapist's job is to help understand what problem is
> being solved by the self-abusive behavior, and then to help the sys-
> tem find a more adaptive solution. (1997, p. 429)

Persecutor EPs generally have a high level of mental energy, but insufficient mental efficiency. Thus they are often vehemently rageful, disdain-
ful, or even sadistic. They typically have severe time and reality distortions,
being fixed in the past, believing or simulating they *are* the perpetrator(s).
In other words, they place the perpetrator part's actions too high in the
hierarchy of degrees of reality, and the price is intense suffering and a
lowering mental energy and efficiency. Persecutor EPs are often unwilling to participate in therapy directly, and work "behind the scenes" to
sabotage progress, which they regard as dangerous, as a threat to a pre-
carious balance of the inner system. They have little or no ability to engage in reflective actions; to mentalize or verbalize their fears or expectations. Though it may take years of hard work, once these parts personify
their own painful affects and memories and no longer need to defend
against them, the mental level of the patient as a whole is raised considerably, and sometimes dramatically. The personality system as a whole can
become remarkably more able to cooperate, problem solve, and make
adaptive decisions.

The therapist works to improve the mental efficiency of these parts (and others) of the personality by making them aware of the present, helping them feel safer, creating a safe therapeutic relationship with them, correcting cognitive errors, helping them understand the origins of their shame and internal hatred, and reducing internal hatred and fear of other parts of the personality toward them. These parts can learn that their sadism is a powerful substitute action, a defense against profound vulnerability and helplessness.

The therapist is at great risk to appease, submit to, or fight with these parts—all maladaptive actions. Thus, the therapist must maintain a high level of mental efficiency and make every effort to remain empathically attuned to the patient instead of having his or her defenses provoked. That is, the therapist uses empathy and curiosity about the dissociative part as prime emotions that support his or her direct, respectful contact with these EPs. This contact is paired with firm limit setting on aggressive behavior, postponement of maladaptive behaviors, and skills building (cf., Van der Hart et al., 1998). If the therapist becomes chronically defensive with persecutor parts that verbally attack or threaten him or her, an intractable negative therapeutic reaction can ensue. When the therapist inevitably become defensive, he or she must admit it when a mistake has been made, seek reattunement with the patient, and continue to try to engage the persectory part. It cannot be emphasized enough that the therapist must not avoid these parts, but rather be fully engaged with persecutor EPs in order for treatment to be successful.

Working with protector (fight) parts of the personality. Much of what pertains to working with persecutor parts also applies to protector (fight) parts. However, there are some minor differences. The therapist responds empathically to the fact that fight parts, the EPs stuck in the action subsystem of fight, sometimes have more mental energy than mental efficiency, and thus become inappropriately angry and defensive, especially when traumatic memories are reactivated. Such parts may provoke people and other internal parts, and are easily agitated by the slightest perceived threat. The therapist must help fight parts learn to perceive the therapeutic relationship through the lens of secure attachment rather than through the lens of threat. Thus the therapist must be as respectful, predictable, and consistent as possible, not making unexpected moves in the session, for example. Thus a therapist might say, "I'm going to get up and get my schedule book from my desk now. Is that all right?" The therapist learns not sit in a way that blocks the patient from direct access to the door, and learns whether the patient feels safer with the blinds open or closed. When the therapist directly contacts fight parts, he or she should deal with the vehement emotivity of rage, and help transform it into adaptive anger that is expressed appropriately and directed toward the correct target. These parts need to become more reflective about their anger instead of lashing out reflexively. For example, the therapist might say:

> I understand that pounding the wall might give you some immediate relief from your rage, but we both know that is only temporary and not something that is useful to do here. Would you be willing to focus with me on your breathing for a moment? . . . And now that you are a bit more present with me, could you try to put some words to (or draw) how you experience that feeling inside and what it is like to have that rage with you? Perhaps there are parts inside that could help you with this rage right now, so that you are getting help not only from me, but from within yourself?

Fight (and persecutory) parts often have strong negative evaluative conditioning toward submissive or needy parts, defending against helplessness and unmet core needs. Psychoeducation about the survival value of total submission, and of the universality of human needs is helpful in building internal empathy. The therapist does well to state to the patient that he or she will regularly consult these parts on whether it is safe to engage in work with traumatic memories and welcomes these parts to voice their objection to or approval of any course of therapeutic action (i.e., the therapist enlists their active participation in therapy). Time and again the therapist must empathically attune with the defensive stance of these parts, using reframing and positive labeling: Persistent repetition is essential.

Working with "child" parts of the personality. Work with "child" parts that typically hold traumatic memories must be carefully paced according to the mental level of the patient. EPs fixed in attachment cry may attach too quickly to the therapist, activating strong defensive responses by attachment phobic parts. Working with "child" EPs too soon or too intensely can lead to undue reactivation of traumatic memories and substitute actions such as self-mutilation from fight EPs and persecutory parts, as well as further decompensation of ANP (Boon & Van der Hart, 2003).

There are several other difficulties in working with "child" EPs. First, the therapist tends to most easily reify child parts, treating them like actual children, and can be pulled into undue reflexive parenting actions, including inappropriate caretaking. Second, child parts often hold the most intense pain, loneliness, terror, and shame, which can easily overwhelm the therapist, who responds by withdrawing or becoming enmeshed.

Finally, child parts typically operate at lower levels of action tendencies, sometimes having little capacity to verbalize, abstract, understand basic concepts, and engage in systematic, prolonged actions to achieve long-term goals. Childlike or other "needy" EPs may present early in therapy because they are conditioned to be activated when the patient attends to traumatic memories. In addition, these EPs are fixed in attachment-related action systems and are thus strongly pulled to engage in attachment (or prevent attachment loss) with therapist. The patient as ANP may wish that the therapist will be a caretaker of these disowned and needy EPs, and thus present them to the therapist to "fix."

The therapist may work with these parts to help them become more oriented to the safe present and to regulate themselves, but must keep in mind that it is the primary responsibility of the patient as a whole to learn to accept and cope with these parts of him- or herself.

Fostering Fusion

Ultimately overcoming the phobia of dissociation parts should involve *fusion*, "the act or instance of bringing together two or more [parts of the personality] personalities or fragments in order to blend their essence into a single entity" (Braun, 1986, p. xv; cf., Kluft, 1993c). Survivors often fear and avoid fusion. This aversion can be understood as a specific subtype of the phobia of dissociative parts. For the patient to overcome this phobia, the therapist must diligently explore resistances to fusion, and not insist parts fuse before the patient's mental level can tolerate it.

Complete fusion of all dissociative parts is the transformation of the patient's personality in which ongoing integrative actions come together into a complete realization. The patient's action systems and perception–motor action cycles become significantly more inclusive, coordinated, flexible, and cohesive, and ANP and EP are no longer unduly divided. The patient then has a wider array of action tendencies from which to choose reflectively in a given situation, and a higher level of mental efficiency with which to act. Survivors thus realize their own past, present, and future, and experience all parts of their personality as one whole. The integrative actions that result in fusion of two or more dissociative parts involves Phase 3 work (see Chapter 17). However, such partial fusions of the personality may occur earlier in treatment as a brief excursion into Phase 3.

Using Reflective, Higher-order Mental Actions:
The "Inner Source of Wisdom"

The concept of accessing inner wisdom is not new to psychology or to the dissociative disorders field (Comstock, 1991). Ellenberger (1970) noted that Janet's patient, Justine, internalized Janet as a wise figure. When she asked this mental representation for advice, "he answered with good counsel which, interestingly enough, was more than a mere repetition of what he [Janet] had actually said, but proved to be of a novel and

TABLE 15.1
Interventions to Overcome the Phobia of Dissociative Parts

- Generally begin treatment with ANP first to improve daily life in primary, secondary, and tertiary structural dissociation (increase mental energy and efficiency for daily life functioning)
  - In tertiary structural dissociation, begin by encouraging cooperation among ANPs that are active in daily life (foster social action tendencies among ANPs at the levels of reflective, prolonged, and experimental action tendencies)
- Expose parts to each other gradually, not exceeding the mental level of the parts involved (gradual exposure with prevention of relapse symptoms; fostering integrative actions though safe experimentation)
- Focus first on relationships between parts that are least phobic of each other and move toward those that are most phobic of each other (gradual exposure and successive approximation)
- Encourage reflective actions that lead to internal empathy, regulation, and guidance (mentalization, internal social skills development)
- Talk through to all parts (Kluft, 1982; Ross, 1997), using ANP as a "mediator" (intervention at the level of the whole personality system, fostering higher mental efficiency)
- Invite child EPs to "listen and watch" or look through the eyes of an "adult" ANP part (foster synthesis and realization by experimenting with new social actions; internal cooperation; skills development)
- Develop a collective safe space or individual safe spaces, e.g., for EPs, with a communal gathering place, and have parts discuss under what circumstances specific parts need to be in their safe place (increase synthesis and realization; foster mentalization and experimental action tendencies by using symbols and other imaginary tools)
- Help parts to develop inner meeting places, such as conference rooms (G. A. Fraser 1991, 2003; Krakauer, 2001) that include structured meeting times between parts (foster social action tendencies at the levels of prolonged reflective and experimental action tendencies by using symbolic imagery as a tool)
- Use imaginary intercom or phone systems for internal communication among parts [fostering integrative action tendencies by using symbolic imagery as a tool]
- Use nonverbal modes of communication for low functioning EPs (join such parts in lower level, i.e., nonverbal, presymbolic action tendencies)
  - Use ideomotor finger signals to communicate with parts reluctant to speak directly in therapy (Hammond & Cheek, 1988; Putnam, 1989)
  - Use drawing or other artwork to help parts communicate with each other
  - Ask another part to speak for a nonverbal or unresponsive part

(continued)

TABLE 15.1
(Continued)

- When parts switch, allow them to come forward, but always ask why the switch occurred and if the part that "left" can continue to listen and participate (foster synthesis and realization through increased openness and flexibility among parts of the personality)
- Help parts practice collaborative problem solving regarding daily life issues, e.g., using group discussions (skills development; foster social action tendencies among parts at the levels of prolonged reflective action tendencies)
- Stimulate joint execution of tasks in daily life among various parts (foster cooperation to promote a higher level of action tendencies and integration of action systems; internal social skills development)
- Invite an individual part to "come forward" for specific therapeutic work. Some patients need hypnotic support, e.g., counting from 5 to 1. (Increase the mental efficiency of one part in order to effect change in all parts of the personality)
- Ground and orient a part to the present with all five senses (enlarge the field of consciousness at a sensorimotor level; give the present the highest degree of reality)
- Make orienting statements: "You are safe here. You are in my office. You are not being hurt anymore, and the person who has hurt you is not here" (give the safe present the highest degree of reality; foster safe attachment)
- Provide psychoeducation to a specific part; e.g., teach that physical response is normal to a part that feels sexual and is ashamed of it, and invite other parts to listen as well (improve mental efficiency for dealing with difficult emotional problems)
- Discuss relationships of one part with other parts, e.g., "Can you help me understand why you don't like or avoid that other part?" (explore resistances and conditioned responses)
- Avoid content-oriented discussions and stay focused on the relationships among parts (gradual exposure)
- Ask an observer part for information regarding other parts or issues in the patient's life (Boon & Van der Hart, 2003) (utilize the patient's capacity for reflection)
- Discuss with a caretaker part how needy parts might be more effectively addressed internally (encourage the integration of action systems for internal purposes; foster social action tendencies, including mentalization)
- Engage attachment-phobic parts in gradual relationship with other parts and with the therapist (foster secure attachment)

wise nature" (p. 369). Many dissociative patients appear to have higher order mental actions of wisdom and reflection that are most often contained in observer EPs. They have as yet been unable to put these mental actions into behavioral practice, but can nevertheless share them verbally. The therapist may find it helpful to identify these parts, because they may help promote inner cooperation, including increasing self-reliance.

This approach is rooted in the tradition of psychotherapy using "permissive" hypnosis, in which the therapist may suggest that the patient to check with his or her "unconscious mind" (or "inner mind," or "wizard") for the solution of existential problems (Erickson, 1980; Van der Hart, 1988a). Krakauer (2001) extended this approach to the treatment of patients with complex dissociative disorders, in which she suggests that parts of the personality consult the "inner wisdom of the unconscious mind" for guidance. Linehan (1993) has used the concept of "wise mind" in the borderline patient. Of course, the therapist does not relegate all responsibility for the therapy to the patient's "inner wisdom," but takes this inner resource seriously because it can enhance the patient's sense of autonomy, and thus counteract maladaptive dependency on the therapist (cf., Steele et al., 2001).

Table 15.1 lists a selection of other treatment principles and techniques, which are related to those discussed above, and also to the basic treatment principles presented in Chapter 12.

SUMMARY

As with overcoming the phobia of attachment and of trauma-derived mental actions, the therapist gradually exposes dissociative parts of the personality to each other in a paced and respectful manner. The key to success is for the therapist to empathically attune to the beliefs, experiences, and resistances of the patient while maintaining a strong sense of reality (i.e., dissociative parts comprise a single personality). Thus, the therapist thinks systemically, realizing that all interventions have systemic implications. A thorough and ongoing functional analysis of all parts, their roles, and their interrelationships guides the interventions of the therapist. Interventions may be made at the level of the personality as a whole system, among two or more subsystems (parts) of the personality, or with a single dissociative part. However, all interventions are geared toward the purpose of decreasing structural dissociation and increasing the realization of the patient as a whole. Treatment of several common types of EPs has been discussed: persecutory, fight, child, and observer parts.

CHAPTER 16

Phase 2 Treatment

Overcoming the Phobia of Traumatic Memory

*But how are you going to make me suffer the pain that I have man-
aged to avoid in the trauma without a renewed split, that is, without any repetition of mental disorder. . .? Does it not seem an impossible undertaking?*
—Anonymous woman. Quoted by Sandor Ferenczi (1988, p. 181)

T HE TREATMENT OF TRAUMATIC MEMORIES may commence once the goals of
Phase 1 have been met. During Phase 2, the following phobias must
be systematically and gradually addressed: phobias related to insecure attachment to perpetrators; phobias related to therapist attachment and attachment loss in emotional parts of the personality (EPs); and the core
phobia of traumatic memories. Overcoming the phobia of traumatic memories involves guided synthesis that is directed by the therapist, and realization of traumatic memories among various parts of the personality.
This gradually renders structural dissociation unnecessary. The principal
elements of the traumatic experience must be synthesized, shared among
apparently normal parts (ANPs) and EPs, and realized. That is, the memory is transformed into a symbolic verbal account that is personified and
presentified. This realization results in an autobiographical narrative
memory of traumatic events, and in actions that can be adapted to the
present rather than to the traumatic past.

OVERCOMING PHOBIAS RELATED
TO INSECURE ATTACHMENT
TO THE PERPETRATOR(S)

For the survivor abused within the family, secure attachment to the therapist may conflict with the insecure attachment to the perpetrator, at least for some parts of the personality. This may become evident early in therapy, but may become heightened when attachment-related traumatic memories become the focus of treatment in Phase 2. The patient (or various dissociative parts) may feel he or she has to "choose" between the therapist and the perpetrator because of the intense loyalty and enmeshed bonds involved in a dysfunctional family. In addition, various dissociative parts alternate between attachment and defense with perpetrators, a pattern accentuated when traumatic memories are reactivated. Some dissociative parts, such as ANP, may be enmeshed with their abusive or neglectful parents even to the present, while other EPs have strong feelings of hatred, anger, or terror toward the same individuals. EPs fixed in attachment cry may engage in clinging, maladaptive dependence, and submission with perpetrators, and may be unable to realize the associated dangers (Steele, Van der Hart, & Nijenhuis, 2001).

The survivor as ANP attempts to suppress dissociative parts that hate the perpetrator, while defensive EPs attempt to sabotage ANP's contact with the perpetrator. The survivor as ANP may experience extreme guilt and shame when trying to set limits with his or her family, and experience abandonment panic when considering separation, while EPs strive to avoid and even shun the perpetrator. The therapist must not be caught in this dilemma by taking the side of the patient against the perpetrator, but empathically explore *all* the patient's feelings toward the abuser. Psychoeducation about healthy boundaries is essential in gradually guiding patients to set more adaptive limits with intrusive or enmeshed families.

However, if the patient is currently being abused by a perpetrator, the therapist must support the patient in becoming safe. But this must be done without force, or a power struggle will likely ensue and the therapist will lose. Thus the therapist does not forbid the patient to have contact with his or her family, nor to confront perpetrators or even express anger in therapy prematurely. Instead, dissociative parts are encouraged to communicate their feelings and beliefs about the perpetrator to each other, and learn to be empathic with each other's positions. In this way the patient as a whole can contain his or her strong ambivalence and eventually resolve it.

Initial Interventions with EPs Fixed
in Traumatic Memories

Many EPs are fixed in defensive and recuperative action subsystems, experiencing themselves as continuing to interact with the perpetrator in the past. The initial goal of the therapist with these parts is not attach-ment per se, as attempts at immediate attachment will only trigger more defense. But rather the therapist seeks to eliminate the fixed nature of the defensive system in these parts. First, all parts involved should begin to have a sense of being in the safe present, even though they may not di-rectly interact with the therapist. The therapist recurrently "talks through" to these EPs fixated in the past, encouraging them to watch and listen to the therapist to experience whether they are safe. These parts can be en-couraged to communicate with other parts that do have a relationship with the therapist and that are more oriented to the present. But as noted before, much work must occur with aggressive parts of the personality before they can actually become empathic and cooperative, and the sur-vival value of their goals must be appreciated. Flexibility gradually devel-ops among rigidly fixated defensive parts of the personality when the therapist stimulates them to engage in context evaluation of the present, and encourages them to be more present (presentification) (see Chapter 10). As a more fluid and less dissociative defensive system is developed, and as parts become better oriented in the present, there is less need for defensive action. This change allows for a degree of attachment to the therapist, which gradually raises the mental efficiency of these parts. It is vital that the EPs and ANP(s) also become more securely attached with each other. Otherwise, a fantasy of rescue by the therapist may intensify with the building alliance.

OVERCOMING THE PHOBIA
OF TRAUMATIC MEMORY

This is one of the most difficult phobias to overcome, requiring high and sustained integrative capacity of the survivor as ANP *and* EP. Careful pac-ing of therapy and regulation of the patient's hyper- and hypoarousal is crucial to success. Contraindications to initiation of this phase should be strictly followed (Boon, 1997; Kluft, 1997; Steele & Colrain, 1990; Van der Hart & Boon, 1997). These contraindications include psychosis, fixa-tion in lower action tendencies, rapid switching, physical conditions that lower the mental level, malignant regression, unstable life, ongoing abuse, and other issues that involve the patient's mental level being inad-equate. The lower the patient's mental level, the slower this treatment step will be, with frequent returns to Phase 1 interventions.

The treatment of traumatic memories consists of two major compo-nents: *guided synthesis* and *guided realization of the traumatic mem-ory*. Guided synthesis involves modulated and controlled exposure to the traumatic memory. The patient is actively helped by the therapist to re-main oriented to the present while simultaneously synthesizing the previ-ously dissociated mental actions and content of the traumatic memory (Van der Hart & Steele, 2000). That is, the cognitive, sensorimotor, and affective, and behavioral components of the memory are shared by various parts of the personality with each other. Guided realization is the ongoing therapeutic process of helping the patient to realize his or her history, grieve the inherent losses, and move toward higher levels of personification and presentification.

Most importantly, the therapist does not begin the treatment of traumatic memories when the patient is having a flashback. The therapist explains that the traumatic memory need not be reexperienced as the original overwhelming event; that is, *it need not and should not be relived.* The patient (and various dissociative parts) must be oriented and grounded in the safe present, and the flashback contained first. Only then can therapist and patient together make a collaborative decision about whether the patient is ready to proceed with a guided and controlled synthesis.

Although expressions such as *controlled abreactions* or *abreactive work* are often used to describe this process in the dissociative disorders field (e.g., Fine, 1993; Kluft, 1988, 1994a; Putnam, 1989; C.A. Ross, 1989), we prefer the concepts of *guided synthesis* and *realization of traumatic memory*. These emphasize the integrative nature of the mental actions involved and eschew the idea that catharsis of vehement emotion is therapeutic in itself (Howell, 2005; Huber, 2003; Van der Hart, Steele, Boon, & Brown, 1993; cf. Van der Hart & Brown, 1992, for a critical analysis).

The therapist can be susceptible to two countertransference positions in dealing with traumatic memories (Van der Hart & Steele, 1999). First, he or she may develop undue fascination with the content of and a counterphobic attitude toward the patient's traumatic memories. This may result in undue and premature focus on trauma material, and neglect of the development of the patient's essential daily life and regulatory skills. Second, the therapist may overidentify with the patient's lack of realization, colluding to avoid dealing with traumatic memories at all. The therapist should assiduously examine his or her motivations and how these intersect with standard of care interventions and the therapeutic process. It is easy for the therapist to become overwhelmed with patients' traumatic experiences, and find their emotional suffering and extreme loneliness difficult to bear. Thus the therapist should regularly engage in consultation or personal therapy, and have colleagues with whom they can resolve their own overwhelming feelings.

Traumatic memory is treated in several stages (Van der Hart, Steele et al., 1993): (1) *preparation*, in which careful planning occurs; (2) *guided synthesis*, the sharing of all components of the traumatic memory among dissociative parts; and (3) *guided realization*, that includes a beginning narrative account that eventually encompasses all parts of the personality and increasing levels of personification and presentification. This last stage is much more process oriented and occurs over a period of time. It is often a crucial missing link in the treatment of traumatic memories, as some therapists view the "retrieval" or synthesis of memory as the end of the process. In reality, it is merely the beginning of a difficult and longer course of realization in survivors of chronic traumatization. It is essential to include the survivor as ANP(s) in this work, although there may occasionally be times when synthesis and various levels of realization may first occur among EPs. For example, several defensive subsystems might be integrated prior to work with the ANP on realization of the traumatic memories.

Preparation

The therapist prepares the patient for work with traumatic memories by helping him or her be well oriented and grounded in the present, in good contact with the therapist. This grounding is carefully maintained throughout work with traumatic memories as much as is feasible. Ideally, a cognitive overview of the memory can be obtained from some part of the personality; for example, observing EPs, without the risk of uncontrolled reexperiencing. Such reexperiences or flashbacks are to be avoided. It is essential that the patient's level of arousal not become too high or too low, and that both patient and therapist have sufficient control: Panic and redissociation of the traumatic memory, as well as remaining stuck in the memory in a hypoaroused state, should be prevented.

It is especially helpful for the therapist to have an idea of the beginning and end of the memory, which offers a time boundary that can be used to help the patient realize the memory had a beginning, a middle, and an end (cf., Sachs & Peterson, 1996). Dissociative parts may be unable to realize that an experience has indeed ended, and helping them with this realization is a crucial part of Phase 2 work. It is also useful for the therapist to know, if possible, the *pathogenic kernels* or *hot spots* (Chapter 1), i.e., the most threatening parts of the traumatic memory that the patient wants to avoid at all costs. If this can be done with an observer EP, other dissociative parts not yet ready to listen imagine themselves in their safe places to prevent reexperiences. In order to resolve and integrate the traumatic memory, it is essential for the patient to synthesize these pathogenic kernels.

Apart from content, planning focuses on the question of which parts should initially participate. Generally these include one or more of the parts that contain the traumatic memory and parts that can fulfill a helping role, such as offering courage, structure, or comfort during and after the synthesis. For some patients, however, Phase 1 work has been sufficient such that all parts can participate in guided synthesis simultaneously.

There are many patients for whom an observing part can share content on a purely cognitive level. These patients can be prepared by helping all parts explore their beliefs, which may help identify pathogenic kernels: "What have you come to believe about yourself based on this memory?" "What do you believe about others?" The therapist also helps the patient predict worst case possibilities: "What is the worst thing that you could imagine you might have to deal with in regards to what you remember?; and "If that happened, how could we both help you best deal with it?"; "What are some other things you might find difficult to cope with?"

Careful preparation of guided synthesis maximizes the probability that the patient's mental level is high enough to support integrative mental actions. Thus the therapist and patient aim to prevent substitute actions, ranging from lowering of the level of consciousness, to vehement emotions, to self-destructive behaviors.

It may be helpful to plan extended sessions, not to increase intensity and duration of experiences, but rather to more slowly expose the patient to the traumatic memories, and to leave the patient with plenty of time to become regrounded and fully reoriented to the present. The patient should have a thorough understanding of the purposes and experience of integrating traumatic memories. Hypnosis may be used to control and support this aspect of the process, but only if the therapist is formally trained in the use of hypnosis in psychotherapy, hypnosis has already been successfully used with the patient on previous occasions, and he or she has given informed consent (Hammond, 1990; Kluft, 1988, 1989; Putnam, 1989; Van der Hart, Boon, & Van Everdingen, 1990). EMDR is an important technique that may be a suitable alternative for the guided synthesis described below, provided that the guidelines of phase-oriented treatment are strictly followed, and the therapist is trained in using EMDR with dissociative patients (e.g., Gelinas, 2003; Twombly, 2005).

Guided Synthesis of Traumatic Memory

The essence of guided synthesis is that the therapist guides dissociative parts in a series of experiences in which dissociated aspects of the traumatic memory are evoked and shared (cf., Foa, 2006; Leskin et al., 1998; Rothbaum & Schwartz, 2002). *Exposure is conducted such that its intensity and duration are adapted to the survivor's mental level.* The mental level and motivation of the survivor and the subjective severity of the event define how many trauma-related stimuli the survivor can synthesize at a given time, and can subsequently realize—whether massed or graduated exposure is indicated. The therapist cannot and should not force the patient to engage in synthetic action; he or she can only expose the patient to the stimuli if the patient is willing. Thus it is common that several rounds of guided synthesis need to occur more than once for a single traumatic memory. The cases of Martha and Frieda at the end of the chapter offer additional practical examples of guided synthesis.

There are several ways of approaching guided synthesis, depending on the skills of the therapist and the needs of the individual patient. Some patients work most effectively by synthesizing memories with only some parts present, while other parts remain in a safe place until their mental level is high enough at a later time. For example, Steve had five distinguishable EPs. One was extremely terrified and highly resistant to recalling his brutal physical abuse without reliving it. The therapist worked previously with Steve to develop an imaginary safe space for this EP. The other four EPs and Steve as ANP felt prepared to share these painful memories, and did so while the scared EP remained in a soundproof safe space. This guided synthesis improved the mental level of all parts involved, and they were subsequently able to better support the scared EP in becoming more oriented and to gradually realize what had happened without reliving it.

Other patients find it more effective to synthesize with all parts present at a given time. Some patients will become more "lost" in a memory than others during guided synthesis, despite the best efforts of the therapist. Given the enormous variations among patients, it is essential to individualize the process of working with traumatic memories.

In general, the therapist and patient should understand that all sessions, including synthesis sessions, are divided into three parts—"the rule of thirds" (Kluft, 1993b). The first third of the session involves preparation for and perhaps the beginning of synthesis. The second third is dedicated to the guided synthesis, while the last third is used for wrapping up, cognitive work, and reorienting the patient fully to the present. The therapist should never allow the synthesis to continue to the end of session. This ensures the work can be better contained within the patient's mental level. The therapy frame should remain secure, and the sessions should be ended on time. Of course, the time needed at the end for the patient to ground varies from person to person.

The initial stage of guided synthesis might include "gathering" all parts together, while the therapist first facilitates a strong feeling of connection and empathy among them (e.g., suggesting being close and holding hands together, in the same way a very loving and close family might grieve together). Additional suggestions can be added, such as that each part has particular strengths, and being together makes each part stronger, as those different strengths are woven together so that each part gives to and receives help and support from every other part. Then suggestions for connection with the safe present and the therapist can be made, and a slow introduction of the traumatic memory can commence, with frequent reminders for parts to remain together and in the present.

It may be helpful for the patient to take short rest periods between times of synthesis within a session. During these breaks the patient is encouraged to concentrate on relaxation and controlled breathing, and on making contact with the therapist. Suggestions for time distortion, such as experiencing the actual synthesis as much shorter than it actually is (e.g., "the minutes can seem like mere seconds, hardly noticeable in the passage of time"), and experiencing the breaks in between as much longer, can be helpful (e.g., "the minutes can seem like hours of leisurely time, and the hours like long, lazy, relaxing days"). Suggestions for rest and restoration may also be given; for example, imagining being surrounded by white light or safely floating in pool of water with healing powers, or other metaphors that come from the patient.

Guided synthesis can take place in a more encompassing and rapid way or in a very gradual way, depending on the patient's mental level. Whatever the pacing, it is essential for the therapist to provide therapeutic stimulation, such as expressing encouragement and confidence in the patient's abilities to accomplish the task of synthesis at his or her own tempo.

Rapid guided synthesis. Van der Hart and colleagues (1993) described a rapid variant of guided synthesis. During a thorough preparation with an observing part of the personality, a cognitive, rather depersonalized narrative account of the traumatic memory is constructed, including at least the pathogenic kernels. This account is divided into a number of segments, each accompanied by a number (e.g., from 1 to 5, or 1 to 10). Following the suggestion to start the synthesis ("Begin!"), the therapist counts, and with each count relates to the patient a successive kernel of the trauma, encouraging dissociative parts to share their respective partial experiences with each other. When the end of a round has been reached, the therapist announces "Stop: let it go for now" and gives suggestions for controlled breathing and for grounding in the present. After a few rounds, the therapist may inquire about what percentage of the whole traumatic memory has been shared and which aspects still remain unshared. When crucial aspects of the traumatic memory, including pathogenic kernels, remain unshared, other rounds can be negotiated or a joint decision can be made to postpone the remainder for the another session.

Fractionated guided synthesis. There is a much more gradual approach, *fractionated guided synthesis*, in which the synthesis of one traumatic memory or one series of traumatic memories is divided into a number of smaller steps, which may encompass several or even many sessions (Fine, 1993; Huber, 2003; Kluft, 1988, 1994a, 1999; Sachs & Peterson, 1996; Van der Hart, Steele et al., 1993). Such an approach is especially indicated when the patient's mental efficiency is very limited, but when the task of synthesizing a specific traumatic memory seems unavoidable (Kluft, 1989). Variations of this fractionated synthesis are endless. For example, see the case of Frieda described at the end of this chapter.

A session of guided synthesis may be limited only to the sensorimotor aspects (Ogden & Minton, 2000; Ogden et al., 2006). Or the focus may be on fear, pain, or anger, or might involve the sharing of only one EP's experience, or a specific time segment of the traumatic experience. The therapist may structure the synthesis in shorter counts; for instance, 5 instead of 10 counts, each one punctuated by suggestions for rest and comfortable breathing and connection with the therapist. Fractionated synthesis can also be paired with training in relaxation and calmness (Kluft, 1989; Van der Hart & Spiegel, 1993): systematic desensitization. Finally, in addition to fractionated synthesis, suggestions can be given for a very gradual or slow sharing of affect over time (Kluft, 1989). For example, Mary was instructed to allow all parts of herself to experience no more than five percent of the affect that was related to a specific traumatizing event. The therapist suggested to Susan, who loved to cook, that she remember no more and no less than just enough, like the exact amount of yeast needed to make bread rise. Carl, a computer engineer, was encouraged to let himself have just 10 bytes of information regarding a traumatic combat experience. In such cases, the patient makes his or her own subjective determination of the amount of affect (or sensation, etc.) to be experienced and is able to regulate it with the support of the therapist. Titrated synthesis may also occur with the use of EMDR and ample use of the subjective units of discomfort (SUDS) scale during the process (e.g., Gelinas, 2003; Twombly, 2000, 2005). However, the risk inherent with the use of EMDR with chronically traumatized individuals is that it often reactivates too much traumatic memory too quickly. Therefore, extreme care needs to be taken to use it within the frame described here.

Guided synthesis of pathogenic kernels. Conscious substitute beliefs regarding perpetrators and traumatic experiences must be addressed eventually with all parts. They often involve idealization of the caretaker/perpetrator and devaluation of self (e.g., "My father loved me; he would never hurt me. I seduced him; it was my fault"; "I was a bad child; I deserved it"; "I am so stupid and incompetent"). Various protector and persecutory EPs internally hound child parts and ANPs with these destructive messages. These substitute beliefs help the patient to maintain nonrealizations of the unbearable experiences underlying them (Janet, 1945).

The treatment of these beliefs includes several steps. First, the substitute beliefs are identified. Second, the dissociative parts that contain these beliefs are explored. Third, the therapist does not necessarily directly or immediately contradict the belief (e.g., "No, you were not a bad child"), but instead expresses curiosity as to how the patient came to that particular belief (e.g., "What makes you believe you were a bad child?"). Fourth, the therapist helps the dissociative part explore the feelings associated with the belief (e.g., "Could you share something of how it feels for you to believe you were a bad child and it was your fault?"). Thus the therapist engages in empathic attunement prior to confronting the maladaptive belief. Finally, the therapist helps the patient find more adaptive beliefs and objective evidence to the contrary in the present, and encourages parts to support each other in realizing that these beliefs are inaccurate.

Parts may be asked to share more positive statements, experiences, or characteristics with each other (e.g., "I am good at my work"; "I am a kind person"; "I did not cause the abuse to happen to me"). This can be done as a positive guided synthesis (e.g., Twombly, 2000, 2005).

Many substitute beliefs have at their root *pathogenic kernel statements* embedded with traumatic experiences that are not within ANP's awareness. These may be statements made by the perpetrator during abuse ("You're a slut; you like it"; "If you tell, I'll know and I'll kill you") or a belief by the patient at the time of traumatization ("I am going to die"; "This will never end"; "This is unbearable"). Such statements can operate like malignant hypnotic suggestions, resistant to cognitive therapy alone. These statements or beliefs are made when a dissociative part is in an extreme state of arousal with a very restricted field of consciousness, with no possibility to realize they are not true in the present. Guided synthesis of these pathogenic kernel statements together along with related affect and sensorimotor experiences will enable the patient to overcome their influence (e.g., "He can't know anymore if I tell"; "I did not want to be raped"; "It did end!").

> Léonie, a patient with DID, was raped at age 15 by her father, who subsequently killed her rabbit with a knife, then put the knife to her throat and threatened to do the same to her if she ever told anyone. When Léonie began to tell the therapist about this abuse as the EP who received the threat, she became extremely anxious and suicidal. Léonie as ANP was able to realize the impossibility of her father finding out that she had told of the abuse, let alone kill her for doing so. But the degree of reality of the threat for Léonie as EP was far too high to be resolved by cognitive interventions alone. Rather it required synthesis of the whole memory and realization of the EP that she was now in the present and was an adult.

Guided synthesis of dominant trauma-related affect. Guided synthesis can also be done with generalized negative affects (which often are also related to pathogenic kernel statements), such as intense feelings of loneliness, worthlessness, or suicidal feelings. These affects may not be connected to any specific traumatizing event but rather can be pervasive, such as the loneliness related to severe neglect. Guided synthesis consists of sharing this affect in degrees within the mental level of the patient. Sometimes substitute actions related to these affects, such as suicidal gestures, can be treated the same way.

Guided synthesis of trauma-related total submission. Traumatic memories may involve EPs that engaged in the animal defense of total submission or "playing dead" that involves an increase in dorsal vagal tone (Porges, 2001, 2003; Nijenhuis & Den Boer, in press). These parts are completely unresponsive and limp. Traumatic memories involving total submission and its inherent hypoarousal are very hard to treat, including memories that involved abuse when the victim was sedated through the use of drugs or alcohol. Synthesis of traumatic memories demands strenuous mental action, which is by definition mostly absent in this condition. Even the therapist's verbal encouragement is not sufficient.

Elsie, a patient with DDNOS, would become extremely sleepy and unable to move and think whenever a particular part of a traumatic memory was approached in guided synthesis. Grounding efforts by the therapist were not successful. The therapist understood this condition as one of total submission when the traumatic experience had become completely overwhelming. This EP had no elaborations, but was only described as a "limp little girl," that the survivor as ANP felt was "not me." The patient as ANP was able to report after one of these episodes that this "little girl" believed she was dead, that no one was coming to help her, and obviously did not realize the traumatizing event was over. This statement illuminated two pathogenic kernels that served as malignant hypnotic suggestions: "I am dead," and "No one will help." The therapist asked if the survivor as ANP, along with her inner wisdom, could bring the "little girl" into the present. The patient answered no, but she could go to the little girl. The therapist then asked if she could "accompany" the patient, and the patient answered yes. Through imagery, the therapist, the patient as ANP, and her inner wisdom as a figure in flowing robes went to the little girl. ANP shared with the EP that the event was over and that she was safe now and grown up: "Even though you might not understand that, I ask you to trust me. We are here to help you now." The little girl did not respond. The therapist reflected to the patient that the little girl could be surrounded on either side by her "fighting self" (fight action subsystem) that was active earlier in the event, and her "healing self" (recuperative action subsystem) that was active following the event, and that both aspects of her were very much alive and helped her survive. The ANP came up with an image of breathing life into the little girl, which she did, and the EP "woke up" and saw herself surrounded by caring "people" who could help her, and support her ability to fight and to heal. She was encouraged to feel her breathing and heartbeat, then to make tiny movements, such as blinking her eyes. She was grounded in the present in the therapist's office. ANP continued to reassure EP that she was safe and taken care of now. Following this synthesis session, the patient never had another episode of "shutting down" in session and reported much more physical and mental energy in daily life.

However, when the traumatic memories pertain to abuse in which sedatives or heavy doses of alcohol were used, hypoarousal may be so acute that more direct intervention is needed. The therapist can ask the patient if it is possible that an index finger could make a slight movement as an indication that the therapist has permission to touch the patient's hand. Following this minimal signal, the therapist does so and makes small squeezing movements on the patient's hand while counting and encouraging the parts inside to share this experience and to respond back to the therapist with small movements of his or her hand. This intervention involves appropriate physical contact which may help to activate the social engagement system involving the ventral vagal system (Porges, 2001, 2003; see Chapter 9), inducing an increase in mental efficiency that gradually makes successful synthesis possible.

Containment. During guided synthesis, the patient's arousal may be modulated and contained by using the image of a rheostat or scale. Distress, for example, can be gauged to a degree of 3 on a scale of 1 to 5. The therapist frequently checks with the patient about his or her level of arousal throughout the course of the synthesis, and closely monitors physical indications of hyper- or hypoarousal. Parts may be instructed that they "need only experience what is necessary to know, to understand, and to heal," or "to remember only what you are ready to remember." The therapist and patient make strenuous and consistent efforts to stay in contact, helping dissociative parts remain in the present. Parts may be asked not "to go back there in the past, but rather bring the memory here in the present with us."

In general, the unshared portions of traumatic memories that remain after a guided synthesis session should be dealt with in the next session, or soon thereafter. Precautions are taken that these aspects of the traumatic memory do not overwhelm the patient in between sessions. They may be contained with imagery, by having them stored in an imaginary bank vault, or by having parts agree not to share them with each other between sessions. These precautions involve using the patient's dissociative skills for therapeutic purposes, for gradual exposure. It is often useful to have cognitive processing sessions interspersed with guided synthesis sessions, because there needs to be time and support for the patient to fully realize (i.e., personalize) the traumatic memory. The patient should have learned the skills to manage arousal between sessions.

Guided Realization

With adequate synthesis, the traumatic memory no longer operates at an intrusive sensorimotor level. However, synthesis alone is insufficient for integration. In order for the traumatic memory to become an autobiographical memory, it must be realized; that is, personified and presentified (see Chapter 8). During or after a synthesis session, a survivor often will suddenly exclaim, "That happened to *me*!" indicating personification of the traumatic memory. At times, ANP may begin to personify EP: "That little girl is *me*!" Such statements indicate the patient is well on his or her way toward full realization.

But realization is not complete without presentification. The therapist supports the patient in realizing what can now be different in the present: "I don't have to be afraid anymore"; "I don't have to worry about making someone angry"; "It's OK that I have needs now." The survivor thus makes an accounting of the present that is shaped by the past, but no longer dictated by it. He or she finds meaning in what has happened and creates a more cohesive sense of time, reality, self, and experience that changes how the survivor acts in the present.

The therapist encourages the patient to make these statements of realization, and then supports him or her in following them up with new and creative actions, so that the cognitive belief can be accompanied by new feelings, perceptions, and behaviors (i.e., new perceptual–motor action cycles). One patient was able to start his own business because he realized, "No one will hit me if I make a mistake. I am smart enough to do this." Another was able to decide to have children because she realized, "I am not like my mother and won't hurt my children." A third began to feel comfortable for the first time with the opposite sex: "I realize no one is likely to hurt me now; I know how to seek out safe people." These kinds of realizations reverberate throughout the lives of survivors in Phases 2 and 3 of treatment. The therapist encourages the patient to continue talking about and acting upon these realizations in new and adaptive ways. And without the need to avoid the traumatic memory, the patient's mental energy and efficiency should be improved. Alterations in consciousness such as spacing out are diminished because the survivor can experience him- or herself being more present and mindful of the moment. The therapist monitors and encourages this presentification in the daily life of the patient.

The patient can now experience the present when giving an account of former traumatic experience(s). After becoming less avoidant and more accepting of EPs (Phase 1), the survivor as ANP needs to develop this ability to own (personify) past experiences, making a narrative account of traumatic experiences without dissociating any longer. In short:

> The patient must know how to associate the [traumatic] happening with the other events of his life, how to give it its place in that life-history which each of us is perpetually building up and which for each of us is an essential element of our personality. A situation has not been satisfactorily liquidated, has not been fully assimilated, until we have achieved, not merely an outward reaction through our movements, but also an inward reaction through the words we address to ourselves, through the organization of the recital of the events to others and to ourselves, and through the putting of this recital in its place as one of the chapters of our personal history. (Janet, 1919/1925, p. 662)

There has been much controversy over the veracity of recovered memories: Some can be corroborated, while others cannot (D. Brown, Scheflin, & Hammond, 1998; Courtois, 1999; Kluft, 1996b). Realization typically means the patient must accept the reality of what has happened to him or her. However, some survivors are unable to fully know cognitively what happened, but this need not impede full realization. One patient, who apparently had a preverbal traumatic experience, came up with a multitude of different scenarios, none of which she was sure were real. Yet, with the therapist's reassurance that she could use these stories to heal without either of them making a judgment about their veracity, she said, "I know something bad happened to me. I was hurt and scared. I was completely overwhelmed. I didn't get help when I needed it. That's enough for me to know and move on." The therapist may never know the veracity of some memories, and should not be the one who decides on objective truth (Courtois, 1999). Nevertheless, the therapist may eventually develop a reflective belief on this matter, which sometimes needs to be shared with, rather than being withheld from, the patient (Van der Hart & Nijenhuis, 1999).

Realization involves confrontation with enormous loss. The successful passage through grief work is essential for the ultimate integration of the patient's personality. The completion of these integrative mental actions is essential for the resolution of structural dissociation, and their failure underlies continuation of structural dissociation. In Phase 2 the therapist helps the patient grieve a shattered childhood with support. But the therapist must engage in his or her own realization that there is nothing that can replace the patient's losses. Instead, the therapist helps the patient turn to new experiences in the present as grieving for the past continues and gradually subsides. In Phase 3, many survivors may have a renewed and more profound sense of grief as they realize that traumatic experiences prevented a life well-lived up until the present time, and that some hopes and dreams are no longer realistic.

MARTHA: A CASE EXAMPLE
OF GUIDED SYNTHESIS

Martha is a 48-year-old patient with DID, who illustrates how Phase 1 work may easily proceed to Phase 2 treatment, when the patient is ready. Her therapy also illustrates the use of imagery techniques. Over the course of Phase 1, there was an ongoing cycle of increasing cooperation between therapist and patient and among dissociative parts. Following the therapist's advice, dissociative parts developed inner safe spaces and an inner meeting room in which they met twice a day, planning and evaluating their activities of the day, but without sharing traumatic material.

When Martha as ANP had to undergo a series of intrusive medical procedures, she was unable to complete them, once running away in the middle of a procedure, as traumatic memories of violent abuse were reactivated. The therapist suggested that EPs could create an imaginary gate between their inner world and the outside world. Then he asked which parts could tolerate being present during a medical procedure scheduled for the next week, encouraging as many as possible of Martha's dissociative parts to be present at once based on her mental level. Once Martha identified these parts, the therapist suggest that the rest of the parts should practice staying behind the soundproof gate, and encouraged Martha to practice this technique every day. In the next session Martha reported never having been so quiet during such an intrusive medical procedure.

This corrective experience formed the basis for the treatment of her traumatic memories. The therapist explained the rationale and procedure of protecting parts from information that was, as yet, too threatening. Three parts that had undergone a particular traumatic experience and two helper parts came together in an inner "soundproof room," and shared together the factual information of the traumatizing event. Martha listed four of the most painful moments, the *pathogenic kernels*, which she gave to the therapist in the next session.

After explaining the guided synthesis procedure again, the therapist invited the five parts to come forward, with all other parts safely behind the inner gate. He asked them to stay in constant contact with him and to raise a hand if a break was needed. He then read the text regarding the first pathogenic kernel and, with each count (from 1 to 5) suggested that they share that experience with each other and "make it one whole." Following the count of 5, he suggested stopping the synthesis and asked Martha to control her breathing, with "all parts breathing together." When Martha indicated she was ready, they continued the experience. The therapist asked if he should read the same text again or could continue with the next. In this way the whole guided synthesis, experienced by the patient as very intense, took approximately 15 minutes. At the end the therapist asked what percentage of the whole experience had been shared, and the answer was "all of it." He then gave suggestions for comfort and well-being. Martha as ANP and the other parts involved were impressed by the intensity of the task and by their own successful performance.

The next session was used to cognitively process the synthesis session and the traumatic memory, which still needed to get "a place in the system," as Martha said. To the therapist's surprise, Martha needed a brief hospitalization following the synthesis session, because she reported the memory had been too overwhelming. Following a brief return to Phase 1 work, another guided synthesis was attempted one month later. Again, Martha required a brief hospitalization. The therapist expressed surprise and asked how the memory of the event could be overwhelming following a highly successful synthesis. An EP noted that participating parts had encouraged the parts behind the soundproof gate to "listen in" for the purpose of further realization. This information was too overwhelming for some of those parts, hence the need for hospitalization. This pointed to the therapist's oversight regarding how the traumatic experience was to be shared with the parts which had not participated in the synthesis. It also highlights the extent to which a patient might over- or underestimate his or her overall mental level based upon the mental level of only some dissociative parts. The extent to which the patient has successfully engaged in synthesis and realization can only become evident with time. Fortunately, Martha was able to find a suitable solution.

After a number of successful synthesis sessions, always interspersed with sessions dedicated to Phase 1 tasks, the patient wrote that she had successfully learned to regulate her experiences herself:

> We now come together long before the synthesis session (i.e., one or two weeks in advance) in a soundproof room, where we discuss the next synthesis with those parts who want to share the traumatic memory. . . . We have created a semipermeable wall ("membrane") between us and the other parts which wasn't present at the guided synthesis. In this way, dewdrop by dewdrop, very smoothly, by osmosis, the information of the shared traumatic experience will enter the system and the others, who can receive and understand it better. Thus, we don't confront them directly with the hard truth, and in this way we don't have to be admitted [to a crisis center] anymore.

This solution involved the patient's own graduated exposure to balance the limited mental level of the parts that needed to synthesize and realize the traumatic experiences more slowly. Martha subsequently stated that the differences between "normal" sessions and guided synthesis sessions became less. In short, the patient had been able to break down the complex task of synthesizing and realizing traumatic experiences into manageable steps by setting up her own form of graduated exposure to the traumatic memories. The quality of her life increased significantly, with Phase 2 work alternating with that of Phase 1.

FRIEDA: A CASE OF FRACTIONATED GUIDED SYNTHESIS

Frieda, a 31 year old woman who had been chronically traumatized as a child, had been in psychiatric care for more than 15 years when she was eventually diagnosed as DID. She engaged in frequent self-destructive acts, and was seriously suicidal. It became apparent in Phase 1 treatment that her suicidality related to an inability to regulate intense sadness and anger, and to a pervasive phobia of attachment. None of her EPs dared express affect. They feared that crying would never end once it started, would drive Frieda crazy, and that she would be severely punished for crying and showing anger. They frequently intruded into her several ANPs with flashbacks and overwhelming feelings, making daily life difficult. The therapist and Frieda worked on the objectives of Phase 1 treatment: stabilization, skills building, and the therapeutic relationship. Frieda had been unable to create an inner safe space for any part of herself. She had been chronically traumatized and neglected in childhood by her caretakers, abused by a psychiatrist in her teens, and subjected to long-term seclusion in isolation rooms. Thus, safety seemed to have no meaning for her. The therapist encouraged her to think of times when she had felt a little less unsafe than other times instead of beginning with the foreign concept of safety. He helped her gradually realize that she did not feel unsafe in session, and indeed sometimes experienced a new feeling which she was eventually able to label as one of safety. Over time, some ANPs were able to imagine being in the therapist's office and feeling safe. The therapist began to use this image to help EPs become more oriented and safe, and to encourage ANPs to do the same internally. The ANPs were also encouraged to be more empathic and open to the difficult feelings of the EPs, which they previously avoided. Next, the therapist intervened to stop EPs that were chronically intruding into Frieda's daily life with flashbacks by using fractionated guided synthesis. He assisted ANPs to experience and tolerate small portions of the intruding affect of EPs, and encouraged these EPs to express their affect in small amounts. He suggested that the ANP that seemed to have the highest relative integrative capacity could allow just a few tears of one sad EP, if only just for a few seconds. When Frieda succeeded in this challenge, he complimented her, and focused on her joy in action: Frieda smiled. Next, he suggested that she could have a few more tears, for a somewhat longer period. A further step was to allow a little cognitive content to her tears, i.e., short glimpses of realization about the reasons why she was sad. These and subsequent steps were interspersed with actions of triumph such as Frieda laughing and joking.

Therapy proceeded in recurrent alternation between Phase 1 and Phase 2 interventions. Phase 2 interventions allowed Frieda to very slowly integrate her traumatic memories. For example, Frieda needed to realize the abuse by the psychiatrist in very small segments. One session was dedicated to her fear and awe of him; another to her dread of his touch; another to the pain of forced penetration; and yet others to her mixed feelings of shame and pride at his attention. In this way, small portions of the memory were realized over time until Frieda could make a complete narrative and was no longer phobic of the memories. In the process, her dissociative parts experienced that affect is neither lethal nor endless, and that it can be met with empathy and support, not only from another, but from within. This realization also served to strengthen her sense of secure attachment with the therapist and a new sense of confidence and trust in herself.

SUMMARY

The treatment of traumatic memories is a difficult phase of therapy. Over the course of Phase 2 treatment, various phobias must be systematically and gradually addressed: phobias related to insecure attachment to perpetrators; phobias related to attachment and attachment loss in EPs; and the core phobia of traumatic memories. The major goal of the treatment of traumatic memories is their integration in the patient's personality as a whole (synthesis and realization, with the components of personification and presentification). Guided synthesis is the systematic (graduated) exposure of parts of the personality to traumatic memories with prevention of redissociation or avoidance. This must be done within the patients' mental level. Rapid and fractionated synthesis are the two major types of guided synthesis, although there are countless variations. The technique is not only used for discrete traumatic memories but also for pathogenic kernel statements, malignant posthypnotic suggestions, pervasive trauma-related affect, and even for the integration of positive experiences. Synthesis is necessary but not sufficient for full integration, but requires further work toward realization, including personification and presentification.

CHAPTER 17

Phase 3 Treatment

Integration of the Personality and Overcoming the Phobias of Normal Life

> *[W]e come to the more ambitious methods of treatment which aim not only at using and saving what a patient already possesses but also at enabling the patient to acquire further tendencies or to recuperate those which he has lost.*
>
> —Pierre Janet (1919/1925, p. 709)

ONCE ENOUGH HAS BEEN DONE in Phase 2 to allow the patient to integrate most of his or her traumatic memories such that these memories have become autobiographical narratives, Phase 3 can be initiated. This phase is geared toward maximum integration. It involves unification of the personality in most cases and focusing on the highest action tendencies that contribute to the most adaptive life possible. Generally there is rather spontaneous movement back and forth into Phase 2, taking place when the patient begins to initiate exploration of Phase 3 issues.

Extensive descriptions of Phase 3 treatment are often absent in the literature, in part because intensive focus is placed on Phases 1 and 2 due to the many complex skills needed in these phases by both patient and therapist (but see L. Brown, Russell, Thornton, & Dunn, 1999; Kluft, 1993b, 1993c). There is also the persistent myth that merely integrating traumatic experiences is sufficient for overcoming traumatization. In fact, Phase 3 may contain some of the most difficult work yet (Van der Hart, Steele, Boon, & Brown, 1993). The patient engages in painful grieving, along with the relinquishment of long-held core substitute beliefs, and the struggle to adapt to life with new mental and behavioral actions.

These actions require high degrees of sustained mental efficiency, especially until they become more familiar and habitual. The patient must be encouraged to practice regularly actions that involve increasing levels of personification and presentification, and a widening field of consciousness and raising the level of consciousness. The highest levels of action tendencies are encouraged, especially those involving systematic exploration and experimentation in life, and those which contribute to the quality and meaning of the patient's life.

FUSION OF DISSOCIATIVE PARTS
OF THE PERSONALITY

In some patients, fusions among some dissociative parts of the personality proceed on their own with little prompting from the therapist. Martha, a DID patient with strongly elaborated parts, noted with some satisfaction following years of intense resistance to fusion, "once integration [among parts] is on its way, you can't stop it." Emotional parts of the personality (EPs) mediated by the same action system(s) may more easily fuse with each other than parts that are guided by discrepant action systems. In more severe cases of secondary structural dissociation and in DID (tertiary structural dissociation), parts of the personality generally make a more gradual approach toward fusion with each other, needing more interventions by the therapist to help them become less divided and emancipated over time. This occurs as they slowly overcome their phobias of each other, of traumatic memories, and of other trauma-derived actions.

Some dissociative patients are invested in separateness and thus have a *phobia of fusion*, which is a specific aspect of the phobia of dissociative parts of the personality. They may have come to value various "separate" parts as powerful internal transitional objects, and strongly grieve their loss. They may experience loneliness, emptiness, and complain of "too much quiet" internally, having been accustomed to the "company" of other parts (Somer & Nave, 2001). Debby, a patient with complex PTSD, expressed the fear as EP that "I will no longer be myself," while Martha as ANP initially was more vehement in her fear about the therapist "murdering my inner people." When this resistance is the case, the therapist helps the patient (or dissociative parts) express fears and concerns of loss and reminds the patient of previous fusions among parts that have been helpful. Fusions will inevitably fail if they are forced, because the patient does not have the motivation or sufficient mental level to sustain them, or fears the losses he or she perceives is involved in fusion. In general, patients do not lose skills and attributes of particular parts when they fuse, but learn to use them in more adaptive ways, often within higher levels of integration of action systems.

As ANP, Martin had been able to engage in highly focused and successful work because he was able to avoid internal distractions and conflicts. When his dissociative parts began to fuse, he was confronted with the need to tend not only to exteroceptive, but also to interoceptive stimuli. His ability to focus exclusively on work was disrupted and he complained that he had lost his capacity to focus. Actually, he lost his capacity to completely avoid and ignore interoceptive stimuli while working. He felt this loss until he gradually learned a more adaptive balance between his own personal needs and those of work.

Some patients will manifest great reluctance to engage in the mental actions of final fusions (unification), up to the point of leaving therapy. This is often based on a phobia of the most traumatic experiences or condition in their life, such as the realization, with full personification and presentification, that their parents have always rejected them, never loved them, and that they have always been unbearably lonely. Such realization demands the highest mental level, yet is necessary in order to overcome their phobia of intimacy, to completely transform "surviving life" to "living life." In order to help the patient with taking this final hurdle, the therapist needs to be very understanding and patient. Thus he or she should be highly respectful of the patient's decision to abstain from this major integrative challenge, while keeping the option open of a return to it: Good timing is essential.

There are several ways in which the therapist can guide the fusion of dissociative parts: formal, planned fusion rituals, with or without hypnosis; or the encouragement of temporary blendings of parts (e.g., Kluft, 1993c). As the patient gradually overcomes the phobia of dissociative parts, the ensuing internal empathy and cooperation will go a long way toward diminishing the patient's phobia of fusion. Dissociative parts can be encouraged, as an experiment, to simulate fusion for a short period in a session (Fine & Comstock, 1989), and then later to practice this simulation in daily life. Parts can be asked to "feel a feeling all together," or "think a thought all together," or "engage in an action together."

Some patients prefer or need formal rituals to complete the fusion of dissociative parts. Fusion metaphors may be helpful, especially when they come from the patient. The therapist suggests confidence that the patient can find his or her own unique way to "become whole." Some common metaphors include "holding hands," "stepping into each other," "being in a circle together," "walking into a healing white light together and becoming one whole." As the therapist searches for hidden and final resistances, he or she begins to ask the patient if there are any reasons why parts should *not* be together.

Therapeutic actions need to continue to support these integrative steps, which may be disrupted by external life crises or the emergence of new traumatic memories. In fact, during Phase 3 it is quite common for more traumatic memories to emerge, as well as additional parts of the personality. The latter is particularly common in tertiary structural dissociation (DID). This return to traumatic memories is an expected evolution of treatment in complex cases of traumatization, and during such times there will be a temporary revisiting of Phases 1 and 2. Previously unresolved substitute beliefs emerge and become available for change, such as, "I am incapable of having relationships"; "Nothing good will happen to me." The patient must reevaluate and change basic assumptions and beliefs regarding safety, meaning, aloneness, causality and locus of control, power, trust and intimacy, autonomy and interdependence, and a sense of the future and sense of belonging (L. Brown et al., 1999; Janoff-Bulman, 1992; McCann & Pearlman, 1990).

The therapist often prematurely assumes that fusion of all previously dissociative parts has occurred, when he or she may have overlooked further work that still needs to be done. As a general rule, what appears to be "final fusion" between dissociative parts of the personality is not the last one. Based on his observation of a large treatment cohort, Kluft (1993c) stated that only after 27 months of no further manifestations of dissociation in DID patients may one safely assume that integration is indeed secure, indicating a need for thorough and prolonged follow-up.

OVERCOMING THE PHOBIAS
OF NORMAL LIFE

The phobias that are addressed in Phase 3 involve learning to live a normal life that is relatively free of traumatic intrusion. This involves gradual exposure to more of normal life for the survivor, who has lived in chaos or who has avoided life. And most importantly, the survivor learns to engage in the higher levels of action tendencies in a sustained manner, which requires high levels of mental energy and efficiency.

Overcoming Resistances to Normal Life

Prior to Phase 2 work, the survivor has chronically reacted to conditioned stimuli in normal life that reactivate traumatic memories. Thus the survivor learned to avoid and constrict many aspects of life. Normal life involves a requirement to adapt to and integrate a wide variety of complex and sometimes difficult and conflicting actions. This can be a daunting task to a patient whose life has been organized around restriction, avoidance, denial, and structural dissociation.

In Phase 3, the patient's life must first be appraised for its level of actual normalcy (obviously, there is a wide range of what is considered "normal"), including what the patient wishes to achieve. During this phase the patient may develop new goals that he or she could not have imagined previously, such as having an intimate relationship, going back to school, or getting a better job. It is imperative to determine if the patient has a relatively balanced life in terms of work, play, rest, and relationships, and that these experiences are meaningful and personalized. In other words, the patient needs to be able to adaptively engage in action systems according to the desires and needs in his or her own unique life. Often this is not the case, because normal life requires high integrative capacity and flexibility and coordination among action systems. Although much synthesis and realization may have occurred by Phase 3, there remains the work of fully activating and refining action systems and their interdependence.

> As ANP, Terri, a patient with complex PTSD, was an excellent mother who was able to successfully integrate several child EPs. However, neither ANP nor EPs had much experience with the exploratory and play action systems (although Terri as ANP was quite adept in supporting her children in play and exploration as part of her caretaking functions). Thus there remained an absence of recreation, humor, and playfulness in relationship in Terri's life. Her play and exploration systems were progressively activated through psychoeducation, practice of increasingly prolonged and complex tasks (Van der Hart et al., 1989), observation of other people, and the gradual development of several friendships with people who were more adept in these areas, and at times, additional resolution of substitute beliefs and traumatic memories.

The patient must learn to deal with routines, and some degree of monotony in a new life that is no longer chaotic, and thus not always exciting or hyperarousing. At first, he or she may confuse being calm and peaceful with hypoarousal and numbness, and be reluctant to settle into a quieter, more stable life. The patient must also learn the differences between interest and obsession (e.g., with work), between a constricted life and adaptive stability, and between rigidity and healthy routines. Angela, a patient with resolved DID both enjoyed and struggled with a new kind of life in this final phase of treatment:

> This morning I went to the market and thought, this is becoming my normal life, work, comfortable companionship with other people who are dear to me, and then doing what I want during the weekend. And I thought, I have received a new future and I hope that it will last a long time. A new future means taking on things not only to survive or to drive the misery away for a short while, but just being here and now and living. I can do something about the things in life that I wish for. I can carefully give form to some of my life as I want it and I can do it consciously and purposefully, because I have a future perspective. This is new for me. I don't know how I must fit this in emotionally. I am moved by it and I am emotional about it: It's so new and also so confusing because I am not used to it. Everything falls together now and I can finally become myself. I can only cry, I am finally here.

Adaptive Grieving

Immersion in normal life often brings heightened joy and excitement with each new gain and positive experience. But simultaneously there occurs profound grief about missing out on normal life for so long. *Both the joy and sadness are related to the realization of the new gains as well as having missed them so long.* With each new gain, this grieving is recurrent, as the patient further realizes the losses related to the cumulative miseries of traumatization. The survivor also begins to realize more strongly that normal life is sometimes fraught with loss, pain, disappointments, and other difficult experiences. It is not the golden fantasy for which he or she had hoped.

Grieving may involve a period of traumatic rage and anger, in which the patient is not yet ready to accept losses, but rather seeks retribution or focuses on the injustices done to him or her. The survivor struggles with the reality that life is not fair. Mere expression of this rage is not sufficient: The patient must be supported in adaptive grieving, which means he or she must eventually find ways in which to let go of anger and resentment. This may be through forgiveness, though this is not a necessary step. Sometimes a strong realization that the past cannot be changed is enough to propel the survivor to focus his or her mental energy on the present, and in adaptive planning for the future. In other words, the patient engages more strongly in core and extended presentification.

Adaptive grieving is accompanied by strong awareness of the present, the ability to self-soothe, to receive comfort from others, and to become satisfied with new gains in life and connection with others. The survivor must accept the reality of his or her losses, experience the pain, grief, anger, and disappointment, and then adjust to life after these losses, and redirect emotional energy toward the real present (Worden, 2001). But this is more easily said than done. Grief is hard; it is a task for the emotionally hardy and takes tremendous and sustained mental energy and efficiency. It can be overwhelming at times, and has a strong physical component that mimics sensations of traumatization: anxiety, anger, restlessness, dread, suspense, despair, loneliness, guilt, shame. As C. S. Lewis noted in his essay on grief following the death of his wife, "No one ever told me grief felt so like fear" (1961, p. 7). Feelings of grief can be similar to feelings that occurred during traumatization and thus may be conditioned stimuli that survivors have long avoided and make it even more difficult for them to enter the grief process. And grief is long-lived. Though the therapist may feel impatient with the occasional slow pace of the survivor in this stage, grief "turns out to be not a state but a process. It needs not a map but a history" (C. S. Lewis, 1961, p. 47).

The therapist can play an essential role in successful grief work by empathically *bearing witness* to the survivor's suffering (and subsequent healing) while helping him or her remain in the present, thus restoring the empathic connection with self, others, and the world that was lost during traumatization (Herman, 1992b; Laub & Auerhahn, 1989; Van der Hart, Steele et al., 1993; Van der Hart & Nijenhuis, 1999). The therapist also explores resistances to moving through grieving and associated core beliefs: "I can't tolerate the sadness"; "I've lost so much I'll never get over it"; "Life really isn't worth living." Then the therapist assists the patient in integrating the sadness and losses by gradual exposure to the feelings, and encouragement for the patient to own them (personification), and realize and act adaptively upon the consequences for the present (presentification). Leave-taking rituals in which the patient is able to symbolically let go of a loss from the past can be powerful (Van der Hart, 1988a, 1998b). Gradually, the patient realizes "that loss is an inevitable part of trauma, and that it is ultimately a lifelong task to assimilate the ebb and flow of re-experienced grief with equanimity" (Van der Hart, Steele et al., 1993, p. 173).

As any remaining dissociative parts become available, the patient works toward the goals of integrating action systems in an internally cooperative and cohesive manner, and internal states become less conflicted. Gradual exposure to situations in which new adaptations and learning can occur is essential to resolving the phobia of normal life, but such experiences evoke yet another related phobia: That of healthy risk taking and change.

Overcoming the Phobia of Healthy Risk-Taking and Change

Risk taking and change are necessary for continued adaptation to current circumstances. However, many traumatized patients fear change in general, leading to a monotonous and restricted lifestyle, albeit chaotic at times, since chaos is familiar to most patients. Janet (1903, 1909a) noted that a phobia related to adapting to new situations was one of the first difficulties that signals a lowering of the mental level. At more severe levels, this phobia can manifest in intense avoidance and fear of any internal or external change. Some degree of pain and anxiety is normal as individuals take chances to grow and develop in various areas of their lives, and as they move toward progressive individuation, the highest levels of action tendencies (Firestone & Catlett, 1999). It is a natural human tendency to ignore, avoid, or resist change (Caissy, 1998). Mostly, we are able to overcome our normal fears of change and move ahead. But survivors learned to avoid the anxiety and uncertainty inherent in change and developed habitual patterns of inhibition and self-sabotage that prevent change, become ever more fearful of risk taking.

The phobia of change is often particularly evident in certain ANPs. Survivors have tried and failed to change irrevocable *external* circumstances because they cannot accept their reality. One of the most important aspects of adapting to change is the ability to accept reality as it is (Caissy, 1998), to realize the present (core presentification) and also to realize the past and future (extended presentification). The survivor has had little understanding of the necessity to adapt to prevailing situations by making adaptive internal changes: "Not being able to control events, I control myself; and I adapt myself to them, if they do not adapt themselves to me" (De Montaigne, 1993, p. 981).

In this third phase of treatment some patients begin to realize that they are afraid of "getting better," because they have associated it with negatively evaluated change. The therapist must be alert to this possibility and explore with the patient possible resistances and their associated substitute beliefs. For example, one patient was afraid if she got better no one would ever help her again because she would be completely independent. Another was afraid getting better meant leaving his therapist, which seemed intolerable. A third was afraid getting better meant becoming someone other than herself. Each of these patients had an extremely maladaptive view of what it meant "to get better" that entailed pain, loss, and abandonment.

Treatment consists of correcting substitute beliefs regarding change (e.g., it is dangerous, is intolerable, is irrevocable, will induce helplessness and incompetence). Sometimes these beliefs are rooted in remaining traumatic memories, requiring a return to Phase 2.

> Rachel, a patient with complex PTSD, made a very clear and concrete connection between her fear of *any* change and the onset of abuse: "When my father started having sex with me, *everything* changed. Change to me represents the most awful thing that could happen. Sex hurt, so change will hurt."

Change is thus often perceived as a severe threat. Practice and graduated exercises involving activation of the exploration through exposure to change are essential. Also, the patient should be supported in developing an increased awareness and personalization of safe changes that have occurred throughout therapy, and a sustained mental effort related to change and risk. Transitional rituals that mark change can be helpful (Van der Hart, 1983).

Overcoming the Phobia of Intimacy

Overcoming the phobia of intimacy is perhaps the pinnacle of successful treatment. The patient should be assisted in approaching intimacy in a graduated manner, overcoming fear of emotional intimacy prior to physical and sexual intimacy, as the last two generally require the first to be in place. Intimacy requires the integration of many action systems within the field of personal consciousness and the highest levels of sustained personification and presentification. For example, intimacy is at its best when it includes not only attachment, but when each person is open and curious about the other (exploration), playful (play), sociable with others outside the intimate relationship, engages in good physical and emotional self-care (energy regulation), and can engage in healthy caretaking when necessary (caretaking).

To be intimate means to be in a relationship with our whole self. For mature intimacy to occur one must have overcome phobias of trauma-derived mental actions, of attachment, of traumatic memories, of risk taking and change, and of normal life. We most often think of intimacy in terms of our ability to love well, which is one of our central human challenges.

Intimacy takes various forms, such as emotional, physical (nonsexual), and sexual. Phobias may be related to some or all of these forms: Different survivors will experience various permutations of the phobia of intimacy. To a large degree, the phobia of emotional intimacy will have been addressed within the therapeutic relationship, which should offer the experience of secure attachment within which the survivor can be truly known in all his or her aspects. However, overcoming the phobia of intimacy implies the realization that one's own capacity for intimacy is not limited to a relationship with a single individual (i.e., the therapist). This realization is only complete when intimacy can be experienced in less controlled situations—in the "real" world with other individuals.

An analysis of the patient's substitute beliefs and pathogenic kernel statements regarding intimacy is essential. The patient can be asked to explore his or her beliefs about closeness, sexual relationships, and emotional vulnerability with others. In this way the therapist can empathically challenge core reflexive beliefs. Some involve effects of classical conditioning, such as, "I will never trust another man again" and entail negative predictions such as, "Love is just another way to get hurt" and "It's better never to share feelings because they will be used against you." These trauma-related core beliefs often inspire promises (other reflexive beliefs), to avoid conditioned stimuli such as "I will never get close to anyone again" and "I will never share my deepest feelings." Reflexive beliefs can also represent conditioned negative evaluations such as, "Bodies and sex are awful; I hate my body, I loathe sex." The treatment of these reflexive beliefs will depend on their status. Conditioned predictions can be proven false through exposure, in which conditioned avoidance reactions are blocked. Thus, a survivor can learn that showing his or her deepest feelings is not generally dangerous by receiving support rather than rejection. Conditioned negative evaluations can be changed by counterconditioning. For example, a survivor can learn in small self-controlled steps that bodies and sex have different and positive qualities from those he or she previously experienced.

Various parts of the personality may have conflicting beliefs; for example, with ANP wanting an intimate relationship and EP being distrustful of everyone. The patient may become increasingly aware of the discrepancy between the tendency to cling to these ideas and the tendency to become gradually more intimate with other people. The development of more reflective beliefs may involve experiencing ambivalence. Experiencing doubt, uncertainty, and confusion is occasionally one consequence of engaging in more than one action (sub)system at a time (e.g., "Should I rest today or go out with friends?"). Dissociative individuals have typically avoided such ambivalence by having different parts that represent different interests. During and after fusion, survivors begin to experience more conflicts and ambivalence as they simultaneously synthesize and realize different goals/actions. Ambivalence is a price of increasing integration.

The therapist helps the patient examine the quality (and quantity) of his or her everyday relationships as the patient can now integrate far more, and may be able to work on relational issues that previously were not possible to resolve. As the patient changes and becomes more emotionally healthy, many relationships may fall by the wayside. The patient begins to want healthier relationships, and this can affect friendships, partnerships, and marriages. Often, couples and family therapy is an important part of Phase 3. In some cases, the therapist supports the patient in deciding whether or not a relationship must be (dis)continued. The therapist obviously does not decide for the patient whether or not he or she should end a negative relationship but does discuss the issue with the survivor, and helps him or her take stock of the pros and cons of such a relationship. The therapist also helps the patient with the phobia of change in this regard. The patient is also supported in grieving the loss of relationships and is encouraged to move through periods of isolation and to seek out new and healthier relationships. The therapist must be highly sensitive to what is reasonable and desired by the patient in terms of a healthy support system.

Usually the patient has extreme resistance to the experience of loss, a universal and very human risk associated with intimacy. Increasing levels of presentification will prevent the patient from living in the perceived catastrophic future, full of unbearable loss, or in the past, in which relational loss or hurt was predominant. In addition, the patient must be able to tolerate the very ordinary glitches and difficulties that arise within normal intimate relationships *in the present*. The patient must come to a realization of the costs of avoiding relationships, or engaging in unboundaried relationships. These high level relational actions require adequate conflict resolution skills, empathy, self-soothing, reflective thought rather than reflexive action, and the ability to distinguish gradations of difficulty in relationship, so that over- or underreaction does not occur. In other words, they require the patient to operate at the highest levels of action tendencies.

Intimacy requires flexible but stable limits and boundaries, both internal and relational. Patients generally have to learn the importance of personal boundaries, how and when to apply them, and how to respond effectively to others' boundaries without feeling rejected by recognizing that "good fences make good neighbors." Effective boundaries reduce fear of intimacy, giving some sense of personal control, and equalizing the balance of power in relationships. The therapist encourages the survivor to rehearse healthy interactions in imagination or in role play (D. Brown & Fromm, 1986). That is, he or she fosters more adaptive mental and behavioral simulations of the future. In this way, the therapist helps the survivor to anticipate the near future in more realistic ways. In many cases, this engagement in more adaptive presentification is a first step in changing the survivor's actions in real life. The patient gradually realizes the paradox that real intimacy is not in merging or twinship, or being taken care of by another, but instead requires strong individuation and autonomy, which depends on developing high level action tendencies. Thus, the patient learns to balance adaptive dependency and adaptive autonomy (Steele et al., 2001).

Intimacy and the body. Intimacy involves being noticed by others, including in physical ways. Survivors are often acutely sensitive about their looks and their bodies. In Phase 3 the patient needs to learn to accept and care for his or her physical well-being more adequately as part of feeling like a desirable human being and as a result of feeling more self-intimacy. This involves overcoming the phobia of physical and emotional feelings. This can often be achieved through counterconditioning, such as helping the survivor associate emotions and physical sensations with ever more pleasant experiences. For example, emphasis is now placed on physical self-care and enjoyment of the body, as well as a gradual increase in intimate physical interaction with a loving partner. Control on behalf of the survivor regarding the form, degree, and duration of such exposure to previously avoided stimuli is pivotal.

Unfortunately, enduring and sometimes serious physical problems are common for adult survivors of childhood traumatization (Felitti et al., 1998; Landau & Litwin, 2000; Romans, Belaise, Martin, Morris, & Raffi, 2002; Schnurr & Jankowski, 1999). In later phases of treatment, some survivors may struggle with ongoing physical problems they had hoped would dissipate with the resolution of traumatic memories. Or they may be diagnosed with serious and chronic disorders as they age. There may be grief, anger, depression, and fear related to poor health as the patient struggles to realize that the present is not always what was wished for. Such physical problems may reactivate fears about pain, death, helplessness, rejection, and dependency. These problems must be worked through in brief returns to Phase 2 because these fears are often rooted in still unresolved traumatic memories. Nonetheless, some survivors have good health, and with the support of the therapist and others they can begin to enjoy their physical body as they establish healthy and regular patterns of exercise, eating, and relaxation.

Sexual intimacy. Sexual intimacy presents a particular set of obstacles to survivors, particularly those who were sexually abused. First, it involves the survivor's body, which has often been a source of distress, shame, and other negative experiences (Chapter 15). Second, it typically involves attachment, which has its own set of phobias (Chapter 14). Finally, sexual acts in themselves may be extreme conditioned stimuli that reactivate traumatic memories of sexual abuse and associated catastrophic reflexive beliefs. Maria, a patient with BPD exclaimed, "Of all things, I hate sex the most! It reminds me that I am just a dirty 'thing' to be used by somebody else." These are conditioned negative evaluations of her body, of sexual feelings, and of sex itself.

The unified patient may begin to have sexual feelings for the first time, which had previously been sequestered in a dissociative part, or to feel safe and enjoy them. He or she can be encouraged to find the right pace in being sexual, learning to respect boundaries (e.g., D. Brown & Fromm, 1986). A number of techniques exist for helping survivors to overcome their phobia of sexuality (e.g., Brown & Fromm, 1986; Maltz, 2001). Many of these interventions involve gradual exposure with relapse prevention, relaxation training, and systematic desensitization, all within the mental level of the patient.

> Toni, a DID patient who was stably integrated, was still phobic of sex with her partner. Yet she wanted to experience the intimacy of a sexual relationship. The therapist encouraged her to talk with her partner and develop an agreement in which Toni would initiate nonsexual touch and as she felt comfortable, she could initiate more sexual touch, which included planning and execution of gradual, self-controlled exposure in a safe environment to create new associations between touch, control, and pleasure. For several months Toni and her partner practiced regularly, with Toni in control of all touch. When Toni felt anxious she was instructed to stop, be aware of her maladaptive thoughts (e.g., "It's going to hurt"; "I'll be raped"), and engage in pleasurable, progressive relaxation. Then she was to return to the exercise with her partner (prevention of avoidance tendencies, gentle return to exposure and practice). During therapy sessions, she and her therapist worked on her substitute beliefs about sex and sexuality ("cognitive" interventions). Gradually Toni felt more comfortable with nonsexual physical touch (self-generated positive reinforcement of touch). She began to initiate more sexual touch, at first fearfully. But as she followed the protocol of stopping, relaxing, and moving forward again, she felt increasingly in con-

trol, and could allow herself to feel sexual pleasure for the first time with another person. She was proud of herself, and her partner was proud of her too (act of triumph; positive reinforcement).

Fostering the Highest Levels
of Action Tendencies

When individuals operate at the highest action tendencies, they engage in new, innovative, and highly complex mental and motor actions. This requires high and sustained mental energy and efficiency. They are able to work, play, and love well. They are curious about their world and themselves, create lives that are interesting and stimulating, and are not afraid to try new things. Life at this level can be described as relatively rich and full. This does not mean, of course, that life is perfect by any means. Yet regardless of what comes their way for better or worse, healthy individuals are able to derive meaning and purpose, stay connected with those whom they love, and can face life with equanimity, humor, and humility.

There is a Zen saying, "Before enlightenment, chop wood, carry water; after enlightenment, chop wood, carry water." This koan speaks to the need for full presentification and personification even in the most mundane actions of our lives if we are to find meaning and satisfaction, and to explore the more profound experiences of life. The level of *prolonged reflective actions* involves the ability to sustain mindful actions over time, with focus, purpose, and initiative. We can work for ideals and long-term goals. Such reflective actions are necessary not only for work that interests us, but for chores and other mundane but necessary activities of daily life.

Much of the survivor's difficulties with routines and chores is that they continue to persist in alterations in consciousness that lower their interest and focus. Treatment consists of supporting the patient in practicing mindful awareness of activities in the moment (e.g., washing dishes, paying bills), and attaining ever more conscious control over undue alterations in consciousness that are conditioned reactions. This encourages more sustained personification and presentification. Such work should have begun in Phase 1, and now is applied more pervasively across the patient's life as he or she begins to live as a more unified human being.

The patient at this level has a sense of logic and a relatively accurate perception of self and others. This is because action systems are well coordinated and the patient is able to engage in perception–motor cycles that are most appropriate to the moment. At the level of prolonged reflective actions we also develop a sense of duty and responsibility for ourselves and others. The survivor may become more interested in the responsibilities of self-care for its own rewards. And he or she may want to engage in social action and care of others, not in codependent ways, but with genuine altruism, out of a sense of moral responsibility.

At this level, a patient has come to a place of coherent "acts and a unity of life" (Ellenberger, 1970, p. 393). However, unless a survivor is able to reach even higher levels of action tendencies, he or she may become pedantic, rule-bound, and impractical. He or she can be prone to fundamentalist thinking, a person whose judgment is overly reliant upon theories and rigid moral principles.

The *experimental tendencies* are the next level of actions. We explore ourselves and our world, learning new skills in a playful, exciting way, curious way (Brown & Fromm, 1986). This involves very high levels of integration among action systems: exploration and play, attachment, sociability, and energy regulation. We learn from experience and our mistakes and take them into account in planning for the future and in how we act in the present. We have an open mind to options and can creatively exercise our ability to take them. We consciously evaluate and adjust our actions based upon our continual learning. This is often a level at which survivors struggle because of their phobias of change and risk taking. Treatment consists of very gradual exposure to change and risk taking, with ongoing encouragement of the patient to view both success and failures as learning experiences. But survivors who do not progress beyond this level of action tendencies may be prone to experimentation to the point of instability in life, trying too many new things without fully integrating them.

The *progressive tendencies* are the highest anyone is able to achieve. At this level he or she has a strong sense of individuality, and may engage in spiritual or other higher order meaningful pursuits. The patient grasps highly abstract ideas and may have more freedom and energy to explore existential and philosophical issues. He or she is able to mentalize and have good insight into motivations which translates into enduring behavioral changes.

When patients have begun to function at the higher levels, they are able to develop and solidify a strong personal theory of reality (Steele & Van der Hart, 1994). That is, they are able to realize the past, present, and future, realize their own identity and understand others, and act intentionally and reflectively. A personal theory of reality involves six capacities that derive from strong personification and presentification. The first is the ability to maintain consistent relatedness by finding an optimal balance with others between closeness and distance. This capacity involves the patient's highest tendencies in the realms of attachment, sociability, and caretaking action systems. He or she learns to balance care for self with that of others. Second, the patient is able to accurately integrate the data of reality: He or she fully realizes what is happening and adapts by adjusting perception–motor action tendencies to the present moment. This not only implies core presentification but also an accurate placement of the past, present, and future in the hierarchy of degrees of reality (extended presentification). It also means the patient is consciously aware of the differences between internal and external realities.

Third, the patient is able to find a balance between pleasure and pain. He or she does not merely react, but can tolerate pain in order to reach longer term goals, and even understand that pain can have value in what it teaches us. This balance implies that the patient has reflective beliefs about him- or herself, others, and the world. Fourth, the patient is able to accept realistically and with humility his or her human limitations and frailties along with personal strengths and uniqueness. The patient does not strive for perfection in all things, but for adaptive and realistic functioning. This means he or she must reconcile the ideal fantasy of self and the world with the real, reaching the highest level of the hierarchy of degrees of reality. Fifth, the patient has a healthy sense of humor (Kohut, 1971), implying a high mental level in which he or she can mentalize an existential predicament and still feel safe enough to connect with others in a humorous way. It also indicates the patient's ability to symbolize and be creative. Finally, the patient develops a well-defined personal (and professional) ethic. He or she integrates morality, ethics, spirituality, and the most reflective and empathic understanding of self, others, and the world. The patient strives to consciously make the world a better place as much as possible. He or she understands the future is uncertain and keeps an open mind about it and is open to the inevitable changes it will bring. The patient pursues self-knowledge, which presupposes a willingness to face aspects of him- or herself that may be unpleasant.

The survivor may still struggle with historical issues. But on the whole, he or she is able to function in a highly coordinated and cohesive way, no longer haunted continually by the ghosts of the past.

TERMINATION OF TREATMENT

The successful termination of a long-term therapy can be as difficult as it is rewarding, and is an intervention in itself. It models for the patient the natural cycle of secure attachment that sometimes includes endings. The therapeutic relationship has likely weathered many times of despair, anger, futility, sadness, grief, shame, and hopelessness, and therapist and patient have had intense bonding experiences. This relationship has served as a port in the storm for the survivor along the way of recovery, and he or she is unlikely to relinquish it easily. But therapy is time-limited by nature, so patient and therapist alike must determine when the time is right for ending.

Trauma survivors are generally able to terminate therapy when they have a sense of internal cohesion and wholeness, can resign themselves to their history, take charge of their present, and make plans for the future. They should no longer be haunted by the past in general, even though it may be reactivated occasionally in less intense ways. Survivors should no longer feel inhibited or phobic of most experiences. They should be able to engage in healthy relationships in work, play, rest, and relaxation, and take pleasure in their lives. They can repeatedly experience the act of triumph in their lives because they are more successful in their day-to-day living. And they can resign themselves to the vagaries of life that continue over the course of their lifetime.

Yet, even though a survivor may meet the criteria for termination, the process of ending can be difficult (D. Brown et al., 1998; Courtois, 1988; Herman, 1992b). The prospect of ending often evokes previous losses and the patient can easily become depressed or overwhelmed if termination is pushed too quickly. A long period of grieving may precede termination.

Termination can be accomplished in a number of ways. It can occur over the period of an agreed upon number of sessions or be more open-ended. It can begin with the patient coming less often: every other week instead of weekly, then every month instead of twice a month. This slow process gradually exposes the patient to increasingly long periods of time without the direct presence of the therapist.

Termination of therapy should itself mirror the highest level of action tendencies in both patient and therapist. Thus, ending needs to be a well-completed action, fully discussed in every way. The patient is encouraged to process their relationship with the therapist, including wishes that some things had been different, times when the therapist was particularly attuned, and when he or she was especially unhelpful or even hurtful. The patient and therapist should have a sense of completeness. The patient can learn warning signs that a return to therapy might be wise and be alert to these. The therapist remains available for the future possibility that the patient may temporarily return to do other kinds of work (Herman, 1992b). Whether the therapist and patient will have any contact after termination is based on the needs and preferences of both parties, as well as what would be therapeutic to the patient. Occasional contact based on the patient catching up the therapist with his or her life is permissible.

SUMMARY

Using gradual exposure, the patient is supported in engaging in activities of daily life that were previously avoided. Therapeutic exposure to previously avoided stimuli is not a goal in itself, but serves to foster integrative action. Integrative actions typically add new perceptions, ideas, feelings, and behavioral actions to previously rigid, restrictive, and maladaptive perception–motor action cycles. Complete fusion (unification) of all parts of the personality into a more coordinated and cohesive personality is a goal for patients in this phase, such that there is no longer any subjective sense of separateness, and action systems are well coordinated and cohesive. Fusions can be accomplished in a variety of ways, limited only by the creativity of the patient and therapist. The patient who cannot successfully complete Phase 3 work often continues to have difficulty with normal life, despite significant relief from traumatic intrusions. Phase 3 is dedicated to overcoming phobias related to normal life, particularly regarding change and healthy risk taking, and intimacy. Severely traumatized patients persist in tendencies to dissociate and engage in alterations of consciousness under stress. Thus, continued relapse prevention, including stress inoculation and self-care activities are essential ongoing tasks in Phase 3. The patient is encouraged to engage in the highest levels of action tendencies. Appropriate termination of therapy is a major transition that should receive careful and long term attention by both therapist and patient. Its successful navigation is necessary for a well-completed therapy.

Epilogue

There is no short cut to reparation and attempts to find one may merely lead to further denial and disillusionment.
—Jeremy Holmes (1991, p. 104)

WRITING THIS BOOK HAS BEEN a combination of a relay race, passing off one draft after another to each other, and a four-year marathon of reading, discussions, e-mails, phone conferences, and writing. It has been an exciting, frustrating, illuminating, sometimes confusing, and most often, a rewarding journey. The development of a new theory with practical applications is no small undertaking, and one that requires nearly insatiable curiosity, patience, stamina, and modesty. And of course, a high mental level! Our hope and desire is to have made a significant contribution to our beloved field; one that can support clinicians and researchers alike in providing more effective help to traumatized patients. After all, that has been our main objective all along, even in our mistakes and sometimes fumbling attempts to "get it right."

In this epilogue, we address two final issues. First, our theory needs further development and scientific scrutiny, and controlled validation of the treatment based on the theory is yet to begin. Second, we cannot end without speaking about the actions of the therapist as a major contributor to the success (or failure) of therapy with chronically traumatized individuals.

THE EVOLVING NATURE OF THE THEORY AND TREATMENT MODEL

As we stated at the beginning of this book, the theory of structural dissociation in combination with a Janetian psychology of action, and the treatment model derive from our extensive clinical experience with chronically traumatized patients, theoretical reflections, empirical studies, and the influence of many colleagues. We have paid close attention to some of the great masters from the past whose literary heritages contain little noticed treasures, particularly Pierre Janet. Neither the theory nor the treatment model based upon it are fixed and closed systems, but are works in progress, as our successive publications on these matters testify. In turn, we invite interested colleagues to join us in further developing and improving the theory. Most importantly, we hope that others will also begin to empirically test the basic hypotheses of the theory.

The theory of structural dissociation is a rich heuristic. Some hypotheses that were derived from it have been succesfully put to scientific test (e.g., Reinders et al., 2003, Reinders et al., in press; see Chapter 10), and several others are currently under investigation. However, much more work remains to be done to validate the theory or correct its errors. One major challenge is the development and testing of a measurement instrument that assesses the degree of structural dissociation.

How effective is the presented phase-oriented treatment model for survivors of chronic child abuse and neglect? Our own combined clinical experiences, as well as those of colleagues trained in the theory and practice described in this book, testify to its effectiveness with many patients otherwise deemed untreatable. There is no evidence that ignoring symptoms of structural dissociation resolves them (Coons & Bowman, 2001; Kluft, 1993c, 2006). Several uncontrolled studies suggest that phase-oriented of complex structural dissociation can be effective (Coons & Bowman, 2001). Ehling, Nijenhuis, and Krikke (2003) studied 14 women who had completely recovered from DID, all of whom had been treated with a long term phase-oriented approach. Prior to this, many of these patients had received other treatment that included ignoring dissociative symptoms or the mere administration of antipsychotic medication that was ineffective or that had further impaired them. It would be wonderful if we could present randomized controlled trials on the efficacy of the proposed phase-oriented treatment. Unfortunately, these studies do not yet exist, and one major reason is that outcome research of long-term, complex therapies is extraordinarily difficult. There are simply too many variables involved over too long a period of time and it seems almost impossible to construct an acceptable comparison modality. A waiting list control group is out of the question, and it seems equally unethical to treat chronic trauma survivors for years according to treatment practices that, as clinical observations tell, fail time and again. Still, it would be good practice and not overly complicated to begin to build a database of measurements taken, for instance, every six months over the course of therapy, with pre- and postmeasures and follow-up measures.

We have presented this treatment model in terms of (long-term) individual psychotherapy. However, such individual approaches can be combined very well with structured group therapies, especially in Phase 1 treatment. Adjunct group therapies may consist of systematic psychoeducation and skills training; for example, with regard to action regulation and the ability to be more present. These groups should be tailored to the specific needs of their members. For instance, DID patients, characterized by tertiary structural dissociation, might need different groups from those that are appropriate for BPD and complex PTSD patients who are characterized by secondary structural dissociation. Many of the treatment principles presented in Chapter 12 apply to these types of groups.

THE THERAPIST

Onc of the most important lessons we have learned in our journey is that a Janetian psychology of action is relevant to everyone, including the person of the therapist. We have paid ever more attention to our own mental levels, our own maladaptive and adaptive actions, our own capacities to synthesize and realize, our own successes and failures in attaining higher levels of action tendencies both in therapy and various other areas of life.

We discovered the most effective way to utilize this psychology of action with traumatized patients is for the therapist to apply it to his or her own mental and behavioral actions in relation to the patient. Psychotherapy of survivors of chronic childhood abuse and neglect constitutes an ongoing major challenge to both patient and therapist, and it is the therapist who must remain responsible for maintaining the standard of care and the highest ethical principles. The therapist thus needs to function in therapy at a consistently high level in the hierarchy of tendencies. This means, among other things, that when the patient engages in rigid and lower level action tendencies, the therapist does not respond in kind, but rather engages in more flexible, adaptive actions.

At the least, the therapist must master prolonged reflective action tendencies, which include a strong sense of personal duty and ability, reflective actions, initiative, perseverance, and patience. The therapist also must engage in experimental tendencies, which include the ability to patiently await the outcomes of actions (i.e., therapeutic interventions over an extended period of time), to recognize intellectual errors and personal limitations, to have a healthy respect for him- or herself and for patients. The therapist learns from experience, for example, that a certain timing is needed in everything, that resistance to change is nearly universal and to be expected, that patients may take particular and rather predicable courses of action when they are engaged in lower levels of action tendencies, that the therapist works best with one kind of patient and not so well with another. The therapist needs to be humble and modest, with a strong desire to listen to and learn from both patients and colleagues instead of believing he or she has all the anwers. And the therapist should have a firmness of character that includes a strong sense of personal and professional ethics and adaptive dedication and self-control across long periods of time.

To put it in slightly different words, the therapist involved in the long-term treatment of survivors of chronic childhood traumatization needs to be characterized by a high degree of mental health. Being a therapist in general is no easy undertaking, and being a therapist to chronically traumatized individuals is even more demanding. The therapist has to take into account so many variables, not only with regard to the complex world of the patient, but also personal life circumstances that might impact his or her actions as a therapist. These include social factors such as current relationships with family and friends, current stressors, financial status, work situation, health, personal strengths and weaknesses, including the usual level of mental energy and efficiency, and professional expertise or lack thereof.

When the therapist is unable for whatever reason to maintain a high mental level in regards to a patient, he or she will tend to engage in lower level actions. Some of these maladaptive actions can be considered to be countertransference, a phenomenon well-described in the trauma literature (Dalenberg, 2000; J. M. Davies & Frawley, 1994; Figley, 1995; Kluft, 1994a; Loewenstein, 1991; McCann & Pearlman, 1990; Pearlman & Saakvitne, 1995; Rothschild, 2006; Tauber, 1998; J. P. Wilson & Lindy, 1994; J. P. Wilson & Thomas, 2004). For instance, the therapist may generally be able to function at the level of the higher tendencies, but suddenly drop to the level of reflexive actions when a patient becomes very angry because the therapist was five minutes late in beginning the session. The therapist thinks, "It's only five minutes; it's ridiculous for this patient to be controlling me so!" He or she then becomes angry and defensive, further provoking the patient. In this situation, the therapist has temporarily lost the ability to mentalize, to empathize, to understand the fears that are at the root of the patient's unrealistic expectations. Such mentalization is a high level action. The therapist's lower level actions may also complement the patient's actions, leading to fixed victim–perpetrator, or victim–rescuer roles, for example. And the therapist may sometimes be inclined to use the treatment frame too rigidly or allow too much laxity because his or her own defense system or insecure attachment become evoked with patients. He or she may desire to avoid unpleasant confrontations, to appease the patient, or to assuage his or her own negative feelings toward the patient, such as guilt, helplessness, disgust, or rage.

Such drops in the therapist's mental efficiency might be attributed to current personal experience, such as being tired or ill, being faced with too many demands, or professional lack of experience or knowledge. They may also involve countertransference. The therapist engages in countertransferential, thus lower level actions when his or her own unresolved past is evoked by the patient's behavior. The therapist then engages in rigid, conditioned actions in the same way as the patient. It is possible that these actions may sometimes stem from a rudimentary emotional part (EP) in the therapist, which generally remains in a latent state. For example, a therapist experienced intense feelings of guilt and inadequacy and a tendency to withdraw when an EP of one of his patients expressed intense suffering and blamed him for her overwhelming pain. When such incidents took place, the therapist became less able to think clearly and maintain the therapeutic frame. The therapist's withdrawal and silence only served to heightened the patient's fear, anger, and pain, which in turn, heightened the therapist's withdrawal and guilt. Thus, the patient and therapist became stuck in a recurring cycle of trauma-related transference–countertransference actions. The therapist's realization of this maladaptive pattern motivated him to seek personal therapy, in which he became aware how the patient's suffering and blame reactivated intense feelings of failure and fear—belonging to a rudimentary child part—regarding a life-threatening and most painful illness from which his mother had suffered greatly during his childhood. This realization stimulated him to improve his self-care, to have empathy and care for this overwhelmed and unduly burdened part of his personality.

In fact, a substantial minority of therapists have their own history of traumatization (Elliott & Guy, 1993) and may find the theory of structural dissociation and a psychology of action useful in their own healing. We believe that, more than any other type of therapy, the long-term treatment of survivors of childhood abuse and neglect will reactivate unresolved painful experiences in the therapist, including traumatic experiences. We are strong proponents of consultation and supervision, and of psychotherapy for the therapist if needed (J. G. Allen, 2001; Pearlman & Saakvitne, 1995).

Phase 2 treatment, with its main focus on the synthesis and realization of traumatic memories, may constitute a major hazard for trauma-related countertransference drops in the therapist's mental efficiency. As mentioned in Chapter 16, there are two a priori countertransference errors related to the patient's traumatic memories (Van der Hart & Steele, 1999). First, the therapist may have a countertransference attitude to the patient's traumatic memories that may result in inappropriate, reflexive pressure on the patient to face his or her traumatic past. For the patient who does not yet have a sufficient mental level, this can be disastrous, resulting in decompensation or other extremely serious negative outcomes. To the patient who is more able, it can be reexperienced as being forced to participate in something painful, against his or her will. The second countertransference error is an overidentification with the patient, with development of a secondary phobia of the patient's traumatic memories. This secondary phobia should not be confused with a more or less accurate assessment that the patient's mental level is still insufficient for a successful synthesis and realization of a particular traumatic memory. Rather, it may be based on the therapist's avoidance of his or her own unresolved traumatic memories, avoidance of the patient's loss and pain because the therapist believes it would be too painful for him- or herself.

In conclusion, the theory of structural dissociation focuses on the integrative actions that the traumatized individual has failed to achieve, and on the maladapative actions that substitute for these more adaptive actions. A psychology of action describes how an individual can be encouraged to engage in more integrative actions, and which actions are adaptive. After all, to live well, we must learn to be concerned about and care for ourselves and others, to know ourselves and others, to own our experience and value the experiences of others, and to make the most of the present by acting in the best way we know how. This ability to act well is, in the end, all we have and what defines our very humanity. The psychology of action thus can be summed up in the powerful words of Rabbi Hillel: "If I am not for myself, then who am I? If I am not with others, what am I? If not now, then when?"

References

Abelson, R. P. (1963). "Computer simulation of "hot cognitions." In S. Tomkins & S. Messick (Eds.), *Computer simulation and personality: Frontier of psychological theory.* (pp. 277–298) New York: Wiley.

Aderibigbe,Y. A., Bloch, R. M., & Walker, W. R. (2001). Prevalence of depersonalization and derealization experiences in a rural population. *Social Psychiatry and Psychiatric Epidemiology, 36,* 63–69.

Agrawal, H. R., Gunderson, J., Holmes, B. M., & Lyons-Ruth, K. (2004). Attachment studies with borderline patients: A review. *Harvard Review of Psychiatry, 12,* 94–104.

Alexander, P. C. (1992). Application of attachment theory to the study of sexual abuse. *Journal of Consulting & Clinical Psychology, 60,* 185–195.

Alexander, P. C., & Anderson, C. L. (1994). An attachment approach to psychotherapy with the incest survivor. *Psychotherapy, 31,* 665–675.

Allen, J. G. (2001). *Traumatic relationships and serious mental disorders.* New York: Wiley.

Allen, J. G., Console, D. A., & Lewis, L. (1999). Dissociative detachment and memory impairment: Reversible amnesia or encoding failure? *Comprehensive Psychiatry, 40,* 160–71.

Allen, J. G., Coyne, L., & Console, D. A. (1997). Dissociative detachment relates to psychotic symptoms and personality decompensation. *Comprehensive Psychiatry, 38,* 327–334.

Allen, J. G., Coyne, L., & Console, D. A. (1996). Dissociation contributes to anxiety and psychoticism on the Brief Symptom Inventory. *Journal of Nervous and Mental Disease, 184,* 639–641.

Allen, J. G., Coyne, L., & Huntoon, J. (1998). Complex posttraumatic stress disorder in women from a psychometric perspective. *Journal of Personality Assessment, 70,* 277–298.

Allen, S. N. (1994). Psychological assessment of post-traumatic stress disorder. Psychometrics, current trends, and future directions. *Psychiatric Clinics of North America, 17,* 327–349.

Allport, G. W. (1961). *Pattern and growth in personality.* New York: Holt, Rinehart, & Winston.

American Psychiatric Association. (1994). *Diagnostic and statistical manual of mental disorders* (4th ed.). Washington, DC: Author.

Anda, R. F., Felitti, V. J., Bremner, J. D., Walker, J. D., Whitfield, C., Perry, B. D., Dube, S. R., & Giles, W. H. (2006). The enduring effects of abuse and related adverse experiences in childhood: A convergence of evidence from neurobiology and epidemiology. *European Archives of Psychiatry and Clinical Neuroscience, 256,* 174–186.

Anderson, C. M., & Stewart, S. (1983). *Mastering resistance: A practical guide to family therapy.* New York: Guilford.

Anderson, G., Yasenik, L., & Ross, C. A. (1993). Dissociative experiences and disorders among women who identify themselves as sexual abuse survivors. *Child Abuse & Neglect, 17*(5), 677–686.

Anderson, M. C., & Green, C. (2001). Suppressing unwanted memories by executive control. *Nature, 410*, 366–369.

Anderson, M. C., Ochsner, K. N., Kuhl, B., Cooper, J., Robertson, E., Gabrieli, S. W. et al. (2004). Neural systems underlying the suppression of unwanted memories. *Science, 303*, 232–235.

Andreski, P., Chilcoat, H., & Breslau, N. (1998). Post-traumatic stress disorder and somatization symptoms: A prospective study. *Psychiatry Residency, 79*, 131–138.

Andrews, B. (2002). Body shame and abuse in childhood. In P. Gilbert & J. Miles (Eds.), *Body shame: Conceptualisation, research and treatment* (pp. 256–266). New York: Brunner-Routledge.

Andrews, B., Brewin, C. R., Rose, S., & Kirk, M. (2000). Predicting PTSD symptoms in victims of violent crime: The role of shame, anger, and childhood abuse. *Journal of Abnormal Psychology, 109*, 69–73.

Appelfeld, A. (1994). *Beyond despair.* New York: Fromm.

Armstrong, J. (1991). The psychological organization of multiple personality disordered patients as revealed in psychological testing. *Psychiatric Clinics of North America, 14*, 533–546.

Armsworth, M. T., Stronk, K., & Carlson, C. D. (1999). Body image and self-perception in women with histories of incest. In J. Goodwin & R. Attias (Eds.), *Splintered reflections: Images of the body in trauma* (pp. 137–153). New York: Basic Books.

Arnold, M. B. (1960). *Emotion and personality.* New York: Columbia University Press.

Atlas, J. A., Wolfson, M. A., & Lipschitz, D. S. (1995). Dissociation and somatization in adolescent inpatients with and without history of abuse. *Psychology Reports, 76*(2), 1101–1102.

Azam, A. (1876). *Le dédoublement de la personnalité, suite de l'histoire de Félida X***. Revue Scientifique* [Doubling of the personality, followed by the history of Félida X***]. 2nd series, 265–269.

Baeyens, F., Eelen, P., Van den Berg, O., & Crombez, G. (1989). Acquired affective-evaluative value: Conservative but not unchangeable. *Behavioral Research & Therapy, 27*, 279–287.

Baeyens, F., Hermans, D., & Eelen, P. (1993). The role of CS–US contingency in human evaluative conditioning. *Behavioral Research & Therapy, 31*, 731–737.

Bailey, P. (1928). The psychology of human conduct: A review. *American Journal of Psychiatry, 8*, 209–234.

Bain, A. (1855). *The senses and the intellect.* London: Parker.

Baker, D., Hunter, E., Lawrence, E., Medford, N., Patel, M., Senior, C., Sierra, M., Lambert, M. V., Phillips, M. L., & David, A. S. (2003). Depersonalisation disorder: Clinical features of 204 cases. *British Journal of Psychiatry, 182*, 428–433.

Barach, P. (2004, November*). "If love be good, from whence comes my woe?"* Third Annual Pierre Janet Memorial Lecture. Presented at the 21st Annual Meeting of the International Society for the Study of Dissociation, New Orleans, LA.

Barkley, R. A. (2001). The executive functions and self-regulation: An evolutionary neuropsychological perspective. *Neuropsychology Review, 11*, 1–29.

Barkow, J., Cosmides, L., & Tooby, J. (Eds.) (1992). *The adapted mind: Evolutionary psychology and the generation of culture*. New York: Oxford University Press.

Bartlett, A. B. (1996). Clinical assessment of sexual trauma: Interviewing adult survivors of childhood abuse. *Bulletin of the Menninger Clinic, 60*, 147–159.

Beaunis, H. (1887). *Le somnambulisme provoqué* [Instigated somnambulism]. (2nd., enlarged ed.). Paris: J.-B. Bailière & Fils.

Becker-Blease, K. A., Deater-Deckard, K., Eley, T., Freyd, J. J., Stevenson, J., & Plomin, R. (2004). A genetic analysis of individual differences in dissociative behaviors in childhood and adolescence. *Journal of Child Psychology and Psychiatry, 45*, 522–532.

Benyakar, M., Kutz, I., Dasberg, H., & Stern, M. (1989). The collapse of a structure: A structural approach to trauma. *Journal of Traumatic Stress, 2*, 431–450.

Berk, J. H. (1998). Trauma and resilience during war: A look at the children and humanitarian aid workers of Bosnia. *Psychoanalytic Review, 85*, 639–658.

Berlucchi, G., & Aglioti, S. (1997). The body in the brain: Neural bases for corporeal awareness. *Trends in Neurosciences, 20*, 560–564.

Bernstein, E. M., & Putnam, F. W. (1986). Development, reliability, and validity of a dissociation scale. *Journal of Nervous and Mental Disease, 174*, 727–735.

Berrington, W. P., Liddell, D. W., & Foulds, G. A. (1956). A re-evaluation of the fugue. *Journal of Mental Science, 102*, 280–286.

Berthoz, A. (2000). *The brain's sense of movement*. Cambridge, MA: Harvard University Press.

Binet, A. (1977). *Alterations of personality*. Washington, DC: University Publications of America. (Original work published 1892–1896).

Birmes, P., Brunet, A., Carreras, D., Ducasse, J. L., Charlet, J. P., Lauque, D. et al. (2003). The predictive power of peritraumatic dissociation and acute stress symptoms for posttraumatic stress symptoms: A three-month prospective study. *American Journal of Psychiatry, 160*, 1337–1339.

Blake, D. D., Weathers, F. W., Nagy, L. M., Kaloupek, D. G., Gusman, F. D., Charney, D. S. et al. (1995). The development of a clinician-administered PTSD scale. *Journal of Traumatic Stress, 8*, 75–90.

Bleich, A., & Moskowits, L. (2000). Post traumatic stress disorder with psychotic features. *Croatian Medical Journal, 41*, 442–445.

Blizard, R. A. (1997). The origins of dissociative identity disorder from an object relations and attachment theory perspective. *Dissociation, 10*, 223–229.

Blizard, R. A. (2001). Masochistic and sadistic ego states: Dissociative solutions to the dilemma of attachment to an abusive caretaker. *Journal of Trauma and Dissociation, 2*(4), 37–58.

Blizard, R. A. (2003). Disorganized attachment: Development of dissociated self states and a relational approach to treatment. *Journal of Trauma and Dissociation, 4*, 27–50.

Blum, H. P. (Ed.). (1986). *Defenses and resistances: Historical perspectives and current concepts*. Madison, CT: International Universities Press.

Bolstad, B. R., & Zinbarg, R. E. (1997). Sexual victimization, generalized perception of control, and posttraumatic stress disorder symptom severity. *Journal of Anxiety Disorders, 11*, 523–540.

Boney-McCoy, S., & Finkelhor, D. (1996). Is youth victimization related to trauma symptoms and depression after controlling for prior symptoms and family relationships? A longitudinal, prospective study. *Journal of Consulting and Clinical Psychology, 64*, 1406–1416.

Boon, S. (1997). The treatment of traumatic memories in DID: Indications and contra-indications. *Dissociation, 10*, 65–79.

Boon, S., & Draijer, N. (1993). *Multiple personality disorder in the Netherlands.* Lisse, the Netherlands: Swets & Zeitlinger.

Boon, S., & Van der Hart, O. (2003). De behandeling van de dissociatieve identiteitsstoornis [Treatment of dissociative identity disorder]. In O. Van der Hart (Ed.), *Trauma, dissociatie en hypnose* [Trauma, dissociation and hypnosis] (4th ed., pp. 193–238). Lisse, the Netherlands: Swets & Zeitlinger.

Borkovec, T. D., & Sharpless, B. (2004). Generalized anxiety disorder: Bringing cognitive–behavioral therapy into the valued present. In S. C. Hayes, V. M. Folette, & M. M. Linehan (Eds.), *Mindfulness and acceptance: Expanding the cognitive–behavioral tradition* (pp. 209–243). New York: Guilford.

Borys, D. S. (1994). Maintaining therapeutic boundaries: The motive is therapeutic effectiveness, not defensive practice. *Ethics and Behavior, 4*, 267–273.

Bouton, M. E. (2004). Context and behavioral processes in extinction. *Learning and Memory, 11*, 485–494.

Bouton, M. E., Westbrook, R. F., Corcoran, K. A., & Maren, S. (2006). Contextual and temporary modulation of extinction: Behavioral and biological mechanisms. *Biological Psychiatry,* in press.

Bowlby, J. (1982). *Attachment* (2nd ed., Vol. 1). New York: Basic Books. (Original work published in 1969).

Bowman, E. (2006). Why conversion seizures should be classified as a dissociative disorder. *Psychiatric Clinics of North America, 29*(1), 185–211.

Bowman, E. S., & Markand, O. N. (1996). Psychodynamics and psychiatric diagnoses of pseudoseizure subjects. *American Journal of Psychiatry, 153*, 57–63.

Brady, K. T. (1997). Posttraumatic stress disorder and comorbidity: Recognizing the many faces of PTSD. *Journal of Clinical Psychiatry, 58*(Suppl. 9), 12–15.

Brady, K. T., Killeen, T. K., Brewerton, T., & Lucerini, S. (2000). Comorbidity of psychiatric disorders and posttraumatic stress disorder. *Journal of Clinical Psychiatry, 61*(Suppl. 7), 22–32.

Brand, B. L., Armstrong, J. G., & Loewenstein, R. J. (2006). Psychological assessment of patients with dissociative identity disorder. *Psychiatric Clinics of North America, 29*, 145–168.

Braude, S. E. (1995). *First person plural: Multiple personality and the philosophy of mind* (Rev. ed.). London/New York: Routledge.

Braun, B. G. (1984). The transgenerational incidence of dissociation and multiple personality disorder; A preliminary report. In R. P. Kluft (Ed.), *Childhood antecedents of multiple personality* (pp. 127–150). Washington, DC: American Psychiatric Press.

Braun, B. G. (1986). Introduction. In B. G. Braun (Ed.), *Treatment of multiple personality disorder* (pp. xi–xxi). Washington, DC: American Psychiatric Press.

Braun, B. G. (1990). Dissociative disorders as sequelae to incest. In R. P. Kluft (Ed.), *Incest-related syndromes of adult psychopathology* (pp. 227–245). Washington, DC: American Psychiatric Press.

Bremner, J., Southwick, S., Darnell, A., & Charney, D. (1996). Chronic PTSD in Vietnam combat veterans: Course of illness and substance abuse. *American Journal of Psychiatry, 153*, 369–375.

Bremner, J. D. (1999). Acute and chronic responses to psychological trauma: Where do we go from here? *American Journal of Psychiatry, 156*, 349–351.

Bremner, J. D., Southwick, S. M., Brett, E., Fontana, A., Rosenheck, R., & Charney, D. S. (1992). Dissociation and posttraumatic stress disorder in Vietnam combat veterans. *American Journal of Psychiatry, 149*, 328–332.

Bremner, J. D., Southwick, S. M., Johnson, D. R., Yehuda, R., & Charney, D. (1993). Childhood physical abuse in combat-related posttraumatic stress disorder. *American Journal of Psychiatry, 150*, 235–239.

Bremner, J. D., Steinberg, M., Southwick, S. M., Johnson, D. R., & Charney, D. S. (1993). Use of the Structured Clinical Interview for DSM-IV Dissociative Disorders for systematic assessment of dissociative symptoms in posttraumatic stress disorder. *American Journal of Psychiatry, 150*, 1011–1014.

Bremner, J. D., Vermetten, E., Southwick, S. M., Krystal, J. H., & Charney, D. S. (1998). Trauma, memory, and dissociation: An integrative formulation. In J. D. Bremner & C. R. Marmar (Eds.), *Trauma, memory, and dissociation* (pp. 365–402). Washington, DC: American Psychiatric Press.

Breslau, N., Davis, G. C., Andreski, P., & Peterson, E. (1991). Traumatic events and posttraumatic stress disorder in an urban population of young adults. *Archives of General Psychiatry, 48*, 216–222.

Breslau, N. (2001). The epidemiology of posttraumatic stress disorder: What is the extent of the problem? *Journal of Clinical Psychiatry, 62*(Suppl. 17), 16–22.

Breslau, N., Chilcoat, H. D., Kessler, R. C., Peterson, E. L., & Lucia, V. C. (1999). Vulnerability to assaultive violence: Further specification of sex difference in post-traumatic stress disorder. *Psychology and Medicine, 29*, 813–821.

Breslau, N., Davis, G., & Andreski, P. (1995). Risk factors for PTSD-related traumatic events: A prospective analysis. *American Journal of Psychiatry, 152*, 529–504.

Brett, E. A. (1996). The classification of posttraumatic stress disorder. In B. A. Van der Kolk, A. C. McFarlane, & L. Weisaeth (Eds.), *Traumatic stress: The overwhelming experience on mind, body, and society* (pp. 117–128). New York: Guilford.

Brett, E. A., & Ostroff, R. (1985). Imagery and posttraumatic stress disorder: An overview. *American Journal of Psychiatry, 142*, 417–424.

Breuer, J., & Freud, S. (1955a). Studies on hysteria. In J. Struchey (Ed. & Trans.), *The standard edition of the complete psychological works of Sigmund Freud* (Vol. 2). London: Hogarth Press. (Original work published in 1893–1895).

Breuer, J., & Freud, S. (1955b). On the psychical mechanism of hysterical phenomena: Preliminary communication. In J. Strachey (Ed. & Trans.), *The standard edition of the complete psychological works of Sigmund Freud* (Vol. 2, pp. 3–17). London: Hogarth Press. (Original work published in 1893).

Brewin, C. R. (2001). A cognitive neuroscience account of posttraumatic stress disorder and its treatment. *Behaviour Research and Therapy, 39*, 373–393.

Brewin, C. R. (2003). *Posttraumatic stress disorder: Malady or myth?* New Haven, CT: Yale University Press.

Brewin, C. R. (2005a). Systematic review of screening instruments for adults at risk of PTSD. *Journal of Traumatic Stress, 18*, 53–62.

Brewin, C. R. (2005b, November). "Voices" in PTSD: A window of identity. *Proceedings of the 21st Annual Meeting of the International Society for Traumatic Stress Studies*, p. 79. Toronto, Canada.

Brewin, C. R., Andrews, B., Rose, S., & Kirk, M. (1999). Acute Stress Disorder and Posttraumatic Stress Disorder in victims of violent crime. *American Journal of Psychiatry, 156*, 360–366.

Brewin, C. R., Andrews, B., & Valentine, J. D. (2000). Meta-analysis of risk factors for posttraumatic stress disorder in trauma-exposed adults. *Journal of Consulting and Clinical Psychology, 68*, 748–766.

Brewin, C. R., Dalgleish, T., & Joseph, S. (1996). A dual representation theory of post traumatic stress. *Psychological Review, 103*, 670–686.

Brewin, C. R. & Holmes, E. A. (2003). Psychological theories of posttraumatic stress disorder. *Clinical Psychology Review, 23*, 339–376.

Brewin, C. R. & Smart, L. (2005). Working memory capacity and suppression of intrusive thoughts. *Journal of Behavior Therapy and Experimental Psychiatry, 36*, 61–68.

Bridges, N. A. (1999). Psychodynamic perspective on therapeutic boundaries: Creative clinical possibilities. *Journal of Psychotherapy Practice & Research, 8*, 292–300.

Briere, J. (1997). *Psychological assessment of adult posttraumatic states*. Washington, DC: American Psychological Press.

Briere, J. (2004). *Psychological assessment of adult posttraumatic states: Phenomenology, diagnosis, and measurement* (2nd ed.). Washington, DC: American Psychological Association.

Briere, J., & Scott, C. (2006). *Principles of trauma therapy: A guide to symptoms, evaluation, and treatment*. Thousand Oaks, CA: Sage.

Briere, J., & Spinazzola, J. (2005). Phenomenology and psychological assessment of complex posttraumatic states. *Journal of Traumatic Stress, 18*, 401–412.

Brodsky, B. S., Cloitre, M., & Dulit, R. A. (1995). Relationship of dissociation to self-mutilation and childhood abuse in borderline personality disorder. *American Journal of Psychiatry, 152*, 1788–1792.

Brown, D., & Fromm, E. (1986). *Hypnotherapy and hypnoanalysis*. Hillsdale, NJ: Lawrence Erlbaum.

Brown, D., Scheflin, A. W., & Hammond, D. C. (1998). *Memory, trauma treatment, and the law*. New York: Norton.

Brown, L., Russell, J., Thornton, C., & Dunn, S. (1999). Dissociation, abuse and the eating disorders: Evidence from an Australian population. *Australian & New Zealand Journal of Psychiatry, 33*, 521–528.

Brown, R. J., Schrag, A., & Trimble, M. R. (2005). Dissociation, childhood interpersonal trauma, and family functioning in patients with somatization disorder. *American Journal of Psychiatry, 162*, 899–905.

Brown, W. (1919). War neuroses: A comparison of early cases seen in the field with those seen at the base. *Lancet, ii*, 833–836.

Brunet, A., Weiss, D. S., Metzler, T. J., Best, S. R., Neylan, T. C., Rogers, C. et al. (2001). The peritraumatic distress inventory: A proposed measure of PTSD criterion A2. *American Journal of Psychiatry, 158*, 1480–1485.

Bryant, R. A., & Harvey, A. G. (2000). *Acute stress disorder: A handbook of theory, assessment, and treatment*. Washington, DC: American Psychological Association.

Bryant, R. A. & Panasetis, P. (2001). Panic symptoms during trauma and acute stress disorder. *Behavioural Research and Therapy, 39*, 961–966.

Buchheim, A., Strauss, B., & Kachele, H. (2002). The differential relevance of attachment classification for psychological disorders. *Psychotherapy & Psychosomatic Medical Psychology, 52*, 128–133.

Buckley, T. C., Blanchard, E. B., & Hickling, E. J. (1998). A confirmatory factor analysis of posttraumatic stress symptoms. *Behavior, Research, and Therapy, 36*, 1091–1099.

Buckley, T. C., Blanchard, E. B., & Neill, W. T. (2000). Information processing and PTSD: A review of the empirical literature. *Clinical Psychology Review, 20*, 1041–1065.

Burney, J., & Irwin, H. J. (2000). Shame and guilt in women with eating-disorder symptomatology. *Journal of Clinical Psychology, 56*, 51–61.

Buss, D. M. (2004). *Evolutionary psychology: The new science of the mind*. (2nd ed.). Boston: Allyn & Bacon.

Buss, D. M. (2005). *The handbook of evolutionary psychology*. Hoboken: Wiley.

Butler, L. D., Duran, R. E. F., Jasiukaitis, P., Koopman, C., & Spiegel, D. (1996). Hypnotizability and traumatic experiences: A diathesis-stress model of dissociative symptomatology. *American Journal of Psychiatry, 153*(Festschrift Suppl.), 42–63.

Butler, R. W., Mueser, K. T., Spock, J., & Braff, D.L . (1996). Positive symptoms of psychosis in posttraumatic stress disorder. *Biological Psychiatry, 39*, 839–844.

Butzel, J. S., Talbot, N. L., Duberstein, P. R., Houghtalen, R. P., Cox, C., & Giles, D. E. (2000). The relationship between traumatic events and dissociation among women with histories of childhood sexual abuse. *Journal of Nervous and Mental Disease, 188*, 547–549.

Caffo, E., & Belaise, C. (2003). Psychological aspects of traumatic injury in children and adolescents. *Child and Adolescent Psychiatric Clinics of North America, 12*, 493–535.

Caissy, G. (1998). *Unlock the fear: How to open yourself up to face and accept change.* New York: Insight Books.

Cameron, C. (2000). *Resolving childhood trauma: A long-term study of abuse survivors.* Thousand Oaks, CA: Sage.

Cardeña, E. (1994). The domain of dissociation. In S. J. Lynn & J. W. Rhue (Eds.), *Dissociation: Clinical and theoretical perspectives* (pp. 15–31). New York: Guilford.

Cardeña, E. (2000). Hypnosis in the treatment of trauma: A promising, but not fully supported, efficacious intervention. *International Journal of Clinical and Experimental Hypnosis, 48*, 225–238.

Cardeña, E., & Spiegel, D. (1993). Dissociative reactions to the San Francisco Bay Area earthquake of 1989. *American Journal of Psychiatry, 150*, 474–478.

Carlson, E. A. (1998). A prospective longitudinal study of disorganized/disoriented attachment. *Child Development, 69*, 1107–1128.

Carlson, E. B. (1994). Studying the interaction between physical and psychological states with the Dissociative Experiences scale. In D. Spiegel (Ed.), *Dissociation: Culture, mind, and body* (pp. 41–58). Washington, DC: American Psychiatric Press.

Carlson, E. B. (1997) *Trauma assessments: A clinician's guide.* New York. Guilford.

Carlson, E. B., & Dalenberg, C. (2000). A conceptual framework for the impact of traumatic experiences. *Trauma, Violence, and Abuse, 1*, 4–28.

Carlson, E. B., & Putnam, F. W. (1993). An update on the Dissociative Experiences scale. *Dissociation, 6*, 16–27.

Carlson, E. B., Putnam, F. W., Ross, C. A., Torem, M., Coons, P. M., Dill, D. L., Loewenstein, R. J., & Braun, B. G. (1993). Validity of the Dissociative Experiences Scale in screening for multiple personality disorder: A multicenter study. *American Journal of Psychiatry, 150*, 1030–1036.

Carrion, V. G., & Steiner, H. (2000). Trauma and dissociation in delinquent adolescents. *Journal of the American Academy of Child and Adolescent Psychiatry, 39*, 353–359.

Carver, C. S., & Scheier, M. F. (2000). Scaling back goals and recalibration of the affect system are processes in normal adaptive self-regulation: Understanding "response shift" phenomena. *Social Science and Medicine, 50*, 1715–1722.

Carver, C. S., Sutton, S. K., & Scheier, M. F. (2000). Action, emotion, and personality: Emerging conceptual integration. *Personality and Social Psychology Bulletin, 26*, 741–751.

Cassidy, J. (1994). Emotion regulation: Influences of attachment relations. In N. A. Fox (Ed.), *The development of emotion regulation: Biological and behavioral considerations* (Vol. 59, pp. 228–249). Chicago: University of Chicago Press.

Cassidy, J. (1999). The nature of the child's ties. In J. Cassidy & P. R. Shaver (Eds.). *Handbook of attachment: Theory, research, and clinical applications* (pp. 3–20). New York: Guilford.

Cattell, J. P., & Cattell, J. S. (1974). Depersonalization: Psychological and social perspectives. In S. Arieti (Ed.), *American Handbook of Psychiatry* (2nd ed., pp. 766–799). New York: Basic Books.

Charcot, J. M. (1887). *Clinical lectures on diseases of the nervous system.* London: New Sydenham Society.

Chefetz, R. A. (2000). Affect dysregulation as a way of life. *Journal of the American Academy of Psychoanalysis, 28*, 289–303.

Chemtob, C. M., Tolin, D. F., Van der Kolk, B. A., & Pitman, R. K. (2000). Eye movement desensitization and reprocessing. In E. B. Foa, T. M. Keane, & M. J. Friedman (Eds.), *Effective treatments for PTSD* (pp. 139–154). New York: Guilford.

Christianson, S. A. (1992). Emotional stress and eye-witness memory: A critical review. *Psychological Bulletin, 112*, 284–309.

Chu, J. A. (1988a). Ten traps for therapists in the treatment of trauma survivors. *Dissociation, 1*(4), 24–32.

Chu, J. A. (1988b). Some aspects of resistance in the treatment of multiple personality disorder. *Dissociation, 1*(2), 34–38.

Chu, J. A. (1996). Dissociative symptomatology in adult patients with histories of childhood physical and sexual abuse. In J. D. Bremner & C. R. Marmar (Eds.), *Trauma, memory, and disssociaton* (pp. 179–203). Washington, DC: American Psychiatric Press.

Chu, J. A. (1998a). *Rebuilding shattered lives: The responsible treatment of complex post-traumatic and dissociative disorders.* New York: Wiley.

Chu, J. A. (1998b). Dissociative symptomatology in adult patients with histories of childhood physical and sexual abuse. In J. D. Bremner & C. R. Marmar (Eds.), *Trauma, memory, and dissociation* (pp. 179–203). Washington, DC: American Psychiatric Press.

Chu, J. A., & Dill, D. L. (1990). Dissociation, borderline personality disorder, and childhood trauma. *American Journal of Psychiatry, 148*, 812.

Chu, J. A., Frey, L. M., Ganzel, B. L., & Matthews, J. A. (1999). Memories of childhood abuse: Dissociation, amnesia, and corroboration. *American Journal of Psychiatry, 156*, 749–763.

Classen, C., Cheryl, K., Hales, R., & Spiegel, D. (1998). Acute stress disorder as a predictor of posttraumatic stress symptoms. *American Journal of Psychiatry, 155*, 620–624.

Cloete, S. (1972). *A Victorian son: An autobiography.* London: Collins.

Clohessy, S., & Ehlers, A. (1999). PTSD symptoms, response to intrusive memories and coping in ambulance service workers. *British Journal of Clinical Psychology, 38*, 251–265.

Cloitre, M., Chase Stovall-McClough, K., Miranda, R., & Chemtob, C. M. (2004). Therapeutic alliance, negative mood regulation, and treatment outcome in child abuse-related posttraumatic stress disorder. *Journal of Consulting and Clinical Psychology, 72*, 411–416.

Cloitre, M., Koenen, K., Cohen, L., & Han, H. (2002). Skills training in affective and interpersonal regulation followed by exposure. *Journal of Consulting and Clinical Psychology, 70*, 1067–1074.

Cohen, J. A., Perel, J. M., De Bellis, M. D., Friedman, M. J., & Putnam, F. W. (2002). Treating traumatized children: Clinical implications of the psychobiology of posttraumatic stress disorder. *Trauma, Violence, and Abuse: A Review Journal, 3*, 91–108.

Comstock, C. M. (1991). The inner self helper and concepts of inner guidance: Historical antecendents, its role within dissociation, and clinical utilization. *Dissociation, 4,* 165–177.

Conlon, L., Fahy, T. J., & Conroy, R. (1999). PTSD in ambulant RTA victims: A randomized controlled trial of debriefing. *Journal of Psychosomatic Research, 46,* 37–44.

Coons, P. M. (1984). Children of parents with multiple personality disorder. In R. P. Kluft (Ed.), *Childhood antecedents of multiple personality* (pp. 151–165). Washington, DC: American Psychiatric Press.

Coons, P. M. (1992). Dissociative disorder not otherwise specified: A clinical investigation of 50 cases with suggestions for typology and treatment. *Dissociation, 5*(4), 187–196.

Coons, P. M. (1994). Confirmation of childhood abuse in child and adolescent cases of multiple personality disorder and dissociative disorder not otherwise specified. *Journal of Nervous and Mental Disease, 182,* 461–464.

Coons, P. M. (1996). Depersonalization and derealization. In L. Michelson & W. J. Ray (Eds.), *Handbook of dissociation: Theoretical, empirical, and clinical perspectives* (pp. 291–605). New York: Plenum Press.

Coons, P. M., & Bowman, E. S. (2001). Ten-year follow-up study of patients with dissociative identity disorder. *Journal of Trauma and Dissociation, 2,* 73–89.

Coons, P. M., & Milstein, V. (1992). Psychogenic amnesia: A clinical investigation of 25 cases. *Dissociation, 4,* 73–79.

Cosmides, L., & Tooby, J. (1992). Cognitive adaptations for social change. In J. Barkow, L. Cosmides, & J. Tooby (Eds.), *The adaptive mind* (pp. 162–228). New York: Oxford University Press.

Courtois, C. A. (1988). *Healing the incest wound: Adult survivors in therapy.* New York: Norton.

Courtois, C. A. (1999). *Recollections of sexual abuse: Treatment principles and guidelines.* New York: Norton.

Courtois, C. A. (2004). Complex trauma, complex reactions: Assessment and treatment. *Psychotherapy: Theory, Research, Practice, and Training, 41,* 412–425.

Crabtree, A. (1993). *From Mesmer to Freud: Magnetic sleep and the roots of psychological healing.* New Haven, CT: Yale University Press.

Craine, L. S., Henson, C. E., Colliver, J. A., & MacLean, D. G. (1988). Prevalence of a history of sexual abuse among female psychiatric patients in a state hospital system. *Hospital & Community Psychiatry, 39,* 300–304.

Crocq, L. (1999). *Les traumatismes psychiques de guerre.* [Psychological trauma of war]. Paris: Editions Odile Jacob.

Culpin, M. (1931). *Recent advances in the study of the psychoneuroses.* Philadelphia: P. Blakiston's Son.

Dalenberg, C. J. (2000). *Countertransference and the treatment of trauma.* Washington, DC: American Psychological Association.

Damasio, A. (1999). *The feeling of what happens: Body and emotion in the making of consciousness.* Orlando, FL: Harcourt Brace.

Darves-Bornoz, J. M., Degiovanni, A., & Gaillard, P. (1999). Validation of a French version of the Dissociative Experiences scale in a rape-victim population. *Canadian Journal of Psychiatry, 44,* 271–275.

Darves-Bornoz, J. M., Delmotte, I., Benhamou, P., Degiovanni, A., & Gaillard, P. (1996). Syndrome secondaire à un stress traumatique (PTSD) et conduites addictives [Syndrome secondary to post-traumatic stress disorder and addictive behaviors]. *Annales Médico-Psychologiques, 154,* 190–194.

Darves-Bornoz, J. M., Lépine, J. P., Choquet, M., Berger, C., Degiovanni, A., & Gaillard, P. (1998). Predictive factors of chronic post-traumatic stress disorder in rape victims. *European Psychiatry, 13*, 281–287.

David, D., Kutcher, G. S., Jackson, E. I., & Mellman, T. A. (1999). Psychotic symptoms in combat-related posttraumatic stress disorder. *Journal of Clinical Psychiatry, 60*, 29–32.

Davies, J. M., & Frawley, M. G. (1994). *The psychoanalytic treatment of adult survivors of childhood sexual abuse*. New York: Basic Books.

Davies, M. I., & Clark, D. M. (1998). Thought suppression produced a rebound effect with analogue post-traumatic intrusions. *Behaviour, Research, and Therapy, 36*, 571–582.

Delbo, C. (1985). *La mémoire et les jours*. [Days and memory] Paris: Berg International.

Dell, P. F. (1998). Axis II pathology in outpatients with dissociative identity disorder. *Journal of Nervous and Mental Disease, 186*, 352–356.

Dell, P. F. (2002). Dissociative phenomenology of dissociative identity disorder. *Journal of Nervous and Mental Disease, 190*, 10–15.

Dell, P. F. (2006a). A new model of dissociative identity disorder. *Psychiatric Clinics of North America, 29*, 1–26.

Dell, P. F. (2006b). The multidimensional inventory of dissociation (MID): A comprehensive measure of pathological dissociation. *Journal of Trauma and Dissociation, 7*(2), 77–106.

De Montaigne, M. (1993). *Michel de Montaigne: The complete essays* (Trans. M. A. Screech). New York: Penguin Books.

Dickinson, L. M., DeGruy, F. V., Dickinson, P., & Candib, L. (1999). Health-related quality of life and symptom profiles of female survivors of sexual abuse. *Archives of Family Medicine, 8*, 35–43.

Donovan, B. S., Padin-Rivera, E., Dowd, T., & Blake, D. D. (1996). Childhood factors and war zone stress in chronic PTSD. *Journal of Traumatic Stress, 9*, 361–368.

Donovan, B. S., Padin-Rivera, E., & Kowaliw, S. (2001). "Transcend:" Initial outcomes from a post traumatic stress disorder/substance abuse treatment program. *Journal of Traumatic Stress, 14*, 757–772.

Draijer, N. (1990). *Seksuele traumatisering in de jeugd: Gevolgen op lange termijn van seksueel misbruik van meisjes door verwanten* [Sexual traumatization in childhood: Long-term sequelae of sexual abuse of girls by relatives]. Amsterdam: SUA.

Draijer, N., & Boon, S. (1993). Trauma, dissociation, and dissociative disorders. In S. Boon & N. Draijer (Eds.), *Multiple personality in the Netherlands: A study on reliability and validity of the diagnosis* (pp. 177–193). Amsterdam/Lisse: Swets & Zeitlinger.

Draijer, N., & Boon, S. (1999). The imitation of dissociative identity disorder: Patients at risk, therapists at risk. *Journal of Psychiatry & Law, 11*, 301–322.

Draijer, N., & Langeland, W. (1999). Childhood trauma and perceived parental dysfunction in the etiology of dissociative symptoms in psychiatric inpatients. *American Journal of Psychiatry, 156*, 379–385.

Drever, J. (1952). *Penguin dictionary of psychology*. Harmondsworth, Middlesex: Penguin Books.

Driessen, M., Beblo, T., Reddemann, L., Rau, H., Lange, W., Silva, A. et al. (2002). Ist die Borderline-Persönlichkeitsstörung eine komplexe posttraumatische Störung? [Is borderline personality disorder a complex posttraumatic disorder?] *Nervenartz, 73*, 820–829.

Dube, S. R., Anda, R. F., Felitti, V. J., Chapman, D. P., Williamson, D. F., & Giles, W. H. (2001). Childhood abuse, household dysfunction, and the risk of attempted suicide throughout the life span: Findings from the Adverse Childhood Experiences Study. *Journal of the American Medical Association, 286,* 3089–3096.

Dube, S. R., Felitti, V. J., Dong, M., Chapman, D. P., Giles, W. H., & Anda, R. F. (2003). Childhood abuse, neglect, and household dysfunction and the risk of illicit drug use: The Adverse Childhood Experiences Study. *Pediatrics, 111*(3), 564–572.

Dube, S. R., Felitti, V. J., Dong, M., Giles, W. H., & Anda, R. F. (2003). The impact of adverse childhood experiences on health problems: Evidence from four birth cohorts dating back to 1900. *Preventive Medicine, 37,* 268–277.

Dutton, M. A., Burghardt, K. J., Perrin, S. G., Chrestman, K. R., & Halle, P. M. (1994). Battered women's cognitive schemata. *Journal of Traumatic Stress, 7,* 237–255.

Edelman, G. M. (1989). *Bright air, brilliant fire: On the matter of the mind.* New York: Basic Books.

Edelman, G. M., & Tononi, G. (2000). *A universe of consciousness: How matter becomes imagination.* New York: Basic Books.

Ehlers, A., Mayou, R. A., & Bryant, B. (2003). Cognitive predictors of posttraumatic stress disorder in children: Results of a prospective longitudinal study. *Behavior, Research, and Therapy, 41,* 1–10.

Ehling, T., Nijenhuis, E. R. S., & Krikke, A. P. (November, 2003). *Volume of discrete brain structures in florid and recovered DID, DDNOS, and healthy controls.* Presentation at the 20th International Fall Conference of the International Society for the Study of Dissociation, Chicago, IL.

El-Hage, W., Darves-Bornoz, J.-M., Allilaire, J.-F., & Gaillard, P. (2002). Posttraumatic somatoform dissociation in French psychiatric outpatients. *Journal of Trauma and Dissociation, 3*(3), 59–73.

Ellason, J. W., & Ross, C. A. (1995). Positive and negative symptoms in dissociative identity disorder and schizophrenia: A comparative analysis. *Journal of Nervous and Mental Disease, 183,* 236–241.

Ellason, J. W., Ross, C. A., & Fuchs, D. L. (1996). Lifetime axis I and II comorbidity and childhood trauma history in dissociative identity disorder. *Psychiatry, 59,* 255–266.

Ellenberger, H. F. (1970). *The discovery of the unconscious.* New York: Basic Books.

Elliott, D., & Guy, J. D. (1993). Mental health professionals versus non-mental health professionals: Childhood trauma and adult functioning. *Professional Psychology: Research and Practice, 24,* 83–89

Ellis, A. (1962). *Reason and emotion in psychotherapy.* New York: Lyle-Stuart.

Ellis, G. F. R. (2005). *Physics and the real world.* Paper presented at Science and Religion: Global perspectives. Philadelphia: Metanexus Institute, http://www.metanexus.net.

Ellis, G. F. R., & Toronchuk, J. (2005). Affective neural Darwinism. In R. D. Ellis, & N. Newton (Eds.), *Consciousness and emotion: Agency, conscious choice, and selective perception* (pp. 81–119). Amsterdam: John Benjamins.

Emily, J. O., Best, S. R., Lipsey, T. L., & Weiss, D. S. (2003). Predictors of posttraumatic stress disorder and symptoms in adults: A meta-analysis. *Psychological Bulletin, 129,* 52–73.

Engelhard, I. M., & Arntz, A. (2005). The fallacy of ex-consequentia reasoning and the persistence of PTSD. *Journal of Behavioral Therapy and Experimental Psychiatry, 36,* 35–42.

Epstein, R. S. (1994). *Keeping boundaries: Maintaining safety and integrity in the therapeutic process.* Washington, DC: American Psychiatric Press.

Epstein, S. (Ed.) (1991). *The self concept, the traumatic neurosis, and the structure of personality* (Vol. 3). London: Jessica Kingsley Publishers.

Erickson, M. H. (1980). *The collected papers of Milton H. Erickson on hypnosis* Ed. by E. L. Rossi, (Vols. 1–4). New York: Irvington.

Eulenberg, A. (1878). *Lehrbuch der Nervenkrankheiten* [Textbook of nervous disorders]. Berlin: August Hirschwald.

Fallot, R., & Harris, M. (2002). The trauma recovery and empowerment model (TREM). *Community Mental Health Journal, 38,* 475–485.

Fanselow, M. S., & Lester, L. S. (1988). A functional behavioristic approach to aversively motivated behavior: Predatory imminence as a determinant of the topography of defensive behavior. In R. C. Bolles & M. D. Beecher (Eds.), *Evolution and learning* (pp. 185–212). Hillsdale, NJ: Lawrence Erlbaum.

Feeny, N. C., Zoellner, L. A., & Foa, E. B. (2002). Treatment outcome for chronic PTSD among female assault victims with borderline personality characteristics: A preliminary examination. *Journal of Personality Disorders, 16,* 30–40.

Felitti, V. J., Anda, R. F., Nordenberg, D., Williamson, D. F., Spitz, A. M., Edwards, V. et al. (1998). Relationship of childhood abuse and household dysfunction to many of the leading causes of death of adults: The Adverse Childhood Experiences (ACE) Study. *American Journal of Preventive Medicine, 14,* 245–258.

Ferenczi, S. (1919). Die Psychoanalyse der Kriegsneurose [Psychoanalysis of war neuroses] n. In S. Freud et al., *Zur Psychoanalyse der Kriegsneurosen* [Psychoanalysis of war neuroses] (pp. 9–30). Vienna: Internationaler Psychoanalytischer Verlag.

Ferenczi, S. (1926). *Further contributions to the theory and technique of psychoanalysis.* London: Hogarth Press.

Ferenczi, S. (1949). Confusion of tongues between adults and the child. *International Journal of Psychoanalysis, 30,* 225–231.

Ferenczi, S. (1988). *The clinical diary of Sándor Ferenczi.* (J. Dupont, Ed.). Cambridge, MA: Harvard University Press.

Figley, C. R. (1978). *Stress disorders among Vietnam veterans.* New York: Brunner/Mazel.

Figley, C. (1995). *Compassion fatigue: Coping with secondary traumatic stress disorder in those who treat the traumatized.* Philadelphia: Brunner/Mazel.

Fine, C. G. (1993). A tactical integrationist perspective on the treatment of multiple personality disorder. In R. P. Kluft & C. G. Fine (Eds.), *Clinical perspectives on multiple personality disorder* (pp. 135–154). Washington, DC: American Psychiatric Press.

Fine, C. G. (1999). The tactical-integration model for the treatment of dissociative identity disorder and allied dissociative disorders. *American Journal of Psychotherapy, 53,* 361–376.

Fine, C. G., & Berkowitz, A. S. (2001). The wreathing protocol: The imbrication of hypnosis and EMDR in the treatment of dissociative identity disorder and other dissociative responses. *American Journal of Clinical Hypnosis, 43,* 275–290.

Fine, C. G., & Comstock, C. M. (November, 1989). *The completion of cognitive schemata and affective realms through the temporary blending of personalities.* Paper Presented at the Fifth International Conference on Multiple Personality/Disssociative States, Chicago, IL.

Firestone, R. W., & Catlett, J. (1999). *Fear of intimacy.* Washington, DC: American Psychological Association.

Foa, E. B. (2006). Psychosocial therapy for posttraumatic stress disorder. *Journal of Clinical Psychiatry, 67* [Suppl 2], 40–45.

Foa, E. B., Keane, T. M., & Friedman, M. J. (2000). *Effective treatments for PTSD: Practice guidelines from the International Society of Traumatic Stress Studies.* New York: Guilford.

Foa, E. B., & Rothbaum, B. O. (1998). *Treating the trauma of rape: Cognitive–behavioral treatment for PTSD.* New York: Guilford.

Foa, E. B., Zinbarg, R., & Rothbaum, B. O. (1992). Uncontrollability and unpredictability in post-traumatic stress disorder: An animal model. *Psychological Bulletin, 112,* 218–238.

Follette, V. M., Ruzek, J., & Abueg, F. R. (Eds.) (1998). *Cognitive–behavioral therapies for trauma.* New York: Guilford.

Fonagy, P. M. (1997). Multiple voices vs. meta-cognition: An attachment theory perspective. *Journal of Psychotherapy Integration, 7,* 181–194.

Fonagy, P. M., Gergely, G., Jurist, E. L., & Target, M. (2002). *Affect regulation, mentalization, and the development of the self.* New York: Other Press.

Fonagy, P., & Target, M. (1996). Playing with reality: I. Theory of mind and the normal development of psychic reality. *International Journal of Psychoanalysis, 77,* 217–233.

Fonagy, P., & Target, M. (1997). Attachment and reflective function: Their role in self-organization. *Developmental Psychopathology, 9,* 679–700.

Ford, J. (1999). Disorder of extreme stress following war-zone military trauma: Associated features of posttraumatic stress disorder or comorbid but distinct syndromes? *Journal of Consulting and Clinical Psychology, 67,* 3–12.

Ford. J. D., Courtois, C. A., Steele, K., Van der Hart, O., & Nijenhuis, E. R. S. (2005). Treatment of complex posttraumatic self-dysregulation. *Journal of Traumatic Stress, 18,* 437–448.

Ford, J. D., & Kidd, P. (1998). Early childhood trauma and disorders of extreme stress as predictors of treatment outcome with chronic posttraumatic stress disorder. *Journal of Traumatic Stress, 11,* 743–761.

Ford, J. D., Racusin, R., Ellis, C. G., Daviss, W. B., Reiser, J., Fleischer, A., & Thomas, J. (2000). Child maltreatment, other trauma exposure, and posttraumatic symptomatology among children with oppositional defiant and attention deficit hyperactivity disorders. *Child Maltreatment, 5,* 205–217.

Ford, J. D., & Russo, E. (in press). A trauma-focused, present-centered, emotional self-regulation approach to integrated treatment for post-traumatic stress and addiction: Trauma Adaptive Recovery Group Education and Therapy (TARGET). *American Journal of Psychotherapy.*

Fosha, D. (2000). *The transforming power of affect: A model of accelerated change.* New York: Basic Books.

Fosha, D. (2001). The dyadic regulation of affect. *Journal of Clinical Psychology, 57,* 227–242.

Fraser, G. A. (1991). The dissociation table technique: A strategy for working with ego states in dissociative disorders and ego-state therapy. *Dissociation, 4,* 205–213.

Fraser, G. A. (2003). Fraser's "Dissociative Table Technique" revisited, revised: A strategy for working with ego states in dissociative disorders and ego-state therapy. *Journal of Trauma and Dissociation, 4*(4), 5–28.

Fraser, S. (1987). *My father's house: A memoir of incest and of healing.* Toronto: Doubleday Canada.

Freeman, L., & Power, M. J. (2005). *Handbook of evidence-based psychotherapy.* New York: Wiley.

Freyd, J. J. (1996). *Betrayal trauma: The logic of forgetting childhood trauma.* Cambridge, MA: Harvard University Press.

Frijda, N. (1986). *The emotions.* Cambridge, UK: Cambridge University Press.

Fromm, E. (1965). Hypnoanalysis: Theory and two case excerpts. *Psychotherapy: Theory, Research, and Practice, 2*, 127–133.

Fuster, J. M. (1997). *The prefrontal cortex: Anatomy, physiology, and neuropsychology of the frontal lobe*. Philadelphia: Lippincott-Raven.

Fuster, J. M. (2003). *Cortex and mind: Unifying cognition*. New York: Oxford University Press.

Gabbard, G. O., & Lester, E. P. (1995). *Boundaries and boundary violations in psychoanalysis*. New York: Basic Books.

Gallese, V. (2003). The roots of empathy: The shared manifold hypothesis and the neural basis of intersubjectivity. *Psychopathology, 36*, 171–180.

Gallese, V., Keysers, C., & Rizzolatti, G. (2004). A unifying view of the basis of social cognition. *Trends in Cognitive Science, 8*, 396–403.

Galloucis, M., Silverman, M. S., & Francek, H. M. (2000). The impact of trauma exposure on the cognitive schemas of a sample of paramedics. *International Journal of Emergency Mental Health, 2*, 5–18.

Garbarini, F., & Adenzato, M. (2004). At the root of embodied cognition: Cognitive science meets neurophysiology. *Brain and Cognition, 56*, 100–106.

Garcia, J., Forthman-Quick, D., & White, B. (1984). Conditioned disgust and fear from mollusk to monkey. In D. L. Alkon & J. Farley (Eds.), *Primary neural substrates of learning and behavioral change* (pp. 47–61). New York: Cambridge University Press.

Gelinas, D. J. (1983). The persisting negative effects of incest. *American Journal of Psychiatry, 46*, 312–332.

Gelinas, D. J. (2003). Integrating EMDR into phase-oriented treatment for trauma. *Journal of Trauma & Dissociation, 4*(3), 91–135.

Gershuny, B. S., Cloitre, M., & Otto, M. W. (2003). Peritraumatic dissociation and PTSD severity: Do event-related fears about death and control mediate their relation? *Behaviour Research and Therapy, 41*, 157–166.

Gershuny, B. S., & Thayer, J. F. (1999). Relations among psychological trauma, dissociative phenomena, and trauma-related distress: A review and integration. *Clinical Psychology Review, 19*, 631–657.

Gilbert, P. (1989). *Human nature and suffering*. London: Lawrence Erlbaum Associates.

Gilbert, P. (2000). The relationship of shame, social anxiety, and depression: The role of evaluation and social rank. *Clinical Psychology and Psychotherapy, 7*, 174–189.

Gilbert, P. (2001). Evolution and social anxiety. The role of attraction, social competition, and social hierarchies. *Psychiatric Clinics of North America, 24*(4), 723–751.

Gilbert, P. (2002). Body shame: A biopsychosocial conceptualization and overview with treatment implications. In P. Gilbert & J. N. V. Miles (Eds.), *Body shame: Conceptualization, Research & Treatment* (pp. 3–54). Hove: Brunner Routledge.

Gilbert, P., & Gerlsma, C. (1999). Recall of shame and favouritism in relation to psychopathology. *British Journal of Clinical Psychology, 38*, 357–373.

Glaser, D. (2000). Child abuse and neglect and the brain: A review. *Journal of Child Psychology and Psychiatry, 41*, 97–116.

Gleaves, D. H. (1996). The sociocognitive model of dissociative identity disorder. *Psychological Bulletin, 120*, 42–59.

Gold, S. N. (2000). *Not trauma alone*. Philadelphia: Brunner/Routledge.

Goldstein, A. J., & Chambless, D. L. (1978). A reanalysis of agoraphobia. *Behavior Therapy, 9*, 47–59.

Golier, J. A., Yehuda, R., Lupien, S. J., Harvey, P. D., Grossman, R., & Elkin, A. (2002). Memory performance in Holocaust survivors with posttraumatic stress disorder. *American Journal of Psychiatry, 159*(10), 1682–1688.

Golier, J. A., Yehuda, R., Schmeidler, J., & Siever, L. J. (2001). Variability and severity of depression and anxiety in post traumatic stress disorder and major depressive disorder. *Depression and Anxiety, 13*, 97–100.

Golynkina, K., & Ryle, A. (1999). The identification and characteristics of the partially dissociated states of patients with borderline personality disorder. *British Journal of Medical Psychology, 72*(4), 429–445.

Goodman, L., & Peters, J. (1995). Persecutory alters and ego states: Protectors, friends, and allies. *Dissociation, 8*, 91–99.

Goodman, L. A., Rosenberg, S. D., Mueser, K. T., & Drake, R. E. (1997). Physical and sexual assault history in women with serious mental illness: Prevalence, correlates, treatment, and future research directions. *Schizophrenia Bulletin, 23*(4), 685–696.

Goodman, L. A., Thompson, K., Weinfurt, K., Corl, S., Acker, P., & Mueser, K. T. (1999). Reliability of reports of violent victimization and posttraumatic stress disorder among men and women with serious mental illness. *Journal of Traumatic Stress, 12*, 587–599.

Goodwin, J., & Attias, R. (1999). Conversations with the body: Psychotherapeutic approaches to body image and body ego. In J. M. Goodwin & R. Attias (Eds.). *Splintered reflections: Images of the body in trauma* (pp. 167–182). New York: Basic Books

Gould, J. L. (1982). *Ethology: The mechanisms and evolution of behavior*. New York: Norton.

Graham, C., & Thavasotby, R. (1995). Dissociative psychosis: An atypical presentation and response to cognitive–analytic therapy. *Irish Journal of Psychological Medicine, 12*, 109–111.

Grey, N., Holmes, E., & Brewin, C.R. (2001). Peritraumatic emotional "hot-spots" in memory. *Behavioural and Cognitive Psychotherapy, 29*, 367–372.

Grieger, T. A., Staab, J. P., Cardeña, E., McCarroll, J. E., Brandt, G. T., Fullerton, C. S., & Ursano, R. I. (2000). Acute stress disorder and subsequent post-traumatic stress disorder in a group of exposed disaster workers. *Depression & Anxiety, 11*, 183–184.

Grigsby, J., & Stevens, D. (2000). *Neurodynamics of personality*. New York: Guilford.

Gunderson, J. (1996). The borderline patient's intolerance of aloneness: Insecure attachments and therapist availability. *American Journal of Psychiatry, 153*, 752–758.

Gunderson, J. G., & Sabo, A. (1993). The phenomenological and conceptual interface between borderline personality disorder and post-traumatic stress disorder. *American Journal of Psychiatry, 150*, 19–27.

Guralnik, O., Schmeidler, J., & Simeon, D. (2000) Feeling unreal: Cognitive processes in depersonalization. *American Journal of Psychiatry, 157*, 103–109.

Hahn, W. K. (2004). The role of shame in negative therapeutic reactions. *Psychotherapy: Theory, Research, Practice, Training, 41*, 3–12.

Haley, J. (1963). *Strategies of psychotherapy*. New York: Grune & Stratton.

Hammond, D. C. (1990). (Ed.). *Handbook of hypnotic suggestions and metaphors*. New York: Norton.

Hammond, D. C., & Cheek, D. B. (1988). Ideomotor signaling: A method for rapid unconscious exploration. In D. C. Hammond (Ed.), *Hypnotic induction and suggestion: An introductory manual* (pp. 90–97). Des Plaines, IL: American Society of Clinical Hypnosis.

Hamner, M. B., Frueh, B. C., Ulmer, H. G., Huber, M. G., Twomey, T. J., Tyson, C., et al. (2000). Psychotic features in chronic posttraumatic stress disorder and schizophrenia: Comparative severity. *Journal of Nervous and Mental Disease, 188*, 217–221.

Hamner, M. B., Frueh, B. C., Ulmer, H. G., & Arana, G. W. (1999). Psychotic features and illness severity in combat veterans with chronic posttraumatic stress disorder. *Biological Psychiatry, 45*, 846–852.

Harter, S. (1999). *The construction of the self: A developmental perspective.* New York: Guilford.

Harvey, A. G., & Bryant, R. A. (1998). The relationship between acute stress disorder and posttraumatic stress disorder: A prospective evaluation of motor vehicle accident survivors. *Journal of Consulting and Clinical Psychology, 66*, 507–512.

Harvey, A. G., & Bryant, R. A. (1999a). A qualitative investigation of the organization of traumatic memories. *British Journal of Clinical Psychology, 38*(4), 401–405.

Harvey, A. G., & Bryant, R. A. (1999b). Dissociative symptoms in acute stress disorder. *Journal of Traumatic Stress, 12*, 673–680.

Haugen, M. C., & Castillo, R. J. (1999). Unrecognized dissociation in psychotic outpatients and implications of ethnicity. *Journal of Nervous and Mental Disease, 187*, 751–754.

Hayes, S. C., Wilson, K.G., Gifford, E. V., Folette, V. M., & Strohsahl, K. (1996). Emotional avoidance and behavioral disorders: A functional dimensional approach to diagnosis and treatment. *Journal of Consulting and Clinical Psychology, 64*, 1152–1168.

Hayes, S. C., Folette, V. M., & Linehan, M. M. (Eds.) (2004). *Mindfulness and acceptance: Expanding the cognitive-behavioral tradition.* New York: Guilford.

Hayes, S. C., Luoma, J. B., Bond, F. W., Masuda, A., & Lillis, J. (2006). Acceptance and commitment therapy: Model, processes and outcomes. *Behavioral Research and Therapy, 44*, 1–25.

Hedges, L. E. (1997). Surviving the transference psychosis. In L. E. Hedges, R. Hilton, V. W. Hilton, & O. B. Caudill, Jr. (Eds.), *Therapists at risk: Perils of the intimacy of the therapeutic relationship* (pp. 109–145). Northvale, NJ: Jason Aronson.

Heim, G., & Bühler, K. E. (2003). Les idées fixes et la psychologie de l'action de Pierre Janet. [Fixed ideas and Pierre Janet's action psychology] *Annales Médico Psychologiques, 161*, 579–586.

Henry, D. L. (2001). Resilient children: What they tell us about coping with maltreatment. *Social Work in Health Care, 34*, 283–298.

Herman, J. L. (1992a). Complex PTSD: A syndrome in survivors of prolonged and repeated trauma. *Journal of Traumatic Stress 5*, 377–392.

Herman, J. L. (1992b). *Trauma and recovery.* New York: Basic Books.

Herman, J. L. (1993). Sequelae of prolonged and repeated trauma: Evidence for a complex posttraumatic syndrome (DESNOS). In J. R. T. Davidson & E. B. Foa (Eds.), *Posttraumatic stress disorder: DSM-IV and beyond* (pp. 213–228). Washington, DC: American Psychiatric Press.

Herman, J. L., Perry, J. C., & Van der Kolk, B. A. (1989). Childhood trauma in borderline personality disorder. *American Journal of Psychiatry, 146*, 490–495.

Herman, J. L., & Van der Kolk, B. A. (1987). Childhood trauma in borderline personality disorder. *American Journal of Psychiatry, 146*, 490–495.

Hermans, E. J., Nijenhuis, E. R. S., Van Honk, J., Huntjens, R., & Van der Hart, O. (2006). State dependent attentional bias for facial threat in dissociative identity disorder. *Psychiatry Research, 141*, 233–236.

Hesse, E. (1999). The adult attachment interview: Historical and current perspective. In J. Cassidy & P. R. Shaver (Eds.), *Handbook of attachment: Theory, research, and clinical applications* (pp. 395–433). New York: Guilford.

Hilgard, E. R. (1977). *Divided consciousness: Multiple controls in human thought and action.* New York: Wiley.

Hillis, S. D., Anda, R. F., Dube, S. R., Felitti, V. J., Marchbanks, P. A., & Marks, J. S. (2004). The association between adverse childhood experiences and adolescent pregnancy, long-term psychosocial consequences, and fetal death. *Pediatrics, 113*, 320–327.

Holbrook, T. L., Hoyt, D. B., Stein, M. B., & Sieber, W. J. (2001). Perceived threat to life predicts posttraumatic stress disorder after major trauma: Risk factors and functional outcome. *Journal of Trauma-Injury Infection & Critical Care, 51*, 287–293.

Holbrook, T. L., Hoyt, D. B., Stein, M. B., & Sieber, W. J. (2002). Gender differences in long-term posttraumatic stress disorder outcomes after major trauma: Women are at higher risk of adverse outcomes than men. *Journal of Trauma, 53*, 882–888.

Hollender, M. H., & Hirsch, S. J. (1964). Hysterical psychosis. *American Journal of Psychiatry, 120*, 1066–1074.

Holmes, J. (1991). Psychotherapy 2000: Some predictions for the coming decade. *British Journal of Psychiatry, 159*, 149–155.

Holmes, E. A., Brown, R. J., Mansell, W., Fearon, R. P., Hunter, E. C., Frasquilho, F., & Oakley, D. A. (2005). Are there two qualitatively distinct forms of dissociation? A review and some clinical implications. *Clinical Psychology Review, 25*, 1–23.

Holowka, D. W., King, S., Saheb, D., Pukall, M., & Brunet, A. (2003). Childhood abuse and dissociative symptoms in adult schizophrenia. *Schizophrenia Research, 60*, 87–90.

Horner, A. J. (2005). *Dealing with resistance in psychotherapy.* Lanham, MD: Jason Aronson.

Horevitz, R., & Loewenstein, R. J. (1994). The rational treatment of multiple personality disorder. In S. J. Lynn & J. W. Rhue (Eds.), *Dissociation: Clinical and theoretical perspectives* (pp. 289–316). New York: Guilford.

Hornstein, N. L., & Putnam, F. W. (1992). Clinical phenomenology of child and adolescent dissociative disorders. *Journal of the American Academy of Child and Adolescent Psychiatry, 31*, 1077–1085.

Horowitz, M. J. (1986). *Stress response syndromes* (2nd ed.). Northvale, NJ: Jason Aronson.

Howell, E. (2005). *The dissociative mind.* Mahwah, NJ: Analytic Press.

Huber, M. (1995). *Multiple Persönlichkeiten: Überlebenden extremer Gewalt* [Multiple personalities: Survivors of extreme violence]. Frankfurt: Fischer.

Huber, M. (2003). *Wege der Traumabehandlung: Trauma und Traumabehandlung, Teil 2* [Trauma treatment: Trauma and trauma treatment, Part 2]. Paderborn, Germany: Junfermann Verlag.

Hunter, M., & Struve, J. (1998). *The ethical use of touch in psychotherapy.* Thousand Oaks, CA: Sage.

Hurley, S. L. (1998). *Consciousness in action.* Cambridge, MA: Harvard University Press.

Ide, N., & Paez, A. (2000). Complex PTSD: A review of current issues. *International Journal of Emergency Mental Health, 2*, 43–49.

International Society for the Study of Dissociation (2005). [Chu, J. A., Loewenstein, R., Dell, P. F., Barach, P. M., Somer, E., Kluft, R. P., Gelinas, D. J., Van der Hart, O., Dalenberg, C. J., Nijenhuis, E. R. S., Bowman, E. S., Boon, S., Goodwin, J., Jacobson, M., Ross, C. A., Şar, V., Fine, C. G., Frankel, A. S., Coons, P. M., Courtois, C. A., Gold, S. N., & Howell, E.] Guidelines for treating dissociative identity disorder in adults. *Journal of Trauma & Dissociation, 6*(4), 69–149.

Irwin, H. J. (1996). Traumatic childhood events, perceived availability of emotional support, and the development of dissociative tendencies. *Child Abuse & Neglect, 20*, 701–707.

Irwin, H. J. (1998). Affective predictors of dissociation. II: Shame and guilt. *Journal of Clinical Psychology, 54*, 237–245.

Irwin, H. J. (1999). Pathological and nonpathological dissociation: The relevance of childhood trauma. *Journal of Psychology, 133*, 157–164.

Izquierdo, I., Cammarota, M., Vianna, M. M., & Bevilaqua, L. R. (2004). The inhibition of acquired fear. *Neurotoxicity Research, 6*, 175–188.

Jackson, J. H. (1931–1932). *Selected writings of John Hughlings Jackson* (Vol. 1–2). London: Milford.

Janet, P. (1887). L'anesthésie systématisée et la dissociation des phénomènes psychologiques [Systematic anesthesia and the dissociation of psychological phenomena]. In P. Janet, *Premiers écrits psychologiques* [First psychological writings] (pp. 87–112) (edited by S. Nicolas). Paris: L'Harmattan (Original work published in 1887).

Janet, P. (1889). *L'automatisme psychologique* [Psychological automatism]. Paris: Félix Alcan.

Janet, P. (1898a). *Névroses et idées fixes*, Vol. 1., [Neuroses and fixed ideas]. Paris: Félix Alcan.

Janet, P. (1898b). Un cas de possession et l'exorcisme moderne [A case of possession and modern exorcism]. In P. Janet (1898), *Névroses et idées fixes*, Vol. 1 [Neuroses and fixed ideas]. (pp. 375–406). Paris: Félix Alcan. (Original work published in 1894–1895).

Janet, P. (1898c). Histoire d'une idée fixe [History of a fixed idea]. In P. Janet, *Névroses et idées fixes* [Neuroses and fixed ideas], Vol. 1. Paris: Félix Alcan. (Original work published in 1894).

Janet, P. (1898d). L'amnésie continue [Continuous amnesia]. In P. Janet, *Névroses et idées fixes* [Neuroses and fixed ideas], Vol. 1 (pp. 109–155). Paris: F. Alcan. (Original work published in 1893).

Janet, P. (1903). *Les obsessions et la psychasthénie* [Obsessions and psychasthenia], Vol. 1. Paris: Félix Alcan.

Janet, P. (1907). *The major symptoms of hysteria.* London & New York: Macmillan.

Janet, P. (1909a). Problèmes psychologiques de l'émotion [Psychological problems of emotion]. *Revue Neurologique, 17*, 1551–1687.

Janet, P. (1909b). *Les névroses* [The neuroses]. Paris: E. Flammarion.

Janet, P. (1910–1911). Les problèmes de la suggestion [The problems of suggestion]. *Medizinische Psychologie und Psychotherapie* [Medical Psychology and Psychotherapy], *17*, 323–343.

Janet, P. (1921–1922). La tension psychologique, ses degrés, ses oscillations. [Psychological tension, its degrees, its oscillations] *British Journal of Psychology, Medical Section, 1*, 1–15, 144–164, 209–224.

Janet, P. (1922). The fear of action. *Journal of Abnormal and Social Psychology, 16*, 150–160.

Janet, P. (1925). *Psychological healing.* New York: Macmillan. (Original work published as *Les médications psychologiques.* (1919). Paris: Félix Alcan).

Janet, P. (1926a). *Les stades de l'évolution psychologique et le rôle de la faiblesse dans le fonctionnement de l'esprit* [Stages of psychological evolution and the role of weakness in the functioning of the mind]. Paris: A. Chahine.

Janet, P. (1926b). *De l'angoisse à l'extase*, Vol. 1, *Un délire religieux, La croyance.* [From agony to ecstasy, Vol. 1, A religious delirium, belief]. Paris: F. Alcan.

Janet, P. (1927). *La pensée intérieure et ses troubles* [Inner thought and its troubles]. Paris: A. Chahine.

Janet, P. (1928a). *L'evolution de la mémoire et de la notion du temps* [The evolution of memory and of the notion of time]. Paris: A. Chahine.

Janet, P. (1928b). *De l'angoisse à l'extase*, Vol. 2, *Les sentiments fondamentaux* [From agony to ecstasy, Vol. 2, The fundamental feelings]. Paris: F. Alcan.

Janet, P. (1929a). *L'évolution psychologique de la personnalité* [The psychological evolution of the personality]. Paris: A. Chahine.

Janet, P. (1929b). Les sentiments régulations de l'action [The regulating feelings of action]. *Bulletin de la Société Française de Philosophie, 29*, 73–103.

Janet, P. (1932a). On memories which are too real. In C. MacFie Campbell (Ed.), *Problems of personality* (pp. 141–150). New York: Harcourt, Brace, and Company.

Janet, P. (1932b). *La force et la faiblesse psychologiques* [Psychological strength and weakness]. Paris: N. Maloine.

Janet, P. (1932c). *L'amour et la haine* [Love and hate]. Paris: N. Maloine.

Janet, P. (1934). *La tension psychologique et ses oscillations* [Psychological tension and its oscillations]. In G. Dumas (Ed.), *Nouveau traité de psychologie* [New textbook of psychology] (pp. 386–411). Paris: F. Alcan.

Janet, P. (1935a). Réalisation et interprétation [Realization and interpretation]. *Annales Médico-Psychologiques, 93*, 329–366.

Janet, P. (1935b). *Les débuts de l'intelligence* [The beginnings of intelligence]. Paris: Flammarion.

Janet, P. (1936). *L'intelligence avant le language* [Intelligence before language]. Paris: Flammarion.

Janet, P. (1937). Psychological strength and weakness in mental diseases. In R. K. Merton (Ed.), *Factors determining human behavior* (pp. 64–106). Cambridge, MA: Harvard University Press.

Janet, P. (1938). La psychologie de la conduite [The psychology of action]. In H. Wallon (Ed.), *Encyclopédie Française* [The French encyclopedia] (pp. 808-11–808.16). Paris: Société de Gestion de l'Encyclopédie Française.

Janet, P. (1945). La croyance délirante [Delirious beliefs]. *Schweizerische Zeitschrift für Psychologie, 4*, 173–187.

Janet, P. (1977). The mental state of hystericals: A study of mental stigmata and mental accidents (edited and with prefaces by D. N. Robinson). Washington, DC: University Publications of America. (Original work published in 1901).

Janet, P. (1983a). *L'état mental des hystériques* [The mental state of hystericals], 2nd ed. Marseille: Lafitte. (Original work published in 1911).

Janet, P. (1983b). L'amnésie et la dissociation des souvenirs par l'émotion [Amnesia and the dissociation of memories by emotion]. In P. Janet, *L'état mental des hystériques* [The mental state of hystericals], 2nd ed. (pp. 506–544). Marseille: Lafitte. (Original work published in 1904).

Janet, P. (1983c). Le traitement psychologique de l'hystérie [Psychological treatment of hysteria]. In P. Janet (1911), *L'état mental des hystériques* [The mental state of hystericals], 2nd ed. (pp. 619–688). Marseille: Lafitte. (Original work published in 1898/1911).

Jang, K. L., Stein, M. B., Taylor, S., Asmundson, G. J., & Livesley, W. J. (2003). Exposure to traumatic events and experiences: Aetiological relationships with personality function. *Psychiatry Research, 120*, 61–69.

Janoff-Bulman, R. (1992). *Shattered assumptions: Towards as new psychology of trauma*. New York: The Free Press.

Janssen, I., Krabbendam, L., Hanssen, M., Bak, M., Vollebergh, W., de Graaf, R. et al. (2005). Are apparent associations between parental representations and psychosis risk mediated by early trauma? *Acta Psychiatrica Scandinavica, 112*, 372–375.

Jenkins, M. A., Langlais, P. J., Delis, D. A., & Cohen, R. A. (2000). Attentional dysfunction associated with posttraumatic stress disorder among rape survivors. *Clinical Neuropsychology, 14*, 7–12.

Johnson, D. M., Pike, J. L., & Chard, K. M. (2001). Factors predicting PTSD, depression, and dissociative severity in female treatment-seeking childhood sexual abuse survivors. *Child Abuse & Neglect, 25*, 179–198.

Joseph, B. (1975). The patient who is difficult to reach. In P. L. Giovacchini (Ed.), *Tactics and techniques in psychoanalytic therapy:* Vol. 2. *Countertransference* (pp. 205–216). New York: Jason Aronson.

Kardiner, A. (1941). *The traumatic neuroses of war*. New York: Hoeber.

Kardiner, A., & Spiegel, H. (1947). *War stress and neurotic illness*. New York: Hoeber.

Kellerman, N. P. (2001). Psychopathology in children of Holocaust survivors: A review of the research literature. *Israel Journal of Psychiatry and Related Sciences, 38*, 36–46.

Kellogg, N. D., & Hoffman, T. J. (1997). Child sexual revictimization by multiple perpetrators. *Child Abuse & Neglect, 21*, 953–964.

Kessler, R. C., Sonnega, A., Bromet, E., Hughes, M., & Nelson, C. B. (1995). Posttraumatic stress disorder in the National Comorbidity Survey. *Archives of General Psychiatry, 52*, 1048–1060.

Keysers, C., & Perrett, D. I. (2004). Demystifying social cognition: A Hebbian perspective. *Trends in Cognitive Science, 8,* 501–507.

Keysers, C., Wicker, B., Gazzola, V., Anton, J. L., Fogassi, L., & Gallese, V. (2004). A touching sight: SII/PV activation during the observation and experience of touch. *Neuron, 42,* 335–346.

Kihlstrom, J. F. (1992). Dissociation and conversion disorders. In D. J. Stein & J. E. Young (Eds.), *Cognitive science and clinical disorders* (pp. 247–270). San Diego, CA: Academic Press.

Kinsler, P. J. (1992). The centrality of the therapeutic relationship: What's *not* being said. *Dissociation, 5,* 166–170.

Kirshner, L. A. (1973). Dissociative reactions: An historical review and clinical study. *Acta Psychiatrica Scandinavia, 49,* 698–711.

Kleber, R. J., & Brom, D. (1992). *Coping with trauma: Theory, prevention and treatment*. Lisse, The Netherlands: Swets & Zeitlinger.

Kluft, R. P. (1982). Varieties of hypnotic interventions in the treatment of multiple personality. *American Journal of Clinical Hypnosis, 24,* 230–240

Kluft, R. P. (1984). An introduction to multiple personality disorder. *Psychiatric Annals, 14*, 19–24.

Kluft, R. P. (1985). The natural history of multiple personality disorder. In R. P. Kluft (Ed.), *Childhood antecedents of multiple personality* (pp. 197–238). Washington, DC: American Psychiatric Press.

Kluft, R. P. (1987a). First-rank symptoms as a diagnostic clue to multiple personality disorder. *American Journal of Psychiatry, 144*, 293–298.

Kluft, R. P. (1987b). The simulation and dissimulation of multiple personality disorder. *American Journal of Clinical Hypnosis, 30*, 104–118.

Kluft, R. P. (1988). The dissociative disorders. In J. A. Talbot, R. E. Hale, & S. C. Yudofsky (Eds.), *The American Psychiatric Press Textbook of Psychiatry* (Vol. 10, pp. 557–584). Washington, DC: American Psychiatric Press.

Kluft, R. P. (1989). Playing for time: Temporizing techniques in the treatment of multiple personality disorder. *American Journal of Clinical Hypnosis, 32*, 90–98.

Kluft, R. P. (1991). Multiple personality disorder. In A. Tasman & S. M. Goldfinger (Eds.), *American Psychiatric Press Review of Psychiatry* (Vol. 10, pp. 161–188). Washington, DC: American Psychiatric Press.

Kluft, R. P. (1992). Hypnosis with multiple personality disorder. *American Journal of Preventive Psychiatry and Neurology, 3*, 19–27.

Kluft, R. P. (1993a). The initial stages of psychotherapy in the treatment of multiple personality disorder patients. *Dissociation, 6*, 145–161.

Kluft, R. P. (1993b). Basic principles in conducting the psychotherapy of multiple personality disorder. In R. P. Kluft & C. G. Fine (Eds.), *Clinical perspectives on multiple personality disorder* (pp. 19–50). Washington, DC: American Psychiatric Press.

Kluft, R. P. (1993c). Clinical approaches to the integration of personalities. In R. P. Kluft & C. G. Fine (Eds.), *Clinical perspectives on multiple personality disorder* (pp. 101–133). Washington, DC: American Psychiatric Press.

Kluft, R. P. (1994a). Countertransference in the treatment of multiple personality disorder. In J. P. Wilson & J. D. Lindy (Eds.), *Countertransference in the treatment of PTSD* (pp. 122–150). New York: Guilford.

Kluft, R. P. (1994b). Treatment trajectories in multiple personality disorder. *Dissociation, 7*, 63–76.

Kluft, R. P. (1996a). Dissociative identity disorder. In L. Michelson & W. J. Ray (Eds.), *Handbook of dissociation: Theoretical, empirical, and clinical perspectives* (pp. 337–366). New York: Plenum Press.

Kluft, R. P. (1996b). The confirmation and disconfirmation of memories of abuse in DID patients: A naturalistic clinical study. *American Journal of Psychiatry, 153*(Festschrift Suppl.), 103–110.

Kluft, R. P. (1997). On the treatment of traumatic memories: Always? Never? Sometimes? Now? Later? *Dissociation, 10*, 80–90.

Kluft, R. P. (1999). An overview of the psychotherapy of dissociative identity disorder. *American Journal of Psychotherapy, 53*, 289–319.

Kluft, R. P. (2006). Dealing with alters: A pragmatic clinical perspective. *Psychiatric Clinics of North America, 29*, 281–304.

Kohut, H. (1971). *The analysis of the self: A systematic approach to the psychoanalytic treatment of narcissistic personality disorder*. New York: International Universities Press.

Kopelman, M. D. (1987). Crime and amnesia: A review. *Behavioral Sciences and the Law, 5*, 323–342.

Koss, M. P., Figueredo, A. J., & Prince, R. J. (2002). Cognitive mediation of rape's mental, physical, and social health impact: Test of four models in cross-sectional data. *Journal of Consulting and Clinical Psychology, 70*, 926–941.

Kowal, J. (2005). QEEG comparisons of persons with and without DID. *Proceedings of the 22nd Fall Conference of the International Society for the Study of Dissociation*, p. 47. Toronto, November 6–8.

Krakauer, S. Y. (2001). *Treating dissociative identity disorder: The power of the collective heart*. Philadephia: Brunner-Routledge.

Kramer, N. A. (1990). Comparison of therapeutic touch and casual touch in stress reduction of hospitalized children. *Pediatric Nursing, 16*, 483–485.

Krinsley, K. E., Gallagher, J. G., Weathers, F. W., Kaloupek, D. G., & Vielhauer, M. (1997). *Reliability and validity of the Evaluation of Lifetime Stressors Questionnaire*. Unpublished manuscript.

Kroll, J. (2001). Boundary violations: A culture-bound syndrome. *Journal of the American Academy of Psychiatry and Law, 29*, 274–283.

Krystal, J. H., Bannett, A., Bremner, J. D., Southwick, S. M., & Charney, D. S. (1996). Recent developments in the neurobiology of dissociation: Implications for posttraumatic stress disorder. In L. Michelson & W. J. Ray (Eds.), *Handbook of dissociation: Theoretical, empirical, and clinical perspectives* (pp. 163–190). New York: Plenum Press.

Krystal, J. H., Bremner, J. D., Southwick, S. M., & Charney, D. S. (1998). The emerging neurobiology of dissociation: Implications for the treatment of posttraumatic stress disorder. In J. D. Bremner & C. R. Marmar (Eds.), *Trauma, memory, and dissociation* (pp. 321–363). Washington DC: American Psychiatric Press.

Kubany, E. S., Hill, E. E., & Owens, J. A. (2003). Cognitive trauma therapy for battered women with PTSD: Preliminary findings. *Journal of Traumatic Stress, 16*, 81–91.

Kuipers, T. (1992). *Stille waters . . . over de meting en beoordeling van negatieve symptomen.* [Still waters . . . on the measurement and evaluation of negative symptoms] Utrecht, the Netherlands: Department of Medicine, Utrecht University.

Kuyk, J. (1999). *Pseudo-epileptic seizures: Differential diagnosis and psychological characteristics.* Amsterdam: Vrije Universiteit.

Kuyk, J., Spinhoven, P., van Emde Boas, W., & Van Dyck, R. (1999). Dissociation in temporal lobe epilepsy and pseudo-epileptic seizure patients. *Journal of Nervous and Mental Disease, 187*, 713–720.

Kundakci, T., Şar, V., Kiziltan, E., Yargic, L. I., & Tutkun, H. (1998). *The reliability and validity of the Turkish version of the SCID-D.* Paper presented at the 15th Annual Meeting of the International Society got the Study of Dissociation, Seattle.

Laddis, A., Dell, P. F., Cotton, M., & Fridley, D. (2001, December 4). *A comparison of the dissociative experiences of patients with schizophrenia and patients with DID.* Presented at the annual meeting of the International Society for the Study of Dissociation. New Orleans, LA.

Landau, R., & Litwin, H. (2000). The effects of extreme early stress in very old age. *Journal of Traumatic Stress, 13*, 473–487.

Lang, P. J. (1995). The emotion probe: Studies of motivation and attention. *American Psychologist, 50*, 372–385.

Lang, P. J., Bradley, M. M., & Cuthbert, B. N. (1998). Emotion, motivation, and anxiety. Brain mechanisms and psychophysiology. *Biological Psychiatry, 44*, 1248–1263.

Lang, P. J., Davis, M., & Öhman, A. (2000). Fear and anxiety: Animal models and human cognitive psychophysiology. *Journal of Affective Disorders, 61*, 137–159.

Langer, L. L. (1999). *Holocaust testimonies: The ruins of memory.* New Haven, CT: Yale University Press.

Lanius, R. A., Hopper, J. W., & Menon, R. S. (2003). Individual differences in a husband and wife who developed PTSD after a motor vehicle accident: A functional MRI case study. *American Journal of Psychiatry, 160*, 667–669.

Laporte, L., & Guttman, H. (1996). Traumatic childhood experiences as risk factors for borderline and other personality disorders. *Journal of Personal Disorders, 10*, 247–259.

Laposa, J. M., & Alden, L. E. (2003). Posttraumatic stress disorder in the emergency room: Exploration of a cognitive model. *Behavior, Research, and Therapy, 41*, 49–65.

Laub, D., & Auerhahn, N. C. (1989). Failed empathy—A central theme in the survivor's Holocaust experiences. *Psychoanalytic Psychology, 6*, 377–400.

Laub, D., & Auerhahn, N. C. (1993). Knowing and not knowing massive psychic trauma: Forms of traumatic memory. *International Journal of Psycho-Analysis, 74*, 287–302.

Laufer, R. S. (1988). The serial self: War trauma, identity and adult development. In J. P. Wilson, Z. Harel, & B. Kahana (Eds.), *Human adaptation to extreme stress: From the Holocaust to Vietnam* (pp. 33–53). New York: Plenum Press.

Lazarus, A. A. (1994). How certain boundaries and ethics diminish therapeutic effectiveness. *Ethics and Behavior, 4*, 255–261.

Leahy, R. L. (2001). *Overcoming resistance in cognitive therapy.* New York: Guilford.

Leavitt, F. (2001). MMPI profile characteristics of women with varying levels of normal dissociation. *Journal of Clinical Psychology, 57*, 1469–1477.

Léri, A. (1918). *Commotions et émotions de guerre* [Commotions and emotions of war]. Paris: Masson & Cie.

Leskela, J., Dieperink, M., & Thuras, P. (2002). Shame and posttraumatic stress disorder. *Journal of Traumatic Stress, 15*, 223–226.

Leskin, G. A., Kaloupek, D. G., & Keane, T. M. (1998). Treatment for traumatic memories: Review and recommendations. *Clinical Psychology Review, 18*, 983–1001.

Lewis, C. S. (1961). *A grief observed.* New York: The Seabury Press.

Lewis, D. O., Yeager, C. A., Swica, Y., Pincus, J. H., & Lewis, M. (1997). Objective documentation of child abuse and dissociation in 12 murderers with dissociative identity disorder. *American Journal of Psychiatry, 154*, 1703–1710.

Levin, R., & Sprei, E. (2003). Relationship of purported measures of pathological and nonpathological dissociation to self-reported psychological distress and fantasy immersion. *Assessment, 11*, 160–168.

Liberzon, I. & Phan, K. L. (2003). Brain-imaging studies of posttraumatic stress disorder. *CNS Spectrum, 8*, 641–650.

Linehan, M. M. (1993). *Cognitive behavioral treatment of borderline personality disorder.* New York: Guildford.

Liotti, G. (1992). Disorganized/disoriented attachment in the etiology of dissociative disorders. *Dissociation, 5*, 196–204.

Liotti, G. (1995). Disorganized/disoriented attachment in the psychotherapy of the dissociative disorders. In S. Goldberg, R. Muir, & J. Kerr (Eds.), *Attachment theory: Social, developmental and clinical perspectives* (pp. 343–363). Hillsdale, NJ: Analytic Press.

Liotti, G. (1999a). Disorganization of attachment as a model for understanding dissociative psychopathology. In J. Solomon & C. George (Eds.), *Attachment disorganization* (pp. 297–317). New York: Guilford.

Liotti, G. (1999b). Understanding the dissociative process: The contributions of attachment theory. *Psychoanalytic Inquiry, 19*, 757–783.

Liotti, G., & Pasquini, P. (2000). Predictive factors for borderline personality disorder: Patients' early traumatic experiences and losses suffered by the attachment figure. The Italian Group for the Study of Dissociation. *Acta Psychiatrica Scandanavia, 102*, 282–289.

Lipschitz, D. S., Winegar, R. K., Hartnick, E., Foote, B., & Southwick, S. M. (1999). Posttraumatic stress disorder in hospitalized adolescents: Psychiatric comorbidity and clinical correlates. *Journal of the American Academy of Child and Adolescent Psychiatry, 38*, 385–392.

Llinás, R. R. (2001). *I of the vortex: From neurons to self.* Cambridge, MA: MIT Press.

Loevinger, J. (1976). *Ego development.* San Francisco: Jossey-Bass.

Loewenstein, R. J. (1991). An office mental status examination for complex chronic dissociative symptoms and multiple personality disorder. *Psychiatric Clinics of North America, 14*, 567–604.

Loewenstein, R. J. (1993). Psychogenic amnesia and psychogenic fugue: A comprehensive review. In D. Spiegel (Ed.), *Dissociative disorders: A clinical review* (pp. 45–78).Lutherville, MD: Sidran Press.

Loewenstein, R. J. (1996). Dissociative amnesia and dissociative fugue. In L. Michelson, & W. J. Ray (Eds.), *Handbook of dissociation: Theoretical, empirical, and clinical perspectives* (pp. 307–336). New York: Plenum Press.

Lotterman, A. C. (1985). Prolonged psychotic states in borderline personality disorder. *Psychiatric Quarterly, 57*, 33–46.

Lou, H. C., Luber, B., Crupain, M., Keenan, J. P., Nowak, M., Kjaer, T. W. et al. (2004). Parietal cortex and representation of the mental self. *Proceedings of the National Academy of Sciences U.S.A, 101*, 6827–6832.

Luria, A. R. (1968). *The mind of a mnemonist.* New York: Avon.

Lyons-Ruth, K. (1999). Two person unconscious: Intersubjective dialogue, enactive relational representation, and the emergence of new forms of relational organization. *Psychoanalytic Inquiry, 19*, 576–617.

Lyons-Ruth, K. (2001). The two person construction of defense: Disorganized attachment strategies, unintegrated mental states and hostile/helpless relational processes. *Psychologist Psychoanalyst, 21*, 40–45.

Lyons-Ruth, K. (2003). Dissociation and the parent–infant dialogue: A longitudinal perspective from attachment research. *Journal of the American Psychoanalytic Association, 51*, 883–911.

Lyons-Ruth, K., Yellin, C., Melnick, S., & Atwood, G. (2003). Childhood experiences of trauma and loss have different relations to maternal unresolved and hostile-helpless states of mind on the AAI. *Attachment and Human Development, 5*, 330–352.

Lyons-Ruth, K., Yellin, C., Melnick, S., & Atwood, G. (2005). Expanding the concept of unresolved mental states: Hostile/helpless states of mind on the Adult Attachment Interview are associated with disrupted mother–infant communication and infant disorganization. *Developmental Psychopathology, 17*, 1–23.

Macfie, J., Cicchetti, D., & Toth, S. L. (2001a). The development of dissociation in maltreated preschool-aged children. *Development and Psychopathology, 13*, 233–254.

Macfie, J., Cicchetti, D., & Toth, S. L. (2001b). Dissociation in maltreated versus nonmaltreated preschool-aged children. *Child Abuse & Neglect, 25*, 1253–1267.

Main, M. (1995). Recent studies in attachment: Overview with selected implications for clinical work. In S. Goldberg, R. Muir, & J. Kerr (Eds.). *Attachment theory: Social, developmental and clinical perspectives* (pp. 407–472). Hillsdale, NJ: Analytic Press.

Main, M., & Morgan, H. (1996). Disorganization and disorientation in infant Strange Situation behavior: Phenotypic resemblance to dissociative states? In L. Michelson & W. Ray (Eds.), *Handbook of dissociation* (pp. 107–137). New York: Plenum.

Main, M., & Solomon, J. (1986). Discovery of a new, insecure-disorganized/disoriented attachment pattern. In T. B. Brazelton & M. W. Yogman (Eds.), *Affective development in infancy* (pp. 95–124). Norwood, NJ: Ablex.

Maltz, W. (2001). *The sexual healing journey: A guide for survivors of sexual abuse* (rev. ed.). New York: HarperCollins.

Marmar, C. R., Weiss, D. S., Schlenger, W. E., Fairbank, J. A., Jordan, K., Kulka, R. A. et al. (1994). Peritraumatic dissociation and posttraumatic stress in male Vietnam theater veterans. *American Journal of Psychiatry, 151*, 902–907.

Marmar, C. R., Weiss, D. S., Metzler, T. J., Ronfeldt, H. M., & Foreman, C. (1996). Stress responses of emergency services personnel to the Loma Prieta earthquake Interstate 880 freeway collapse and control traumatic incidents. *Journal of Traumatic Stress, 9,* 63–85.

Marshall, G. N., & Schell, T. L. (2002). Reappraising the link between peritraumatic dissociation and PTSD symptom severity: Evidence from a longitudinal study of community violence survivors. *Journal of Abnormal Psychology, 111,* 626–636.

Marshall, R. D., Spitzer, R., & Liebowitz, M. R. (1999). Review and critique of the new DSM-IV diagnosis of acute stress disorder. *American Journal of Psychiatry, 156,* 1677–1685.

McCann, I. L., & Pearlman, L. A. (1990). *Psychological trauma and the adult survivor: Theory, therapy, and transformation.* New York: Brunner/Mazel.

McClellan, J., Adams, J., Douglas, D., McCurry, C., & Storck, M. (1995). Clinical characteristics related to severity of sexual abuse: A study of seriously mentally ill youth. *Child Abuse & Neglect, 19,* 1245–1254.

McCluskey, U., Hooper, C. A., & Miller, L. B. (1999). Goal-corrected empathic attunement: Developing and rating the concept within an attachment perspective. *Psychotherapy: Theory, Research, Practice, Training, 36,* 80–90.

McCoullough, L. (1991). Davanloo's short-term dynamic psychotherapy: A crosstheoretical analysis of change mechanisms. In R. Curtis & G. Stricker (Eds.), *How people change: Inside and outside of therapy* (pp. 59–79). New York: Plenum.

McCullough, L., Kuhn, N., Andrews, S., Kaplan, A., Wolf, J., Hurley, C. L., & Hurley, C. (2003). *Treating affect phobia: A manual for short-term dynamic psychotherapy.* New York: Guilford.

McDougall, W. (1926). *An outline of abnormal psychology.* London: Methuen.

McDowell, D. M., Levin, F. R., & Nunes, E. V. (1999). Dissociative identity disorder and substance abuse: The forgotten relationship. *Journal of Psychoactive Drugs, 31,* 71–83.

McFarlane, A. C. (2000). Posttraumatic stress disorder: A model of the longitudinal course and the role of risk factors. *Journal of Clinical Psychiatry, 61* (Suppl. 5), 15–20.

McFarlane, A. C., & Papay, P. (1992). Multiple diagnoses in posttraumatic stress disorder in the victims of a natural disaster. *Journal of Nervous and Mental Disease, 180,* 498–504.

McFarlane, A. C., & Van der Kolk, B. A. (1996). Conclusions and future directions. In B. A. Van der Kolk, A. C. McFarlane, & L. Weisaeth (Eds.), *Traumatic stress: The effects of overwhelming experience on mind, body, and society* (pp. 559–575). New York: Guilford.

McFarlane, A. C., Yehuda, R., & Clark, C. R. (2002). Biologic models of traumatic memories and post-traumatic stress disorder. The role of neural networks. *Psychiatric Clinics of North America, 25,* 253–270.

McGloin, J. M., & Widom, C. S. (2001). Resilience among abused and neglected children grown up. *Development and Psychopathology, 13,* 1021–1038.

McLean, L. M., & Gallop, R. (2003). Implications of childhood sexual abuse for adult borderline personality disorder and complex posttraumatic stress disorder. *American Journal of Psychiatry, 160,* 369–371.

McNally, R. (2003). *Remembering trauma.* Boston: Belknap Press.

Meares, R. (1999). The contribution of Hughlings Jackson to an understanding of dissociation. *American Journal of Psychiatry, 156,* 1850–1855.

Meares, R., Stevenson, J., & Gordon, E. (1999). A Jacksonian and biopsychosocial hypothesis concerning borderline and related phenomena. *Australian and New Zealand Journal of Psychiatry, 33,* 831–840.

Messer, S. B. (2002). A psychodynamic perspective on resistance in psychotherapy: Vive la resistance. *Journal of Clinical Psychology, 58*, 157–163.

Metzinger, T. (2003). *Being no one: The self-model theory of subjectivity*. Cambridge, MA: MIT Press.

Migdow, J. (2003). The problem with pleasure. *Journal of Trauma and Dissociation, 4*(1), 5–25.

Miller, F. T., Abrams, T., Dulit, R., & Fyer, M. (1993). Psychotic symptoms in patients with borderline personality disorder and concurrent Axis I disorder. *Hospital and Community Psychiatry, 44*, 59–61.

Mineka S. & Öhman A. (2002). Phobias and preparedness: The selective, automatic, and encapsulated nature of fear. *Biological Psychiatry, 52*, 927–937.

Misslin, R. (2003). The defense system of fear: Behavior and neurocircuitry. *Neurophysiology Clinic, 33*, 55–66.

Mitchell, T.W. (1922). *Medical psychology and psychical research*. London: Society of Psychical Research.

Modai, I. (1994). Forgetting childhood: A defense mechanism against psychosis in a Holocaust survivor. *Clinical Gerontologist, 14*, 67–71.

Modell, A. (1990). *Other times, other realities: Towards a theory of psychoanalytic treatment*. Cambridge, MA: Harvard University Press.

Moene, F. C., Spinhoven, P., Hoogduin, C. A. L., Sandijck, P., & Roelofs, K. (2001). Hypnotizability, dissociation, and trauma in patients with a conversion disorder: An exploratory study. *Clinical Psychology and Psychotherapy, 8*, 400–410.

Moradi, A. R., Taghavi, M. R., Neshat Doost, H. T., Yule, W., & Dalgleish, T. (1999). Performance of children and adolescents with PTSD on the Stroop colour-naming task. *Psychological Medicine, 29*, 415–419.

Moreau, C., & Zisook, S. (2002). Rationale for a posttraumatic stress spectrum disorder. *Psychiatric Clinics of North America, 25*, 775–790.

Moreau de Tours, J. J. (1845). *Du haschish et de l'aliénation mentale: Études psychologiques* [Hashish and Mental derangement: Psychological studies]. Paris: Fortin, Masson, & Cie. English edition: *Hashish and mental illness*. New York: Raven Press, 1973.

Moreau de Tours, J. J. (1865). *De la folie hystérique et de quelques phénomènes nerveux propres à l'hystérie convulsive, à l'hystérie-épilepsie et à l'épilepsie* [On hysterical madness and some of its nervous phenomena in hysterical convulsions, hysterical epilepsy, and epilepsy]. Paris: Masson.

Morgan III, C. A., Hazlett, G., Wang, S., Richardson, E. G., Schnurr, P., & Southwick, S. (2001). Symptoms of dissociation in humans experiencing acute uncontrollable stress: A prospective investigation. *American Journal of Psychiatry, 158*, 1239–1247.

Morgan III, C. A., Hill, S., Fox, P., Kingham, P., & Southwick, S. M. (1999). Anniversary reactions in Gulf war veterans: A follow-up inquiry 6 years after the war. *American Journal of Psychiatry, 156*, 1075–1079.

Mueser, K. T., Goodman, L. B., Trumbetta, S. L., Rosenberg, S. D., Osher, C., Vidaver, R., et al. (1998). Trauma and posttraumatic stress disorder in severe mental illness. *Journal of Consulting & Clinical Psychology, 66*, 493–499.

Mulder, R. T., Beautrais, A. L., Joyce, P. R., & Fergusson, D. M. (1998). Relationship between dissociation, childhood sexual abuse, childhood physical abuse, and mental illness in a general population sample. *American Journal of Psychiatry, 155*, 806–811.

Myers, C. S. (1916a, March 18). Contributions to the study of shell shock. *The Lancet*, 608–613.

Myers, C. S. (1916b, September 9). Contributions to the study of shell shock. *The Lancet*, 461–467.

Myers, C. S. (1940). *Shell shock in France 1914–1918*. Cambridge: Cambridge University Press.

Najavits, L. (2002). *Seeking safety*. New York: Guilford.

Nathan, P., & Gorman, J. (2002). *A guide to treatments that work*. Oxford: Oxford University Press.

Nathanson, D. L. (Ed.). (1987). *The many faces of shame*. New York: Guilford.

Nemiah, J. C. (1989). Janet redivivus: The centenary of *L'automatisme psychologique*. *American Journal of Psychiatry, 146*, 1527–1529.

Nemiah, J. C. (1991). Dissociation, conversion, and somatization. In A. Tasman & S. M. Goldfinger (Eds.), *American Psychiatric Press review of psychiatry* (Vol. 10, pp. 248–260). Washington, DC: American Psychiatric Press.

Nemiah, J. C. (1998). Early concepts of trauma, dissociation, and the unconsciousness: Their history and current implications. In: J. D. Bremner & C. R. Marmar (Eds.), *Trauma, memory, and dissociation* (pp. 1–26). Washington, DC: American Psychiatric Press.

Newman, E., Kaloupek, D., & Keane, T. M. (1996). Assessment of posttraumatic stress disorder in clinical and research settings. In B. A. Van der Kolk, A. C. McFarlane, & L. Weisaeth (Eds.). *Traumatic stress: The effects of overwhelming experience on mind, body, and society* (pp. 242–275). New York: Guilford.

Nietzsche, F. (1901). *The will to power* (Trans. W. Kaufmann and R. J. Hollingdale). New York: Vintage, 1968.

Nijenhuis, E. R. S. (1994). *Dissociatieve stoornissen en psychotrauma* [Dissociative disorders and psychological trauma]. Houten, The Netherlands: Bohn Stafleu Van Loghum.

Nijenhuis, E. R. S. (1996). Dissociative identity disorder in a forensic psychiatric patient: A case report. *Dissociation, 9*, 282–288.

Nijenhuis, E. R. S. (2004). *Somatoform dissociation: Phenomena, measurement, and theoretical issues*. Norton, New York, 2004. (Original work published in 1999).

Nijenhuis, E. R. S. & Den Boer, J. A. (in press). Psychobiology of traumatization and trauma-related structural dissociation of the personality. In E. Vermetten, M. J. Dorahy, and D. Spiegel (Eds.), *Traumatic Dissociation: Neurobiology and treatment*. Arlington, VA: American Psychiatric Press.

Nijenhuis, E. R. S., Matthess, H., & Ehling, T. (2004, November). Psychobiological studies of structural dissociation. *Proceedings of the 21st International Society for the Study of Dissociation*, pp. 19–20. New Orleans, LA.

Nijenhuis, E. R. S., Quak, J., Reinders, S., Korf, J., Vos, H., & Marinkelle, A. B. (1999). Identity dependent processing of traumatic memories in dissociative identity disorder: Converging regional blood flow, physiological and psychological evidence. *Proceedings of the 6th European Conference on Traumatic Stress: Psychotraumatology, clinical practice, and human rights*, Istanbul, Turkey.

Nijenhuis, E. R. S., Spinhoven, P., Vanderlinden, J., Van Dyck, R., & Van der Hart, O. (1998). Somatoform dissociative symptoms as related to animal defense reactions to predatory imminence and injury. *Journal of Abnormal Psychology, 107*, 63–73.

Nijenhuis, E. R. S., Spinhoven, P., Van Dyck, R., Van der Hart, O., & Vanderlinden, J. (1996). The development and psychometric characteristics of the Somatoform Dissociation Questionnaire (SDQ–20). *Journal of Nervous and Mental Disease, 184*, 688–694.

Nijenhuis, E. R. S., Spinhoven, P., Van Dyck, R., Van der Hart, O., & Vanderlinden, J. (1997). The development of the Somatoform Dissociation Questionnaire (SDQ–5) as a screening instrument for dissociative disorders. *Acta Psychiatrica Scandinavica, 96*, 311–318.

Nijenhuis, E. R. S., Spinhoven, P., Van Dyck, R., Van der Hart, O., & Vanderlinden, J. (1998a). Psychometric characteristics of the Somatoform Dissociation Questionnaire: A replication study. *Psychotherapy and Psychosomatics, 67*, 17–23.

Nijenhuis, E. R. S., Spinhoven, P., Van Dyck, R., Van der Hart, O., & Vanderlinden, J. (1998b). Degree of somatoform and psychological dissociation in dissociative disorders is correlated with reported trauma. *Journal of Traumatic Stress, 11*, 711–730.

Nijenhuis, E. R. S., & Van der Hart, O. (1999a). Forgetting and reexperiencing trauma. In J. Goodwin & R. Attias (Eds.), *Splintered reflections: Images of the body in trauma* (pp. 39–65). New York: Basic Books.

Nijenhuis, E. R. S., & Van der Hart, O. (1999b). Somatoform dissociative phenomena: A Janetian perspective. In J. Goodwin & R. Attias (Eds.), *Splintered reflections: Images of the body in trauma* (pp. 89–127). New York: Basic Books.

Nijenhuis, E. R. S., Van der Hart, O., & Kruger, K. (2002). The psychometric characteristics of the Traumatic Experiences Questionnaire (TEC): First findings among psychiatric outpatients. *Clinical Psychology and Psychotherapy, 9*, 200–210.

Nijenhuis, E. R. S., Van der Hart, O., Kruger, K., & Steele, K. (2004). Somatoform dissociation, reported abuse, and animal defence–like reactions. *Australian and New Zealand Journal of Psychiatry, 38*, 678–686.

Nijenhuis, E. R. S., Van der Hart, O., & Steele, K. (2002). The emerging psychobiology of trauma-related dissociation and dissociative disorders. In H. D'Haenen, J. A. den Boer, & P. Willner (Eds.), *Biological Psychiatry* (pp. 1079–1098). London: Wiley.

Nijenhuis, E. R. S., Van der Hart, O., & Steele, K. (2004). Trauma-related structural dissociation of the personality: Traumatic origins, phobic maintenance. Available at http://www.trauma-pages.com.

Nijenhuis, E. R. S., Vanderlinden, J., & Spinhoven, P. (1998). Animal defensive reactions as a model for trauma-induced dissociation. *Journal of Traumatic Stress, 11*(2), 243–260.

Nijenhuis, E. R. S., & Van Duijl, M. (2001, December). Dissociative symptoms and reported trauma among Ugandan patients with possessive trance disorder. *Proceedings of the 18th International Fall Conference of the International Society for the Study of Dissociation*, New Orleans, LA.

Nijenhuis, E. R. S., Van Dyck, R., Spinhoven, P., Van der Hart, O., Chatrou, M., Vanderlinden, J., & Moene, F. (1999). Somatoform dissociation discriminates among diagnostic categories over and above general psychopathology. *Australian and New Zealand Journal of Psychiatry, 33*, 511–520.

Nijenhuis, E. R. S., Van Engen, A., Kusters, I., & Van der Hart, O. (2001). Peritraumatic somatoform and psychological dissociation in relation to recall of childhood sexual abuse. *Journal of Trauma and Dissociation, 2*(3), 49–68.

Noë, A. (2004). *Action in perception.* Cambridge, MA: MIT Press.

Noll, J. G., Horowitz, L. A., Bonanno, G. A., Trickett, P. K., & Putnam, F. W. (2003). Revictimization and self-harm in females who experienced childhood sexual abuse: Results from a prospective study. *Journal of Interpersonal Violence, 18*, 1452–1471.

Noyes, R., Hoenk, P. R., Kupperman, B. A., & Slymen, D. J. (1977). Depersonalization in accident victims and psychiatric patients. *Journal of Nervous and Mental Disease, 164*, 401–407.

Noyes, R., & Kletti, R. (1976). Depersonalization in the face of life-threatening danger; An interpretation. *Omega, 7*, 103–114.

Noyes, R., & Kletti, R. (1977). Depersonalization in response to life-threatening danger. *Comprehensive Psychiatry, 18*, 375–384.

Ogata, S. N., Silk, K. R., Goodrich, S., Lohr, N. E., Westen, D., & Hill, E. M. (1990). Childhood physical and sexual abuse in adult patients with borderline personality disorder. *American Journal of Psychiatry, 147,* 1008–1013.

Ogawa, J. R., Sroufe, L. A., Weinfield, N. S., Carlson, E. A., & Egeland, B. (1997). Development and the fragmented self: Longitudinal study of dissociative symptomatology in a nonclinical sample. *Development and Psychopathology, 9,* 855–879.

Ogden, P., & Minton, K. (2000). Sensorimotor psychotherapy: One method for processing trauma. *Traumatology, 6;* see also http://www.trauma-pages.com.

Ogden, P., Minton, K., & Pain, C. (2006). *Trauma and the body: A sensorimotor approach to psychotherapy.* New York: Norton.

Ohan, J. L., Myers, K., & Collett, B. R. (2002). Ten-year review of rating scales. IV: Scales assessing trauma and its effects. *Journal of the American Academy of Adolescent Psychiatry, 41,* 1401–1422.

Olio, K., & Cornell, W. (1993). The therapeutic relationship as the foundation for treatment of adult survivors of sexual abuse. *Psychotherapy, 30,* 512–523.

Orne, M. T. (1959). The nature of hypnosis: Artifact and essence. *Journal of Abnormal and Social Psychology, 58,* 277–299.

Ozer, E. J., Best, S. R., Lipsey, T. L., & Weiss, D. S. (2003). Predictors of posttraumatic stress disorder and symptoms in adults: A meta-analysis. *Psychological Bulletin, 129,* 52–73.

Panksepp, J. (2003). At the interface of the affective, behavioral, and cognitive neurosciences: Decoding the emotional feelings of the brain. *Brain and Cognition, 52,* 4–14.

Panksepp, J. (1998). *Affective neuroscience: The foundations of human and animal emotions.* New York: Oxford University Press.

Parson, E. R. (1984). The reparation of self: Clinical and theoretical dimensions in the treatment of Vietnam combat veterans. *Journal of Contemporary Psychotherapy, 14,* 4–56.

Parson, E. R. (1998). Traumatherapy 2001, Part I: "The reparation of the self" revisited on the way into the 21st century. *Journal of Contemporary Psychotherapy, 28,* 239–279.

Pavlov, I. P. (1927). *Conditioned reflexes.* London: Oxford University Press.

Pearlman, L. A., & Saakvitne, K. W. (1995). *Trauma and the therapist: Countertransference and vicarious traumatization in psychotherapy with incest survivors.* New York: Norton.

Pelcovitz, D., Van der Kolk, B. A., Roth, S., Mandel, F., Kaplan, S., & Resick, P. (1997). Development of a criteria set and a structured interview for the disorders of extreme stress (SIDES). *Journal of Traumatic Stress, 10,* 3–16.

Peri, T., Ben Shakhar, G., Orr, S. P., & Shalev, A. Y. (2000). Psychophysiologic assessment of aversive conditioning in posttraumatic stress disorder. *Biological Psychiatry, 47,* 512–519.

Perry, B. D. (1994). Neurobiological sequelae of childhood trauma: Posttraumatic stress disorders in children. In M. Murberg (Ed.), *Catecholamine function in post traumatic stress disorder: Emerging concepts* (pp. 233–255). Washington, DC: American Psychiatric Press.

Perry, B. D. (1999). The memories of states: How the brain stores and retrieves traumatic experience. In J. M. Goodwin & R. Attias (Eds.), *Splintered reflections: Images of the body in trauma* (pp. 9–38). New York: Basic Books.

Perry, B. D., & Pate, J. E. (1994). Neurodevelopment and the psychobiological roots of posttraumatic stress disorder. In L. F. Koziol & C. E. Stout (Eds.), *The neuropsychology of mental illness: A practical guide* (pp. 129–147). Washington, DC: American Psychiatric Press.

Perry, B. D., & Pollard, R. (1998). Homeostasis, stress, trauma, and adaptation. A neurodevelopmental view of childhood trauma. *Child & Adolescent Psychiatric Clinics of North America, 7*, 33–51.

Perry, J. C. (1985). Depression in borderline personality disorder: Lifetime prevalence at interview and longitudinal course of symptoms. *American Journal of Psychiatry, 142*, 15–21.

Peterson, J. A. (1996). Hypnotherapeutic techniques to facilitate psychotherapy with PTSD and dissociative clients. In L. K. Michelson & W. J. Ray (Eds.), *Handbook of dissociation: Theoretical, empirical, and clinical perspectives* (pp. 449–474). New York: Plenum.

Phillips, M. (2001). Potential contributions of hypnosis to ego-strengthening procedures in EMDR, Eye Movement Desensitization Reprocessing. *American Journal of Clinical Hypnosis, 43*, 247–262.

Polan, H. J., & Hofer, M. A. (1999). Psychobiological origins of infant attachment and separation responses. In J. Cassidy & P. R. Shaver (Eds.), *Handbook of attachment: Theory, research, and clinical applications* (pp. 162–180). New York: Guilford.

Pope, C. A., & Kwapil, T. (2000). Dissociative experiences in hypothetically psychosis-prone college students. *Journal of Nervous and Mental Disease, 188*, 530–536.

Pope, K. S., & Brown, L. S. (1996). *Recovered memories of abuse: Assessment, therapy, forensics.* Washington, DC: American Psychological Association.

Porges, S. W. (2001). The polyvagal theory: Phylogenetic substrates of a social nervous system. *International Journal of Psychophysiology, 42*, 123–146.

Porges, S. W. (2003). The polyvagal theory: Phylogenetic contributions to social behavior. *Physiology and Behavior, 79*, 503–513.

Power, K., McGoldrick, T., Brown, K., Buchanan, R., Sharp, D., Swanson, V., & Karatzias, A. (2002). A controlled comparison of eye movement desensitization and reprocessing versus exposure plus cognitive restructuring versus waiting list in the treatment of post-traumatic stress disorder. *Clinical Psychology and Psychotherapy, 9*, 299–318.

Prince, M. (1905). *The dissociation of a personality.* London: Longmans, Green.

Prince, M. (1927). Suggestive repersonalization. *Archives of Neurology and Psychiatry, 21*, 159–189.

Prueter, C., Schultz-Venrath, U., & Rimpau, W. (2002). Dissociative symptoms and associated psychopathological symptoms in patients with epilepsy, pseudoseizures, and both seizure forms. *Epilepsia, 43*, 188–192.

Putnam, F. W. (1989). *Diagnosis and treatment of multiple personality disorder.* New York: Guilford.

Putnam, F. W. (1991). Recent research on multiple personality disorder. *Psychiatric Clinics of North America, 14*, 489–502.

Putnam, F. W. (1993). Diagnosis and clinical phenomenology of multiple personality disorder: A North American perspective. *Dissociation, 6*, 80–86.

Putnam, F. W. (1997). *Dissociation in children and adolescents: A developmental perspective.* New York: Guilford.

Putnam, F .W. (2005, November). *States of being.* Third Pierre Janet Memorial Lecture. Presented at the International Society for the Study of Dissociation's 22nd International Fall conference. Toronto, ON, CA.

Putnam, F. W., Guroff, J. J., Silberman, E. K., Barban, L., & Post, R. M. (1986). The clinical phenomenology of multiple personality disorder: Review of 100 recent cases. *Journal of Clinical Psychiatry, 47*, 285–293.

Putnam. F. W., Helmers, K, & Trickett, P. K. (1993). Development, reliability, and validity of a child dissociation scale. *Child Abuse and Neglect, 17*, 731–741.

Raine, N. V. (1998) *After silence: Rape and my journey back*. New York: Crown.

Rau, V., DeCola, J. P., & Fanselow, M. S. (2005). Stress-induced enhancement of fear learning: An animal model of posttraumatic stress disorder. *Neuroscience & Biobehavior Review, 29*, 1207–1223.

Ray, W., & Faith, M. (1995). Dissociative experiences in a college age population. *Personality and Individual Differences, 18*, 223–230.

Read, J., Perry, B. D., Moskowitz, A., & Connolly, J. (2001). The contribution of early traumatic events to schizophrenia in some patients: A traumagenic neurodevelopmental model. *Psychiatry, 64*, 319–345.

Read, J. & Ross, C. A. (2003). Psychological trauma and psychosis: Another reason why people diagnosed schizophrenic must be offered psychological therapies. *Journal of the American Academy of Psychoanalytic & Dynamic Psychiatry, 31*, 247–268.

Read, J., Van Os, J., Morrison, A. P., & Ross, C. A. (2005). Childhood trauma, psychosis and schizophrenia: A literature review with theoretical and clinical implications. *Acta Psychiatrica Scandinavica, 112*, 330–350.

Reinders, A. A. T. S., Nijenhuis, E. R. S., Paans, A. M., Korf, J., Willemsen, A. T., & Den Boer, J. A. (2003). One brain, two selves. *Neuroimage, 20*, 2119–2125.

Reinders, A. A. T. S., Nijenhuis, E. R. S., Quak, J., Korf, J., Paans, A. M. J., Haaksma, J., Willemsen, A. T. M., & Den Boer, J. (in press). Psychobiological characteristics of dissociative identity disorder: A symptom provocation study. *Biological Psychiatry*.

Remarque, E. M. (1982). *All Quiet on the Western Front*, New York: Ballantine Books. (Original work published 1929).

Resch, F. (2004). Entwicklungspsychopathologie und Strukturdynamik [Psychopathology of development and structural dynamics]. *Fortschritte der Neurologie und Psychiatrie, 72*, S23–S28.

Rescorla, R. A. (1998). Pavlovian conditioning: It's not what you think it is. *American Psychologist, 43*, 151–160.

Rescorla, R. A. (2003). Contemporary study of Pavlovian conditioning. *Spanish Journal of Psychology, 6*, 185–195.

Resick, P. A., & Schnicke, M. K. (1993). *Cognitive processing therapy for rape victims*. Newbury Park, CA: Sage.

Resnick, H. S. (1996). Psychometric review of trauma assessment for adults (TAA). In B. H. Stamm (Ed.), *Measurement of stress, trauma, and adaptation* (pp. 362–364). Lutherville, MD: Sidran Press.

Resnick, H. S., Falsetti, S. A., Kilpatrick, D. G., & Foy, D. W. (1994, November). *Associations between panic attacks during rape assaults and follow-up PTSD or panic attack outcomes*. Presentation at the 10th Annual Meeting of the International Society of Traumatic Stress Studies, Chicago.

Ribot, T. (1885). *Les maladies de la personnalité* [Diseases of the personality]. Paris: Félix Alcan.

Rivers, W. H. R. (1920). *Instinct and the unconscious: A contribution to a biological theory of the psycho-neuroses*. Cambridge, UK: Cambridge University Press.

Rizzolatti, G., & Craighero, L. (2004). The mirror-neuron system. *Annual Review of Neuroscience, 27*, 169–192.

Roelofs, K., Keijsers, G. P. J., Hoogduin, C. A. L., Näring, G. W. B., & Moene, F. C. (2002). Childhood abuse in patients with conversion disorder. *American Journal of Psychiatry, 159*, 1908–1913.

Roelofs, K., Spinhoven, P., Sandijck, P., Moene, F., & Hoogduin, K. A. L. (2005). The impact of early trauma and recent life-events on symptom severity in patients with conversion disorder. *Journal of Nervous and Mental Disease, 193*, 508–514.

Romans, S., Belaise, C., Martin, J., Morris, E., & Raffi, A. (2002). Childhood abuse and later medical disorders in women. An epidemiological study. *Psychotherapy and Psychosomatics, 71*, 141–150.

Rosenberg, S., Mueser, K., Friedman, M., Gorman, P., Drake, R., Vidaver, R., Torrey, W., & Jankowski, M. K. (2001). Developing effective treatments for posttraumatic stress disorder among people with severe mental illness. *Psychiatric Services, 52*, 1453–1461.

Rosenfeld, H. (1987). *Impasse and interpretation.* London: Routledge.

Ross, C. A. (1989). *Multiple personality disorder: Diagnosis, clinical features, and treatment.* Toronto, Canada: Wiley.

Ross, C. A. (1996). History, phenomenology, and epidemiology of dissociation. In L. K. Michelson & W. J. Ray (Eds.), *Handbook of dissociation* (pp. 3–24). New York: Plenum.

Ross, C. A. (1997). *Dissociative identity disorder: Diagnosis, clinical features, and treatment of multiple personality.* New York: Wiley.

Ross, C. A. (2004). *Schizophrenia: Innovations in diagnosis and treatment.* Binghamton, NY: Haworth.

Ross, C. A., & Joshi, S. (1992). Schneiderian symptoms and childhood trauma in the general population. *Comprehensive Psychiatry, 33*, 269–273.

Ross, C. A., Miller, S. D., Bjorson, L., Reagor, P., Fraser, G., & Anderson, G. (1991). Abuse histories in 102 cases of multiple personality disorder. *Canadian Journal of Psychiatry, 36*, 97–101.

Ross, C. A., Miller, S. D., Reagor, P., Bjornson, L., Fraser, G. A., & Anderson, G. (1990). Schneiderian symptoms in multiple personality disorder and schizophrenia. *Comprehensive Psychiatry, 31*, 111–118.

Ross, C. A., Norton, G. R., & Wozney, K. (1989). Multiple personality disorder: An analysis of 236 cases. *Canadian Journal of Psychiatry, 34*, 423–418.

Roth, S., Newman, E., Pelcovitz, D., Van der Kolk, B., & Mandel, F.S. (1997). Complex PTSD in victims exposed to sexual and physical abuse: Results from the DSM-IV Field trial for posttraumatic stress disorder. *Journal of Traumatic Stress 10*, 539–556.

Rothbaum, B. O., & Davis, M. (2003). Applying learning principles to the treatment of post-trauma reactions. *Annals of the New York Academy of Sciences, 1008*, 112–121.

Rothbaum, B., Meadows, E., Resick, P., & Foy, D. (2000). Cognitive–behavioral therapy. In E. Foa, T. Keane, & M. Friedman (Eds.), *Effective treatments for PTSD: Practice guidelines from the International Society for Traumatic Stress Studies* (pp. 60–83). New York: Guilford.

Rothbaum, B. O., & Schwartz, A. C. (2002). Exposure therapy for posttraumatic stress disorder. *American Journal of Psychotherapy, 56*, 59–75.

Rothschild, B. (2006). *Help for the helper: The psychophysiology of compassion fatigue and vicarious trauma.* New York: Norton.

Roussy, G., & Lhermitte, J. (1917). *Psychonévroses de guerre* [Psychoneuroses of war]. Paris: Masson & Cie.

Rowe, C. E. (1996). The concept of resistance in self psychology. *American Journal of Psychotherapy, 50*, 66–74.

Rowe, C. E., & Mac Isaac, D. S. (1991). *Empathic attunement: The "technique" of psychoanalytic self psychology.* Northvale, NJ: Aronson.

Rows, R. G. (1916). Mental conditions following strain and nerve shock. *British Medical Journal, ii*, 441–443.

Runtz, M., & Schallow, J. R. (1997). Social support and coping strategies as mediators of adult adjustment following childhood maltreatment. *Child Abuse & Neglect, 21*, 211–226.

Sachs, R. G., & Peterson, J. A. (1996). Memory processing and the healing experience. In L. K. Michelson & W. J. Ray (Eds.), *Handbook of dissociation: Theoretical, empirical, and clinical perspectives* (pp. 475–498). New York: Plenum.

Salter, A. C. (1995). *Transforming trauma: A guide to understanding and treating adult survivors of child sexual abuse.* Thousand Oaks, CA: Sage.

Sandman, C. A., Barron, J. L., & Colman, H. (1990). An orally administered opiate blocker, naltrexone, attenuates self-injurious behavior. *American Journal of Mental Retardation, 95*, 93–102.

Şar, V., Akyuz, G., Kundakci, T., Kiziltan, E., & Dogan, O. (2004). Childhood trauma, dissociation, and psychiatric comorbidity in patients with conversion disorder. *American Journal of Psychiatry, 161*, 2271–2276.

Şar, V., Kundakci, T., Kiziltan, E., Bakim, B., & Bozkurt, O. (2000). Differentiating dissociative disorders from other diagnostic groups through somatoform dissociation. *Journal of Trauma and Dissociation, 1*(4), 67–80.

Şar, V., & Ross, C. (2006). Dissociative disorders as a confounding factor in psychiatric research. *Psychiatric Clinics of North America, 29*, 129–144.

Şar, V., Tutkun, H., Alyanak, B., Bakim, B., & Baral, I. (2000). Frequency of dissociative disorders among psychiatric outpatients in Turkey. *Comprehensive Psychiatry, 41*, 216–222.

Sautter F. J., Brailey, K., Uddo, M. M., Hamilton, M. F., Beard, M. G., & Borges, A. H. (1999). PTSD and comorbid psychotic disorder: Comparison with veterans diagnosed with PTSD or psychotic disorder. *Journal of Traumatic Stress, 12*, 73–89.

Schachtel, E. G. (1947). On memory and childhood amnesia. *Psychiatry, 10*, 1–26.

Schmahl, C. G., Elzinga, B. M., Vermetten, E., Sanislow, C., McGlashan, T. H., & Bremner, J. D. (2003). Neural correlates of memories of abandonment in women with and without borderline personality disorder. *Biological Psychiatry, 54*, 142–151.

Schnurr, P. P., & Jankowski, M. K. (1999). Physical health and post-traumatic stress disorder: Review and synthesis. *Seminal Clinical Neuropsychiatry, 4*, 295–304.

Schore, A. N. (1994). *Affect regulation and the origin of self: The neurobiology of emotional development.* Hillsdale, NJ: Lawrence Erlbaum.

Schore, A. N. (2002). Dysregulation of the right brain: A fundamental mechanism of traumatic attachment and the psychopathogenesis of posttraumatic stress disorder. *Australian & New Zealand Journal of Psychiatry, 36*, 9–30.

Schore, A. N. (2003a). *Affect dysregulation and disorders of the self.* New York: Norton.

Schore, A. N. (2003b). *Affect regulation and the repair of the self.* New York: Norton.

Schuengel, C., Bakermans-Kranenburg, M. J., & Van IJzendoorn, M. H. (1999). Frightening maternal behavior linking unresolved loss and disorganized infant attachment. *Journal of Consulting and Clinical Psychology, 67*, 54–63.

Schwartz, H. L. (2000). *Dialogues with forgotten voices: Relational perspectives on child abuse trauma and treatment of dissociative disorders.* New York: Basic Books.

Schwartz, L. (1951). *Die dynamische Psychologie von Pierre Janet* [The dynamic psychology of Pierre Janet]. Basel, Switzerland: B. Schwabe.

Shalev, A. Y., Freedman, S., Peri, T., Brandes, D., Sahar, T., Orr, S. P., & Pitman, R. K. (1998). Prospective study of posttraumatic stress disorder and depression following trauma. *American Journal of Psychiatry, 155*, 630–637.

Shalev, A. Y., Ragel-Fuchs, Y., & Pitman, R. K. (1992). Conditioned fear and psychological trauma. *Biological Psychiatry, 31*, 863–865.

Shephard, B. (2000). *A war of nerves: Soldiers and psychiatrists in the twentieth century.* Cambridge, MA: Harvard University Press.

Siegel, D. J. (1999). *The developing mind: Toward a neurobiology of interpersonal experience.* New York: Guilford.

Silberg, J. (1996). *The dissociative child.* Lutherville, MD: Sidran Press.

Simeon, D., Guralnik, O., Gross, S., Stein, D. J., Schmeidler, J., & Hollander, E. (1998). The detection and measurement of depersonalization disorder. *Journal of Nervous and Mental Disease, 186*, 536–542.

Simeon, D., Guralnik, O., Hazlett, E. A., Spiegel-Cohen, J., Hollander, E., & Buchsbaum, M. S. (2000). Feeling unreal: A PET study of depersonalization disorder. *American Journal of Psychiatry, 157*, 1782–1788.

Simeon, D., Guralnik, O., Schmeidler, J., Sirof, B., & Knutelska, M. (2001). The role of childhood interpersonal trauma in depersonalization disorder. *American Journal of Psychiatry, 158*, 1027–1033.

Simmel, E. (1919). Zweites Korreferat [Second co-lecture]. In S. Freud et al., *Zur Psychoanalyse der Kriegsneurosen* [Psychoanalysis and the war neuroses]. (pp. 42–60). Leipzig and Vienna: Internationaler Psychoanalytischer Verlag.

Simon, R. I. (2001). Commentary: Treatment boundaries—Flexible guidelines, not rigid standards. *Journal of the American Academy of Psychiatry and Law, 29*, 287–289.

Singer, T., Seymour, B., O'Doherty, J., Kaube, H., Dolan, R. J., & Frith, C. D. (2004). Empathy for pain involves the affective but not sensory components of pain. *Science, 303*, 1157–1162.

Skinner, B. F. (1988). The operant side of behavior therapy. *Journal of Behavior Therapy and Experimental Psychiatry, 19*, 171–179.

Slade, A. (1999). Attachment theory and research: Implications for the theory and practice of individual psychotherapy with adults. In J. Cassidy & P. R. Shaver (Eds.), *Handbook of attachment: Theory, research, and clinical applications* (pp. 575–594). New York: Guilford.

Sloman, L., & Gilbert, P. (Eds.) (2000). *Subordination and defeat: An evolutionary approach to mood disorders and their therapy.* Mahwah, NJ: Erlbaum.

Smith, L., & Gasser, M. (2005). The development of embodied cognition: Six lessons from babies. *Artificial Life, 11*, 13–29.

Solomon, M. F. & Siegel, D. J. (Eds). (2003), *Healing trauma: Attachment, mind, body, and brain.* New York: Norton.

Somer, E. (2002). Maladaptive daydreaming: A qualitative study. *Journal of Contemporary Psychotherapy, 32*, 197–212.

Somer, E. & Dell, P. F. (2005). Development of the Hebrew-Multidimensional Inventory of Dissociation (H-MID): A valid and reliable measure of pathological dissociation. *Journal of Trauma and Dissociation, 6*(1), 31–53.

Somer, E., & Nave, O. (2001). An ethnographic study of former dissociative disorder patients. *Imagination, Cognition, and Personality, 20*, 315–346.

Southwick, S. M., Bremner, D., Krystal, J. H., & Charney, D. S. (1994). Psychobiologic research in post-traumatic stress disorder. *Psychiatric Clinics of North America, 17*, 251–264.

Southwick, S., Yehuda, R., & Giller, E., Jr. (1993). Personality disorders in treatment-seeking combat veterans with posttraumatic stress disorder. *American Journal of Psychiatry, 150*, 1020–1504.

Spiegel, D. (1984). Multiple personality as a post-traumatic stress disorder. *Psychiatric Clinics of North America, 7*, 101–110.

Spiegel, D. (1986). Dissociation, double binds, and post-traumatic stress in multiple personality disorder. In B.G. Braun (Ed.), *Treatment of multiple personality disorder* (pp. 61–77). Washington, DC: American Psychiatric Press.

Spiegel, D. (1993). Multiple posttraumatic personality disorder. In R. P. Kluft & C. G. Fine (Eds.), *Clinical perspectives on multiple personality disorder* (pp. 87–99). Washington, DC: American Psychiatric Press.

Spiegel, D., & Cardeña, E. (1991). Disintegrated experience: The dissociative disorders revisited. *Journal of Abnormal Psychology, 100*, 366–378.

Spiegel, D., Classen, C., Thurston, E., & Butler, L. (2004). Trauma-focused versus present-focused models of group therapy for women sexually abused in childhood. In L. Koenig, L. Doll, A. O'Leary, & W. Pequegnat (Eds.), *From child sexual abuse to adult sexual risk: Trauma, revictimization, and intervention* (pp. 251–268). Washington, DC: American Psychological Association.

Spiegel, D., Frischholz, E. J., & Spira, J. (1993). Functional disorders of memory. In American Psychiatric Press (Ed.), *American Psychiatric Press Review of Psychiatry* (Vol. 12, pp. 747–782). Washington, DC: Author.

Spinazzola, J., Blaustein, M., & Van der Kolk, B. A. (2005). Posttraumatic stress disorder treatment outcome research: The study of unrepresentative samples? *Journal of Traumatic Stress, 18*, 425–436.

Spitzer, C., Haug, H. J., & Freyberger, H. J. (1997). Dissociative symptoms in schizophrenic patients with positive and negative symptoms. *Psychopathology, 30*, 67–75.

Stamenov, M. I., & Gallese, V. (2002). *Mirror neurons and the evolution of brain and language.* Amsterdam/Philadelphia: John Benjamins.

Stamm, B. H. (Ed.) (1996). *Measurement of stress, trauma, and adaptation.* Lutherville, MD: Sidran Press.

Stark, M. (1994). *Working with resistance.* Northvale, NJ: Jason Aronson.

Steele, K., & Colrain, J. (1990). Abreactive work with sexual abuse survivors: Concepts and techniques. In M. A. Hunter (Ed.), *The sexually abused male,* (Vol. 2, pp. 1–55). Lexington MA: Lexington Press.

Steele, K., Dorahy, M., Van der Hart, O., & Nijenhuis, E. R. S. (in press). Dissociation and alterations in consciousness: Different but related concepts. In P. F. Dell, J. O'Neill, & E. Somer (Eds.), *The ISSD sourcebook on dissociation and the dissociative disorders.* McLean, VA: International Society for the Study of Dissociation.

Steele, K., & Van der Hart, O. (1994, November). *Beyond shattered assumptions: Towards a new theory of personal reality.* Paper presented at the 11th Annual Conference of the International Society for the Study of Dissociation. Chicago, IL.

Steele, K., & Van der Hart, O. (2004). The hypnotherapeutic relationship with traumatized patients: Pierre Janet's contributions to current treatment. *Janetian Sudies, 1*(1). http://www.pierre-janet.com/JanetianStudiesBody.htm.

Steele, K., Van der Hart, O., & Nijenhuis, E. R. S. (2001). Dependency in the treatment of complex posttraumatic stress disorder and dissociative disorders. *Journal of Trauma and Dissociation, 2*(4), 79–116.

Steele, K., Van der Hart, O., & Nijenhuis, E. R. S. (2005). Phase-oriented treatment of structural dissociation in complex traumatization: Overcoming trauma-related phobias. *Journal of Trauma and Dissociation, 6*(3), 11–53.

Stein, M. B., Walker, J. R., Anderson, G., Hazen, A. L., Ross, C. A., Eldridge, G. et al. (1996). Childhood physical and sexual abuse in patients with anxiety disorders and in a community sample. *American Journal of Psychiatry, 153*, 275–277.

Steinberg, M. (1994). *Structured clinical interview for DSM-IV dissociative disorders,* (Rev.) Washington, DC: American Psychiatric Press.

Steinberg, M. (1995). *Handbook for the assessment of dissociation: A clinical guide.* Washington, DC: American Psychiatric Press.

Steinberg, M. (2000). Advances in the clinical assessment of dissociation: The SCID-D-R. *Bulletin of the Menninger Clinic, 64*, 146–163.

Steinberg, M., Cicchetti, D., Buchanan, J., Rakfeldt, J., & Rounsaville, B. (1994). Distinguishing between multiple personality disorder (dissociative identity disorder) and schizophrenia using the Structured Clinical Interview for DSM-IV dissociative disorders. *Journal of Nervous and Mental Disease, 182*, 495–502.

Stern, C. R. (1984). The etiology of multiple personalities. *Psychiatric Clinics of North America, 7*, 149–160.

Stern, D. (1985). *The interpersonal world of the infant*. New York: Basic Books.

Stern, D. N. (2004). *The present moment in psychotherapy and everyday life*. New York: Norton.

Stiglmayr, C. E., Shapiro, D. A., Stieglitz, R. D., Limberger, M. F., & Bohus, M. (2001). Experience of aversive tension and dissociation in female patients with borderline personality disorder: A controlled study. *Journal of Psychiatric Research, 35*, 111–118.

Strean, H. S. (1993). *Resolving counterresistance in psychotherapy*. New York: Brunner/Mazel.

Stuss, D. T., & Knight, R. T. (Eds.). (2002). *Principles of frontal lobe function*. Oxford: Oxford University Press.

Taine, H. (1878). *De l'intelligence* [Concerning intelligence]. (3rd ed.). Paris: Hachette.

Tauber, Y. (1996). The traumatized child and the adult: Compound personality in child survivors of the Holocaust. *Israel Journal of Psychiatry & Related Sciences, 33*, 228–237.

Tauber, Y. (1998). *In the other chair: Holocaust survivors and the second generation as therapists and clients*. Jerusalem: Gefen.

Teicher, M. H., Andersen, S. L., Polcari, A., Anderson, C. M., & Navalta, C. P. (2002). Developmental neurobiology of childhood stress and trauma. *Psychiatric Clinics of North America, 25*(2), 397–426.

Terr, L. (1983). Time sense following psychic trauma: A clinical study of ten adults and twenty children. *American Journal of Orthopsychiatry, 53*, 244–261.

Terr, L. C. (1984). Time and trauma. *The Psychoanalytic Study of the Child, 39*, 633–665.

Tichener, J. L. (1986). Posttraumatic decline: A consequence of unresolved destructive drives. In C. R. Figley (Ed.), *Trauma and its wake: Vol. 2. Traumatic stress, theory, research, and intervention* (pp. 5–19). New York: Brunner/Mazel.

Timberlake, W. (1994). Behavior systems, associationism, and Pavlovian conditioning. *Psychonomic Bulletin & Review, 1*, 405–420.

Timberlake, W., & Lucas, G. R. (1989). Behavior systems and learning: From misbehavior to general principles. In S. B. Klein & R. R. Mowrer (Eds.), *Contemporary leaning theories: Instrumental conditioning theory and the impact of biological constraints on learning* (pp. 237–275). Hillsdale, NJ: Erlbaum.

Toates, F. M. (1986). *Motivational systems*. Cambridge, UK: Cambridge University Press.

Tomkins, S. S. (1963). *Affects, imagery, consciousness*, Vol. 2. *Negative affects*. New York: Springer.

Tournier, M. (1972). *The ogre*. New York: Pantheon.

Tucker, D. M., Luu, P., & Pribram, K. H. (1995). Social and emotional self-regulation. *Annals of the New York Academy of Sciences, 769*, 213–239.

Tulving, E. (2002). Episodic memory: From mind to brain. *Annual Review of Psychology, 53*, 1–25.

Tutkun, H., Yargic, I., & Şar, V. (1996). Dissociative identity disorder presenting as hysterical psychosis. *Dissociation, 9*, 244–252.

Twombly, J. H. (2000). Incorporating EMDR and EMDR adaptations into the treatment of clients with dissociative identity disorder. *Journal of Trauma & Dissociation, 1*(2), 61–80.

Twombly, J. H. (2005). EMDR for clients dissociative identity disorder, DDNOS, and ego states. In R. Shapiro (Ed.), *EMDR solutions: Pathways to healing* (pp. 86–120). New York/London: Norton.

Uchino, B. N., Cacioppo, J. T., & Kiecolt-Glaser, J. K. (1996). The relationship between social support and physiological processes: A review with emphasis on underlying mechanisms and implications for health. *Psychological Bulletin, 119,* 488–531.

Van Gerven, M., Van der Hart, O., Nijenhuis, E. R. S., & Kuipers, T. (2002). Psychose, trauma en trauma-gerelateerde psychopathologie [Psychosis, trauma, and trauma-related psychopathology]. *Tijdschrift voor Psychiatrie, 44,* 533–540.

Van der Hart, O. (1983). *Rituals in psychotherapy: Transition and continuity.* New York: Irvington Publishers.

Van der Hart, O. (1985). Metaphoric and symbolic imagery in the hypnotic treatment of an urge to wander: A case report. *Australian Journal of Clinical and Experimental Hypnosis, 13,* 83–95.

Van der Hart, O. (1988a). An imaginary leave-taking ritual in mourning therapy. *International Journal of Clinical and Experimental Hypnosis, 36,* 63–69.

Van der Hart, O. (Ed.) (1988b). *Coping with loss: The therapeutic use of leave-taking rituals.* New York: Irvington Publishers.

Van der Hart, O. (Ed.) (1991), *Trauma, dissociatie en hypnose* [Trauma, dissociation, and hypnosis]. Lisse, The Netherlands: Swets & Zeitlinger.

Van der Hart, O., Bolt, H., & Van der Kolk, B. A. (2005). Memory fragmentation in patients with dissociative identity disorder. *Journal of Trauma & Dissociation, 6*(1), 55–70.

Van der Hart, O., & Boon, S. (1997). Treatment strategies for complex dissociative disorders: Two Dutch case examples. *Dissociation, 10,* 157–165.

Van der Hart, O., Boon, S., & Everdingen, G. B. (1990). Writing assignments and hypnosis in the treatment of traumatic memories. In M. L. Fass & D. Brown (Eds.), *Creative matery in hypnosis and hypnoanalysis: A Festschrift for Erika Fromm* (pp. 231–253. Hillsdale, NJ: L. Erlbaum Associates.

Van der Hart, O., Boon, S., Friedman, B., & Mierop, V. (1992). De reactivering van traumatische herinneringen [The reactivation of traumatic memories] *Directieve Therapie, 12,* 12–55.

Van der Hart, O., & Brom, D. (2000). When the victim forgets: Trauma-induced amnesia and its assessment in Holocaust survivors. In A. Y. Shalev, R. Yehuda, & A. C. McFarlane (Eds.), *International handbook of human response to trauma* (pp. 233–248). New York: Kluwer Academic/Plenum Publishers.

Van der Hart, O., & Brown, P. (1990). Concept of psychological trauma. *American Journal of Psychiatry, 147,* 1691.

Van der Hart, O., & Brown, P. (1992). Abreaction re-evaluated. *Dissociation, 5,* 127–140.

Van der Hart, O., Brown, P., & Van der Kolk, B. A. (1989). Pierre Janet's treatment of post-traumatic stress. *Journal of Traumatic Stress, 2,* 379–396. Also in G. S. Everly, Jr., & J. M. Lating (Eds.), *Psychotraumatology: Key papers and core concepts in post-traumatic stress* (pp. 195–210. New York: Plenum Publishing Corporation.

Van der Hart, O., & Dorahy, M. (in press). Dissociation: History of a concept. In P. F. Dell, J. O'Neill, & E. Somer (Eds.), *The ISSD sourcebook on dissociation and dissociative disorders.* McLean, VA: The International Society for the Study of Dissociation.

Van der Hart, O., & Friedman, B. (1989). A reader's guide to Pierre Janet on dissociation: A neglected intellectual heritage. *Dissociation, 2*, 3–16.

Van der Hart, O., & Friedman, B. (1992). Trauma, dissociation and triggers: Their role in treatment and emergency psychiatry. In J. B. van Luyn et al. (Eds.), *Emergency psychiatry today* (pp. 137–142). Amsterdam: Elsevier.

Van der Hart, O., & Nijenhuis, E. R. S. (1995). Amnesia for traumatic experiences. *Hypnos, 22*, 73–86.

Van der Hart, O., & Nijenhuis, E. R. S. (1999). Bearing witness to uncorroborated trauma: The clinician's development of reflective belief. *Professional Psychology: Research and Practice, 30*, 37–44.

Van der Hart, O., & Nijenhuis, E. R. S. (2001). Generalized dissociative amnesia: Episodic, semantic, and procedural memories lost and found. *Australian and New Zealand Journal of Psychiatry, 35*, 589–600.

Van der Hart, O., Nijenhuis, E. R. S., & Steele, K. (2005). Dissociation: An insufficiently recognized major feature of complex posttraumatic stress disorder. *Journal of Traumatic Stress, 18*, 413–424.

Van der Hart, O., Nijenhuis, E. R. S., Steele, K., & Brown, D. (2004). Trauma-related dissociation: Conceptual clarity lost and found. *Australian and New Zealand Journal of Psychiatry, 38*, 906–914.

Van der Hart, O., & Op den Velde, W. (1995). Traumatische herinneringen [Traumatic memories]. In O. Van der Hart (Ed.), *Trauma, dissociatie en hypnose* [Trauma, dissociation and hypnosis] (pp. 71–90). Amsterdam/Lisse: Swets & Zeitlinger.

Van der Hart, O., & Spiegel, D. (1993). Hypnotic assessment and treatment of trauma-induced psychoses: The early psychotherapy of H. Breukink and modern views. *International Journal of Clinical and Experimental Hypnosis, 41*, 191–209.

Van der Hart, O., & Steele, K. (1997). Time distortions in dissociative identity disorder: Janetian concepts and treatment. *Dissociation, 10*, 91–103.

Van der Hart, O., & Steele, K. (1999). Reliving or reliving childhood trauma?: A commentary on Miltenburg and Singer (1997). *Theory & Psychology, 9*, 533–540.

Van der Hart, O., & Steele, K. (2000). The integration of traumatic memories versus abreaction: Clarification of terminology. *ISSD News, 18*(2), 4–5.

Van der Hart, O., Steele, K., Boon, S., & Brown, P. (1993). The treatment of traumatic memories: Synthesis, realization and integration. *Dissociation, 6*, 162–180.

Van der Hart, O., Van der Kolk, B. A., & Boon, S. (1998). Treatment of dissociative disorders. In J. D. Bremner & C. R. Marmar (Eds.), *Trauma, memory, and dissociation* (pp. 253–283). Washington, DC: American Psychiatric Press.

Van der Hart, O., & Van der Velden, K. (1995). Over het waarheidsgehalte van traumatische herinneringen [On the truth content of traumatic memories]. In O. van der Hart (Ed.), *Trauma, dissociatie en hypnose* [Trauma, dissociation, and hypnosis]. Lisse: Swets & Zeitlinger.

Van der Hart, O., Van Dijke, A., Van Son, M., & Steele, K. (2000). Somatoform dissociation in traumatized World War I combat soldiers: A neglected clinical heritage. *Journal of Trauma and Dissociation, 1*(4), 33–66.

Van der Hart, O., Witztum, E., & Friedman, B. (1993). From hysterical psychosis to reactive dissociative psychosis. *Journal of Traumatic Stress, 6*, 43–64.

Van der Kolk, B. A. (1994). The body keeps the score: Memory and the evolving psychobiology of posttraumatic stress. *Harvard Review of Psychiatry, 1*, 253–265.

Van der Kolk, B. A. (1996). The complexity of adaptation to trauma: Self-regulation, stimulus discrimination, and characterological development. In B. A. Van der Kolk, A. C. McFarlane, & L. Weisaeth (Eds.), *Traumatic stress: The effects of overwhelming experience on mind, body, and society* (pp. 182–213). New York: Guilford.

Van der Kolk, B. A. (2003). The neurobiology of childhood trauma and abuse. *Child & Adolescent Psychiatric Clinics of North America, 12,* 293–317.

Van der Kolk, B. A., & Fisler, R. (1995). Dissociation and the fragmentary nature of traumatic memories: Overview and exploratory study. *Journal of Traumatic Stress, 8,* 505–525.

Van der Kolk, B. A., Hopper, J. W., & Osterman, J. E. (2001). Exploring the nature of traumatic memory: Combining clinical knowledge with laboratory methods. *Journal of Aggression, Maltreatment & Trauma, 4*(2), 9–31.

Van der Kolk, B. A., McFarlane, A. C., & Van der Hart, O. (1996). A general approach to treatment of posttraumatic stress. In B. A. Vaz der Kolk, A. C. McFarlane, & L. Weisaeth (Eds.), *Traumatic stress: The effects of overwhelming experience on mind, body, and society* (pp. 417–440). New York: Guilford.

Van der Kolk, B. A., Pelcovitz, D., Roth, S., Mandel, F. S., McFarlane, A. C., & Herman, J. L. (1996). Dissociation, somatization, and affect dysregulation: The complexity of adaptation of trauma. *American Journal of Psychiatry, 153*(FestschriftSuppl), 83–93.

Van der Kolk, B. A., Roth, S., Pelcovitz, D., & Mandel, F. (1993). *Complex PTSD: Results of the PTSD field trials for DSM-IV.* Washington, DC: American Psychiatric Association.

Van der Kolk, B. A., Roth, S., Pelcovitz, D., Sunday, S., & Spinazzola, J. (2005). Disorders of extreme stress: The empirical foundation of a complex adaptation to trauma. *Journal of Traumatic Stress, 18,* 389–399.

Van der Kolk, B. A., & Van der Hart, O. (1989). Pierre Janet and the breakdown of adaptation in psychological trauma. *American Journal of Psychiatry, 146,* 1530–1540.

Van der Kolk, B. A., & Van der Hart, O. (1991). The intrusive past: The flexibility of memory and the engraving of trauma. *American Imago, 48,* 425–454.

Van der Kolk, B. A., Van der Hart, O., & Marmar, C. R. (1996). Dissociation and information processing in posttraumatic stress disorder. In B. A. Van der Kolk, A. C. McFarlane, & L. Weisaeth (Eds.), *Traumatic stress: The effects of overwhelming experience on mind, body and society* (pp. 302–327). New York: Guilford.

Van Derbur, M. (2004). *Miss America by day: Lessons learned from ultimate betrayals and unconditional love.* Denver, CO: Oak Hill Ridge Press.

Van IJzendoorn, M., & Schuengel, C. (1996). The measurement of dissociation in normal and clinical populations: Meta-analytic validation of the Dissociative Experiences Scale (DES). *Clinical Psychology Review, 16,* 365–382.

Vanderlinden, J. (1993). *Dissociative experiences, trauma, and hypnosis: Research findings and applications in eating disorders.* Delft, the Netherlands: Eburon.

Vanderlinden, J., Van Dyck, R., Vandereycken, W., & Vertommen, H. (1993). Dissociation and traumatic experiences in the general population of the Netherlands. *Hospital & Community Psychiatry, 44,* 786–788.

Vasterling, J. J., Brailey, K., Constans, J. I., & Sutker, P. B. (1998). Attention and memory dysfunction in posttraumatic stress disorder. *Neuropsychology, 12*(1), 125–133.

Vasterling, J. J., Duke, L. M., Brailey, K., Constans, J. I., Allain, A. N., & Sutker, P. B. (2002). Attention, learning, and memory performances and intellectual resources in Vietnam veterans: PTSD and no disorder comparisons. *Neuropsychology, 16,* 5–14.

400   *The Haunted Self*

Vermetten, E., & Bremner, J. D. (2000). Dissociative amnesia: Re-remembering traumatic memories. In G. E. Berrios & J. R. Hodges (Eds.), *Memory disorders in psychiatric practice* (pp. 400–431). Cambridge/New York: Cambridge University Press.

Vermetten, E., & Bremner, J. D. (2002). Circuits and systems in stress. II. Applications to neurobiology and treatment in posttraumatic stress disorder. *Depression and Anxiety,16*, 14–38.

Vermetten, E., Schmahl, C., Lindner, S., Loewenstein, R. J., & Bremner, J. D. (2006). Hippocampal and amygdalar volume in dissociative identity disorder. *American Journal of Psychiatry, 163*, 1–8.

Waelde, L. C., Koopman, C., Rierdan, J., & Spiegel, D. (2001). Symptoms of acute stress disorder and posttraumatic stress disorder following exposure to disastrous flooding. *Journal of Trauma and Dissociation, 2*(2), 37–52.

Wald, J., & Taylor, S. (2005). Interoceptive exposure therapy combined with trauma-related exposure therapy for post-traumatic stress disorder: A case report. *Cognitive Behavior Therapy, 34*, 34–40.

Waller, G., Hamilton, K., Elliott, P., Lewendon, J., Stopa, L., Waters, A. et al. (2000). Somatoform dissociation, psychological dissociation and specific forms of trauma. *Journal of Trauma and Dissociation, 1*(4), 81–98.

Waller, G., Ohanian, V., Meyer, C., Everill, J., & Rouse, H. (2001). The utility of dimensional and categorical approaches to understanding dissociation in the eating disorders. *British Journal of Clinical Psychology, 40*(4), 387–397.

Waller, N. G., Putnam, F. W., & Carlson, E. B. (1996). Types of dissociation and dissociative types: A taxonomic analysis of dissociative experiences. *Psychological Methods, 1*, 300–321.

Wang, S., Wilson, J. P., & Mason, J. W. (1996). Stages of decompensation in combat-related posttraumatic stress disorder: A new conceptual model. *Integrative Physiolology & Behavioral Science, 31*, 237–253.

Wenninger, K., & Ehlers, A. (1998). Dysfunctional cognitions and adult psychological functioning in child sexual abuse survivors. *Journal of Traumatic Stress, 11*, 281–300.

Weze, C., Leathard, H. L., Grange, J., Tiplady, P., & Stevens, G. (2005). Evaluation of healing by gentle touch. *Public Health, 119*, 3–10.

Wildgoose, A., Waller, G., Clarke, S., & Reid, A. (2000). Psychiatric symptomatology in borderline and other personality disorders: Dissociation and fragmentation as mediators. *Journal of Nervous and Mental Disease, 188*, 757–763.

Wilson, J. P., & Lindy, J. D. (Eds.). (1994). *Countertransference in the treatment of PTSD*. New York: Guilford.

Wilson, J. P., & Keane, T. M. (Eds.). (2004). *Assessing psychological trauma and PTSD*. New York: Guilford.

Wilson, J. P., & Thomas, R. B. (2004). *Empathy in the treatment of trauma and PTSD*. New York: Brunner Routledge.

Wilson, M. (2001). The case for sensorimotor coding in working memory. *Psychonomic Bulletin and Review, 8*, 44–57.

Wilson, M. (2002). Six views of embodied cognition. *Psychonomic Bulletin and Review, 9*, 625–636.

Winnicott, D. W. (1965). *The maturational process and the facilitating environment*. New York: International Universities Press.

Winnik, H. Z. (1969). Second thoughts about "psychic trauma." *Israel Journal Psychiatry and Related Disciplines, 1*, 82–95.

Witzum, E., Margalit, H., & Van der Hart, O. (2002). Combat-induced dissociative amnesia: Review and case example of generalized dissociative amnesia. *Journal of Trauma and Dissociation, 3*(2), 35–55.

Witztum, E. & Van der Hart, O., & Friedman, B. (1988). The use of metaphors in psychotherapy. *Journal of Contemporary Psychotherapy, 18*, 270–290.

Worden, J. W. (2001). *Grief counseling and grief therapy* (3rd. ed.). New York: Springer Publishing Company.

World Health Organisation (1992). *ICD-10: The ICD-10 classification of mental and behavioural disorders. Clinical descriptions and diagnostic guidelines.* Geneva, Switzerland: Author.

Yargic, L. I., Şar, V., Tutkun, H., & Alyanak, B. (1998). Comparison of dissociative identity disorder with other diagnostic groups using a structured interview in Turkey. *Comprehensive Psychiatry, 39*, 345–351.

Yehuda, R. (2002). Posttraumatic stress disorder. *New England Journal of Medicine, 346*, 108–114.

Yen, S., Shea, M. T., Battle, C. L., Johnson, D. M., Zlotnick, C., Dolan-Sewell, R. et al. (2002). Traumatic exposure and posttraumatic stress disorder in borderline, schizotypal, avoidant, and obsessive–compulsive personality disorders: Findings from the collaborative longitudinal personality disorders study. *Journal of Nervous and Mental Disease, 190*, 510–518.

Zanarini, M. C., Ruser, T., Frankenburg, F. R., & Hennen, J. (2000). The dissociative experiences of borderline patients. *Comprehensive Psychiatry, 41*, 223–227.

Zanarini, M. C., Yong, L., Frankenburg, F. R., Hennen, J., Reich, D. B., Marino, M. F. et al. (2002). Severity of reported childhood sexual abuse and its relationship to severity of borderline psychopathology and psychosocial impairment among borderline inpatients. *Journal of Nervous and Mental Disease, 190*, 381–387.

Zanarini, M. C., Williams, A. A., Lewis, R. E., Reich, R. B., Vera, S. C., Marino, M. F. et al. (1997). Reported pathological childhood experiences associated with the development of borderline personality disorder. *American Journal of Psychiatry, 154*, 1101–1106.

Ziegler, D. J., & Leslie, Y. M. (2003). A test of the ABC model underlying rational emotive behavior therapy. *Psychological Reports, 92*, 235–240.

Zlotnick, C., Zakriski, A. L., Shea, M. T., Costello, E., Begin, A., Pearlstein, T. et al. (1996). The long-term sequelae of sexual abuse: Support for a complex posttraumatic stress disorder. *Journal of Traumatic Stress, 9*, 195–205.

Index

fostering realization, 259–60
  fusion of dissociative parts, 338–339
grief work in groups, 332, 356–357
  guided realization. *see* realization,
    guided
  guided synthesis. *see* synthesis, guided
in groups, 356–57
improving mental efficiency in, 246–59
indications, 216, 217
initiation of phase three, 337
intervention with mental actions. *see*
    trauma-derived mental actions, pho-
    bia of
intervention with phobia of traumatic
    memory, 321–32
interventions to complete actions,
    258–59, 261
manifestations of attachment phobia,
    266–67
overcoming substitute actions, 252
paying off "debts", 246
phase 1, stabilization and symptom re-
    duction, 16–17, 240, 257, 266, 281
phase 2, treatment of traumatic memo-
    ries, 18, 240, 257, 266–67, 282
phase 3, personality integration and reha-
    bilitation, 18, 240, 257, 267, 283
phases, 15, 240
phobia interventions, 256–57
principles of mental economy in, 240,
    260–61
psychoeducation interventions, 247–48
relapse prevention, 353
resistance in, 248–50
simplifying daily life, 245
skills development, 15, 250–52
stress inoculation, 353
theoretical and technical development,
    216
therapeutic goals, *ix, xi,* 16–19, 216, 240,
    260–61, 337
therapeutic relationship, 241–42, 260
therapeutic stimulation in, 247
therapist factors, 357–60
therapy frame, 241, 242–43, 260
phobia(s), *xi,* 211–12
  of action, 193–94
  of affect, 282, 289–294, 299
  assessment of, 234–35
  of attachment and attachment loss, 12,
    194, 207–8, 249, 272, 278
  of change, 208–9
  classical conditioning and, 195–99
  conditioned escape and avoidance in, of
    traumatic memory, *xi,* 15–16, 53–54,
    194, 204–5
    containment in work with, 330
    contraindications to work with, 321

countertransference risk, 322
guided realization interventions, 321,
    322, 330–32
guided synthesis interventions, 321–22,
    324–30, 332–35
intervention strategies, 321–22, 335
preparation for work with, 323–24
treatment goals, 335
treatment stages, 322–23
of dissociative parts of personality, *x,*
    194, 205–7, 284
of fantasies, 295, 299
of fusion, 338, 339
generalization learning and, 202–3
goals of stabilization phase of treatment,
    17
interoceptive defenses and, 36–37
of intimacy, 208, 283, 344–49
in maintenance of structural dissociation,
    13, 14, 193
of mental actions, 13
of needs, 294–95, 299
of normal life, *xi,* 16, 208, 340–41
of one's body, 295–96, 299
operant conditioning and, 200–204
phase two interventions and, 319
in primary structural dissociation, 53
of risk taking, 343–44
severity assessment, 257
of sexuality, 208, 345–46, 348–49
therapeutic interventions, 256–57
of thoughts, 294, 299
of trauma-derived (mental) actions, *xi,*
    205, 249, 281–83
    trauma-related, 194, 212, 225, 244
treatment goals, *xi,* 13–14, 212, 215, 335
verbalization, 257
of wishes and fantasies, 295
see also attachment and attachment loss,
    phobias of; dissociative parts, phobia
    of; trauma-derived mental actions,
    phobia of
phylogeny, 172
physical illness or impairment
  mental energy and, 10
  motor dysfunction, 96
  negative somatoform dissociative symp-
    toms, 95–97
  sensory impairment, 96–97
  somatization disorder, 123–24
play
  as action system of daily life, 35, 47, 60,
    81, 85, 345
  behavior, 81–82
posttraumatic decline, 46, 142
posttraumatic stress disorder (PTSD),
  action systems in, 4
  amnesia in, 93